NO PASSING GLORY

NO PASSING GLORY

The full and authentic biography
of Group Captain Cheshire
V.C., D.S.O., D.F.C.

BY
ANDREW BOYLE

THE REPRINT SOCIETY LONDON

FIRST PUBLISHED 1955
THIS EDITION PUBLISHED BY THE REPRINT SOCIETY LTD.
BY ARRANGEMENT WITH WM. COLLINS, SONS & CO. LTD.
1957

PRINTED IN GREAT BRITAIN
BY R. & R. CLARK, LTD., EDINBURGH

For
Edmund Campion

FOREWORD

I HAVE not attempted to carry the detailed story of Leonard Cheshire's life beyond the summer of 1952, preferring instead to summarise in a short epilogue the present phase of his mission for the relief of suffering. My main concern has been to unfold as objectively as possible the elusive and sometimes inscrutable character of a great man of action. Since his work during and after his grave illness belongs to a chapter that has barely begun, it obviously lies outside the scope of this book.

I am indebted to Leonard Cheshire, who has read the finished text, for his patient collaboration and for the comparatively free hand he has given me ; to both his parents for making available original family documents, and all the wartime letters ; to Dr. Cheshire, his father, for suggestions now incorporated in the early chapters ; and to Christopher Cheshire, Mrs. Edith Dichter, Prebendary C. Cheshire, and Sir Patrick and Lady Cadell for much additional information.

More than five hundred people aided me in compiling a vast hoard of original matter only part of which could be used. I should like to name the late Mr. J. F. Roxburgh, the first head-master of Stowe ; his successor, Mr. E. V. Reynolds ; the Warden of Merton College, Oxford ; the Steward ; Cheshire's tutor, Professor F. H. Lawson ; and his servant, Mr. Bert Gardiner. To Mr. Douglas Baxter, Major D. H. L. Parker, Mrs. Mavis Lowndes, the Donellis and Miss P. Piehler, I owe much for the vigour and clarity of their evidence of the Oxford period.

The testimony of Group Captain J. N. H. Whitworth, who taught Cheshire how to fly and has been in intermittent touch with him since, was of the utmost value. Of the surviving members of Cheshire's early air crews I owe most to George Roberts (" Taffy ") and to Squadron Leader A. M. M. Hill (" Jock ") for the inspiration of their accounts and for Jill's care in correcting the chapters entitled " The Leader " and " The Legend ". Nor can I overlook the contributions, oral and

7

written, of Colonel Basil Ivor Jones ; Squadron Leader " Pop "
Bligh ; Mr. Geoffrey Harmsworth ; Mr. Vernon Noble ;
Lieutenant-Colonel Halle of the Royal Norwegian Air Force ;
Air Vice-Marshals MacNeece Foster, Whitley, and Patch ;
Group Captain " Willie " Tait ; Air Chief Marshal Sir Roderick
Carr ; Sir Frederick Handley Page ; and Air-Commodore
John Kirby.

One of my objects in the long chapter entitled " The
Perfectionist " was to trace as accurately as possible the influence
of Cheshire's unique tactical ideas, as a lowly Wing Commander,
on the staging of the vital air prelude to D-Day. The personal
operational diary he kept for much of the time he led 617
Squadron was an indispensable source for the day-to-day details
of individual raids, but for essential background material, some
of which has not been officially recorded, I wish to express my
appreciation to Air Chief Marshal Sir Robert Saundby ; to
Air Vice-Marshal D. C. T. Bennett ; and to Air Chief Marshal
Sir Ralph Cochrane, who read the completed chapter with a
finely critical eye. The responsibility for interpreting events,
political and military, is mine alone. The principal works of
reference I consulted are given at the end of this book.

Of Cheshire's colleagues in 617 Squadron who helped me I
should like to single out Wing Commander Danny Walker, now
of the Royal Canadian Air Force ; Mr. Arthur Pollen ; and Mr.
David Shannon, who also read the completed chapter.

If almost every page acknowledges the ready assistance
offered and given to me, I am under a special obligation to Sir
Charles Symonds, Field Marshal Lord Wilson, Marshals of the
Royal Air Force Sir John Slessor and Sir Arthur Harris, Sir
William Penney, Mr. Barnes Wallis, Mr. Robert Cockburn,
Mr. Clement Attlee, and Sir Desmond Morton. Either by
interview or through correspondence, they answered my many
questions, enabling me to keep the record balanced and straight.
I am obliged to Mr. J. C. Nerney of the Air Ministry Historical
Section who cleared the manuscript for security ; to Mr. T.
Parsons of the Air Ministry Records ; and to the Public Relations
Department of the United States Air Force in Washington, for
their combined help in leading me to important witnesses on
both sides of the Atlantic.

Of the scores of men and women who sharpened my

understanding of Cheshire's outlook in the immediate post-war years before I knew him, I must mention Mr. Noel Holland, Bishop Hugh Embling, Mrs. Frances Jeram, Mr. and Mrs. Cyril Cowey, Canon L. John Collins and Mr. R. W. Tyler. The bulky records and papers of V.I.P., Cheshire's abortive colony experiment, together with the recollections of a representative cross-section of colonists, provided me with authoritative material for the chapter entitled " The Idealist ".

Father Henry Elliot Clarke, Monsignor Valentine Elwes, Flight Lieutenant Bob Dickinson, Mr. and Mrs. Douglas King and individual patients, staff members and helpers, living and dead, of Le Court, St. Teresa's and Holy Cross, were amongst those instrumental in deepening my personal appreciation of Leonard Cheshire's work in more recent years, thus preparing the groundwork of this book. I have also drawn liberally on hundreds of personal letters which Dr. John Keevil and others kindly put at my disposal.

Finally I must thank Father Joseph Crehan, S.J., Professor of Fundamental Theology at Heythrop College, for advice on the historical background of the Holy Shroud ; Father Thomas Holland, C.M.S., a friend of Cheshire's and mine, for reading the final chapter and epilogue ; the editors of the *Sunday Graphic* and *News Chronicle* for permission to quote from articles by Cheshire ; Messrs. Macmillan and the executors of the estate for permission to use a short extract from the late Richard Hillary's *The Last Enemy* ; Messrs. Hutchinson for permission to use a short extract from Cheshire's *Bomber Pilot* ; Mr. and Mrs. B. C. L. Keelan for the more than adequate index ; and Christina without whom there would probably have been no book at all.

ANDREW BOYLE

PUTNEY,
October 1953/*June* 1955

CONTENTS

PROLOGUE

BEHIND them, buried in his thoughts, the rear-gunner was humming a dance tune. He was wholly responsible for any sudden attack on the giant Superfortress : there were no other guns on board, only the cameras, the other members of the crew, a distinguished British scientist, and Cheshire. But the restful feeling of confidence in their invulnerability was absolute. They knew that no Japanese fighter could touch them. They might have been on a pleasure cruise through space, except for the hour and the sharp expectancy that gave heightened meaning to every idle thought. This was war in a new dimension, where fear, pity and the primitive reflexes of the human animal in danger had no place.

Outside in the darkness, the sudden storm which had struck them five miles above the trackless Pacific was abating. An occasional shaft of lightning exposed the naked silver belly of the B29, but the following gentle dips through space were fewer now. Somewhere ahead in the gusty void where sea met sky the other two aircraft were leading the way—the second carrying scientific instruments, the first carrying the plutonium bomb. It was not yet four o'clock in the morning on August 9th, 1945.

Beside Cheshire, his head occasionally drooping forward, Penney, the scientist, was dozing fitfully. The seats were hard, but the air in the pressurised cabin was almost too warm and relaxing for watchfulness. They had discarded ties soon after take-off, and were sitting in shirt sleeves. They needed no oxygen masks or microphones. Normal conversation could be carried on above the rush of air and the whir of the compressor without raising the voice ; but Cheshire was content for the moment to take stock of the position, this strange, almost unbelievable position of privilege in which he found himself. For it had seemed distinctly probable several times during the past two or three frantic days that Penney and himself would be elbowed out and left behind. The simple matter of fitting in two Englishmen, of providing them with seats in an aircraft bound for the final kill, had set an almost insuperable problem for American pride and had proved an exasperating distraction from the main task.

Since Hiroshima's destruction three days earlier, the tension on the secret atomic base of Tinian, the small coral island in the Marianas which had been transformed into the greatest bomber airfield on earth, had been strung to an unbearable pitch. The success of that first operation had been so overwhelming that it was feared a second would be unnecessary. The longing for peace was strong in the minds of all the airmen and scientists living and working in the heavily guarded compound of tents and air-conditioned Nissen huts, where the cores of the weapons were stored ready for assembly ; but the obsession to see what the second bomb could do was far stronger.

To Cheshire, with his considerable experience of bombing operations, this obsession was something subtle yet compelling, defying cold, clear analysis. It had been allowed to feed on the prolonged uncertainty during the days of waiting like a malignant maggot in the brain. Even here, aloft in the B29, he was uneasily aware of it still. More palpable than fear or hatred, it seemed to affect the air crew and even Bill Penney. As the Prime Minister's special observer, Cheshire blessed his infallible luck in having so companionable a person as Penney beside him. For his sole benefit and as artlessly as a man playing patience, the scientist had predicted, within two decimal places, the exact amount of energy that would be released by the uranium bomb over Hiroshima without stirring from the rough table in the tent they shared together on Tinian.

The pilot, Major James Hopkins, a big taciturn Texan, passed back the message that he was coming down to a lower ceiling. The winds were swinging behind in their favour, and the pale dawn had begun to finger the far horizon in front. About breakfast time the wireless operator slipped off the headphones and announced excitedly that both targets were uncovered by cloud. The special weather planes had just come through with a reassuring signal. . . .

2

" There's Japan, sir," said the rear-gunner.

Penney peered out of the starboard window, but all he could see was water, miles and miles of sparkling dark blue with here and there a shallow patch of green.

Not a puff of smoke, nor a sail nor a sign of life in that infinite expanse.

" You won't find a thing on that side, Bill," said Cheshire. " But take a look down here."

He and the rear-gunner were standing side by side pointing to a minute pinpoint of ink on the port beam—so minute that a short-sighted man might easily have dismissed it as a spot before the eyes. " Japan, I suppose," said Penney with a smile of resignation. " I'm in your hands."

They all laughed together. It was Yakoshima, their appointed rendezvous, a white curdled rim round a black lozenge, growing visibly larger as they dropped nearer. There were no defences. That was something they knew from the final detailed briefing, something that made it possible to laugh now without false bravado.

Hopkins called out, " Keep an eye open for the others. We're due to make contact in two minutes." But the sky was as empty as the sea. Finally the B29 captain's phlegmatic calm was ruffled. " Those bastards have run out on us," he said. " We must find out why. Get a message back to base."

The sun was well up in a flawless blue sky when they broke strict radio silence. For over half an hour they had been circling that dark sea-bound speck of an island off the south-east tip of Kyushu. Their unspoken fears increased as the slow minutes passed and the other two B29s still failed to appear. Had they been forced down on the way ? Were they straggling behind, trying to make up the leeway ? Should they themselves take a chance and proceed alone to the primary target ? The hidden depth of their anxiety conveyed itself to General Farrell and his staff in the terse question that Major Hopkins ordered the wireless operator to send to Tinian : " Has the aircraft with the bomb aborted ? "

They were not to know the agony of irrelevant doubt their message had created, an agony which had to be endured until

shortly after noon, when the hush in Tinian's great communications' centre was suddenly shattered by the automatic click
of instruments, and the remote, disembodied voice of the
wireless operator on the leading aircraft, the *Great Artiste*, uttered
the two laconic words : " Operation successful."

Hopkins had given them the order to put on their polaroid
glasses a few minutes before zero hour. " Anything may happen
—or nothing," he said glumly. They had flown from Yakoshima
straight across the tiny neck of Kyushu to the primary target,
still unsure of their final destination or of what they would find
when they reached it ; and then the weather intervened. An
impenetrable screen of low cloud, stretching across the sky
between themselves and the earth, confirmed what they already
guessed : the hidden city below had been spared by the whim
of the elements. Hopkins had changed course abruptly for the
secondary target, Nagasaki, and the others wondered whether
they would ever get there in time.

It happened when they were only half-expecting it, although
their synchronised watches pointed to zero hour. Through his
thick arc-welder's glasses, Cheshire had been looking towards
the tropical sun, which even in that rarefied atmosphere at nearly
40,000 feet appeared as a small, sharp spot of light. A split
fraction of a second later the darkly glimpsed sunlight was blotted
out by a blinding white flash, and the dim interior of the B29
was plunged in eerie purple radiance. A massive explosion,
rumbling from the doomed city over thirty miles away, assailed
their ears like a blow and rocked the aircraft so violently that it
seemed about to crumble and disintegrate in the blast.

Then they saw the ball of fire, and watched it rise like men in
a trance. It shot up suddenly from the pillar of acrid smoke at
a height of about 2000 feet, but its movements were unlike
anything Cheshire had ever visualised or imagined. As it soared
upwards, it kept expanding, not as a snowball expands by rolling
down a slope, but through its own seething, turbulent inner
power.

He thought of the fireball on top of the smoke as something
like a colossal piece of silk that had been compressed by giant
hands, then suddenly released, expanding, unwrapping and
unrolling as it climbed through the clouds at terrifying speed.
He thought, too, of the harmless ping-pong borne up on those

jets of water, which he had seen people try to dislodge on fair-ground rifle ranges. Beside him, Penney was muttering half audibly. The scientist had begun to make quick, approximate calculations, converting the awesome vision into unreal mathematical terms. Cheshire tried to take in these lifeless abstractions and relate them to the inferno below. But time conceived in millionths of a second, heat considered in tens of millions of degrees, seemed more meaningless than ever.

In two or three minutes the fireball had transformed itself into a vast, luminous mushroom-shaped cloud, two miles wide ; outwardly it was now almost stationary at 60,000 feet. Yet they knew the hideous activity within its sulphurous folds ; and underneath the cloud the column of black smoke and dust particles visibly sucked up from the target area writhed and twisted like a monster in torment.

The air crew remained in their places, and the few words they exchanged were spoken in matter-of-fact tones. Whatever the Americans felt, the routine business of keeping the B29 aloft and orbiting helped to distract their stunned thoughts. For the best part of an hour, they hovered there, watching and saying little. Cheshire, after the early passive feeling of dazed stupefaction, had striven to free his brain from the feverish stranglehold of his imagination. He realised he had a specific task to do as well ; and with Penney's assistance he settled down to do it almost with relief.

Discarding the thick protective eye-shields, he looked through field glasses at the base of the dense pall of smoke where Nagasaki lay. He could see red, glowing patches of flame here and there. Fumbling in his pockets, he brought out a note-book and pencil ; in spite of the aircraft's synchronised cameras, he was determined to make his own rough sketch.

" Can you see that fire, Bill ? " he asked Penney, who was peering through half-closed eyes, straining to accustom them to the convulsions at the foot of the column of smoke. Presently the scientist barely detected the licking tongues of flame that were probably the homes and buildings of Nagasaki.

Penney stood over Cheshire while the drawing took shape, carefully answering a quick stream of questions about estimated areas of blast, the size of the fires, the possible extent of radioactivity. This attempted escape from the terrible nightmare

unleashed by nuclear physics through the harmless, empty
sounding incantations of the scientists who had fathered it was
a curious momentary blessing. Perhaps later, the crude pencilled
impression with the explanatory footnotes supplied by the
practical Penney would mean more than all the photographs
put together.

On the long flight back to Tinian, Cheshire thought of the
fireball and its terrible, destructive symmetry, so evil in its
appearance yet so perfect in its control. What was it the
scientists had talked about ?

" The law of equal and opposite reaction," yes, that was it.
On his first and last war-time raid as a passive spectator, he had
seen that law demonstrated for the benefit of the Mikado and his
subjects. He could work up no honest feeling of pity for their
fate. Bombs were constructed to demolish targets, and sometimes
men, women and even children, perished in the ruins. If this
extraordinary bomb had claimed more than the average haphazard
toll of victims, that was part of the ironic fortune of war.

They flew on across the calm ocean waters, slowly trying to
absorb an experience which beggared description and left the
mind limp and helpless, and the eleven men in the aircraft sat stiff
and silent. In the late afternoon Hopkins and the flight engineer
created a brief diversion by their obvious concern at the precariously low readings on the fuel gauge. In the end, they
landed on Okinawa, the agreed emergency landing place, to
refill the tanks.

The aircraft that dropped the bomb and the second B29 with
the scientific equipment were already down; and this unscheduled
halt on an airfield heedlessly bustling with normal activity
provided a welcome outlet for desperately pent-up feelings.
They clustered together comparing notes, rummaging for the
right words to recreate their individual responses to the lurid
scenes they had witnessed. Only Captain Kermit Beahan, the
Texan bomb-aimer who pressed the button that released the
weapon, had anything plain and non-committal to say. He had
done his job only too well.

While they were standing nervously talking in small groups,
a hatless American officer came running towards the parked
aircraft.

" Have you heard the news ? " he shouted.

" What news ? " someone asked hesitantly.

" We have another ally in this godawful theatre. The Russians have joined in the war."

Nothing could have been farther from their thoughts at that moment. It seemed an unimportant, far-fetched trifle. They were still on the borderland of nightmare, like precocious children roused from sleep who recognise the safe familiar symbols of the nursery but fear that the shadow in the doorway belongs to a stranger. A week ago the news of Soviet Russia's entry into the Far Eastern war would have excited them ; to-day it left them unmoved and indifferent.

Before they left Okinawa a pilot strolled up and spoke casually to Hopkins and his crew.

" You know about the raid ? " he asked.

" What raid ? "

" There's been another of these atomic jobs on Japan. A bomb was dropped this morning somewhere near Nagasaki."

" Yeah," said Hopkins, " could be " : and left it at that.

Among themselves they speculated how the news could have travelled so quickly. Cheshire learned afterwards, without much surprise, that a patrol of U.S. fighters had observed the flash and the mushroom cloud more than 250 miles out over the Pacific.

3

Not until 10.30 that night did they taxi to a standstill on one of Tinian's six wide arterial runways, and welling up through his physical and mental weariness Cheshire felt an overpowering sense of elation and achievement. At the supper table he joined in the artificial raucous chatter : discussing those hours of depressed frustration when they lost contact with the others, hearing in turn how the two leading aircraft waited and waited, and were forced to run a wildly inaccurate gauntlet of Japanese anti-aircraft fire as they flew over the primary target—that unnamed city which had been saved from extinction by cloud. But he noticed that nobody except himself appeared anxious to hark back to the climax of that unforgettable day : it was as if the fulfilment of the obsession had sickened them, so that the very mention of it filled them with inexpressible doubt. Some had been caught on the emotional rebound more quickly than others ; it was easy enough to pick them out, those who ate mechanically without speaking, their mind still numbed by the vision of absolute physical destruction.

This dumb shorthand of remorse was a reaction which Cheshire had hardly bargained for, least of all from these veteran American airmen whom he had come to know and respect. He was no blind lover of American ways and ideas ; but the mighty B29, in which he had completed his 103rd operational mission, was unquestionably the perfect instrument for delivering these crushing atomic blows. It was almost foolproof, and the men who handled it were no fools.

The B29 lifted air operations into a sphere above the dangers of flak and sudden death in which he had formerly revelled. It converted war into a scientific experiment, in which every member of the crew became a technical assistant with a cold, detached part to play. That was why, he reflected, the real centre of strategic gravity had shifted from Washington, London, or even Potsdam—where the decision to use the bomb was taken—to this unknown tropical island of Tinian, 6000 miles from San Francisco. By to-morrow, perhaps, the secret would be out. Millions of war-weary men and women in all the Allied nations, resigned to the probability of a long, bitter struggle to the end against Japan, might learn how the balance of forces had been tipped overnight by the miracle of atomic energy.

It was long past midnight when they went to their tent, but neither Penney nor Cheshire could sleep. " We argued well into the night," the scientist recalls, " and in our talks were raised the same tremendous issues that have been debated ever since."

The two Englishmen had developed a firm friendship in the bare three weeks since they first met on the island. Penney, who had two young sons of his own, was vaguely disturbed by the unqualified, unreflecting enthusiasm of Cheshire for the bomb as a military weapon.

His exultant feelings were understandable, if hardly edifying. He had been concentrating with typical single-mindedness on the FACTS of the bomb ever since he saw it explode. With Penney's help he had conjured up " a remarkably accurate " picture of its military potentialities. But what would be his reactions when he grasped its deeper implications ? And what would the future hold for someone whose only trade was bombing ? Penney found himself wondering about that, too.

He did not have long to wait for the beginnings of an answer and in a form he least expected.

" I've been thinking a lot about what you were saying last night, Bill," Cheshire told him next morning. " I've decided that atomic research—the aeronautical side of it, of course—is the thing for me when I leave the Air Force."

Penney nodded approval.

" But that's not everything, Bill," he continued. " This isn't going to be a government show entirely. What I have in view is a big Anglo-American corporation for promoting atomic research. And I'd like you to come in and help me to organise it. We could go far together."

Penney was accustomed by now to the wildly ingenious schemes for the future which Cheshire threw up regularly without apparent effort. This was one of his more exotic brainwaves. The scientist smiled his gentle, knowing smile, and tactfully said that he would have to think about it. It was a long time since anyone had offered him a job ; and all the omens pointed to his keeping the appointment he now held for a long, long time to come. . . .

4

They heard President Truman's broadcast on the short-wave, announcing the fate that had befallen Nagasaki out of a clear sky. The peroration, with its pious assumption of divine providence at work on behalf of Allied science and righteousness, seemed somehow out of place :

" We thank God," declared the President, " that it has come to us instead of to our enemies, and we pray that He may guide us to use it in His way and for His purpose."

Someone shut off the set. What God's part had been in the affair Cheshire failed to see ; otherwise he fully endorsed the sentiment. It mildly surprised him to find that some of the Americans thought differently. They could not yet rid their minds of the terrifying image of violence—the product of that small mysterious atomic core which a few days before had been assembled before their eyes in one of the Nissen huts. The

President's words skirted the real difficulty and did little to restore hope or allay remorse.

A colonel from New England whom Cheshire particularly liked, said defiantly as if to console himself :

" We can't undo the past, but there must be no more atomic bombs. We can't let innocent people go through that again. Even Japs."

The pink, middle-aged face wore an expression of taut earnestness ; Nagasaki had been a supreme emotional ordeal for everyone. This mood of settled melancholy would surely pass with time. Cheshire himself grudgingly recognised the disproportionate ruthlessness of the weapon, one of the factors which had blasted down the established certainties of men like the colonel. But his own faith in the bomb as a necessary scientific short-cut to peace could not be shaken by incidental detail.

He believed that the nations which created it had every right to use it and an equal duty to develop it so that peace would not be threatened lightly again. When Cheshire attempted to fit words to his thoughts, however, he was contradicted and shouted down. It was disconcerting to face these once nonchalant Americans, Air Force veterans every bit as experienced and brave as himself, who were now truculent and abusive because he could not regard the atomic attack as something almost criminal. But misunderstandings could not touch his elation which was as deeply felt as the artist's appreciation of a new masterpiece prematurely condemned as an unfashionable monstrosity.

He had known the same buoyancy of spirit before : on the first night he piloted his own Whitley ; when he launched his own point-blank target-marking technique in a Lancaster ; again when he perfected the method in a Mosquito and a Mustang. There had been past occasions for elation, but never one so clearly momentous as this. The pride of the technician left no room for moral scruples or sentimental doubts about the purpose of the machine. That was something for preachers and politicians, and somehow politics had always left him as cold as religion. But common sense told him it would be better now to keep the discussion impersonal and general.

" Hiroshima and Nagasaki prove one thing at any rate,"

he told the colonel. " They prove that the man with the biggest gun is the man who will always have the biggest say. The fact that science has given us something new to load the gun with doesn't change the principle. And if we accept it and stick to it, we can't go wrong."

" You make me sick," snapped the colonel. " What price Western civilisation ! You haven't mentioned the casualties. Have you faced the possibility that one day London or New York may take as big a pounding as Hiroshima and Nagasaki if people with your ideas get their way ? How can you stand there and justify the mass killing of innocent people ? You're crazy if you can't see that leads to barbarism."

It all seemed so heavy and irrelevant to Cheshire. Moral delicacy and glib sentimentality were surely inseparable in the crude context of modern warfare. He could not gloat over the dead or rejoice at the sufferings of the wounded, but his peace of mind was immune against doubts about the validity of bombing.

If there was a small discrepancy which he had been subconsciously struggling to reconcile with his own ideas, it was a technical nicety and had nothing to do with fastidious scruples. He had been given the chance in Europe to prove how accurately a bomb could be placed on even the smallest target ; and in proving it he had made an effective contribution to winning the war against Germany, with a minimum loss of lives among civilians on the ground. The sacrificial pyramid of fire over Nagasaki had shown him that the atomic bomb, at least in its earliest form, could not be dropped with any precision.

Britain's extreme vulnerability to atomic attack in any future conflict was an unpleasant implication which he had intuitively grasped in his discussion with Penney the night before. The thought, however, only increased his conviction that there must be no concession to vulgar fears, no turning back in cowardly distaste from the problems of a new scientific revolution.

The advance of atomic warfare was, as he saw it, simply one more step in the logical pattern of events. Total war meant total methods of waging it, and behind the men who flew the planes or manned the guns was the hidden army of mobilised scientists—the men who moulded strategy far more decisively than the politicians or the military leaders. Accept the challenge of war, and you accept all its consequences. There could be no resisting the imperious sweep of circumstances rushing your cause to triumph or tragedy. The atomic bomb was part of this dynamic, inexorable process—like blockbusters or flame-throwers. To argue that their use must be governed independently by abstract moral principles was preposterous nonsense.

" Bill Penney and I have had all this out," he told the colonel. " We kept coming back to the same point."

" And what's that ? "

" Do everything to keep the lead and then there'll be time for wisdom. The principle of the Big Gun is a simple matter of self-preservation."

Outside, a sudden fusillade brought them back to Tinian and the present. They could hear frenzied shouts and laughter amidst the scattered shooting. The door of the mess burst open, and in came a naval officer looking flushed and merry.

" What is it, a mutiny ? " asked a pilot.

" No. Haven't you heard ? The Japs have surrendered."

That evening there were loud celebrations in the big camps surrounding the airfields. Klaxon horns wailed endlessly from hundreds of trucks, lights blazed in tents and headquarters' buildings where men danced, sang and quarrelled at spontaneous victory parties which went on until the supplies of drink ran low. In the medical blocks the bodies of some thirty G.I.s were later laid out for burial among the crosses in the marines' graveyard. The new era of peace had claimed its first stray victims. Cheshire took a stroll with the colonel before turning in. As they walked uneasily together in the warm, damp night air through the shadowy palms to the coral bluff overlooking the Pacific, on the runways behind them rows of great B29s stood glinting, forgotten and strangely silent under the stars.

The declaration of peace was an empty formality. It had solved nothing for most of the men in the atomic compound, who received the news of victory with a flat resignation. The foregone conclusion had robbed them of surprise as it had already robbed them of hope.

Cheshire told his companion that he intended to break into atomic research when he left the R.A.F. The colonel grunted and asked with laboured sarcasm what this had to do with enforcing the principle of the Big Gun. He seemed unimpressed by the casual reply :

" I want Britain to lead the world in atomic energy. It's got nothing to do with personal ambition. I don't want to make a fortune at it. This war has proved all the way through that you have to be strong to cast out fear."

" For Christ's sake, snap out of it, boy," said the colonel in a sudden upsurge of anger. " You're living in a dream-world."

Cheshire looked at him good-naturedly and knew it was useless trying to unravel these tangled issues with a man whom Nagasaki had disillusioned and thrown off balance. For the colonel and others, the experiment had been a grisly failure because they stupidly persisted in mixing emotion with their logic.

When he returned to London, he would call on the Prime Minister with his report and use the same detached military line of reasoning which had somehow upset these Americans. The remote domestic interlude of the General Election, and the displacement of Churchill by Attlee, had made little impression on him : it had taken place at a bad time, when Tinian was in the early grip of the atomic obsession and before anyone knew for certain whether there would be an opportunity to test the bombs on Japan. He remembered now that his assignment had come through Churchill, while his report would have to be made to Attlee, but there was no good reason why this should make any difference to the force or effect of his argument.

Such was the prevailing state of Leonard Cheshire's mind as he watched Penney prepare to leave again for Japan with the other scientists to study on the ground the havoc their handiwork had caused. There had been no melodramatic change in his outlook on war or on the purpose of human life. On the contrary, though Nagasaki's doom had at first stunned his senses, it left his understanding high, dry and elated ; and the subsequent collapse of the Japanese will to resist had justified that elation to the full. War was a grim business, perhaps ; but, being also a condition of mind, war still had its moments of reassuring truth for the hardened strategist.

Facts, alas, are duller and more stubborn things to handle than the tempting fruits of fiction ; and stranger events have happened to unhinge a man's reason than Cheshire's last operational mission on that August morning ten years ago. A few chosen souls have been favoured in the course of history with providential visions which instantly opened their minds to the truth about life or themselves, as the eyes of a man called Saul were once opened as he rode down the road to Damascus. It is a pity for the sake of good melodrama that nothing remotely comparable overtook Cheshire over Japan ; his reason remained sound as a bell, his values remained untouched. The route to Nagasaki was neither the road to Damascus nor a short-cut to bedlam for him.

The basis of a view of existence which events on Tinian served only to crystallise was laid long before, in the years Leonard Cheshire had spent as a pilot in Bomber Command, as a carefree undergraduate at Oxford, as a schoolboy at Stowe, and at the beginning as a child at home.

CHAPTER ONE

THE FAMILY

ONLY the doctor who brought him into the world about dawn on September 7th, 1917, seemed disposed to share the relief of Leonard Cheshire's young mother. The little private nursing home in Chester was a sad, dispiriting place, and the prim nurses who moved in and out of the room like blue and white robots appeared too starched for feeling. Primrose Cheshire, an attractive girl in her early twenties with fair hair and commanding steel-blue eyes, had rarely known a time when she longed so much for company.

Geoffrey, her husband, was in France. The posts were slow and erratic, and she could not be sure where he was or whether he was alive or dead. Life was full of ironies. If he had remained an Oxford don or even a musketry instructor instead of volunteering for the balloon section of the Royal Flying Corps, Geoffrey might have been pacing the corridor downstairs, at this moment, anxious and helpless. But even the tritely absurd picture of the overwrought, expectant father suffering the indirect pangs of child-birth would have been preferable to this inhuman caricature of loneliness.

" He's a lively little chap," said the doctor. " Must be like his father with those brown eyes." His voice trailed cheerfully on. He sounded really interested in the new baby, and genuinely sorry that the father could not be there to add to the mother's somewhat muted joy. Primrose Cheshire was grateful for his thoughtfulness. Nor was she surprised when twenty-four years later an unexpected letter arrived from the doctor congratulating her on the award of his Chester baby's first D.S.O. The old man died not long afterwards, before the infant prodigy he was so proud of won the V.C.

Geoffrey Cheshire learnt the news of the birth of his first son several days later, and prayerfully hoped he would live to see him. A fairly tall, spare man of thirty-one with solemn brown

eyes, bushy brows, a long thin face, and an aloofly studious
manner, which hid a stubborn will and a sometimes explosive
temper, he did not much care for the dangerous, unromantic
work he was doing. He had moved from the Cheshire Regiment
to the R.F.C. on an impulse in 1916. Before that the war had
been a pleasant billet, training with the reserve battalion in
Wales. It had certainly been fraught with fewer risks than
exposing himself daily in an unarmed balloon basket 800 feet
or so above the British front line at Arras, and later at
Ypres.

For months he had been floating perilously in his frail little
observation post, waiting for a shell to blow him into eternity
and slightly envious of the men who flew machines which could
be manœuvred for evasive as well as offensive action.

The tension of " sitting " daily for the German heavy gunners
gradually told on Geoffrey Cheshire ; and he was greatly relieved
when the R.F.C. transferred him home towards the end of
October, in time for his son's christening. Primrose travelled
to London from her mother-in-law's Chester home for the
ceremony in the Grosvenor Chapel. She, too, was glad to move.
A forthright, sensitive person, who liked arranging affairs in her
own way, she had felt hemmed in and frustrated. Now that
Geoffrey was reunited with her and the child, life could start
afresh.

They had no difficulty in choosing Christian names for the
baby : the tiny aged puckered face was unmistakably the face
of a Cheshire, and they called him Geoffrey after his father. The
second name of Leonard was a tribute to a maternal uncle he
would never see, the youngest of his mother's four brothers
who had been killed at Kut-el-Amara in Mesopotamia earlier
in the year at the age of twenty-one. Geoffrey's brother,
Christopher, who is known to Members of Parliament to-day
as chaplain of the House of Commons, baptised the baby and was
mildly astonished that there was no shrill protest when the cold
water was poured over his head.

At the end of his leave, Captain Cheshire took furnished
rooms in Wanstead as near as possible to the site of his new unit.
To tighten the defence of London against future Zeppelin
attacks, a ring of barrage balloons had been placed round the
outer perimeter of the capital. The blind ungainly monsters

nosed the air at the end of their long, steel leads, the wintry sunlight catching their gleaming flanks as they slowly swayed to
and fro above the housetops. Cheshire was curious about their
usefulness as air traps, but his curiosity was not gratified. There
were no raids while he was stationed at Wanstead. Still he was
pleased to be on the ground for a change, letting the balloons
fend for themselves.

Neither at Wanstead nor at Tenby, in Pembrokeshire, where
he was posted early in 1918, did Cheshire have to take up any
more balloons. The R.F.C. discovered that he knew a fair
amount about law ; and until the Armistice he was put to work
in the legal department's offices at Haverfordwest. It was a
more economical use, perhaps, for the brains of an Oxford don
who preferred tennis to flying and had an aura of academic
aloofness even in uniform. But he could still look back to the
early days with a touch of nostalgia, and would at a pinch have
gone out again to stalk for the British guns and to provide
daily shooting practice for the Germans.

2

Geoffrey Cheshire was twenty-seven and a Fellow of Exeter
College, Oxford, when he met his future wife on a tennis court
in Chester in 1914. She had been spending a short holiday with
an army colleague of her father's whose home happened to stand
opposite the tennis court. Primrose Barstow, her two sisters
and four brothers, were rare visitors to England. Her father, a
former colonel in the Seaforth Highlanders, brought his wife
and family home to Edinburgh from the Continent only now and
then. He found it cheaper and generally more stimulating to
live abroad, renting large and inexpensive houses in Italy or
Switzerland for the greater part of the year. At this period only
Leonard, his youngest son, and the three girls were still with
him, enjoying a cosmopolitan existence in the Europe of open
frontiers and learning to speak French, Italian and German as
fluently as English. The three eldest sons had already grown up
and left : Arthur and Thomas were commissioned army officers,
and Jack had disappointed his father by going to India for a
job in textiles. He had been refused a commission owing to
exceptionally weak eyesight ; but his father found it bitterly

degrading to think of any son of his as a businessman. Soldiering was in the Barstow blood.

In spite of that, he developed a sneaking liking for Geoffrey Cheshire as a prospective son-in-law A young man with the law in his blood was virtually an untouchable, someone outside the family pale. The possibilities as he saw them did not extend to the idea of Geoffrey in uniform as a civilian-soldier, even though at that moment an archduke was preparing for a state visit to Bosnia and a group of Serbian nationalists across the Adriatic were planning an assassination that would plunge the world into war within five weeks. What the colonel could not understand was the perverse determination of any eligible bachelor in his senses to wed a daughter of his !

On August 4th, a few hours before Britain's ultimatum to Germany expired, Primrose crossed the Channel to France. It was a characteristic gesture. She had recently returned from Naples with a rather depressed fiancé to spend a few weeks in England, but her anxiety to rejoin the family abroad increased daily with the international tension.

" It's madness, of course," he said with matter-of-fact resignation. " You'll be cut off before you get anywhere near Switzerland."

Various officials told her the same thing on the way, but she swept all objections imperiously aside and reached the Alpine village near Sion, where the Barstows had moved, after a hot chaotic journey in crowded troop trains that took the best part of three days.

That autumn, Oxford relaxed its rigid little rule which obliged young dons to remain unmarried for seven years when Cheshire volunteered, appropriately enough, for the regiment that bore his name. Since he was leaving the University and might not return, the authorities decided that it would be safe enough to lift the formal embargo on his marriage.

" They're going to be peeved if I'm not killed after all," he wrote dryly to Primrose.

In November 1915, a few months after the Barstows packed up and returned to England for the duration, the couple were married in Christ Church, Lancaster Gate. The colonel, reconciled at last to the unavoidable, was there to give his daughter away.

3

Early in 1919, the Cheshires took a house in North Oxford, and Geoffrey was appointed Bursar of Exeter College. Leonard was now an active, bright child, talking and walking at eighteen months ; a second baby was on the way ; and Dr. Cheshire had readjusted himself to the academic routine without effort.

They called the new baby Christopher, a name common to both families, and when he was two Mrs. Cheshire took him and his elder brother to France for fifteen months. The old urge to travel abroad was in her again ; and she easily managed to persuade her husband that the world was a bigger place than Oxford and that there was no reason why the children should not start to see it while still young. At Pau, the fashionable spa near the foothills of the Pyrenees where they stayed with their grandmother, the two boys were soon jabbering together in French. Their education in the Barstow tradition had begun, and they seemed to thrive on it.

The elder boy was very much a Cheshire in manner as well as in looks, whereas Christopher with his blond mop of hair and blue eyes was just as obviously a Barstow. Mrs. Cheshire adored them both, but the younger child naturally claimed more of her attention and affection. Christopher was placid, friendly and utterly uncomplicated. Leonard was his constant companion, teaching him how to balance on a bicycle, climb a tree, and aim straight with a toy gun. He had some of his father's detached alertness and dry humour, so that it was a rare event to find the boys arguing or quarrelling.

There was something almost adult at times in his intuitive desire to please. Yet when he was seven and had been a pupil for two years at Miss Owen's, a private preparatory school in Oxford, he began to show signs of possessing an independent mind of his own. There were occasions, in his mother's words, when he would " just drift off into a separate world." Though he was never sullen or huffy, his mother lost patience with his habit of dreamy moodiness. It seemed unnatural in a boy so young, and clashed with the infectious gaiety and touching thoughtfulness which often characterised him.

" The boy's got a fierce will of his own," said his father.

But his mother insisted that Leonard's will was a wayward legacy from the Cheshire branch of the family.

Unlike most modern middle-class parents, Dr. and Mrs. Cheshire probably knew more about their forebears than was good for them; and the "family trees" provided both with rival clues to the less endearing traits of the children. The Cheshires were a force in the county of that name when Charles I was on the throne; and Sir Thomas Cheshire, who took up arms in the Civil War and fought on the King's side against the Roundheads at Edge Hill in 1642, is the earliest recorded member of the line. The family papers are vague about his fate. It is thought that he paid the penalty for fighting on the wrong side as a Cavalier and was dispossessed of his lands during the dictatorship of Cromwell.

While Sir Thomas was upholding the Royalist cause in the West, a Yorkshire landowner called Thomas Barstow was equally active against the Rebel Parliament. He seems to have been taken prisoner in the rout of Marston Moor, where a Royal Air Force station would one day stand, and a remote modern descendant called Leonard Cheshire would serve as a Group Captain in 1943. Barstow was put on trial in York, and the County Commissioners deprived him, too, of his estates. He was the first in a long line of soldiers.

Young Leonard Cheshire did not share his parents' interest in the family past. Perhaps he was put off by hearing too much about shadowy ancestors who were proudly invoked as living personages.

If there were odd corners in his mind for scenes and dreams of the past they had to be scenes and dreams with no family puppet strings attached. For instance, he never tired of hearing certain stories out of the Bible; and Mrs. Cheshire grew used to seeing him " in tears at the sad bits." The sight of a beggar or a deformed person in the street had an even stronger effect on him; poverty and suffering in the flesh gave a keener edge to the truth of the stories.

Colonel Barstow had been wrong in his hasty surmise that the Cheshires were all lawyers. Until the middle of the 18th century they were small landowners in the Hartford district of Cheshire. The family coat-of-arms contains wheat sheaves to show that they held their estates under the Earls of Chester, and the crest is surmounted by a large Talbot hound with its tongue jutting out and its right paw poised on a miniature blood-red shield. Leonard's parents, whose knowledge of heraldry has always been of the hit and miss variety, would have preferred a Cheshire cat.

The legal strain in the family emerged under pressure of economic necessity, with the big families of early Victorian days. Leonard's great-grandfather, Christopher, was the first lawyer in the field. A practising solicitor in the Northwich region, he gave legal advice to the Council on highways, the destitute poor, and rural sanitation, and became the Registrar of the County Court. He had to earn his living because his father, in old age, had run through a fortune of more than £100,000 in less than a year with the spendthrift collaboration of John, his youngest and favourite son.

John is described by the family chronicler as a " handsome, clever young man, who preferred hunting and other sports to any useful work. He persuaded his father, who had no business head whatever but ample means, to embark on speculative undertakings and invest a large part of his fortune in salt mines." The salt mines which swallowed the Cheshire inheritance were in the Northwich neighbourhood, and the ruins can be seen to this day.

" The charming home at Hartford had to be given up," mourns the family chronicler. " All its treasures were sold, but the creditors could not be fully paid, and debt was a heavy burden for years."

If the family had a spendthrift whose ravages had to be lived down by sheer industriousness, it was also collaterally linked with a romantic adventurer through Leonard's great-grandmother. Her maiden name was Frances Phillips ; and she appeared to be the typically English daughter of exceedingly rich English parents. She was descended in fact from Ian MacPhadraic, a highland chieftain, who followed the standard of Bonnie Prince Charlie from the victorious skirmish of Prestonpans to the catastrophe of Culloden field, where he was killed in 1746. The rebel's estates were forfeited to the Crown, and his clansmen were dispersed or transported as convicts to the colonies. But his eldest son, Thomas, escaped to York, took the Sassenach name of Phillips and turned to a trade in which, as a good Scot, he was

B

presumably a natural adept : the distilling of gin. " He rose
to celebrity as a gin-distiller," says the chronicler, " and was
known by the quodlibet DOCTOR Phillips—gin being drunk at the
time as a cure for stomach complaints—and at his death left a
colossal fortune to his widow."

The family name of Cheshire had to be kept alive by a legal
artifice in 1817. John Widdowson, a gentleman pensioner of
Peterhouse, Cambridge, increased his own riches to the tune
of £45,000 by complying with an injunction in the will of his
maternal great-uncle, the last of the male Cheshires in the direct
line of descent. Applying for a Royal Sign Manual, he changed
his own surname to Cheshire. The family recovered slowly
from the salt mines fiasco half-way through the 19th century.
By hard work and thrift, Christopher Cheshire, the first lawyer,
paid off most of the debts. One of his sons, Walter, became his
legal partner, extended the solicitor's practice, and succeeded
him as Registrar of Northwich County Court. And it was to
the Chester home of Walter, her father-in-law, that Mrs. Cheshire
went for the birth of her first child, when Geoffrey was at the
front with the R.F.C. in 1917. Leonard had some interesting
ancestors. His parents regretted at times that he could work up
no enthusiasm for them.

4

When he was eight, they sent him to the Dragon School in
Oxford as a day-boy. His companions included the sons of
other dons, and some of them wore the permanently worried
look of boys on whom too many exacting demands have been
made. Mr. A. E. Lynam, the headmaster, had a gentle way of
dealing with parents who expected him to discover and bring on
early genius, but the Cheshires were too realistic to regard
Leonard as anything but a boy who might in time learn to use
his brains. He was far from lazy and they knew that he was
a quick thinker with a good memory and plenty of quiet self-
confidence. He settled down as a good, average boy, who held
his own in the middle of his class. Strangely enough Lynam
was pleased. He recognised that Leonard had a mind which in
some mysterious fashion was too big for its books, at any rate
for the groundwork books of the preparatory school. Therefore
he did not force him forward faster than the boy wanted to go.

In March, 1929, after looking at various sites around Oxford, Dr. Cheshire bought a three-acre plot of land at Cothill, near Abingdon, and started to build his own house. It was a novel undertaking for a dignified Oxford don, and there were raised eyebrows and incredulous chuckles over the teacups in many a Fellow's drawing-room. He engaged an architect who was a close personal friend—T. Harold Hughes, the designer of many University buildings, including the new Taylorian, at Oxford— and slowly the walls of a beautiful, modern house in grey Berkshire stone began to rise. They took rooms in a local farm, hired their own labour, appointed their own foreman, and bought their own materials. At week-ends, and in the longer early summer evenings, the boys and their father would put on overalls when the workmen had gone, inspect their work, and even do a bit of overtime for them.

Dr. Cheshire travelled the ten miles to and from Exeter College every day by car, dropping the boys at school in the morning and picking them up again in the evening. Lynam was fascinated by the whole project; and on his occasional visits would stand admiring the energy of Mrs. Cheshire and the nimbleness of the two boys as they sat aloft boarding the unfinished roof and laying tiles. " We worked for hours at it," Leonard recalls. " I remember father losing his footing on the roof one day, slipping half off, and mercifully getting his clothes entangled in the scaffolding. It was hard going at times."

As a diversion, Leonard spent hours in the open with the farmer, learning how to handle a shotgun and pick off a rabbit or a crow from a few yards. The farmer liked his pluck and untiring readiness to learn, but was extremely reserved about his marksmanship.

By November, Grey Walls was ready, and the Cheshires moved in. The world and its problems were forgotten as they laid out the garden, planted sapling trees in the drive, and levelled the ground for tennis courts. Mrs. Cheshire had green fingers and a passion for flowers; the boys were obliging rather than keen understudies; and their father had to be prised out of the big, book-lined study upstairs where he had swiftly installed himself. The domestic upheaval was amply repaid by the self-contained privacy of a comfortable home of their own in the country, within easy reach of school and University. Like their

yeoman ancestors on both sides, the Cheshires felt the independent pride of living in surroundings that had been fashioned
by themselves, steering clear of the house agents and refusing to
be fobbed off with somebody else's notion of an ideal home.

Both boys were now at the Dragon School, and towards the
end of 1930 Dr. Cheshire decided that Leonard should become
a boarder in order to acclimatise him gradually to the routine
and discipline of school life. He was thirteen, still rather small
for his age, but making up for lack of inches with a cool
determination and a poise beyond his years. He was not
particularly good at games ; and Lynam's hope that he would
suddenly be inspired to make a spurt in class had not yet been
realised.

CHAPTER TWO

THE SCHOOLBOY

LEONARD'S father was not too pleased with the reports from the Dragon School. He had hoped for quicker and better results, and several times he asked the headmaster whether the boy was really trying.

Lynam pleaded with Dr. Cheshire to show a little patience and more appreciation. "Some boys with strong wills can't be set a standard pace," he said. "Leonard's got the brains all right, and if he's encouraged to use them without nagging, he'll use them."

It was admittedly all a little galling to a parent of Dr. Cheshire's temperament and academic standing, particularly in the small, cloistered, talkative world of Oxford, where it was implicitly accepted as a law of nature that the son of a don should follow dutifully in his father's footsteps at least as far as the doors of the University.

Leonard instinctively sensed his father's hopes and the store he placed by success in the schoolroom. Though he had little of the average schoolboy's inborn horror of the competitive examination, he realised that he could clear the coming hurdle and qualify for a place in a public school only by pushing himself without reserve. So the late spring and early summer of 1931 found him working harder than ever before, with " Joc " Lynam, the headmaster's son, singling him out for special coaching in mathematics, a subject he detested.

By ordinary worldly standards, the Cheshires were comfortably off ; but the salary of a Fellow and Bursar of an Oxford college, with no private means beyond the royalties trickling in from his first book on Law, could hardly stretch to cover the high cost of educating two sons at a first-class public school. This additional source of income might have done so later, when Cheshire's *Modern Real Property* became an accepted classic among lawyers all over the English-speaking world, but certainly not at this trying period when the father was faced with the nice problem of deciding which school would set a scholarship test simple enough to give Leonard a faint, outsider's chance of winning a place.

Marlborough had been the first choice, and Leonard's name was put down, but later removed because of the expense and the sharp competition for subsidised places. Lynam, who was called in to advise on a more practical choice, rightly decided to take the matter into his own hands. His opening move was a lengthy telephone call one day to Dr. J. F. Roxburgh, the head-master of Stowe, the school which had been founded amidst much bickering and head-shaking only eight years before in a great, dilapidated house on the outskirts of Buckingham.

Lynam was much blunter than Dr. Cheshire would ever have given him credit for. He told Roxburgh :

" The boy is nowhere near first-rate scholarship form, of course, and that's flat. But he's steady and intelligent. My view is that Leonard is one of these late developers, who's likely to come on exceedingly well in time. Will you consider giving him a chance ? " Roxburgh thought it over for a minute or two, and agreed to take the risk.

Whether his father's admonitions, Lynam's support or the extra work Leonard had been doing tipped the scales nobody ever discovered in the Cheshire household ; but their delight was as real as their relief when a formal note arrived one morning from Roxburgh. Leonard had pulled it off by some incom-prehensible fluke, winning the tenth of the ten scholarship places.

On a warm mid-September afternoon, he kissed his mother good-bye, shook hands with his father, and waved with a casual grown-up indifference he did not feel to Christopher. The family car moved slowly down the twisting gravel drive, and he turned away feeling small and lonely. So this was Stowe, his home for the next five years ; and this was Roxburgh, the tall erect man with the strong sensitive face, lips that could relax quickly into a warming smile and eyes like kindly gimlets. The headmaster led him up the steps of the North Front, assuring him in a fatherly way that he would like Chatham House. In time, perhaps, he would ; but at that moment he was just another small, homesick boy perplexed by the vast strangeness of his surroundings and the grey vista of days and weeks before the Christmas holidays.

Between early bouts of homesickness, Cheshire found himself gasping at the incredible size and proportioned beauty of the school buildings and grounds. He had to walk the whole length of the South Front to reach Chatham House, a plain red brick modern block which stood some distance away from the classical miracle of Robert Adam's magnificent central portico ; and the panorama of tree-lined avenues, rolling lawns with the lakes between, and ornamental temples half-glimpsed through gaps in the walls of waving green foliage, helped him to forget how sorry he felt for himself.

Roxburgh had seen the possibilities of Stowe from the beginning, when the first big sale of treasures from the ancestral home of the Temple family took place in 1921. A man of great energy, taste and vision, very much steeped in the humanist spirit of the 18th century, he was determined as a headmaster to recapture the best of it and to revive in a new form the vanished glories of Stowe. He was certain that boys brought up in daily touch with such historic beauty and grandeur, in and about the private palace where the " Grenville Cousinhood " had thriven as the real rulers of England for the long lifetime of a man, would acquire at any rate a subconscious appreciation of its worth.

Every House in the new school was named after leading members of the families which had once made Stowe illustrious. Bruce and Temple, Grenville and Chandos, Cobham and Grafton, Walpole and Chatham. And it was to Chatham, called after the greatest of them all, that Cheshire was allotted by the luck of the draw.

2

Leonard's loneliness gradually wore off, and the rough community life began to appeal to him. A wiry boy, rather small and light for his age, with " eyebrows that met in the middle " above sharp brown eyes and a rather pouting smile, he found his niche in Chatham and made a few friends. Instead of fagging, he had to " office " after the first fortnight, helping to clean out prefects' and monitors' studies, and washing up crockery in the kitchen. At table in the long bright refectory that looked out across rolling lawns of the South Front towards the lake and the

Corinthian Arch on the hill beyond, he sat opposite a big boy
called Taylor, two years his senior. He liked Taylor for his
North Country candour, his useful knowledge of the rules and
the peculiarities of the masters, and his noisy way of eating.
In ordinary gratitude, he pulled Taylor's leg by telling dramatic
stories about imaginary happenings in the Lower House with an
air of solemn innocence and a perfectly straight face. A disarming smile at the last moment usually saved him from a kick
on the shins—or worse.

With Charles and Pat Ashton, twin brothers whose home was
near his at Cothill and new members of Chatham House like
himself, he struck up a quick comradeship. Games and lessons
were necessary evils that had to be accepted, but the Stowe
rules made it possible to cultivate interests that would have been
considered childish or revolutionary in older public schools with
less flexible traditions. That was part of the genius of Roxburgh
as a headmaster. He believed in giving full scope to the individual
interests and tastes of his pupils within the proper limits. The
Ashtons brimmed over with the countryman's inbred love of the
countryside and its ways ; with them Leonard went on the first
of many memorable expeditions : fishing, bird-watching or
nesting in the grounds.

During his first two terms he worked diligently but with
no enthusiasm, and Mr. P. G. Hunter, his tutor, seemed reasonably satisfied. Hunter, a self-effacing scholarly man, gained the
confidence of Leonard and many another new boy before and
since by his wry manner and unexpected firmness. " Piggy ",
as they called him, " knew his stuff " and " got results " without
pressure. He felt that Cheshire was worth watching, though it
was very doubtful whether he would ever win a prize. The
inclination and ambition to shine as a bookworm were not in
him.

" He is a consistently steady worker," Hunter reported.
" His attitude to his studies is conscientious and certainly more
than passive, but he cannot be called outstandingly bright at
any subject. Quite clever, certainly above average, but really not
remarkable."

Nobody except Leonard himself had any serious doubts
about his ability to pass the School Certificate in his first summer
term, and his marks were higher than he judged possible.

Roxburgh sent a satisfactory report to Dr. Cheshire hinting at an untapped reserve of talent which partly explained the credits in English, Latin, Greek, French and elementary mathematics. He was convinced that this had more to do with personality and character than intellectual promise. The headmaster was glad that the boy had found his feet at Stowe ; with some coaxing the latent vigour in this quiet, pleasant, resolute youngster could be drawn out : and Roxburgh was determined to do it.

" I was very happy at Stowe when I got used to it," Cheshire admits. " I liked the surroundings, the masters and many of the boys—and we all worshipped ' J. F.' as everyone called Rox-burgh. Without knowing it at the time I was deeply influenced by him. He was kind, enthusiastic and full of dignity. He made you feel you were letting him down if you did anything stupid and he could see right through you."

Roxburgh in fact was Stowe. He had reversed the hallowed order of things by which even Arnold was forced at first to subordinate himself and his ideals to an institution, building his own community where boys were treated as individuals. Small wonder that some outsiders looked on aghast, confidently predicting that a school run on these heretical lines would very soon close from lack of support. It took a bold man of Roxburgh's stature to experiment with a method of teaching boys to behave while encouraging them to be themselves. And Stowe is one of the few first-class public schools which could have found room under the same roof for masters like T. H. White and boys like Leonard Cheshire, the de Havilland brothers and Jack Anderson.

T. H. White is better known to the public as an established novelist with a flair for whimsy which can be as pungent as Evelyn Waugh's satire or Eric Linklater's rabelaisian sense of the ridiculous. He was wrestling uncomfortably with his first book between taking classes and escaping into the open air from the frustrations of teaching English when Leonard Cheshire came to his notice. And there are flashes of his quizzical regard for the boy here and there in the loose diary pages of *England Have My Bones*. A large, benign, sensitive and florid man in those days, with a sharp zest for life and some healthy hates, he managed somehow to combine teaching with the active pursuits

of the freelance country squire. White's love of the countryside
was as deep and perceptive as Cobbett's ; he revelled in its per-
manence and rhythmic peace. " The whole British island is an
anchorage, if you avoid the towns," he could write, as one
stating a simple, self-evident truth. " So are the birds and beasts
and the sporting seasons . . . When London Bridge has tumbled
down, and the sewers of the hive have ceased to pollute the
waters, there will be salmon opposite the Imperial Chemical
building, but no Imperial Chemical building opposite the
salmon."

White has a single recollection of Cheshire at Stowe which
stands out among many memories of a full life. It dates back to
the autumn term of 1932, within days of the gloomy return from
the summer holidays. Before setting the usual essay : " What I
did in the holidays ", the master eyed his twenty boys with keen
distrust, and warned them that he was not interested in the usual
unimaginative rot that was resurrected year after year like
reheated hash. Anything " from rape to buzzing " would be
preferable to that. He implored them to try using the little bit
of brain they might have been blessed with, but passively
resigned himself to the inevitable deadliness of the dull mixture
as before.

As he glowered over the compositions later, reading how
one blockhead went camping at Aberystwyth and how another
helped a father with more money than sense to build a dinghy,
White came upon a blotted, scrawling essay that was different.
Two pages in a spidery hand—there was very little in it beyond
a description of a French beach on a hot summer's day and of
the only person in the bright crush of sunbathers and children
at play who arrested and stimulated the fancy of the writer : a
girl in a red bathing dress sitting nearby on the sand. But the
essay had the rough vigour of a primitive impressionist landscape.
The girl filled the whole background, blending perfectly with
that shimmering sense of gold and blue ; her skin was coffee-
coloured and she was a year younger than the English boy on
holiday who watched her with dumb admiration. " I gave
Cheshire an alpha-plus for what was quite a sensuous and vivid
piece of life appreciated," said White. " This ' Cheese ' always
did write me good essays after that. He was one of the few
children of fourteen or so who could actually *tell* you that he

liked to lie on his back in a hayfield, smelling clover and wondering what it would be like to fall upward into the clouds."

Cheshire was flattered by the grossly high marks he was given for that first essay, and responded willingly to White's informal methods of teaching, in school and out. Often he would rise before the bell clanged in the morning, stealing on tip-toe out of the dormitory with the Ashtons to accompany the master on a brief fishing or bird-watching expedition.

3

On the playing fields, Cheshire was never entirely himself. Games were compulsory, and the monitors and prefects made sure that everyone " pulled " for his House in the best public school manner. Because he saw the point of this local patriotism and rivalry, Cheshire " pulled " as best he could, without convincing anyone that he would be likely one day to win his cap for England at Twickenham. Unlike Douglas Bader as a boy, Cheshire had neither the physique nor the inclination to become a first-class athlete. Far from being written up in the sporting columns of *The Times*, his name was almost invariably passed over in stony silence by the school magazine. His muscles were often engaged, but seldom his complete interest.

He seemed to prefer parades, drills and practice shooting on the rifle range with the O.T.C. which he joined as soon as they would have him. Nor did he seem impressed when an aero club was started and its first members visited R.A.F. stations in the district for free flights and demonstrations.

Cheshire looked forward to his first summer term and to every subsequent one because of tennis, the game his father had taught him and the one school sport in which he excelled. With Roxburgh's approval he abandoned cricket entirely in favour of it. For his height and reach, he was a fast, forceful player who could turn a point to his advantage by coolly changing the pace of a stroke, lobbing a ball over his opponents' heads or producing a sudden sizzling slam that would raise the chalk from the base line.

Hunter, who took over the twenty boys after their year in White's care, appointed Cheshire acting editor of the school magazine in 1934. The work was casual and the position nominal. There was little writing for the *Stoic* that could not be farmed out to senior boys or masters who had something or other they badly wanted to say. At any rate, in the little matter of submitting articles to himself as editor of the *Stoic*, he compromised only twice with the authorities, and only then because there was no other way out.

However, Cheshire's half-formed views of life seen narrowly from his study in Chatham House as though through the wrong end of a telescope are unimportant beside the positive ideas that he learned from the first educated strangers in his experience, the four masters who had more to do with him than any others. Each in his own way was impressive; and their sharply contrasting outlooks and personalities added spice to the daily round. Nobody could fail to like or respect Roxburgh, genial yet firm in the grand manner, with his photographic memory for names, faces and birthdays, who knew everything that was going on by some sort of trained instinct. He was like a presence breathing everywhere. As regards White, Cheshire was much surer of his ground; there was a solid simplicity in this fastidious man which belied his eccentric ways and sardonic tongue. White put up philosophically with the slow torture of the classroom for the ample leisure it left him to roam the countryside studying birds, beasts and trees, or to burn up the narrow lanes in his old Bentley for private fishing, shooting and flying lessons.

Then there was Hunter, a quiet, even-tempered person, a human chameleon who seemed able to merge into the company or scenery, and who could talk work into the most stubborn brains. And finally there was Ivor Cross, the Chatham housemaster, a stickler for detail, just and rather unpopular with a streak of severity in him.

These four were the dominant influences on Cheshire, and he responded by learning a little from each at his own pace, without attempting to imitate or copy them slavishly. If Roxburgh's high sense of honour was attractive, the flamboyant habits of White probably struck the most responsive chord.

Those who served with Cheshire in the R.A.F., or who remember him at Oxford, will not miss the odd symbolism of the schoolmaster at the wheel of a fast car, or at the controls of an aircraft, proving to himself that timidity is an emotion which can be challenged and surmounted with a little effort.

4

White's fondness for animals was carried to odd lengths at times. Cheshire, who loathed anything slippery or slimy to the touch, shuddered when White gave the freedom of his room to half a dozen grass snakes caught by hand in the grounds during the mating season. For the comfort of his slithering pets, White filled the fireplace with moss, ferns and a tank of water. They in turn became attached to him. He loved to set them loose and watch them pouring their coils over the furniture and skidding across the polished floor.

One Sunday in spring White took a snake with him to chapel " to make him a Christian and to comfort me during the sermon." It lay snugly in his pocket, but did not change its creed as a result. Public school religion was a stiff and solemn and often depressing ritual, which was accepted as a mechanical part of the routine by Cheshire and others. He was not the " Pi " type. Evening prayers and the Sunday services in Lorimer's chapel were an integral part of the rule, but the God of Stowe seemed a rather stern Being who was never brought any closer. Religion became a bore, something that had its familiar place in the time-table but seldom went deeper than the emotional warmth of singing hymns. And even that glow of consolation was denied to Cheshire, who was half tone-deaf and could never keep in tune.

During the winter evenings, the numerous societies and clubs which Roxburgh permitted as part of his liberal policy came into their own. But none of them really appealed to Cheshire, nor did the distant din of orchestras scraping away at rehearsals or the choral society or madrigal singers stumbling on high notes disturb him as he sat alone in his room reading.

Historical novels were his favourite, and Charles Ashton (with whom he shared a study all through 1933-34) remembers him as a " voracious reader ". The adventurous doings of the heroes in the novels of Scott or Stevenson were far more intriguing than the heavy issues of the outside world which were regularly threshed out in the Debating Society or the League of Nations Union. He was not tempted out of curiosity to listen to Lord Cecil or Mr. J. R. Clynes giving expert views on current problems, or moved to a show of interest by the indignation of some of the older boys when a fiery socialist came to preach an

eloquent secular sermon against settling international disputes
by force, under the ægis of " The No War Movement".

Only in his last year did he feel it necessary to give a better
example ; and twice he took part in public discussions. The
second occasion was the more memorable. Stowe still boasts
of a small, distinctive literary society known as " The Twelve "
which meets to hear its members deliver papers on chosen
themes. Mr. John Boyd-Carpenter had been one of its leading
lights in the early pioneering days, and Cheshire sat through
several prodigiously tedious papers in which keen young men
explored " The Critical Method " or dissected the lives of " The
Brontës " or " The Thought of D. H. Lawrence ". In November the president asked him to prepare something of his own,
and he obliged. His paper on " Beer " was sandwiched between
one on " Greek Thinkers " and another on the " Life and Times
of François Villon ", and its clever irreverence pained some of
Stowe's budding intellectuals. He was not asked to take the
floor again.

As head of Chatham House in the autumn and winter of
1935, a position he filled with distinction, Cheshire was respected
rather than popular, especially among the younger boys. The
fact that he was a " good all-rounder ", a kind leader who could
be serious without show or fuss, compensated for his sometimes
distant, off-hand manner. " He certainly raised the standards of
the House, and did so without bullying or driving," said the
Hon. Martin Buckmaster, who was a member of the Lower
school. " You never would have thought such a strong sense of
purpose could go with a quiet, unassuming nature." With his
fellow-prefects and monitors Cheshire was perhaps more of an
enigma. His intelligence had tended in the past to make him
choose companions from among the senior boys. Now that he
was at the top of the House himself, he began to feel a certain
isolation. Only Jack Anderson, his second-in-command, was
drawn to him, as a friend as well as a colleague. And it is a
strange coincidence that Jack also went on to win the V.C. in
1943 as a Major in the Argyll and Sutherland Highlanders. The
award was for capturing Longstop Hill, in Tunisia, with four
officers and less than forty men against very formidable opposition. Anderson lived only six months longer, and was killed in
action in Italy towards the end of 1943.

Cheshire's aim was to protect from the heavy-handed wrath of the housemaster boys who broke minor rules, but considerateness of this personal kind hurt prefectorial pride, and was sometimes denounced behind the scenes as likely to undermine House discipline. In fact it did almost the opposite, increasing the average sense of trust. Roxburgh's personal example was proving potent in Chatham more than it seemed reasonable to expect. Niall MacManus, now a busy London doctor, recalls that " Leonard went to a lot of trouble deciding how to deal with individuals who broke the rules. He would inevitably settle matters in his own fashion, and only after much thought." MacManus was a contemporary of Cheshire's and a monitor under him at Chatham.

Ivor Cross recognised but did not always approve of this strongly individualist approach. Once, in order to stress the importance of " House spirit ", Cheshire rounded up every boy who was not actually in bed with a temperature for an inter-House cross-country race. It was an unprecedented action to which Cross gave his blessing only hesitantly and reluctantly ; for it meant overruling the matron, who was already clucking over the imaginary ailments of a much larger panel of patients than usual.

All the snifflers, the genuine and the backsliders, turned out and ran, none the worse for the fresh air. But the matron's authority was not challenged again. There were seldom any cases at all for her to attend to when a House sporting event was taking place.

Cross attempted at times to damp his head boy's enthusiasm for finding ways of keeping members of the house on their toes. It was not easy to curb him : " If I were asked to assess his character as a boy, I should call him a stranger to *pretence* in any form," the master said. " I am not likely to forget Leonard, and am bound to say that his way of life to-day is *not* out of line with the spirit of his approach to school as I saw it."

Nor is any eyewitness likely to forget one special moment of embarrassment for Ivor Cross on an October night in 1935, when the master (who was an excellent musician) held an impromptu House concert round the piano in the music room. All the members of the Chatham Cabinet and a number of sixth form boys led the audience in the singing of popular songs ;

and not a few of the younger boys were given a pleasant jolt
by the master's light-hearted mood. He seemed relaxed and
friendly, a very different man somehow from the firm disciplin-
arian they knew.

" Now I want some of you to sing solos," said Cross im-
pulsively. " And we'll start with you, Cheshire."

Cheshire lost his composure for a second. " You know I'd
like to, sir," he said apologetically, " but I just can't. I never
seem able to find the right note. Do you mind if I tell a story
instead ? "

" All right," said Cross. " I'm sure that will spare us all
unnecessary pain. The rest of you can think of your songs while
he's reciting."

Cheshire's story went down only too well. It was a hoary
variation on one of the unwritten fables of La Fontaine with a
flippant moral twist in the tail. It slowly described the fate of a
foolish fledgling bird which paid no heed to its mother's warnings
and went hopping and fluttering down a garden path one
peaceful morning, chasing the seeds of a dandelion clock. The
poor bird looked neither to left nor right, ignored the warning
cries from the nest and failed to see in the excitement of the
chase a great black villain of a cat crouching behind the trunk of
a tree ready to pounce. " The little bird, of course, was pinned
down, killed and eaten," he concluded. " And the moral is :
don't lose your head over a little bit of fluff." Cheshire was
taken aback by the immediate roar of laughter, but his grin
faded as he saw Cross's lips tighten in anger. Then he realised
what a tactless idiot he had been. He could not have chosen a
more unfortunate tale if he had tried. For the housemaster had
married only a few weeks earlier. To be humiliated in public
by his own Head boy was insufferable. A public apology here
and now was indicated. Before Cheshire could apologise, however, Cross was off the piano stool and across the room in a
flash, slamming the door hard behind him. For several days
afterwards, relations between the two were correct rather than
cordial.

One of his admirers as head of the house was Christopher,
his brother. A bad attack of osteomyelitis in 1933 had put him
to bed for nearly six months, and he had returned to Stowe
inches taller but no less good-natured than before. Leonard,

who still felt guilty because he had once thought Christopher was shamming and had complained in the early days of the illness that he could not sleep a wink at night for the cries from the next bed, kept a discreet protective watch on him.

The first taste of real responsibility thoroughly agreed with Cheshire. All the evidence Stowe can give shows it ; and nobody was more affirmative on the point than Roxburgh himself. I was fortunate enough to encounter this enlightened man early in 1954, a few weeks before his sudden death. His life had been given to the school he founded ; he was prematurely worn out and still haunted by the negative success of his ideals mirrored in the grim wartime casualty lists of a generation of pupils. " One boy in every seven who joined up lost his life," he kept repeating. " One in every eight was decorated. A new school can be proud of such sacrifice but neither school nor country can afford the loss."

Roxburgh's summing up of Cheshire, with whom he kept in touch to the end of his life, was typically dispassionate. " He was very successful as a schoolboy, in the ordinary sense," he said.

" He became head of his house, a prefect, a member of the sixth form (the august twelve) and captain of lawn tennis. But any first-rate boy can expect a career of that kind at his public school, and I cannot say that he made more impression on what was certainly a distinguished generation than several others did. Leonard could not have reached the position he did among boys like that if he had not been pretty good. But that does not mean that he showed as a schoolboy the extraordinary qualities that he developed later as a fighting man. I personally was much attached to him, and I felt for him not only affection but respect. There was something about him—was it perhaps a kind of moral dignity ?—which made it inconceivable that he would think or do anything which was below top level. He knew how to make other people do the right thing, too, and his courteous, even gentle manner, covered a pretty tough will, which made him a strong ruler in his House and an effective prefect in the school. But all this could be said of other boys who as men never became pre-eminent as Leonard did . . . I should have expected him to do well when tested by war, but I should not have foreseen that he would become what he became or achieve what he

achieved. I doubt if such development and such achievement
could have been predicted of anyone. . . ."

Schoolmasters are normally sound judges of character, and
in the light of Cheshire's later career Roxburgh's appreciation
was not unduly flattering. But schoolmasters rarely have the
time or aptitude to cast good horoscopes ; they are often blind
to the meaning of small symptoms of uneasiness which are plain
enough to parents narrowly wondering how much their children
have changed as they emerge from the cocoon at the end of
every school term. Yet the normal boy, growing up with a
foot in the two conflicting worlds of boarding-school and home,
measuring the frontiers between in months instead of miles, and
accepting the different standards of each as a matter of course,
seldom fails to shake off passing restlessness, like a dog getting
rid of fleas. Marx might have been writing glumly of his own
schooldays when he described man as a product of his environment ; Orwell might have been describing schoolboys instead
of pigs when he coined the slogan " all animals are equal, but
some are more equal than others." For only the schoolboy can
be a snob and a communist at the same time without a pang of
self-conscious guilt.

Cheshire accepted both worlds with a good grace until he
was seventeen. Nor were his parents concerned for the future.
They had every reason to hope the boy would take Oxford and
the bar in the same unhurried stride as he was taking Stowe.
Their brightest memory of his schoolboy adaptability was of the
late summer of 1933, when the outbreak of a contagious disease
at school earned him an unexpected holiday at home. Roxburgh
had sent word to all parents that boys should be reminded to do
a little work, but Leonard needed little coaxing. He would sit
quietly on a deckchair in the sunlit garden, with a Greek or
Latin grammar in his hands and a loaded shotgun between his
knees. Frequently he would come in for tea with Christopher
carrying a wood-pigeon or a rabbit, his bonus for completing
the day's lessons.

Then two or three terms later something suddenly went
wrong. He left for a short holiday with an older friend who
lived near the Scottish border. The family was rich, and the
casual air of taking luxury for granted impressed him greatly.
He returned home to his parents rather moody and critical.

Practically all his conversation revolved ruefully round the big, comfortable house where he had been living in something like the style of the 18th-century Grenvilles at Stowe. His father's dry observation that money could not buy happiness had little effect. And one object in particular seemed to loom in the boy's mind like the symbol of a new set of values—an immense cocktail cabinet which had slid silently out of the wall in the lounge at the pressing of a button, displaying its array of expensive bottles. They did not know it yet, but Leonard had taken his first conscious step into a third world that had little in common with home or school, a world to which wealth was the master-key.

The episode seemed to have left no harmful traces. Leonard was the same unaffected, unobtrusively strong personality as before during the autumn and winter of 1935 at Stowe, working and playing hard and setting high standards for his House. Merely to have crossed the frontier into the old, familiar orbit of masters, dormitories, and roll-calls was enough.

It was a week or two after the episode of the frivolous cautionary tale at Ivor Cross's expense that Roxburgh entered Leonard's name for Merton, his father's old college. In a letter to the warden, the headmaster wrote, " Young Cheshire is an excellent boy. As a scholar he is tasteful and hard-working but not very gifted. But he has ambition."

It would have been premature, perhaps, for Roxburgh to speculate in which direction ambition would lead the boy ultimately, but he had few doubts that Leonard would do well at Oxford. Dr. Cheshire was by now more guarded, though not without hope. All would be well provided Leonard was meanwhile weaned away from idle dreams of luxurious living. Mrs. Cheshire, an excellent linguist, had always wanted him to travel and learn another language. Through a family friend with connections in Germany, the necessary arrangements were made; and on a blustering March day in 1936 Leonard piled into a car with his cases, not knowing that he was turning his back on his schooldays.

CHAPTER THREE

THE UNDERGRADUATE

To a man of Dr. Cheshire's rather saturnine disposition, the idea of breaking the news gently to Leonard that he would not be returning to Stowe was unthinkable. He had discovered from experience that, short of using force, the only effective way of steering the boy from a headstrong to a reasonable course was to resort to a kind of mental bribery. During the Easter holiday Dr. Cheshire made one or two tentative efforts to arouse Leonard's interest in Germany by talking like a travel folder, but had to give it up in disgust. His son was so full of Stowe, his plans for the school tennis season, and his unfinished guerilla campaign with Ivor Cross over House discipline (" I don't think I led him a dog's life, but he never quite knew what was coming next "), that for once drastic action seemed imperative.

On the last day but one of the holiday, Leonard's parents presented him with the *fait accompli*.

" You're going to Potsdam the day after to-morrow," they told him. If they had said Xanadu or Timbuctoo instead, his face would have worn the same set expression of displeasure. He knew it was too late for arguments, and suddenly looked crestfallen. At the silent, restrained leave-taking on the station platform, they detected signs of an underlying youthful bewilderment and could not help wondering whether they had made the right move.

Leonard's glum feeling of having been unceremoniously torn up by the roots did not survive the sea-crossing to Holland. On the long rail journey across Germany to Berlin he had already reconciled himself to the prospect of unsought independence at his father's expense for the next four months. He merely hoped that the von Reuters, his hosts, would not be too tedious to live with.

He was met in Berlin by Admiral Ludwig von Reuter himself, a small cask of a man with white closely-cropped hair, pebbly grey eyes and a square thrusting jaw, who greeted him in the clipped English he had learned as a prisoner-of-war in Britain. Leonard winced involuntarily when his host told him so. He felt as though he was entering a lion's den under false pretences. There were other boys at Stowe whose taste for contemporary history would have forearmed them sufficiently to deal with this retired German sea-lord who had gained notoriety in Allied lands and transitory fame among his own vanquished countrymen by scuttling the surrendered German Grand Fleet at Scapa Flow in 1919. Leonard ruefully admitted to himself that he knew little more about the event at the age of eighteen than he had known at the age of two, when it happened. He did not relish the prospect of being indoctrinated by its author.

His first letters home suggested that he was settling down well in the elegant home of the von Reuters at Potsdam. Frau von Reuter, a comely, house-proud woman, much younger than her husband, was most anxious to put the English visitor at his ease. From the window of his comfortable bed-sitting-room at the top of the house he could look out across the park and the lake and time himself at his desk by the mellow chimes of the Nicolai-Kirche clock striking the quarter hours. At the beginning the von Reuters half smothered him with their kind attentions. They had to be shown that he had come to learn their language, not to teach them his, so he spent the mornings alone upstairs. Leonard would daily cross the park to the home of a woman linguist for lessons, and over meals, with heavy humour, the Admiral would test his knowledge.

The sons were about his own age, but their manner was oddly formal and shy until they got used to the easy manners of the stranger from England. Leonard had smiled to hide his embarrassment when Derfflinger, the eldest, greeted him on the day of his arrival with a stiff bow, a click of the heels and a hard handshake. The second eldest, Emden, and the youngest boy, Hipper, stood in line to go through the same pantomime of welcome. They later satisfied his curiosity about their quaint first names by telling him rather pompously that they had been called after battleships. Sometimes, too, it seemed that their father walked over their feelings as he would over his own quarter-deck. Leonard, by contrast, was treated with unfailing respect and consideration.

The boys were good tennis players, and Leonard made up a foursome with them on a private court near the house practically every day. They often went bicycling together through the flat, wooded country about Potsdam, swimming in the calm, blue Templiner-See or rowing on the other lakes. The young von Reuters were interested in most sports, and through them Leonard met family friends who introduced him to a new enthusiasm which at once captivated him : motor racing. He came back from his first visit to the big circuit in Berlin with shining eyes. He could talk of little else, and went back as often as he could. The thrill of watching begoggled drivers in powerful cars flashing round sharp bends at over one hundred miles an hour with brakes screaming aroused a craving to enjoy the same exhilaration of speed. The next thing was that he wanted to go racing also, but the Admiral refused firmly. It was not his place to give permission ; besides, the allowance from the Cheshires was not intended to cover the extravagance and unpredictable risks.

He spent a fortnight with friends of the von Reuters at Kuremberg and went to the race track every night. Germany seemed to be the home of expert drivers, and in his eager, impressionable way he thought more highly of the nation and people as a result.

"I was greatly impressed by their thoroughness and efficiency."

Only one little matter, which he had foreseen on the very first day, tended to stick in his gullet. Conversation at table had a habit of veering from harmless generalities to political details of German naval history, with the Admiral invariably setting his own spanking pace. For the first time in his life, Leonard was called upon to think and feel patriotically about questions of fact. His ignorance was unashamed and chronic. He made little attempt to conceal it. But a native common sense and quiet humour were probably better weapons than a whole armoury of contrary evidence. His interruptions were rare, pointed, and patient. The Admiral would puff meditatively at one of his fat, short cigars, as though raising steam. Then he would launch forth into reminiscences about his North Sea battles against the Royal Navy. It appeared that on at least three different occasions he had engaged superior enemy forces and fought successful running actions. His wife and sons would

sit hushed and reverent, their eyes downcast or fixed on the
stocky little man pacing his phantom bridge.

"It was amusing to begin with," Leonard discovered.
"Soon, when the novelty wore thin, my incredulity got the
better of me. It didn't make sense, and I had to disagree at the
risk of hurting his feelings.

"The others seemed to accept it all unquestioningly. They
were used to it and I wasn't. But they must have thought me
mad when I at last told him what I really thought about his one-
sided view of the war at sea.

"He was in the middle of a long, involved account of a
particularly ferocious encounter. His flagship was surrounded
by about fifteen British battleships which fired at him night and
day, without managing to sink him. I asked him if he honestly
expected me to swallow that, and he seemed shocked at my
scepticism."

There was a streak of bitterness in the Admiral's attitude to
German politicians. He was sure that but for them the German
Fleet would never have been subjected to the shame of capitulation. His own spectacular part in frustrating the surrender
terms by sending most of his ships to the bottom within sight
of the Scottish shore was a deed in which he still gloried.

Leonard gathered that the Admiral had little time for the
new rulers of the Reich. The Nazis had passed over the claims
of this droll, pleasant but slightly arrogant man, leaving him a
pension, and expected no service in return. Cheshire, for all his
political naïveté and inexperience, became dimly aware, even in
that house of regrets, of the unusual emphasis placed on Germany's military preparedness against a foe or foes unknown.

"They seemed to have an awful lot of tanks and so on," he
noted. "Far more than we seemed to have in Britain." War,
however, was a subject that never seriously crossed his mind.
When he read newspapers, it was only for the sporting columns.
The political news at home and abroad, the speeches of Hitler,
the reports of ecstatic party rallies, and the shrill editorial demands
for a revision of the iniquitous Versailles settlement were matters
he lightly skipped over. They belonged to the dull sphere of the
Debating Society and the League of Nations Union at Stowe.
And if the von Reuters had any strong opinions on current
political trends, they kept them discreetly to themselves.

But the head of the household was an incorrigible old Prussian in his cold, unfeeling contempt for ordinary people. He seemed possessed at times by the monomaniac notion that his country's humiliation and degradation had been made possible by the dwindling morale and swelling defeatism of fickle millions who had never caught the whiff of a bullet fired in anger. " The rabble," he called them, spitting out the German word like poison.

" There's only one thing the rabble understands : discipline. War is a necessity to keep them down. War is a legal method of reducing their numbers. Only five per cent of the human race is worth anything. The other ninety-five per cent are the rabble, fit only for extermination."

It was a far cry indeed from the lofty all-embracing liberalism of Roxburgh, the jovial egalitarian instincts of Tim White, even the guarded friendliness of his father towards the gardener at Grey Walls, the college servants and the undergraduate " rabble " of Oxford. This twisted spirit of intolerance, though rarely uncovered, was something alien and frightening. Unconsciously Leonard began to count it a blessing that he had been born the son of an English scholar and not the son of a Prussian militarist.

Such moments of disagreeable insight were few, however. The only time he felt like defying the Admiral was during the welcome excitement of the Olympic Games. Derfflinger had somehow succeeded in securing precious tickets for one of the most attractive days when several finals were to be held. The three brothers were so excited that they arrived five minutes late for lunch. As they sat down, rather sheepishly, the old man's face grew ugly with anger. " Stand up, all of you," he shouted hoarsely.

The three boys rose meekly and stood to attention behind their chairs.

" Give me the tickets."

Derfflinger fumbled in an inside pocket, and handed them to his father, who snatched them away and slowly tore them into shreds before their eyes. " Perhaps that will teach you to obey me," the Admiral said.

Leonard hardly knew which staggered him more—the savage coldness of that act of rigid justice, or the incredible submissiveness of the young von Reuters. It made him think the less of them, without touching his own general liking for Germans and German ways.

Early in July he decided to take a holiday by himself, and travelled by local train from Berlin to Pomerania, crossing the narrow mile of the Strelasund strait to the Baltic island of Rügen. To his delight, the first person he met in the little *pension* where he put up was an Englishman. Their sense of exile drew them together. They decided to hire bicycles and left early each morning to explore a new area, resting in the woods off the roads to eat their picnic meals and exchange impressions. One evening, as the pair sat talking over long glasses of beer at a pavement café in the seaside resort of Sellin, Leonard noticed a big advertisement announcing the town's annual tennis tournament. " I must look into this," he told his incurious companion.

Leonard discovered that it was an open competition with no conditions of age or nationality, and thanked his lucky stars that he had brought his tennis racket. His stolid English acquaintance was unmoved. He had not come all the way to Germany to watch indifferent tennis, and had no intention of wasting time in Sellin. He wished Leonard good luck and pushed on alone to the next town.

The tournament made an almost perfect climax to the holiday. Against opponents whose skill and experience fell short of what was promised in the glossy programme, the unknown English entrant lobbed and smashed his way into the finals of the men's singles. Before a large crowd of astonished but appreciative German holidaymakers, Leonard fought a hard, clever duel on a hot afternoon against an amateur champion from Berlin, but was narrowly defeated by three sets to two. It was an unexpected sip of fame, and he liked the taste. The next day his plucky display made headlines in the local paper. There was a photograph, too, showing the slight smiling English challenger side by side with the solid champion who had been made to work hard for his title. Leonard read the account until he knew it almost by heart and cut it out to keep. Hans, his opponent, took to the quiet young Englishman. Leonard promised to look him up in Berlin on his return, and did so.

One morning soon after his return, the usual weekly letter came from home with the news that his father and mother would

shortly be motoring across Germany to visit him in Potsdam.
Leonard was fairly pleased. He looked forward to seeing them
and showing them round.

Within an hour of his arrival Dr. Cheshire saw that Leonard
in his irritatingly adaptable way had settled down as though he
was going to stay with the von Reuters for ever. Mrs. Cheshire
admired the fluency of his German but not his easy, familiar
relationship with three of the most awkward German youths
she had ever encountered. They humoured Leonard by letting
him lead them on monotonous sight-seeing expeditions into
Berlin ; they met some of the von Reuters' friends ; and on one
energetic occasion the father partnered his son in a sharp Anglo-
German tennis clash with Derfflinger and Emden. It gave Dr.
Cheshire an obscure sense of satisfaction to win by a handsome
margin. He seemed to play that afternoon on the tennis court
at Potsdam as though Britain's security depended on the outcome.

The Cheshires now found Leonard more opposed to leaving
Germany than he had been to leaving home. His ostrich-like
gift of burrowing his head comfortably in the nearest patch of
sand, blithely cheerful and blind to realities, was somewhat
disconcerting. Mrs. Cheshire's intuition told her that the boy
was reaching manhood " without roots ". After four months in
a recommended German household he had fallen unreflectingly
in love with German modes and ideas. Perhaps, they consoled
themselves, his wide-eyed political innocence was a blessing in
disguise. At least he had seen and heard little enough of the
Nazis, and his veneration for Germanic thoroughness did not
extend to the Hitler régime. Leonard, they concluded ruefully,
might have grown a shade in grace and self-assurance, but not
in wisdom.

His unwillingness to return home was marked by a provoca-
tive silence which he kept up almost unbroken until they reached
Trier. At this point Dr. Cheshire's patience snapped :

" For heaven's sake behave like a man," he said. " You've
carried this moodiness far enough. I'm damned if I'll ever go
on holiday with you again."

That momentary flare-up of annoyance in his father was
sufficient. Leonard apologised, pulled himself together, and was
his charming, polite other-self long before the car brought them
back to Grey Walls.

2

Leonard moved into " Mob Quad," the oldest part of Merton College, on an October afternoon in 1936, with his father's good wishes and prudent advice still buzzing in his head. He had made up his mind to begin his Oxford career cautiously feeling his way, neither frowsting without friends in his narrow room on the second floor of the first staircase, nor wholly neglecting his books. It was not that he sought success for its own, or his father's sake. Subconsciously, he was groping for some definite aim in life which Stowe and the German interlude had failed to provide. He did not care for the family's fixed assumption that he was cut out by nature and tradition for law, and would one day make a great name as a barrister if he gave himself half a chance, but he was ready to give it a fair trial.

Mr. F. M. Lawson, Leonard's tutor for the honours school in jurisprudence, a tidy, accommodating Yorkshireman with a wispy moustache, weighed up his qualities like a careful grocer, and told Dr. Cheshire (who kept a discreet ear very close to the ground) that his son was more than holding his own. Lawson was captivated by Leonard's courtesy and by the accumulating evidence of his planned economy of effort. Whatever the father might hope or say, the son was definitely not the pure intellectual type. In his tutor's eyes, he was that infinitely more intriguing specimen, the individualist, always on nodding terms with his subject, having no natural gift or taste for it, but a rather remarkable compensating flair for making a little knowledge go a long way.

" I saw him as a distinctive character from the first," Lawson recalls. " I cannot think of a single occasion when he wasn't in command of himself and the situation. I may be quite wrong, but I believe that he assessed his abilities and limitations almost at once, deliberately set himself a good, moderate target, and reached it without too much effort. He had the enviable gift of being able to strike his own kind of balance, regardless of other people."

It was by accident that he found his boon companions for the next three years on the first evening he attended dinner in the hall. Leonard was seated opposite a stocky dark-haired, intent young man called Jack Randle and next to a slim, talkative fellow with horn-rimmed spectacles whose name was Douglas Baxter. There were three other freshmen within comfortable hailing distance : Peter Lalor, a high-spirited Australian, Bernard Schwartze, a German who had been at Cheltenham, and Peter Higgs, blond, diminutive and gay.

If their characters and temperaments varied, they professed a common dislike for work and an absorbing interest in drinking, conversation or any other effortless activity which would keep them from it.

In those days public houses were strictly out of bounds to undergraduates. That was a good enough excuse for a regular stroll before lunch to the Chequers or the Turf, often with one or two of the College servants. Leonard would usually join them. As far as he was concerned, stupid rules were invented to be broken. Only his " scout ", Bert Gardiner, knew that he had earned the drink. For though he affected the same mocking horror of prescribed study as the others, he rarely failed, in his first term at least, to do an hour's work every morning.

The University custom of " sporting the oak "—closing the outer door as a notice to all callers that the occupant does not wish to be disturbed—was a custom which Leonard approved within limits. Gardiner, a bald little man in his forties, with a limp, a slight stutter and staring eyes, watched over him like a faithful mongrel. The son of a don at his father's old college is a marked man ; the Fellows expect him to do well, but some rather humanly hope that by doing badly he will bring his father down a salutary peg or two and incidentally provide a refreshing piece of scandal to discuss over the port. College servants are not ingenuous enough to cast themselves lightly in the unpaid rôle of local guardian angels. A benevolent neutrality is their soundest policy. In spite of that, Bert Gardiner, sizing up the problem in the early days, appointed himself Leonard Cheshire's protecting spirit. He proved a staunch, wily ally, and covered up Leonard's tracks so well that months passed before Dr. Cheshire received any whispered hint that his son was flouting college rules and regulations.

Bert found it extremely difficult to rouse him in the morning for roll-call or chapel. Leonard was a heavy sleeper, especially after a late night-out—an increasingly frequent occurrence during his second term.

" Mr. Cheshire never once darkened the door of the chapel,"
said Bert. " He told me prayers didn't agree with him."

The alternative to chapel was the answering of thirty roll-calls
per term, fully dressed, before the old clock in the grey tower
struck eight ; and it demanded all the agility of Cheshire and the
utmost vigilance of Gardiner.

As he worked at his table near the window one January
morning in 1937, Leonard heard the distant clatter of a bicycle
falling on cobble-stones. The din was accompanied by a shout
of pain and a stream of colourful blasphemy. He leaned over
the sill and saw a hefty overalled servant pitching an undergraduate's carelessly parked cycle to one side, and disappearing
in the direction of the Tower pushing a loaded barrow. His
curiosity was piqued : a man who used such interesting language
might have an interesting mind.

" Bert," called Leonard, " who's the chap with the vile
tongue ? "

" Oh, that's the stoker, Fred Hulbert, sir."

Later, Leonard called at the boiler house and introduced
himself. He discovered that Fred was Welsh, a hard drinker, an
ex-coal miner who had been badly wounded and decorated for
gallantry at sea in the war, and had since acquired a withering
contempt for namby-pamby Oxford men. He also had a passion
for the countryside, and put up with his present demeaning job
because the taverns of the city and the leafy lanes of Oxfordshire were both so handy. Then, like a conspirator who is at
last sure of himself, he pointed out the coal-hole which would
offer Leonard his own private entrance to the college after hours.
The pair went off together arm-in-arm that evening to toast one
another at the Chequers.

The Steward of Merton, W. G. Innes, a diplomatic Buddha
with a more accurate insight into the undergraduate mind and
its mysterious workings than all the dons combined, watched
them go. He liked the disarming manners of Cheshire and
knew that there was no trace of bravado or inverted snobbery
in his sudden adoption of Fred.

" We often used to go ferreting together," Cheshire recalls,
" and once we took a woman cousin of his along with us. It
wasn't a very successful afternoon's hunting, and Fred's temper
was tried a bit. I was puzzled when he went off alone five or six

times, returning each time with a more tolerant look on his face. On the way back to College I asked him to explain. He told me he had just to get out of earshot to relieve his feelings with some hard swearing. I laughed a little, but couldn't suppress my admiration for his rough delicacy.

" Fred, with the seaman's rolling swagger and the big feet stuck out at right angles, was a philosopher in his own way and a good influence on me. He lived with his wife and a large family in a very small overcrowded house, and took life uncomplainingly as it came. We got on famously."

Years afterwards, Hulbert spent several weeks convalescing after a serious illness as Cheshire's guest and patient. The ex-Merton stoker had lost his fiery, blustering manner, and the ex-Merton undergraduate had meanwhile changed a good deal, too ; but the friendship between them, forged in the improbable atmosphere of pre-war Oxford, had endured.

If he began by studying fairly conscientiously, Cheshire also made reasonably frequent appearances on the Merton rugby field until his freshman's fervour evaporated early in 1937.

Before he gave up the game he had one or two outings with the Merton Mudlarks, a special combination whose members were selected more for their love of conviviality than for any expertness as ball players. Peter Higgs had been persuaded to take on the club presidency, but soon passed on the honour to Douglas Baxter for the price of a couple of drinks. The team would leave the college by coach, with crates of beer for ballast, to play against local village sides.

The inevitable afternoon came when Baxter had to haunt the taverns in the High for able-bodied volunteers from other colleges willing to sink their pride for a consideration and uphold the honour of Merton ; for Cheshire and the others had by now outgrown their interest in all organised sports with the possible exception of tennis. And the summer was still some months ahead.

3

Though other colleges could equally well have made the same claim, Merton in Leonard's first year was a faithful mirror of the mood of Oxford as a whole. Its undergraduates were no better, no worse, no rowdier and no less vacuous than the undergraduates of Trinity, Magdalen or even Balliol ; but they preened themselves on having a longer record of corporate lawlessness to maintain. Had not Charles II chosen to hold court there and set the Philistines in residence a royal example in Restoration merry-making ? And had not the Merton " smoking concerts " of the twenties, when Cheshire was playing as a child in the garden of his North Oxford home, been the despair and envy of the University ?

Like the majority of men in his year, Leonard looked on his Oxford superiors as a group of well-intentioned old fogeys. The fact that his father happened to be one of them was in itself a stimulating challenge ; on no account must he even appear to be influenced out of consideration for family ties. If he was no docile tool of the dons, neither was he promising material for the canvassers of the various political societies. Politics was a subject for future politicians ; and Oxford seemed to be overpopulated with them already. He had no inclination to get to the bottom of the real issues in the Spanish civil war or to question the folly or otherwise of British non-intervention. As far as he was concerned these and a hundred other dusty topics could remain the monopoly of the wordy young bores who attended the weekly debates of the Union.

Leonard and his set did not pause to rationalise their attitude. Without a tinge of cynicism they purposely steered clear of any- one and anything that seemed self-consciously serious, virtuous or patriotically noble. A common taste for beer, idle conversa- tion and outrageous pastimes was proof against the claims of the politicians of to-morrow and the highbrow *poseurs* of to-day. When the taste could lawfully be indulged in one or other of the small Merton societies, so much the better.

The Richard Steele Society, for instance, ostensibly existed for reciting verse, reading literary papers and informally discuss- ing both over mulled claret in one of the rooms of the College Tower ; in fact it more closely resembled the Shakespearian group in another place whose proceedings invariably began with the passing of a unanimous resolution " that the Bard be not read to-night." Cheshire and his set enjoyed the informal, comfortable atmosphere of the society's weekly meetings, at which ribald irrelevancies took pride of place, gaily aware that their demure eighteenth-century patron would undoubtedly have stormed down the stairs of the Tower like a shocked Roundhead leaving a wild Cavalier party.

Their president that year was G. Airey Neave, a debonair rebel against convention, who represents Abingdon in the House of Commons to-day. A misguided don had asked him to " keep an eye " on the freshmen and Cheshire seemed a receptive pupil with a rich talent for devilry. Neave roused his fitful interest in a small study circle which gathered once a week in his rooms. Sitting decorously on cushions with tall moonbeam-spangled black witches' hats on their heads and tankards of ale on the floor beside them, they would read aloud to each other in turn from the pages of D. H. Lawrence. One visit was sufficient for Cheshire. Cultural charades struck him as a hollow sham.

These fanciful diversions were not original or practical enough. He wanted to patent his own forms of excitement and to share them with like-minded friends. So one lunch-time, in a public house, he took Jack Randle aside and described a pastime which promised to offer the sensational thrills he sought. That evening, when traffic in the High was heavy, they gave it a trial. Keeping a sharp look-out for the police, they stood, hands in pockets, on the crowded kerb until a fast approaching car was only a few yards away : then they leapt without warning into the road across its path. Whoever scraped closest to the bonnet without being touched was the winner ; and a few disputes arose at first because they lacked an impartial judge.

After considerable practice, their ability to assess speeds and distance—and the mixture of skill, boldness and luck involved in hanging back until it was almost too late for the unsuspecting driver to slam down his foot hard on the brake—went like wine to their heads. Then one wet afternoon Cheshire tempted fate too far, and a skidding saloon car tore off his right shoe as it slewed across the road. The irate motorist ran after him, threatened to knock the living daylights out of him, but seeing the small, expectant crowd that had begun to assemble open-mouthed, decided against physical violence. Cheshire limped sheepishly back to Merton with Randle.

His hunger for spectacular escapades was stronger than common sense, and Oxford abounded in opportunities. One day a heated argument broke out in Higgs's room about the deceitfulness of Hollywood film producers.

" Take this ridiculous business of the hero in a melodrama lying down between the rails and letting a train pass over him," someone said. " It's criminal deception. Trains aren't built that way."

" How do you know ? " sneered a second undergraduate. " What makes you think railway companies aren't controlled by men who believe all they see on the pictures ? "

" Besides," said a third, " there must obviously be some kind of regulation clearance under every wagon."

Cheshire's curiosity was piqued, and suddenly he grinned from ear to ear.

" I've got it," he said.

" There's only one way of settling this thing beyond doubt and I don't mean ringing up the G.W.R. Let's all go to the main line outside the town this afternoon, and I'll lie down under the Paddington express."

They howled with delight, but grew hesitant when they saw that he was serious. They told him not to be such a showman, hoping to dissuade him by wounding his vanity. The matter, however, had gone too far ; Cheshire was anxious to prove his point. Their relief was very great when they assembled after tea as arranged and he failed to appear. One of the dons had unwittingly saved the situation by sending for him at the appointed hour.

The Merton authorities gradually came to hear indirect rumours of Cheshire's more imaginative escapades, but half reluctantly dismissed them as exaggerations.

During 1937, their scepticism weakened as the rumours strengthened and spread. His hand was suspected in scores of incidents, the Merton bonfire of lavatory seats on Coronation night for instance, but his alibis were invariably cast-iron.

A good general will secure his lines of communication before committing an army to battle, and Leonard had unconsciously adopted this first principle of strategy in befriending men like Fred Hulbert and Bert Gardiner.

" I was standing by many a night when Mr. Cheshire came in through the coal-hole," Bert admitted. " He was so likeable that we didn't mind taking risks for him."

Cheshire's parents had been dismayed when he introduced them to his friends. They would have preferred companions

C

less boisterous, less addicted to pints of beer in taverns that were
out of bounds, slightly more serious and conscientious. In the
way of all parents from Adam and Eve onwards, they attributed
his restlessness to the bad example of others ; and he in turn told
them no more than he felt was good for them.

Now that his game at the expense of speeding motorists had
lost its point, Cheshire hankered after a car of his own. As an
investment, he put down a small deposit on a Squire which was
lying in pieces in a mews garage. Then he saw a stylish road-
worthy Alfa-Romeo in a car-dealer's window, a bright red 1931
model, 1750 c.c. supercharged, which brought back poignant
memories of the German racing circuits. When a connoisseur
offered him £25 and an old M.G. for the Squire, Leonard leaped
at the offer. He at once sold the M.G. for £100, paid a large
instalment on the Alfa-Romeo, and drove proudly back to
Merton.

One spring morning, in the Oxford Court, the magistrate
sternly asked him to explain the contradiction between his
confident plea of " Not Guilty " to a charge of exceeding the
speed limit and the stout evidence of the police officer that the
car he had stopped in the Abingdon Road had been flying along
at forty miles an hour.

" It wasn't my car, I'm afraid," he replied with a sideways
glance at its owner, Peter Higgs, who was standing beside him
in the dock. " I wasn't watching the speedometer ; but I'm
certain Mr. Higgs's old Austin has never been known to register
more than thirty."

The magistrate was unimpressed and unconvinced. The pair
were fined £1 for being uninsured car users and their licences
were suspended.

This brush with the law was exceptional ; but running a car
on top of his other extravagances was a costly business, as
Leonard's father kept acidly insisting. Yet to exchange his
essential pleasures for the frugal studious life would be a squalid
surrender ; and to cripple himself with debt and his family with
worry would be selfish folly. He decided to take to gambling
with the kindly intention of keeping his bookmaker waiting no
longer than his tailor or the garage proprietor who had sold him
the Alfa-Romeo. He was now confidently striding along in
pursuit of new and gainful excitements, with a lengthening field

of creditors beginning to trail behind in a separate paper-chase of unpaid bills.

Jack, Douglas and the two Peters always accompanied him when they could on his night jaunts to London. The Alfa-Romeo was conveniently garaged in a mews just past Magdalen bridge. They would climb out over the Merton wall about ten o'clock, and be sitting in a West End night club just over an hour later. The Coconut Grove and The Nest were their favourite haunts. The return journey along empty roads and through sleeping villages in the small hours was even faster : " Between forty-three and forty-five minutes for the fifty miles from Marble Arch on average," is Leonard's own recollection.

One May afternoon in 1937 he drove down the Banbury Road with Jack, Mavis his fiancée, and Bernard Schwartze " for a breath of fresh air." As they slowed down at a roundabout Cheshire revved up to forty-five miles an hour, roared round the banked island of flowers in a tight circle, and continued hurtling round until the needle quivered at sixty and Mavis was quite giddy. They lost count of the number of times they whizzed round ; Jack and Bernard were quite enjoying the sensation, but were as mystified as Mavis.

" What the hell was that in aid of ? " one of them asked as Leonard at last bore half-left and continued towards Banbury, ignoring the indignant shouts of a procession of motorists who had pulled in hastily out of harm's way.

" I just wanted to see how many times we could go round on half a gallon of petrol," he said without flickering an eyelid. They marvelled that no police patrols had come to interrupt the experiment. Cheshire had the devil's own luck, and there were times when he took too much for granted.

The unfortunate Schwartze was the only passenger in the car a week or two afterwards when Leonard visited Stowe for the afternoon. Roxburgh provided tea and came out on the North Front steps to shake hands and see him off. The car started up with its usual powerful whine, and a group of admiring boys drew back from the vicious blue jet of exhaust. Their thin cheer of farewell died quickly when the Alfa whipped round the familiar hairpin bend in the narrow gravel drive at nearly sixty miles an hour. In a moment the wheels were locked in an uncontrollable skid, as Cheshire braked hard on the loose surface. A party of cricket enthusiasts who had been quietly watching the game on the boundary behind the bowler's arm scattered like the pigeons at Lord's as the angry red vehicle hurtled across the turf, plunged with a rending crash into the back of the sight screen, and came to a standstill a few yards away in a heap of splintered white wood. Bernard was thrown clear, with a badly bruised arm : Cheshire was still huddled in the driver's seat, miraculously unscratched. Only his pride was wounded. And a formal demand note from Stowe for £20 to replace the ruined sight-screen capped a miserable anti-climax which he badly wanted to forget.

The summer brought a new diversion when he turned entertainer to promote the cultural uplift of the villagers of Marcham, near Cothill. Leonard persuaded two girl-friends, Randle, Higgs and three more undergraduates to organise and take part in a series of local charity concerts. Some of Peter Higgs's jokes were perhaps coldly received, but Jack's conjuring tricks went down very well as did the songs and the dances of the girls. But one memorable evening Randle and Cheshire infuriated the owner of a gold watch, who had been imprudent enough to pass it up to the stage and could not understand why it should be passed back in little pieces. As the bucolic audience sided with the victim, the concert broke up in some disorder ; and another item was added to the ever growing bill of expenses for the term.

4

Cheshire's rapid development as an unthinking, light-hearted scapegrace was not, as it appeared, just another case of a high-spirited young man entering into the feckless spirit of Oxford in the mid-thirties. Nor was it entirely, as the disillusioned wife of a prominent Fellow remarked, " a wholesome reaction against an Alice-in-Wonderland way of living which can be worse in some respects than being brought up in the shadow of a great cathedral."

Behind the insouciant mask was a hard purpose and a vision. He sought and took nobody's advice because he was quite content with a makeshift, crude philosophy of action which he had worked out for himself. The big cocktail cabinet which he had dimly recognised before leaving school as a distant symbol of happiness now became one of a series of readily attainable ends in themselves. The elegant ease of rich undergraduates first unsettled him, then awoke an ambition to be as rich as they were. He saw no reason why this could not be done quickly at Oxford, and believed that by deliberately cultivating a reputation for " cutting a dash " he would speed the process. Parental disapproval was, he felt, entirely misplaced. Indeed, he was conferring a distinct favour on them by enabling his uneasy father to invest liberally in a badly misunderstood goose which was about to lay outsize golden eggs.

Jack Randle and Mavis, his future wife, were among the rare friends to whom Cheshire occasionally opened up. The tolerant good-natured Randle knew, as a devout Anglican, that Cheshire had argued himself from an insipid form of Christianity which was little better than " agnosticism untempered by hymns " to a position of robust materialism. Success in life was the all-important goal, and half measures would not do. It was a question of " nature red in tooth and claw " and the survival of the slickest, with the weakest to the wall, and no regrets. The melancholy truth was that " the weakest " usually meant " the poorest ". Since man was on earth to get the most out of existence, to pluck the day with Horace and to defend himself with Darwin were minimum conditions of progress. What did it matter if Horace and Darwin were only names ? While the devotees of Auden, Day Lewis and the rest brooded over the inevitable break-up of a decadent society, and the politically minded ruminated about rearmament, Fascism and the danger of war, Cheshire blandly cast about for undergraduate short-cuts to fortune.

The time sequence is blurred as in a dream, but the plan to open a Bond Street dress shop seems to be one he toyed with intermittently until the end of his Oxford days. The fashionable establishment called Debutante, with a single exquisite dress to focus attention on its tastefully designed windows, remained an idle hope for lack of capital.

The same inglorious fate overtook his scheme for flying the Atlantic from East to West, emulating the American pilot " Wrong-Way " Corrigan who had recently made an unexpected crossing from West to East. The resulting publicity would bring overnight renown, and fame was a sure means to riches.

Dr. Cheshire began to take it seriously when his son suddenly sold his Alfa-Romeo.

Undeterred by arguments and appeals to reason, Cheshire paid the deposit on a superannuated Puss Moth. For months it took up valuable storage space in a hanger at Abingdon, and was finally sold at a knock-down price. By then the war had come ; but it consoled him slightly to think it had taken a world upheaval to divert him from his purpose.

For all his energy and adolescent dreams of grandeur there were occasional periods when solitude was a balm to Cheshire. Though he seemed the very opposite of introspective he felt at times the compelling need to be left alone to think. This was an incongruous element in his make-up which those who regarded him entirely as a " limelight-seeker " usually overlooked.

Even his small set of close friends did not always recognise it. The healthy kind of communism they practised, drifting in and out of each other's rooms to help themselves to anything, was not designed to encourage solitude. Cheshire's radiogram, for example, was the only one in " Mob Quad " ; and the " hot " music of Duke Ellington, crashing out from the room at the top of the first staircase, where, as a contemporary put it, " a light was always burning and somebody always seemed to be cele-brating something," provoked frequent complaints from the studious and the strait-laced.

Cheshire's extra-mural activities had taken him far afield one evening when Baxter, perched on the window ledge listening to a cracked recording of " Land of Hope and Glory," lost his balance and somersaulted on to the lawn some thirty feet below. To the astonishment of those who saw the accident, he rose to his feet shaken but unhurt. Cheshire noted with irony on his return that the treatment for shock had included three-quarters of a bottle of his best sherry.

Many of his contemporaries knew one or other of his many brave faces, hardly anyone knew him well enough to under-stand the complexity of the man within. To wealthy men like Willi Freund, Noel Agazarian and Bernard Schwartze he was the amusing, sophisticated man-about-town. To servants like Hulbert and Gardiner he was that rare thing, a real gentleman. To the cloth-capped habitués of the dog tracks at Cowley and Reading he was a charming oddity who liked a flutter and was a handsome loser. To Randle, Baxter and his own set he was an adventurous, restlessly gay companion always ready for fresh devilry.

In his own eyes, he was someone still at odds with a feverish world that was for ever throwing out irresistible challenges. He was determined to dominate that world on his own terms, and at the same time be all things to all men. There were no women " in his life ", though several girl friends became very attracted to him. " Jackie " lived in London, but would come up for dances and special occasions ; Philippa he met first at a local dancing school where he took tap-dancing lessons as another possible short-cut to fame in the steps of Fred Astaire. To them and others Leonard was never more than a gallant, courtly, brilliant but fickle and enigmatic escort. Sometimes he seemed almost cold in his detachment, as though he regarded female companionship as a mere glittering accessory to grace a social evening. It was implicitly understood that they took him on his own terms or not at all ; and his terms precluded any serious emotional entanglements.

One particular episode which illustrates at a single swoop Cheshire's ruthless sense of humour and utter disregard for others' feelings when challenged took place in The George at dinner. He had met Charles Ashton at a cocktail party, and they left in an elated mood to dine together. Ashton, who was at Christ Church, had seen little of Leonard since leaving Stowe. He had travelled to London with him once or twice in the Alfa, and had admired his fast, safe, nerveless driving ; but he knew of his exploits as an undergraduate only at second hand.

Between courses, the pair sat discussing their fellow-diners. It was still relatively early, and people were being shepherded to tables by waiters. When a small, lovely girl came in escorted by a massive, fourteen-stone young man with the physique of a weight-lifting blue, Leonard and Charles winked at one another. They tittered impolitely at the next arrivals—a middle-aged horsy lady in tweeds accompanied by a flashily dressed, heavily made-up younger woman. Ashton suddenly snapped his fingers with glee.

" I've got it," he said. " I bet you a bottle of champagne you daren't go across and ask which is the lesbian."

Without a moment's hesitation or a qualifying word of

comment, Leonard pushed back his chair. Instead of crossing the room to where the two women were now giving their orders, he walked purposefully towards the table at which the heavily-built potential blue and his pretty little partner were seated.

" I apologise for this intrusion," he said, " but my friend wants to know whether your friend is a lesbian."

The effect was electrifying. Cheshire stood aside as the insulted escort half-ran across to Ashton, pulled him angrily out of his chair and frog-marched him to the door. Half a dozen waiters and the manager tried to separate them as they rolled about on the floor outside. When the misunderstanding was explained, Charles and his assailant straightened their collars and returned shamefaced to their tables. And there sat Cheshire with a satisfied smile on his face—and the bottle of champagne already opened in front of him.

CHAPTER FOUR

THE LEARNER PILOT

WHEN Cheshire joined the Oxford University Air Squadron within six weeks of going up to Merton, he was prompted by no particular motive, except perhaps a healthy inquisitiveness. This was the short-lived period of cautious settling down ; he had not yet discovered how best to spread his own wings in earnest. But already he felt the need of some simple insurance against the cumulative risk of dying a little each day from boredom. Oxford had few legalised excitements to offer its undergraduates ; and learning to fly with the Air Squadron was the only one likely to attract and hold an undergraduate as mercurial as Cheshire.

For nearly five months, he remained conspicuously on the non-flying inactive list, too preoccupied exploring other outlets for his darting curiosity and abounding vigour to give more than a passing thought to aircraft. His vital interests and those of the Air Squadron did not coincide ; and the fact that Peter Higgs, the only other volunteer among his friends at Merton, shared his wholesome disdain for officialdom and clockwork rules, put an extra brake on his natural eagerness to go flying.

One of the incidental advantages of membership was the gradual widening of his circle of happy-go-lucky acquaintances to include men of other colleges with something of his adolescent lust for full living. Their impatience with the " thinking " type of undergraduate was as rooted as their collective scorn for the things which academic Oxford held sacred. Their breezy conversation reflected an occasionally defiant attitude of knowing worldliness. If there were solemn responsible individuals among them, Cheshire met few at the cheerfully uproarious cocktail parties organised from time to time by the rank and file.

It was at one such party, held in the rooms of C. K. Foxley-Norris of Trinity College one November evening during his first term, that Cheshire was introduced to a young R.A.F. officer whom he liked on sight. Flight-Lieutenant Charles Whitworth had been posted to the Air Squadron as an instructor the previous summer, and his easy social grace matched a delicious sense of humour which made him more of an asset in the sceptical atmosphere of undergraduate Oxford than a wagon-load of regular recruiting specialists.

Cheshire was deep in conversation when Foxley-Norris moved across the crowded room with Whitworth, whose smart blue uniform with the wings above the left breast pocket lent him a dignified look in that motley assembly of corduroys, lounge suits and Oxford bags.

"Hallo, Leonard," said Foxley-Norris. "I'd like you to meet Flight-Lieutenant Whitworth, one of our instructors."

They shook hands, and went on sipping their sherry. Then Whitworth, in his mildly teasing manner, said quizzically :

"You're not a member of the Air Squadron, are you ? "

"Of course I am," replied Cheshire. "You surely don't think I'm a gate-crasher, do you ? "

"Oh, I see," said Whitworth slowly with mock relief. "You must be another of the wingless specimens we have on the books. When are you coming along to do some work at Abingdon ? "

"One day I may find time to look you up," said Cheshire airily. "Learning to fly should be fun, provided the instructors know their business." Then, with a serious air of poker-faced innocence, he looked at Whitworth's wings and said, "I suppose you CAN fly ? "

The unexpectedness of the sally knocked Whitworth momentarily off balance. He did not quite know how to take it. He suppressed his feeling of annoyance as Cheshire's innocent mask was discarded, and looked the slim, smiling, cool and composed young braggart straight between the eyes :

"I'll make a point of remembering you when we meet again," he said evenly. "I can't think of anything I'm more anxious to do now than get you up into the air ! "

They did not meet again until nearly three months later on the apron at Abingdon airfield. It was a sharp, clear day in early February. Cheshire, wearing a leather helmet and flying suit, came towards Whitworth who stood beside his Avro Tutor apparently deep in the enjoyment of some private joke. He looked up from the printed list he held in one ungloved hand, beamed at him and said :

"Oh, it's you.   Good !   I've been looking forward to this."

"So have I," said Cheshire with a broad grin.   "I'm still rather keen to find out whether you're any good."

Whitworth pursed his lips and said nothing more until they were both strapped securely in the twin cockpits.   Then he turned round and shouted :

"Hang on hard.   And if you want to be sick, please avoid messing up the inside of the cockpit.   You and I will be seeing quite a bit of one another.   It's your great good fortune to have me as your instructor."

Tim White at Stowe had taken at least one of Cheshire's schoolboy contemporaries aloft when he was learning to fly, but he had never invited Leonard as a passenger.   That flight with Whitworth on February 5th, 1937, was the first he ever made; and his instructor was icily determined to do everything short of letting the wings fall off to bring him to his senses.   For once Whitworth was happy to ignore the instructors' rule which laid it down in black and white that "air experience" should be confined to the gentlest of turns and circuits.

Minutes later the runway was dropping like a narrowing blue-black ribbon below them, and Cheshire could see beyond the gaunt, bare trees of Frilford, the flags on the golf course where his father played and, nearer, the dwindling grey bulk of his home with its green handkerchief of a tennis court.   In the middle distance, the long line of the Berkshire hills did a series of neat handsprings above the White Horse Vale as the aircraft banked steeply and rolled over.   The instructor eased himself round in the front cockpit, fully expecting to find his pupil queasily blind to the topsy-turvy beauties of his native heath and desperately holding on to the contents of his stomach.

"Wonderful view," shouted Cheshire in the rush of wind. "But what about some real flying ?"

Whitworth's complacency vanished.   He gave the machine full throttle, pulled back the stick firmly, and the Tutor climbed to 4000 feet.   Then, without warning, he put her into an accelerating spin.   As they corkscrewed down, Whitworth thought he heard retching noises in the rear.

He did not turn round to confirm his suspicions, but righted the Tutor, soared swiftly again, banked vertically, looped a few long loops, and finally plunged into a screaming, inverted spin. It was a long time since Whitworth had derived such satisfaction from an instructing period. There was no point yet in turning round ; he would spare himself the sight of those pasty features and the hang-dog look of physical misery he knew so well. Besides, the brittle affront to his vanity had been wiped out in the last ten exhilarating minutes ; his good nature was reasserting itself, and he even felt a stab of compunction that initiation should have to go so far.

When they were level at about 1500 feet, Whitworth twisted round for a good look at his victim, who had been keeping remarkably quiet. As he peered over the leather rim of the cockpit, his sympathetic smile faded. Cheshire was grinning back at him.

" That was grand," he bellowed. " I enjoyed it. What about a few more stunts ? "

Whitworth shrugged resignedly and had to relent. " No, I think that's quite enough for a start," he replied. " We'll do some quieter turns out of the book, then we'll land."

He was certain of one fact. Luck had sent him an exceptionally spirited and promising tyro whose bounce and quick-wittedness were possibly more marked than when they took off forty minutes earlier.

" You're not pulling my leg, are you ? " asked Whitworth as they walked across the tarmac together. " You definitely haven't been up before ? "

" No, never," came the reply.

" Well, I want to see you here more often because there's no reason why you shouldn't fly very quickly. Let's see, it's Friday to-day. Can you manage the same time next week ? " Cheshire promised to try—and kept his word.

This time Whitworth explained the cockpit and the controls on the ground, and let him get the feel of them as soon as they were circling the airfield. He was agreeably surprised by the deft, unflustered movements. The co-ordination of hands, feet and brain was light and graceful for a first effort, and the little Tutor was responding beautifully. Cheshire followed his directions with automatic reflex actions, and for forty minutes handled the machine almost faultlessly.

On the ground again, Whitworth passed on one or two hints for synchronising the action of hands and feet on the stick and rudder. " All you need is practice," he said. " I'll expect you again next week, of course."

Cheshire hedged a little : " I'll try to fit it in," he said. " But I've a lot on my plate at the moment."

He reappeared nearly a month later, unperturbed by Whitworth's scathing comments. Once in the air, the instructor's testiness evaporated. He did not have to convince himself that this fellow was born to the business of flying : it was self-evident.

Spring was dressing the earth at last ; the familiar landscape swept below in a whirl of delicate water-colour browns and greens. Cheshire's appreciation was written all over his radiant face ; and in the next six days he fulfilled the seldom attained Air Squadron ideal of three flights a week by returning on the Tuesday and Wednesday to put in a full hour and fifteen minutes. Whitworth guessed correctly that he would now be pestered with requests for permission to fly solo, but his reply came straight and uncompromisingly :

" You're not nearly ready yet. Don't rush it."

At least it had the good effect of bringing Cheshire out to Abingdon for four periods during May. On the last afternoon of the month the instructor let him take over half-way and was horrified by the fiendish chuckles from behind as the tame Avro described tight, perfect figures of eight among the tree tops on a rise some miles from the airfield. When they were pulling off their flying suits later, Whitworth said :

" I want you to be here without fail on Wednesday week. Scrap all other engagements. You'll be in charge."

Mrs. Cheshire hid her trepidation when Leonard came home with the news, but tried to look pleased and proud. On June 8th, after lunch, she drove along the narrow country road skirting the airfield, and drew in to the grass verge at a point where she could see everything without being seen herself. She watched her son walking with Whitworth towards one of the aircraft, but was too far away to catch the instructor's casual remark as Cheshire settled himself in the front cockpit alone :

" Right. She's all yours. See you bring her back in one piece."

The propeller was swung, the engine snarled into life, the Avro Tutor moved away, and after an eternity of two or three minutes the wheels were off the ground. For half an hour Mrs. Cheshire sat waiting, her ears straining to hold that metallic droning which for eight years had been no more than a background accompaniment to the clamour of poultry behind the house and the bird-calls in the wood. At length, with a final flash of silver, the aircraft's wings dipped, the engine note lost its harsh throatiness, and the wheels touched the runway again. Cheshire in his fitful way had flown solo in seven hours twenty minutes spread unevenly over five months. The ordeal was over. His mother drove back to Grey Walls more slowly than she had come.

" He took to flying like a duck to water," said Whitworth. " I can't remember any member of the University Air Squadron who picked it up so quickly. Great athletes like Prince Obolensky and H. D. Freakes, the South African Rhodes Scholar and rugby blue, were fellow pupils at Abingdon about the same period. By comparison most of them were slow and clumsy. I was sure in Cheshire's case, after three or four lessons, that he had all the makings of an exceptionally daring pilot."

Still strictly in his own time, Cheshire was introduced to the art of aerobatics ; and though the sheer joy of it shut out every other thought while he was in the air, he could rarely be persuaded to yield more than a meagre fraction of his leisure to practice flying. The autumn of 1937 had brought new faces to Oxford, new blood to the Air Squadron, and as a result more acquaintances and more parties. He joined the Volunteer Reserve of the R.A.F. as a matter of course ; it conferred a certain prestige and some paper privileges. He regarded the ability to fly well as a useful string to his commercially bent bow, but still only a secondary string.

His central aim in life was not deflected by the gloomy belief of other undergraduates that war was inevitable. The spur of wealth drove him without respite in search of new means of self-advertisement during his second year at Oxford ; and as we saw in the last chapter his grandiose dream of flying the Atlantic was firm enough to survive even the disillusionment of Munich and persist unbroken until the end of the uneasy peace.

On the other hand, the procession of events which paved

the way to the Munich crisis, and the airy fatalism of Air Squadron acquaintances like Richard Hillary, Noel Agazarian, Frank Waldron and H.M. (" Dinghy ") Young helped to turn his gaze outward a little. Hillary, tall, blond, intense and " always on the go ", was not unlike Christopher Cheshire in looks, though Christopher, now a Freshman at Merton, preferred to choose his own friends, and saw less of Hillary than his brother did. " Dinghy " Young, dark and lean, was addicted to starting involved discussions on improbable subjects at a moment's notice. We shall meet him again in a later chapter.

Hillary and Young were too engaged trying to row themselves into the Oxford boat to be more than casual companions of Cheshire's. Nonetheless they influenced him. For, in addition to sharing his own politely mutinous outlook on life, and similar inhibitions about intellectual snobbery in all its forms, they had an intuitive political wisdom he lacked.

In the pages of *The Last Enemy*, Hillary wrote succinctly of his circle of friends :

" We were cliquey, extremely limited in our horizon, quite conscious of the fact, and in no way dissatisfied about it. We knew that war was imminent. There was nothing we could do about it. We were depressed by a sense of its inevitability but we were not patriotic. While lacking any political training, we were convinced that we had been needlessly led into the present world crisis, not by unscrupulous rogues, but worse, by the bungling of a crowd of incompetent old fools."

That description fairly sums up the transformation that had taken place in Cheshire's breezily nihilistic political attitude by the late summer of 1938, shortly before Chamberlain, armed with his symbolically rolled umbrella, went to Germany on his final mission of appeasement and brought back " peace in our time."

2

Cheshire's conversion to the view that Britain would have to fight, was gradual, but the more he thought of it the more he liked it. His own schemes for making a name and a fortune had not developed too well ; he knew that in 1939 he would have to sit for his honours school of jurisprudence for which he was remarkably unprepared. Always willing to let his principles harmonise with his prospects, he trusted Chamberlain and Hitler between them to solve his immediate personal problems by issuing the necessary ultimatums and calling up all able-bodied young men to vindicate their countries' honour. As a fully fledged member of the R.A.F.V.R., he would escape, for the soundest patriotic reasons, the uncertainty of his finals and the deadliness of a stuffy barrister's office in the event of his passing.

It was therefore in a mood of unaccustomed anger that Cheshire returned to Merton for the start of the 1938 Michaelmas term. The sight of sandbags in the streets and random glimpses of square cardboard boxes containing hastily distributed gas-masks were dispiriting reminders of a war which had not quite happened. The vindictive manner in which he spoke of Chamberlain intrigued his friends, some of whom imagined that a dormant interest in politics had at last been stabbed to life. He wrote an abusive, gratuitously insulting letter to the University Labour Club on learning that its cretinous members were busy denouncing the shame of Munich after having opposed for so long the capitalist wickedness of rearming. It was pitched in terms uncompromising enough for the chairman Howard K. Smith, a Merton man and an American, to seek out Cheshire privately and attempt to explain the difference between propaganda and fact.

Smith, who left Oxford to become one of the ablest and best-known of U.S. radio correspondents and is the present head of the C.B.S. bureau in London, had had little to do with Cheshire before. Their divergent paths rarely crossed. Like Reginald Maudling, the Minister of Supply in the Conservative Government, Smith was a studious, reasonably conventional Merton undergraduate who respected Cheshire's reputation as a local dare-devil without wishing to emulate it. The meeting between Cheshire and Smith was amicable but inconclusive : " We had a pleasant, intelligent and quite brisk exchange of ideas," Smith recalls. " It ended with an agreement to disagree, but it showed me that this reputedly harum-scarum Englishman was not so immunised against the sinister trend of world affairs as his letter had suggested." Cheshire could hardly divulge, above all to a Labour Club official, that the letter was illogically inspired by a deep, personal loathing for Chamberlain, whose chief guilt lay in dashing his private hopes of a world war at once.

Nevertheless the Munich debacle let him see the Air Squadron at last as a practical training organisation for war. Twice a week on average, he drove out to Abingdon for practice flights, but force of habit prevented him from entirely abandoning his other interests : the dog tracks, the public bars, the nocturnal rushes to London by car, and the animated dinner parties with exhibitionist friends.

His rather modest political awareness took a militant turn during the winter of 1938-9. With Jack Randle, who lived in " digs " farther down Iffley Road from the house where he was lodging, Cheshire derived a morbid satisfaction from heckling pacifist speakers in St. Giles. Peaceful co-existence with Fascists, Communists and Socialists was possible because their creeds were unintelligible ; but his contempt for men who condemned violence on grounds of conscience was virulent. One evening, when the pair of them tried to pull a pacifist orator from his portable platform because he refused to " shut up " at their bidding, neither Jack nor Leonard minded being embroiled in the lively little scuffle that followed ; it was a neat way of proving that even pacifists are human enough to think with their fists and forget their principles in the heat of an emergency. Yet it was about this time that Leonard, on a brief visit to Paris, scandalised his Aunt Edith by pretending to be a pacifist himself.

" One thing's quite certain," he said during a conversation about Hitler and his numbing impact on people's nerves. " If there's a war, I shan't fight in it."

His straight face and matter-of-fact tone of voice as he uttered this blasphemy against the soldierly traditions of the Barstows made her see red. She told him sharply to stop being an unpatriotic little prig. Then he flicked on his most inscrutable smile and left her wondering and uncertain.

His landlady, Mrs. Donelli, had never come across a young man with so many conflicting interests—or such an odd assortment of companions to share them. They included bookmakers, racing drivers and chance acquaintances of the dog tracks as well as undergraduates and college servants.

His attendances at Abingdon nevertheless increased, and sometimes he would dip his aircraft in salute over his " digs " in Iffley Road.   One of the younger R.A.F. officers at Abingdon in 1937, Flight-Lieutenant C. W. Bromley, enjoyed Cheshire's extravagant talk and occasionally swopped pints of beer with him in the mess.   Bromley noticed a businesslike glint in his young friend's eye shortly before an official air display due to be held at Northolt early in 1939.   For the benefit of a group of M.P.s and a visiting delegation from abroad, three Fairey Battles were to make a brave show of Britain's puny bomber strength. As one of the pilots Bromley had been spending hours of unrelenting training at Abingdon and elsewhere.   He was rather flattered when Cheshire mentioned the demonstration of air power and bought him a drink :

" I've a confidential proposition to make," said Cheshire.

" What is it ? " asked Bromley, suddenly suspicious.

" I want you to take me up as a stowaway.   You are the Left-Hand Charley, aren't you ? "

" Yes, but I'm damned if you're coming.   This is for big boys only."

" Let me explain first," said Cheshire patiently.   " All I'm asking you to do is to take me up.   Officially you won't know I'm there, of course.   I'll climb out on to your wing, jump across on to the wing of the middle kite, move on to the wing of the next, then come back."

" For God's sake, whatever for ? "

" Well, let's call it experience.   But apart from that it's worth a hundred quid to me."

" You mean you're insured for that sum ? "

" No.   The cameraman has guaranteed me that sum."

" What cameraman ? "

" Oh, a cameraman from one of the national papers.   That reminds me, you'd have to take him, too.   He swears the picture would be worth at least a hundred quid."

Bromley stared at him, finally convinced that the young moron was serious.

" And what about your neck ? "

" What's wrong with my neck ? "

" Nothing, but there would be if you tried this bloody foolish stunt.   Sorry, young Cheshire, nothing doing."

Bromley explained that it was a physical impossibility, that even if he succeeded in getting out on the wing he would be swept away by the slipstream in attempting a jump. Unofficially, and without the chance of a parachute, the idea was suicidal.

Cheshire left the mess looking rather downcast. Bromley's colleagues were incredulous when he told them. They agreed that this unpredictable character from Merton might be as mad as a hatter, but they could not but admire his " guts and shrewdness."

The watchful Lawson advised Cheshire to " do a bit more work " as the spring days lengthened. Since moving to Iffley Road he had hardly opened a law book ; yet his father's repeated warnings that he was going the right way to being sent down without a degree moved him less now than the knowledge that he would need at least a pass to secure a permanent commission as a pilot. He had come to accept as inevitable the war which everyone felt to be imminent.

Only his tutor showed no surprise when the examination results were published. " I expected him to get a second," said Lawson, " and he got a good second." Leonard, despite his appearance of apathy, was relieved. His father's mild astonishment was mingled with disappointment. If only the boy had used his brains properly he could easily have taken first-class honours.

Cheshire celebrated his success by attending the last pre-war Royal Ascot meeting in June with Goldie Barnes and two of the bookmaker's colleagues. They avoided the top hats and finery in the paddock and the stands ; their pitch was on the heath, among the tents, the bars, the gipsies and the tick-tack men. Goldie had come primarily to relieve race-goers of their cash, and Cheshire had obligingly put up most of the money for the book ; but by and large, it was not a very profitable afternoon. The horses, as far as Goldie was concerned, kept " doing all the wrong things, in the wrong order " ; and even before the field lined up for the final race, a crowd of successful punters had gathered menacingly round Cheshire, who looked round nervously for some moral backing from Goldie and his assistants. They were nowhere to be seen. Then he realised with an uncomfortable twinge of apprehension that they had quietly absconded with the little money that was left. To give a plausible explanation to the impatient people now hemming him in called for a skill he did not own. Cheshire suddenly turned and bolted, shaking off the fleetest of his pursuers among the gay confusion of tents and stands. Finally he traced Goldie to a bar well away from the scene of their undoing.

The memory of a costly and humiliating afternoon was partly mellowed by the surprise call Leonard paid on his Aunt Emily who was over from Singapore on holiday. Borrowing a few shillings from a friend, he bought " an enormous bunch of flowers " which he presented to her. " She was absolutely thrilled, and when she stopped saying ' thank you ' I asked her if she could let me have a little money. She did so and was very generous."

3

At Abingdon, during the first fortnight of the long vacation, Cheshire did more flying than he had done during the previous six months. In one day alone he went up five times, returning home about midnight after watching the lights of Oxford from the darkened cockpit of a Hawker Hind. It was his introduction to night flying instruction ; and the very next evening he flew solo in an Audax. His training was interrupted through a visit he paid to the Chequers in Oxford one July evening, when he became involved in an argument with " Jig " Holloway, the landlord, and a lorry driver. Both seemed unduly depressed about Hitler's success in persuading most Britons to take their holidays at home. Cheshire maintained that there was nothing to stop anyone going abroad, and that one could still go to France on next to nothing. Hitler might have affected many things, but hardly holiday traffic.

" You prove it," challenged the landlord. " I bet you a pint of beer you can't go from this pub to Paris inside a week on fifteen bob."

The mere challenge was sufficient. Besides, there were too many witnesses to draw out of it gracefully. Cheshire went home, told his parents of the unforeseen circumstances that had forced him to leave on foot for France that night, and waited hopefully until two in the morning on the main road south before a long-distance truck driver gave him his first lift. The following morning Dr. Cheshire wrote a short note to his sister-in-law in Paris. " Trouble is coming your way," he told her cryptically.

She grasped his meaning three days later on answering a

peremptory ring on the door-bell. There stood her nephew, grimy and travel-stained, with unexpected stubble on his chin but a victorious smile on his face. Cheshire tumbled out the story of his journey : how he had reached Southampton and wasted an entire afternoon in the dock area before hitch-hiking to Newhaven ; how he had spent a willing shilling buying a drink for an informative sailor and sixpence on a pork pie for himself ; how, at the sailor's suggestion, he climbed over the harbour gates after dark and vainly begged the hard-hearted captain of a French ship to let him travel free to Dieppe ; how his lodgings for the night, on borrowed newspaper boards in a public lavatory, had cost him a penny.

She listened while he told how much he had grudged parting with twelve shillings on an excursion ticket early next morning, and how much he had enjoyed the extravagance of a swim in a hired bathing costume when he reached Dieppe. With five-pence left, he had started walking towards Paris in the late afternoon. Motorists whizzed past unseeing. Night fell, and still he walked—20—40—50 kilometres. He tried to rest on the dewy ground. At one point a tramp had followed him in the darkness. With uneasy visions of being attacked and uselessly murdered for his money, he hid behind a tree, jumped out on the tramp, hit him one solid blow and ran until he thought his lungs would burst. By morning he felt exhausted, but the few vehicles heading south towards the French capital ignored his upraised thumbs. Then a Citroën pulled up ; the driver, a Foreign Legion captain on leave, had no difficulty in under-standing the motive of this curiously timed walk.

" Come home and work in my garden for three hours," he said, " I'll give you a meal and pay you."

His home was near enough to Paris to make the delay worth-while and that evening, after one more lift in a wheezy lorry, Leonard slept in a small hotel near the Madeleine in his crumpled underclothes too tired to care.

Cheshire's Uncle Gabriel had to speak at a business luncheon next day and mentioned the exploit as a topical illustration of youthful enterprise. A wakeful journalist saw in it a human-interest story that was well away from the ominous news of the war scare, and the publicity hunt began. He read the reports avidly, accepted an invitation to address the foreign press association, went to the Paris studio of the B.B.C. to prepare a short, carefully edited talk, and promised to consider a tempting offer to advertise the glib fallacy that he owed his energy on the walk to the concentrated food value of a well-known brand of chocolate. Two of his Oxford friends remember his indignation at having to turn the offer down because of the R.A.F.'s rigid rule against publicity for personal gain. Yet the most significant point in the whole episode was that Cheshire had set out for Paris realistically prepared for the worst. The journalists were not told that, in addition to the fifteen shillings, he carried a bank note or two in an inside pocket as an iron ration.

" My aim in life until I left Oxford was the mercenary one of making money," Cheshire freely admits to-day. " I did not have many scruples about the means. But money alone wasn't everything : I was after something spectacular all the time, something in the limelight. I always dreamed of being, so to speak, on the centre court, and in point of fact I always managed to do better on the centre court than anywhere else. I found it easier when I knew people were watching and when more depended on success.

" I was a peculiar mixture of moral and immoral, and the war came at a lucky moment to divert my ambitions, energy and queer ideals into legalised channels of excitement. If it hadn't been for the war I might have done anything. At one point, indeed, I seriously thought of taking up a life of crime. I thought it would be dangerous but rewarding fun. I thought also I'd be rather good at it."

The declaration of war on September 3rd, 1939, changed the course of contemporary history and guided Leonard Cheshire's mind from old thoughts of notoriety to new thoughts of possible glory. Oxford was filling up with undergraduates who would soon be in uniform : Richard Hillary had taken a job in the post office to kill time, Christopher made himself useful as a driver, and for a day or two Leonard sat in the R.A.F.V.R. office sending out call-up notices. It was a whimpering anti-climax to " peace in our time " ; and while the Government machine ground slowly into gear Leonard brooded impatiently at home. Inactivity made him sullenly moody, and his parents were relieved when he was posted to the 9th Flying Training School at Hullavington, Wiltshire, early in October.

CHAPTER FIVE

THE LEADER

WITH a resilience that made his earliest letters home read suspiciously like forgeries, Leonard Cheshire came to terms with himself at Hullavington during the first unsettling fortnight there.

Some semblance of order had been reduced from the chaos involved in converting the establishment to a primitive warlike footing, but living conditions were still far from smooth. He employed a measure of genial diplomacy and crafty cunning in regulating his appearances at parades and on the occasional route marches ; the blind, mechanical discipline of the barrack square might be all very well for the " brown jobs ", but it seemed to serve no sensible purpose for future bombing crews. The technical lectures and regulation periods of flying instruction were a different matter. Here his application was complete.

On the whole 72021 Pilot-Officer Cheshire was happier and easier in his heart than he had been since leaving Stowe. True, he had bartered his tempestuous freedom as an undergraduate for a mere number and a uniform. Yet the uniform gave him an indefinable sense of assurance ; and the number guaranteed him an anonymous place among equals who, like himself, asked only to be turned into efficient front-line flying men with a minimum of red tape and unnecessary ceremonial. Three facts had conspired to reorientate his mind and banish nostalgic regrets for the salad days of Oxford : the permanent commission, the declaration of war, and the novel, rough, but not altogether intolerable conditions of service life. What his parents did not understand, what he was only just beginning to realise himself, was that his personal ambition and his country's needs were in perfect conjunction.

To the casual observer, and most of the ground instructors fell into this category, there was little to distinguish Cheshire from any other recruit on the course. Mathematics had never been his strong subject ; but when he realised that a thorough grasp of simple trigonometry and geometry was indispensable he concentrated on them until they worried him no longer. On the other hand his flying instructors were exasperated by his avid impatience to discover the exact function of every switch, button and lever in the cockpit of the Avro Anson bomber. Flight-Sergeant Boyd, who saw most of him to begin with, was a man of few words. He was not in the least impressed by the University Air Squadron proficiency certificate, by the thin shining braid of the Pilot-Officer, or by the bubbling air of over-confidence which Cheshire exuded every time they left the ground together. The instructor liked his pupil's amiable ways and immunity to criticism, but resented the heedless cocksure manner in which he handled the controls of the machine on his first solo within a week of having the complicated cockpit layout explained to him.

The routine of medium turns, steep turns, power approaches and landings, glide approaches, forced landings and low flying Cheshire mastered quickly, badgering his instructors and even the sceptical flight-commander for more opportunities of practice than the stringently-planned source provided. They admired his " press-on " spirit, but told him forcibly that what was sufficient for real pilots would be more than sufficient for him. He suffered a slight shock to his vanity half-way through November by failing a navigation test that had been made deliberately stiff for his benefit, making amends a week later by sailing through it on a difficult misty morning with the steadiness of a veteran.

December was a month of climbing and gliding through the eroded cliffs of dirty white cloud that brought the first flurry of snow to Wiltshire and southern England ; of instrument tests, formation flying, air-to-ground firing, and cross-country solos. The rhythm of an active life divided fairly evenly between lecture room, link trainer and cockpit, with formal parades thrown in as a necessary reminder that the R.A.F. expected more than lukewarm co-operation from individuals, was a slow but bearable rhythm.

On December 15th he qualified for his wings and felt a surge of justifiable pride for once on the parade ground when the station commander pinned the flying badge to his tunic. He had cleared the early obstacles without turning a hair. He felt he could afford to shrug off with an understanding smile the cutting back-handed assessment written into his log-book : " Average . . . If he can check his tendency to over-confidence, should become Above the Average." It was a good beginning, though the snail's pace had been a trial.

Cheshire went home to what was to prove his first and last wartime Christmas leave with Christopher and his parents. But before returning to Hullavington, he went out of his way to show by one well-planned escapade that his account with Oxford University was by no means closed and that service discipline had not exorcised the old craving for thrusting himself into the limelight, preferably against the familiar backdrop of dreaming spires and discomfited dons.

" It was a fellow on the course in Wiltshire who unintentionally put me up to the idea of spending a night at the top of the Merton College tower," he recalls. " This fellow had been a journalist. He fancied himself a judge of publicity stunts, and his enthusiasm tempted me to try it."

Cheshire tried it on the last night of his leave. Next day the London afternoon newspapers carried a report of the episode.

It appeared that Leonard, instead of catching his train, had visited undergraduate friends at Merton. They agreed to visit the College Tower to inspect Oxford's black-out arrangements, and by an unhappy mischance Leonard had been left behind to spend a cold, miserable night shivering at the top of the Tower inadvertently locked in.

" Early this morning," said the newspapers, " a college scout crossing the quad heard someone shouting for help. . . . The keys of the tower could not be found and Cheshire was rescued with the aid of the college fire escape and a rope. ' I had the wind up,' he said. ' There is a legend that the tower is haunted by the ghost of Duns Scotus.' "

Dr. Cheshire decided bleakly that the exploit was an obvious hoax at the expense of the newspapers and the College authorities. Scotus, the Franciscan schoolman of the high middle ages, had certainly studied at Merton and possibly lectured there, but his ghost seemed to have wandered conveniently far from Cologne where he died in 1308. In fact, the Merton Tower incident was a clever and successful attempt to win a little personal publicity by hoodwinking half a dozen news editors whom

Cheshire did not know to upset a company of dons he did not
like. He had spent much of the night talking and drinking
quite comfortably in the room of Billy Jack, a medical student,
with Dennis Parker and other conspirators. Not until six-thirty
in the morning had they crept silently up to the tower to admit
a willing prisoner and lock the door behind him. It was Bert
Gardiner who first heard his vigorous cries for help about an
hour later. Bert stood below a little uncertainly and called out :

" Would you like a nice cup of tea, sir ? "

" Don't be funny, Bert. Bring a bloody ladder."

Gardiner raised the alarm, and went to prepare the tea ; but
the key of the tower had mysteriously disappeared. Cheshire
waited with every sign of distress and impatience while Parker
and his fellow conspirators hastily superintended the most
elaborate rescue arrangements.

" It seemed a shame to turn a spectacular escape with ropes
and fire escape into a humdrum opening of a door with a key,"
commented Parker.

The arrival of a press photographer at the very moment
Leonard was descending the fire escape excited some comment.
Even Bert Gardiner felt that this was carrying coincidence too
far, and the college authorities drew their own austere conclusions.

Early in January the Dean of Merton wrote a crisp little note
to Leonard at Hullavington warning him off the college precincts
" until further notice ". His plan to attract public attention and
to rouse the dons from their " phony war " torpor had worked
a little too smoothly. " Absolutely incorrigible," one of them
spluttered indignantly. " Mark my words, either Cheshire will
end up in jail or he'll make a name for himself as a remarkable
eccentric." The incident rankled at Grey Walls as well as Merton,
but the Cheshires were indulgent parents. After a frank exchange
of views by post, the subject was gradually allowed to drop.

Leonard was immersed now in the advanced technicalities of
bombing training by night. Half a dozen different instructors
took him through the intensive course of rail reconnaissance
and low-level attacks on imaginary targets. His night vision was
unhesitant and sure ; before the end of January he had done his
first landings in the dark.

In March he made up for time lost through unfavourable

weather with forty-seven flying hours and fewer parades. At the end of the first week in April he drew his leave pass and movement order, genuinely pleased with the latest entry in his log-book : " Proficiency as Pilot : Above Average." Hullavington had given him the " feel " of the R.A.F., an inkling of its traditions and a sense of its ultimate mission when the queer war of words ended ; but the six months' course had by no means cured him of his playboy spirit. In the officers' mess he was regarded as a pleasant but rather unpredictable character, gay and moody by turns, full of sudden quips and weird ideas, yet capable of an almost womanly kindness towards anyone in real need of help or sympathy. When he told his colleagues with an expression of poker-faced gravity that he not only loved the Air Force but intended to go far in it, they laughed appreciatively. The devil of a fellow, Cheshire ! Aloof, maybe, but with such a DRY sense of humour !

Nobody knew him well enough to pierce the charming mask and cut through the controlled emotions to the simple ambition on which his mind and will secretly fed and waxed strong. Nobody at Hullavington knew of the two good Van Gogh prints (the self-portrait and the cornfield scene) which once hung on the wall of his Merton room beside the glossy portraits of leading continental racing drivers. He had bought them at a shop in Turl Street one day in early 1937 without ever having consciously seen a Van Gogh picture or reproduction before. The Irving Stone novel based on the artist's life had roused Cheshire's admiration for someone who combined in his handi-work the uninhibited freshness of the child with the disciplined vision of the master. One perfunctory glance through the plate-glass window lengthened into a stare of thrilling half recognition, as his eyes fastened on Van Gogh's vigorous self-portrait. Here was a great original who could become a practical model, a man whose enviable vitality breathed life even into these pale reproductions.

The prints had since been buried at home with the dusty law books. They were superfluous now that he saw clearly where he was going. Hullavington was the first step towards his aim of flying for the R.A.F. with the instinctive, natural verve of an artist ; he had no need of prints beside the iron bedstead in his bare anchorite's room to advertise what he felt. On April 8th,

1940, he gave up that room for a similar billet in Abingdon, the
" home " airfield where his quest for adventure in the skies
had begun with Charles Whitworth. He was ready for advanced
training on Whitley bombers.

" We are settling down here and flew for a few moments
to-day," he wrote from the operational training unit situated less
than a mile from his home. " Life here is far more amusing . . .
I got 83% in the exams and came second. A sergeant who is a
schoolmaster by profession and had done the stuff before came
first."

The instructors were all strangers ; they were also harder
to please and more businesslike than in the days he had drifted
in and out from Merton as the mood took him. The war, too,
had been brought a little closer by Hitler's decision to invade
Norway. The quickening of the air war across the North Sea
gave point to the daily round of air tests, formation flying and
mock bombing attacks in the squat, two-engined Whitley which
he found a more complicated but no less responsive machine
than the Anson.

The base commander at Abingdon in the late spring of
1940 was Air Commodore F. MacNeece Foster, who, by an odd
twist of fortune, had commanded the R.F.C. balloon section in
which Dr. Cheshire had served on the Western Front in the year
Leonard was born. MacNeece Foster remembered Cheshire
senior as an officer possessing " a certain form of cold-blooded
courage " ; and when he climbed into a Whitley as a passenger
on May 1st, 1940, to assess the skill of Cheshire junior as a pilot,
he felt more than his customary detached interest. Squadron-
Leader Casley, the flight-commander, sat in the second pilot's
seat giving instructions and watching his pupil closely.

A bluff, cheerful man of middle age, MacNeece Foster
believed in " letting my young pilots cart me round the sky like
a sack of coals " on the grounds that it gave them confidence.

The unaccountable whim that led him to " A " Flight that
particular morning and to pick Whitley K 7229 out of the other
training machines warming up near the hangars was at any rate
partly responsible for preventing Cheshire's summary dismissal
from the R.A.F. less than a fortnight later. The incident which
nearly cost him his commission and his life-ambition to fly may
seem of piffling unimportance to-day ; but at that dark period,

when the Wehrmacht's lightning stroke in the West suddenly shattered the lethargy of the " phony war ", action against individuals for mild indiscretions was commonplace enough.

Talk in the mess at Abingdon was no more excited or indiscreet than elsewhere : the fall of Chamberlain, the rise of Churchill, the remorseless advance of the Germans through Belgium and Northern France, and the early caustic comments of Lord Haw-Haw on the decadence of Britain and the retribution in store for her—these displaced the frivolities which had served sufficiently well during the months of inertia. Cheshire joined in the semi-political discussions with zest. He made no secret of his pleasure at the pushing out of Chamberlain ; then one day he proffered the sacrilegious opinion that Haw-Haw, despite his ghastly unctuousness, was probably nearer the truth than our own propagandists in all but his sickening interpretation of the bare facts. During the spirited altercation which followed, nobody noticed two strangers in the background busily taking notes. They were security officers—pouncing on their first case of careless talk in that period of official jitteriness. Later in the day Cheshire was placed under open arrest. His injudicious sentiments had been reported to the base commander, and Air Commodore MacNeece Foster felt himself in a quandary.

There was no question of any loss of secret papers or of divulging confidential information. Cheshire had been merely " shooting an uncalled-for line " at a time when public anxiety and tension were great. Under normal conditions the matter would not even have been brought to his notice. But Ludlow-Hewitt, the Chief of Bomber Command, had given him and other commanders of operational training units full authority to be " utterly ruthless " with trainees for breaches of security and discipline. What should he do ? Use his discretionary powers, as had been done before, and turn Cheshire over to the Army to start his service career all over again as a private ? MacNeece Foster weighed the problem, then rang up Dr. Cheshire at Grey Walls.

" I would like to discuss a serious matter with you," he said. " It concerns your son's future in the R.A.F."

That evening he drove to Grey Walls, and without going into any detail explained to Dr. Cheshire the awkward dilemma in which he was suddenly placed.

" I think it would be useful if you spoke to your son before I see him officially. As it will depend entirely on his own attitude whether I keep him or fire him, perhaps you could warn him."

Leonard, still far more puzzled than contrite, was ordered to go home and see his father next day.

" I suppose you've already guessed why you're here," Dr. Cheshire began. Leonard nodded. He looked bored as well as puzzled.

" There's one thing you possibly don't know. MacNeece Foster is making up his mind whether to make a present of you to the infantry. He'll give you his decision in the morning. That's what he wanted me to tell you."

The effect of this announcement on Leonard was instantaneous. His indifference gave way to speechless astonishment; Dr. Cheshire could not remember when his son had last wilted so abjectly before a verbal threat. He watched him go, not troubling to tell him that the Air Commodore should be treated circumspectly at to-morrow's interview. It was already evident that Leonard would approach him in a suitably humble frame of mind.

MacNeece Foster relented at " the correct and officer-like attitude " Cheshire displayed when he was marched into the base commander's office next morning.

" I told him that he could consider the incident closed, that no record of any kind would be taken, and that I was confident I'd have no cause to regret my decision. In the light of Leonard Cheshire's subsequent career I feel those last words proved to be a remarkable understatement."

The lesson was not lost on Cheshire.

After his " carpeting ", there was little opportunity for self-recrimination, but the sharp knock to his ego put him on his best behaviour for the remainder of the course; and his instructors were gratified by a studied thoughtfulness which complemented his increasingly professional thoroughness. He was training now with a co-pilot, a navigator and cross-country flights by day and night.

When one of his engines cut out above Yatesbury, and he had to carry out a forced landing in a field, there was little bravado about him on his return. He was so apologetic that his crew for the day assured him that they had no intention of reporting him for sabotage. He seemed less concerned about a forced laugh at his own expense than about the forced landing.

On May 21st, the course was transferred to Jurby, about six miles from Ramsey on the north-west coast of the Isle of Man. " It's a funny place here," Cheshire wrote home that evening. " It looks dead from the neck upwards, but the scenery is very lovely. The aerodrome is just underneath a range of high hills which remind me of Scotland, and the sea is only a few yards away.

" As far as amenities go, there aren't many. Papers come a day late, letters probably don't arrive at all, beds are as hard as iron, if not harder, and there is nowhere to go after duty. Still, if that's all there is to complain of, one can call oneself pretty lucky these days."

The weather during Dunkirk Week was " absolutely marvellous." Day after day he was over the coastal bombing range, attacking the white, bobbing targets from high, low and medium level, now in formation, now alone. This was knuckling down to the " real thing " at last—and not a week too soon. The nagging effort of adjusting himself to the average pace, like a Cunarder in a convoy of tramp steamers, had been an ordeal at times, just as drilling on a parade ground had appeared at first to be a ridiculous dissipation of energy.

Yet he had to admit that the R.A.F. was no vicious taskmaster, enforcing discipline with a heavy rod of iron. Its code of rules was more flexible than he had any right to expect in a national emergency ; any lingering doubts on that score had been dissolved by the recent brush with Air Commodore MacNeece Foster.

The R.A.F., too, in a negative way, had come between him and his adolescent dreams of riches by giving him a small, regular income and leaving him no time to spend it. At Hullavington, unprompted by anyone, Cheshire had begun sending home remittances towards the bookmakers' debts that hounded him at Oxford. In the little leisure left him, he had taken up tennis and squash. Service life had not cramped or hobbled his self-contained adventurous nature, but had gradually turned his mind to the challenge of ominously overcast horizons where high technical skill as well as faith in himself and his unfailing luck would be necessary to transcend the perils.

The chief flying instructor at Abingdon during the summer of 1940 was Wing-Commander R. M. W. Clark, a critic unlikely to waste superlatives on mediocre pilots with a sense of their own superiority. Clark, who is still in the R.A.F., recollects how Cheshire stood head and shoulders above every other man on the course both as a personality and a pilot.

" He did exceptionally well on the course, and impressed me as a charming and very high-spirited young officer and a very gifted pilot, full of confidence, who was always most meticulous in his attention to detail in flying as well as ground subjects.

" We quite often played tennis together in our very limited spare time, and I got to know him better than most pupils.

" When he finished the course, and I signed his passing out report, he was the first pilot from No. 10 Operational Training Unit to gain the category ' Exceptional day and night '."

While Wing-Commander Clark was compiling Cheshire's marks at the end of the course, he suddenly remarked to his chief ground instructor :

" This chap's a phenomenon. I swear he'll either kill himself soon or become a very famous pilot."

The chief ground instructor nodded in agreement.

Quite independently, Air Commodore MacNeece Foster had been plagued with similar thoughts since the interview which might so easily have ended Cheshire's R.A.F. career.

" I honestly felt grave doubts as to whether he was really cut out to be a bomber pilot," MacNeece Foster recalls. " Temperamentally and in all his movements he seemed to be much more the type of a fighter pilot."

For the next four years the Air Commodore's admiration for his " star pupil's " soaring success as a bomber leader was conditioned by uncertainty as to how long it could last. Even to-day, a retired Air Vice-Marshal and an Oxford City Councillor, MacNeece Foster feels his doubts were completely justified, since no mortal being could have prudently predicted that Cheshire would be an extraordinary exception to ordinary rules of type and temperament.

" I met on close terms many bomber pilots during the war," he told me not long ago. " Some emphasised that it was not the flak or the risk of enemy fighter attacks which told most on their nerves. Rather it was the strain of flying by night hour after hour over enemy territory, responsible for their crews and for finding their targets, often under the most appalling weather conditions. Always there was the knowledge that they might be shot down at any moment by an unseen foe without a chance to lift a finger in defence.

"To some pilots who were not highly strung this ice-cold courage and subduing of the imagination came more easily than to others. It still remains a mystery to me how Leonard Cheshire, of all men, achieved his iron self-control."

And so within four months of the meticulously planned romp at the top of Merton tower, which had caused an outraged don to predict for him a stretch in a jail or a future of eccentricity, Cheshire was being confidently tipped for an early grave or a meteoric rise to greatness as a flier by his chief flying instructor, while his commanding officer seriously doubted the wisdom of condemning a racehorse to an early, unfitting end between the shafts of a brewer's dray. All Cheshire sought was action. The R.A.F. had given him something attractive to live for, something more tangible than Oxford dons, politicians or patriotic propagandists could give. The thought of having to die for it had not yet seriously entered his head.

2

On June 9th, 1940, five days after the last straggling remnants of the British Expeditionary Force were lifted from the shallows of Dunkirk, Pilot-Officer Leonard Cheshire took off from Driffield, Yorkshire, on his first operational mission of the war. As he sat at the controls of the long, black Whitley bomber passing above Oxford and Abingdon at 3000 feet in the afterglow of a perfect summer evening, the pale ribbon of road near his blacked-out home at Frilford showed up faintly against the shadowy pattern of woods and fields. He was glad that he had told his parents he would not be flying for some time.

Over the English Channel south of Eastbourne, Pilot-Officer "Lofty" Long, the captain of the aircraft, came forward to relieve him. They climbed another thousand feet and in a few minutes were crossing the white-edged line of the French coast. Cheshire gazed spellbound from the front turret at three or four fires blazing on the ground and at streams of red tracer moving

D

below roughly parallel with the track of the Whitley. Down
there the losing land battle was dragging on : it would take more
than bullets to turn back the steel tide of the panzers.

The mouth of the Somme and the contrasting black on either
river bank appeared. " Lofty " ordered the wireless operator
to drop a flare, and it seemed to Cheshire that every other
Whitley captain over Abbeville gave the same order at the
same moment.

The sky was full of floating orange balloons. Cheshire could
hear over the crackle of the intercom garbled scraps of conversation as the aircraft turned and ran up steadily towards the
invisible southern bridge that was their target for the night.

" Christ, what was that ? "

" Another Whitley. Only just missed us though."

Then someone shouted : " The bridge has been blown up
already."

They circled again, dropping a stick of bombs to make
certain, then " Lofty " decided to drop a second stick on the
northern bridge for good measure. Cheshire could not see where
they fell. There was no anti-aircraft fire, and Abbeville huddled
beneath their wings deserted and quiet, as though the Germans
had already left it far behind in their remorseless sweep into
France. The Whitley returned unmolested the way it had come,
with Cheshire again at the controls, roaring above the sleeping
English countryside to land at Driffield soon after sunrise.

It had been a strangely uneventful raid, but he saw no point in
reliving its moments of confused expectation and the somewhat
flat climax. That same morning they were briefed to attack the
crossroads at Poix ; and the dubious experiment of pinpointing
invisible houses to block the highways was repeated two nights
later at Auldnoye. The fourth operation of the week took them
to Charleville, and this time Cheshire did see angry red flashes
as the bombs burst on the railway junction.

Wing Commander Groom, the C.O., and the Squadron
Intelligence Officer had made him feel the general importance
of these small, scattered forays by night. The soldiers had been
snatched from the hopeless battlefield in the nick of time, abandoning their arms and outmanœuvred French allies. It was
entirely up to the airmen now to demonstrate Churchill's stubborn
belief that a campaign might be lost but not the war. If Bomber

Command's " maximum effort " seemed unhappily misdirected to hardened Group Commanders like Coningham and Harris, the flying crews remained in blissful ignorance of the tactical pros and cons.

" The first two trips I did took me slap bang over Sauchie (Grey Walls) but I expect you were in bed," Cheshire wrote in one of his first letters home. " Am going over again in a few moments. It's far better than slopping about doing nothing. And it really is grand fun."

These early letters, most of them hurried notes scribbled in the mess between raids, reflect an unclouded joy in the novel routine of operational flying. There are clear echoes in them, too, of the ill-informed hopes of Driffield's arm-chair strategists, based on imaginary estimates of enemy losses :

June 15th : " Don't worry about the news too much. The French Army is in a tough spot ; but it's still intact. The Germans have lost at least a million men and darn nearly 3000 planes. I don't think they'll be able to keep it up much longer, and the railways behind the lines are just about bombed to hell. . . . Went bathing yesterday. I was sitting on the sand putting my socks on when a little girl of fourteen or so came up and started rubbing the sand off my feet with her handkerchief. She got every single grain off ; brushed my coat and cap, etc.—and said I was doing something for her so why shouldn't she do something for me. Rather sweet, don't you think ? "

June 17th : " Life here still wonderful, although I haven't got very much to do at present. . . . Incidentally, before I forget, if I get taken prisoner I shall send messages to you by code so I want to fix it now. It will be as follows : Fourth letter of first word, third letter of second word, second letter of third word, first letter of fifth word, second letter of sixth word, third letter of seventh word, fourth letter of eighth word, fourth letter of ninth word, third letter of tenth word and so on. . . . If there is a message will put the date in Roman figures."

June 18th : " Now we know where we stand, and thank God there is no one to let us down or betray us so we can fight in confidence. Jerry will come over here with his bombers and give us the same hell as the French, but I think we can take it. I only hope he tries an invasion because that gives us the chance of beating him up. I don't think the navy can stop him getting here—they never claimed to be able to do that—but they can stop him maintaining his communications and he won't succeed in forcing a landing without vast losses, despite his huge numbers of bombers and motor torpedo-boats."

June 20th : " I am afraid that Peter Lalor, the man whom Merton kicked out, has been killed in action. He was one of the Queen Victoria Rifles men who fought the rearguard action in Calais until every one of them was dead. It infuriates me that Merton should kick out a man like that and then pander to seventy or eighty young cissies who get down to their books only because they are too scared to fight. . . . Things are going well here, and I for one am thoroughly enjoying the war. Mind you beat up any fifth columnists you can find : I fear the place is stiff with them, just as France was."

Jack Randle and Douglas Baxter, thinly disguised as lieutenants in the Royal Norfolks, had brought him the sobering news of Peter's death. By a happy chance they were stationed at an emergency camp a mile or two down the road, and had wandered from their usual place of refreshment one evening to The Trout at Wandsworth, seeking new faces and more congenial surroundings. They saw him at the same moment.

" Good grief, it's Cheshire," they called out together.

It was even more incredible to find two more Oxford men helping him to prop up the bar : Melvin Young and Ackroyd-Stuart of the Trinity College clique had been posted to 102 Squadron only a few days previously. They noisily reminisced about the past, swopping information about old friends, and drinking eternal confusion to purblind dons. The most " decadent " of their companions were already winning their spurs : Richard Hillary, Agazarian and Peter Higgs, for example, were fully pledged fighter pilots. No presentiment of what fate might hold in store cast its chill over that gay reunion, although before many months had passed the three fighter pilots would be dead as Lalor, while Young and Ackroyd-Stuart were also doomed to die in action. Nor did it seem even barely conceivable that the placid, immensely loyal Jack Randle, smiling at Cheshire over his tankard, would one day disprove the misplaced taunt of his Oxford contemporaries that he was " just Leonard's shadow " by the final deed of supreme self-sacrifice which won him a posthumous V.C. at Kohima.

During the second half of June and the whole of July Cheshire discovered how fortunate he was in his " skipper " and crew. Thirteen times they took off against oil plants, railway targets and powder factories in Germany. Twice they flew to Gelsenkirchen, twice to Mannheim, twice to Cassel, twice to prolong the insomnia of the stationmaster at Hamm, and once to Duisburg, Frankfurt, Emden, Paderborn, and Kiel, where the *Scharnhorst* lay safe in a floating dock. With every mission Cheshire saw a little more clearly the vital interdependence of the five crew members.

" Lofty " Long was a captain of contagious fearlessness, and Cheshire's immediate liking for the tough New Zealander quickened into affectionate respect. " Lofty " taught him by precept and example how to take easy command of a heavy bomber and its small team of highly trained but fallible specialists, just as Charles Whitworth had once shown him how to make a light aircraft stand gracefully on its wing in the air.

Extremely tall, deceptively indolent in his movements, but watchful as a hawk for the least sign of uncertainty, this imperturbable pilot-officer, who had won one of the first D.F.C.s of the war, possessed an uncanny knack of turning up in the right place at the critical moment to dispel a doubt or anticipate a mistake. " Lofty " punctured Cheshire's early satisfaction with himself by casually taking him through a seemingly endless list of things he did not know about the Whitley. And since four lives apart from his own depended on a complete knowledge of wireless, gunnery, navigating, bomb-aiming and the concealed art of " sub-conscious flying ", Cheshire applied himself to learning all he could with a hard singleness of purpose.

" When I was not with ' Lofty ' I took an aircraft and flew myself by day and sometimes by night as well," he wrote. " I practised flying relaxed till I found it no more tiring than sitting down. I learned to fly on instruments till it was no more tiring than reading a book. . . . I learned about engines, too. . . . For this I turned to the ground crews, and their anxiety to teach me was the greatest stimulus I could ever want."

To be allowed to train at his own pace and in his own way was in itself an inducement. His log book indicated the intensity with which he worked. There were only two days during his two months at Driffield when he failed to practise flying in his own time.

His personal letters, which like the best diary entries recapture the slightest shifts in mood, spoke repeatedly of " the complete freedom " of station routine. But whereas others used their leisure to escape from the war for a few hours, Cheshire would often contrive to " sit in " with a scratch crew, becoming familiar by trial and error with the technical problems of the others. He was a good-humoured and unostentatious part-time student, with nothing of the bristling fanatic about him. An aircraftman second class tinkering with an engine was in his detached view an expert as important as himself ; and as a person that same A.C.2 might be far more interesting than the station commander. Cheshire's unforced consideration for ordinary station " trades-men " and their work was reciprocated. " We fell over ourselves to help him," one of them put it.

Towards regular officers, especially the experienced flight-commanders, his attitude was at first one of polite reserve not unmixed with awe. Gradually, as they accepted him as one of themselves, flashes of his devil-may-care undergraduate spirit balanced his mannered aloofness. Cheshire's quaint, mock-serious brand of humour, for example, manifested itself in odd ways. He had an enormous appetite at table, and frequently would be overheard saying to a mess waiter in a perfectly serious voice, " I really don't think I can manage three eggs this morning, thank you. Two will be sufficient." Sometimes the ruse worked and he would be given two eggs while everyone else had to be content with one.

" Don't get up," he would say with a deprecating movement of the right hand when about to sit down next to someone. And the odd part of it was that the stock phrase and stock gesture, as he used them, never lost a peculiar flavour of originality. The habit of leaning across and interrupting the reading of an obviously private letter with the remark : " After you with that when you've finished " was equally nonplussing to newcomers. Oxford colleagues like Melvin Young were more difficult to catch on the wrong foot. A familiar scene which certain sur-viving flight-commanders of 102 Squadron plainly recall is of Young, seated tailor-wise on the floor of the mess, conducting sarcastic arguments with Cheshire, smiling above him, hands on hips. Only once was Young trapped by a quibble. He was taking part in conversation at a table some distance away from Cheshire and suddenly ejaculated in a shocked tone, " Good God."

" Yes, what is it ? " said Cheshire, looking up quickly.

" I merely said ' Good God '," replied Young.

" I know," said Cheshire haughtily. " You really must not take my name in vain like that. Please address me with more reverence in future."

Visits to the local cinema, a drink in the local inn, or a game of tennis were the limited recreations he allowed himself. A car would have been useful, but it would also have been an extravagance ; and the unpaid Oxford bills still bit deeply into his pay. He was thankful to the R.A.F. for providing the best entertainment of all free of charge, as the following letter, written shortly after an August raid on the Caproni works in Milan, indicates :

" It was a very successful binge and we did a power of damage. Bright moonlight all the way, or very nearly, and I swear I've never seen anything so beautiful as the Alps. They stood out so clearly with their snow-topped caps, and down in the valleys were the towns and villages all lit up. . . . It makes you laugh when you think that the Yanks pay thousands of dollars to see them, and we get paid for it."

On August 15th, at the height of the Battle of Britain, twenty German bombers repaid a few compliments by swooping down on Driffield, killing a horse, a civilian, and four men, injuring twenty-nine more of the two thousand people on the station, and damaging the hangars and a few aircraft : " Jerry didn't even stop us operating," Cheshire's parents were informed. " On the debit side not a single one of his aircraft got away. They were all shot down. The fighters were too good for him. The mess is knocked about, and I've lost some equipment and clothes. It was terrific while it lasted, but was also very funny in parts : I never knew before how fast some people can run when really put to it." He went to the cinema that night and noted : " What a funny war this is. One minute you're in the middle of blood and guns, the next you're watching Bing Crosby play the fool."

The damage to Driffield coupled with the deadlier losses

inflicted by U-boats in the Western Approaches caused the whole squadron to be moved from Yorkshire to Aldergrove, Northern Ireland, early in September. He hated going because it appeared to be a move in the wrong direction, and even spoke to the commanding officer about the possibility of transferring to another squadron. Crews had to stand by permanently ready to take off at any hour of the day or night. The plodding, eye-straining monotony of Atlantic patrols and convoy escorts five hundred feet above the heaving swell and the tossing lines of merchant ships was a grim, thankless duty that drained the mind and frayed the nerves. He missed the flare path, the vagaries of German skies, the groping fingers of searchlights in the clouds, even the rattle of shrapnel and the fountains of tracer rising like harmless coloured bubbles in the darkness among the streaming trails of flak, the hush that descended on everyone as the aircraft was held steady, and the upward kick of relief from the fuselage behind when the bombs dropped. He had done only three raids in charge of his own Whitley (the Milan attack was the second), and objected to being dispensed with so impersonally and summarily by the planners.

"Submarine spotting doesn't suit me at all," he wrote. "The job is dreadful. It's only good for navigational experience. I've applied for a posting and hope to God it goes through."

His commanding officer advised him not to be hasty, pointing out that a posting would reduce the chances of promotion. That was the deciding factor : "It wouldn't be so clever to ask for a change as it would mean starting all over again. Anyway, it looks as though we will go back to our real job before very long. So I'm hanging on."

A negative advantage of the interminable flying through rain squalls or dazzling sunlight was that Cheshire got to know his crew : Desmond Coutts, his co-pilot, fair-haired, stockily built and reliable, with dreaming eyes and a taste for poetry and art which invited mild teasing ; Stokes, one of the squadron's best wireless operators who carried his receiver everywhere with him ; Pike, the rear-gunner ; and George Roberts, his navigator, the inimitable "Taffy", Welsh to the roots of his blonde mop of hair and always grinning amiably as if at some secret frivolity.

Desmond was unaccountably missing on the morning of

October 5th when emergency orders came through to take off inside twenty-five minutes. A convoy had altered position during the night and it had proved impossible to locate it by wireless. Cheshire left in a howling storm with no co-pilot, and only Stokes and Roberts as crew. They had no parachutes and a single flying helmet between the three of them. On an ordinary routine flight these deficiencies might not have mattered ; but soon everything pointed to the depressing fact that this was to be no ordinary routine flight. For though they found the convoy without too much trouble and began patrolling the seething seas around it, the bad weather thickened until visibility was reduced to a few hundred yards.

" I'm going down lower," Cheshire shouted, and quickly lost height until he levelled out just above the boiling fury of the waves. Suddenly he pulled hard and the Whitley's nose shot up, unseating Stokes, as the turret of a destroyer suddenly loomed up grey and solid across their track. After that near-miss, he kept the bomber at mast level, continuing to fly in a wide sweep round the convoy. Five and a half hours after the take-off they were ordered back to base. The advanced landing ground was unsuitable for landing in such weather.

Even at three thousand feet the late afternoon was prematurely dark, and somewhere in the murk between them and base lay hills that rose to the same perilous height. " Taffy " was unable to help ; there were no visible landmarks for him to take a drift. Yet Cheshire dared not come down out of the racing rain clouds for fear of crashing into a peak. Stokes was unable to help ; he had come without his " book of words " and could not re-member the formula to ask base for an approximate position.

They covered and recovered the same swathe of impenetrable clouds for another sixty minutes. The dull throb of the engine was pounding mercilessly inside Cheshire's bare head, raindrops were running down his neck, they were all hungry, cold and thirsty without so much as a coffee flask to share, and the needles of the gauges were sinking fast. Cheshire decided to ignore the order to leap the unseen barrier of hills for a blind landing at base ; instead he asked Stokes to badger control at the advanced landing ground into giving them a rough home bearing.

Then a message from base doubled them up in convulsions

of nervous laughter : " It's O.K. You're over land now. Jump."
The order to leap into space without parachutes was the last
straw. It was " Taffy ", still smiling at a richly comical situation
stage-managed by fate for his private amusement, who first saw
the faint glimmer of flarepath lights through a sudden providential parting in the clouds. They landed with ten minutes' fuel
in the tanks to be greeted coldly by the control officer and with
chilly correctness in the mess. Cheshire had been flouting orders
again, and had no right to be alive.

" We had to put up a front of righteous annoyance," said
Wing-Commander " Jock " McKay, one of the squadron's flight-
commanders. " The whole place was in a flap which a little
forethought on Cheshire's part would have averted. At the same
time there was honest doubt in my mind as to which he deserved
more, a rocket or a commendation."

McKay remembers how his own mixed feelings boiled over
on discovering how impenitent Cheshire was about the entire
affair :

" You'd better watch out, boy," he said in his blunt New
Zealand manner. " One of these days you'll stick your silly neck
out too far. Then you'll be for the chop."

Desmond Coutts, who had spent a miserably anxious evening
in the operations room, took a broader view of his pilot's capa-
bilities. Three trips to Germany and ten Atlantic patrols had
taught him to trust Cheshire implicitly ; this latest episode,
watched nervously from the outside, had taken his breath away :

" Leonard," he said admiringly as they walked out of the
mess together, " you're damned lucky ! If you fell down a
cesspit, I swear you'd come up with a gold watch and chain
round your neck." He explained that all that day the cloud
ceiling had been practically at ground level, with a single break
of fifteen minutes. Cheshire had somehow found that one rift
in the clouds dead above the airfield at the bitter end of a twelve
and a half hour flight.

Dr. and Mrs. Cheshire received a faithful account of the
incident in a letter, the closing sentence of which read, " Stokes,
the wireless operator, was furious at the order to jump. It made
him livid to think that the operations room should consider us
capable of abandoning an aircraft that was undamaged. I must
say it was pretty impertinent." The slight to his professional

pride was keener than rebukes for carelessness ; it was more lasting than Desmond's witticism about his infernal good luck.

"God be praised," begins a letter dated October 6th. "This is great news : we go back to Yorkshire on Tuesday next. I'm in the advance party and with any luck should be operating within a week of arriving."

The squadron crossed the Irish Sea and flew from Prestwick to Linton-on-Ouse, near York, during the second week of the month. The low red brick buildings of this permanent station, with its comfortable mess and living quarters, gave Cheshire a sense of home-coming. For the first two days there was a measure of sorting out to be done : becoming familiar with the lie of the land, replacing lost equipment, testing his new tail-gunner, Pilot-Officer Rivaz, and intermittently cursing the meteorological experts whose forecasts of bad weather proved accurate enough to keep all Whitleys grounded for days.

The 1940 winter seemed to have come providentially early, for, as he well knew, the bad weather " cut both ways." The invasion scare was fading, even though London was still enduring the nightly hammer blows of the blitz. When he went on leave to Grey Walls, Cheshire secretly admired his parents' non-committal acceptance of the war, despite its indirect impact on their hitherto well-ordered existence. He told them a little of his experiences, enough to confirm the impression that he had at last found his true metier. They hid their inner fears well : it was no light burden to live on in that beautiful but empty house, now that Christopher and himself were serving in the R.A.F. For his brother had already left Oxford and was successfully completing his training as a bomber pilot as well.

On November 6th, a night of frosty blackness, the squadron was briefed to attack Lünen, in the Ruhr, and " Taffy " Roberts led them uneventfully to the general target area. The moon, which was in its last quarter, threw a fitful deceiving light over the industrial haze, and Cheshire broke away from the main force to attack from three thousand feet. He told " Taffy " he was determined to identify the aiming point visually and there seemed little risk because the ground defences were weirdly quiet.

Then the inferno opened almost at the same moment as " Taffy " cried " Bombs gone." The darkness below was lit up by dozens of bright flashes, and the air about them became alive with the vicious crackling of shells and tracer bullets. Cheshire took violent evasive action, making the Whitley twist and buck like a creature in pain as splinters came rattling through the fuselage. Only Rivaz in the rear turret saw clearly where the bombs had fallen. The others were too preoccupied. They scored five direct hits on the railway sheds, but simultaneously a random piece of shrapnel pierced the belly of the Whitley, smashed the bomb-sight, and drew a smear of blood from " Taffy " Roberts's cheek as he lay on his stomach peering downward.

In the cramped loneliness of the rear turret, Rivaz felt cheated, cut off and slightly insecure as he listened to the confused chatter on the intercom. When the babble subsided Cheshire called out, " How are you back there, Revs ? " as though conscious of the tail-gunner's uncertainty on his second operation. They were apparently not finished yet. Somehow the rocking, bobbing Whitley was steered gradually nearer to another belt of guns ; and suddenly Rivaz was dazzled by a series of flashes that outshone the searchlights and the flak. He was happy enough to take their word for it, as they flew home with the dawn, that the rest of the bomb-load had landed somewhere in Dortmund.

More than one hundred holes and rents were counted in the Whitley's fuselage on landing at Linton, and in a letter home Cheshire referred briefly to the raid as " Disappointing ". He was more enthusiastic about the visit they paid to Ruhland four nights later. Neither " Taffy " Roberts nor himself could spot the oil refinery they had been briefed to destroy, but eight bombs blew up a very large factory of " doubtful identity ". The weather was clear for a change, and Cheshire told his parents proudly : " All our bombs hit the target causing terrific explosions and a fire which we could see twenty minutes later on the way back. It was a lovely night."

Three raids had sealed his confidence in his crew. They trusted him without reserve, partly because of his quiet genius for the unexpected and partly because they were learning by experience that Cheshire would take no risk that was not thoroughly calculated. He made no secret of his conviction that the surest way of wiping out a factory, a railway junction or an oil refinery was to approach from the lowest level consistent with safety ; and that, for him, meant an average height of 3000 feet. In fact, he was so sure of the validity of his views that he wrote a well-argued paper, advocating the low-level form of attack, and submitted it to the station commander. It was read with some amusement and interest, then pigeon-holed and eventually lost.

Contrary to unfounded suggestions (for which Cheshire's romantic facetiousness has been partly to blame) that he objected to flying at prescribed heights for such whimsical reasons as a fixed dislike of oxygen masks which " scratched my face when I wore them ", he seriously believed that in the large individualistic hit-and-miss conditions of late 1940, when the initiative in the air war was still very much in German hands, every bomb should be placed accurately on its target by careful visual aiming. The chances of being picked off by a misfired shell were probably less at 3000 feet than at 10,000 so that the low-level attack was safer as well as more effective. He was a little pained to find that his opinion was not widely shared ; nor was his faith weakened by one quarter of an hour of agonising danger on November 12th when his Whitley sustained a direct hit and was half burnt out by fire in the flak-riddled air above Cologne. For that night, in spite of instinct, Cheshire approached for his bombing run at the officially prescribed height of 8000 feet.

In the milky light of the full moon, the Rhine uncoiled below like a long jewelled snake. He had rarely seen it so clearly, and the built-up areas on either bank above Wesseling stood out bold against it. The anti-aircraft fire from the ground was not particularly concentrated but a little more accurate than usual, and his senses were keyed up to a fine pitch. It was almost as if fate decreed every link in the little chain of unconnected accidents which overtook them. First, the intercom had gone wrong. While Cheshire hurled inaudible abuse at " Taffy " Roberts for falling asleep, " Taffy " grew purple in the face shouting unheard directions to him. Then, with Coutts acting as a runner between cockpit and navigator's perch, he decided against turning back to attack the target for which they had been briefed.

The others could see the low clouds spreading like a down quilt over Wesseling some miles to the north as Cheshire flew on towards Cologne, passing a blazing bomber which the crew had apparently abandoned already. They were nearly over the city centre when Rivaz in the rear-turret caught the silvery flash of a night fighter prowling uncertainly below them. The ground defences had suddenly closed down. Every gun was silent; every searchlight was switched off. " Taffy " signalled his final bearings for the run up, and Cheshire felt stealing over him " a nasty, creeping feeling ".

The shell which smashed into the front turret of the Whitley blinded and deafened him for a full minute ; the lurch of the stricken aircraft flung his head back hard against the top of the pilot's seat and wrenched the control column out of his limp hands. His brain was in an uncontrollable whirl : the dazzling yellow flash, the petrifying explosion, and the sensation of diving headlong through thick, choking fumes seemed to have paralysed him. Then the instinct of self-preservation seeped back. Slowly removing his gloves, he fumbled for the press stud of the oxygen mask slung round his neck and put it on. The fog before his eyes cleared ; he groped for the control column and pulled it back hard. Miraculously, the Whitley responded without breaking in two ; her two stout-hearted engines were beating as strongly as ever. More gingerly, after attempting a steep, sharp turn which nearly sent the aircraft spinning down on its back, he steered her through the 180 degrees on to the true course.

The wind was whistling in through the broken perspex above his head, numbing his face with cold. Yet his back was running with sweat. Cheshire held his breath as more shells burst beneath and just above. This was one occasion when he could not take the lesser risk of weaving and ducking away into the path of a badly fused or badly aimed missile ; the battered Whitley would not stand up to the strain of weaving and ducking. The heat behind him was increasing, singeing his neck, and he turned his head. There stood Desmond, a tousled, tense Desmond, with blood and black oil besmirching his face, saying that the petrol tank was on fire.

Rivaz, in the isolation of the rear-turret, had been momentarily knocked out by the shock of the explosion. His intercom had been switched on, and as he came to he heard the faint, half-strangled voice of Cheshire ordering him : " Come forward, Revs." Rivaz crawled in a daze through the splintered door to find Roberts and Desmond Coutts working like maniacs, flinging live ammunition out of the gaping, torn fuselage. The littered floor about the petrol tank was half hidden in smoke and licking flames. Only Davidson, the new wireless operator, was nowhere to be seen. He had been crouching over the chute ready to release one of the new experimental flares at the very moment the second shell exploded a few feet above the port wing. A red-hot fragment had penetrated the fuselage, and in a split second every flare in the special rack near Davidson's half-averted head had caught fire. The wireless operator's hands, eyes and face were terribly burnt; he had gone blind; yet he was still conscious and had asked to be led back to his set. Davidson was a London boy, eighteen years of age, and a sergeant on his first operational mission.

The slipstream cutting through the rent sides of the Whitley and the exertion of Coutts, Roberts and Rivaz gradually extinguished the flames. The trio came forward for a consultation and their relief spread the infection of boldness. None of them turned a hair when Cheshire said:

"Oh, I nearly forgot the bombs. They're still on board and it's high time we dropped them."

"Taffy" Roberts, whose headphones were still as useless as Cheshire's, went back again to guide Desmond with taps of his feet, and Desmond passed the directions on verbally. At length, with a recoil that shook them, the bombs sped down into the middle of Cologne's network of railway lines. It was freezing in the cockpit; a film of rime formed on the charred, jagged edges of the fuselage. Davidson, his peeling face glistening with anti-burn jelly, refused to lie wrapped up on the floor. They half carried him to his wireless set, feeling his unbearable pain as he tried to move the key with a raw, stiff, crab-like claw.

When they had shaken off the last gun and the last shell, Cheshire set a rough course for home. The stars, no longer aloof and unfriendly, lit the long way back across Germany and the sea. It was broad daylight when they crossed the Yorkshire coast, and there was a rush of trucks and cars across the airfield to meet them. Very gently they lifted Davidson, whose swollen, blackening lips still fumbled in agony for soundless words, lowered him into a waiting ambulance, and went in for debriefing.

The chief intelligence officer at Linton was an ex-Indian Army Colonel, Basil Ivor Jones, D.S.O., M.C., who had often sparred amiably with Cheshire for interpreting tactical orders flexibly and according to circumstances. The colonel's bluff, articulate " official " manner hid a high regard for Cheshire, but the critical sparring had become a game between them which reached a high point of interest at interrogation after raids.

As the two protagonists faced each other across the table, the older, red-faced, bald-headed man and the pale, lean, tired pilot-officer, Cheshire could not resist informing the colonel with the wan ghost of a smile that they had run into enemy shells predicted and set to explode at the very height recommended at briefing the night before. As for the effectiveness of the experimental flares which Group seemed so concerned about, well—perhaps the colonel would like to judge that for himself by strolling out and examining the charred, twelve-feet gap in the fuselage of Whitley P 5005.

Cheshire went to York in the afternoon with Coutts and Rivaz to see a Fred Astaire-Ginger Rogers film. Sleep had proved impossible, and it was ludicrous to recall what he had written home the day before : " Flying to-night, a nice short trip for once. Weather should be favourable, so I hope we can do some damage."

On November 23rd, a Saturday, he was summoned to the office of the station commander at Watchfield, after his first week on a Lorenz course in blind landing technique. The station commander looked distinctly pleased as he handed him a tele-printed message.

" Here, read it for yourself," he said.

It was from Air Vice-Marshal Coningham, the commanding officer of No. 4 Group. " Many congratulations on the award of the Distinguished Service Order," the message ran. " Your gallantry well deserves this signal honour for you are the first junior officer in Bomber Command to be so decorated after fifteen months of war. Good luck."

The new Chief of Bomber Command, Air Marshal R. E. C. Peirse, had had no hesitation in pushing through Coningham's recommendation for an immediate award on receiving a full report of what happened over Cologne. But Cheshire bridled a little when he heard that the badly wounded Davidson was the only other member of the crew whose gallantry and endurance had been formally recognised.

It was plain to him that an arbitrary line had to be drawn somewhere if the value of decorations was not to be debased, yet it seemed positively unjust to single out the deeds of two men who could hardly have lived to tell the tale had it not been for the equal bravery of the other three.

On returning to Linton he made a point of visiting young Davidson in hospital. Through the thick bandages enveloping his head and hands, the boy told him he was much better and hoped to be up and about before very long. A few days later, among the shoals of letters from friends, came one from Foxley-Norris in whose rooms at Trinity he had been once teased by Charles Whitworth into giving the University Air Squadron a trial.

The letter brought news of Richard Hillary, tragically burned like Davidson but undefeated by the dreadful ordeal of mind and body. He could not have guessed the unconquerable power of will that would lift them both phoenix-like above themselves, giving them strength enough to return and die, flying. A more cheerful note arrived from the discerning Douglas Baxter, at that time a temporary patient in a Yorkshire military hospital. The censored newspaper accounts of the Cologne incident had piqued his curiosity ; he was ready to lay odds of ten to one that the unnamed pilot was Cheshire, and was writing for private confirmation.

When he resumed operations in December, Cheshire experienced a heavy sense of anti-climax. The squadron had moved north to Topcliffe, and the weather was unbelievably bad. It seemed to rain or freeze day and night for nearly a fortnight, and the advanced field where the Whitleys were parked lay deep in mud. To make matters worse, Desmond Coutts had been given a crew of his own, and only " Taffy " Roberts was left of the original team.

It was hardly a good moment for bombing raids that were to be blessed with success. Yet the War Cabinet, stung into vindictive action by the Luftwaffe's prolonged assault on London and the extension of the night blitz to the Midlands and the main ports, allowed Bomber Command little respite. During the second week in December Cheshire took off twice, climbing painfully to the unaccustomed height of 12,000 feet to clear the thick clouds and lightning. On the first occasion Mannheim was the target. Ice rattled off the propellers and lay like white lead on the wings, the perspex and the navigation table. Then a blizzard started to swirl about them. Cheshire turned for home,

ordering " Taffy " to aim his bombs at the dimly flickering outline of Boulogne harbour. The trip to Duisberg was more
depressing still, but by turning back after only twenty minutes
Cheshire could console himself that at least they had saved the
country valuable petrol.

The War Cabinet had also been pressing the Air Staff to
bomb Berlin since the early days of the blitz on London, overlooking the inconvenient fact that six successive nuisance raids
by the R.A.F. on the German capital during the Battle of Britain
in August had helped to precipitate the blitz itself. Token
retaliation with the one long-range weapon available, the heavy
bomber, was speeding up the political tempo of the air war.
On December 15th Cheshire circled blindly three miles above the
Charlottenburg district of Berlin convinced that snow, ice, and
dense cloud were more treacherous foes than all the heavy anti-
aircraft batteries in Germany. They dropped their bombs tentatively and not very proudly, as they returned, on the airfield at
Hildersheim and the railway junction at Minden.

Two further visits to Mannheim on December 16th and 18th
were more rewarding : " I've never seen any place in such a
shambles," he wrote enthusiastically to his parents. " It was
literally a fire from end to end. The moon was bright and the
night lovely. This was our reprisal for Coventry ; and Lofty
Long, who saw Coventry the night it was bombed in November,
reckons Mannheim was infinitely worse. I don't know whether
it will stop their game, I doubt it." The squadron stood by over
Christmas, and the conscious strain of waiting lent a forced note
of gaiety to the festivities. The C.O., Wing Commander F. C.
Cole, looked long and hard at Cheshire on being asked with
off-handed politeness whether there would be any official
objection to a special " mercy mission " dropping Christmas
parcels on British prison camps in Germany. The C.O., who
knew that sometimes it was very difficult to determine whether
Cheshire was talking seriously or was being inscrutably facetious,
pointed out that the scheme was altogether too quixotic and
sudden, despite the undeniable fact that most of the flying crews
were in favour of it. Cheshire felt as crushed by the refusal as he
had been at Abingdon, nearly two years earlier, when his plan
to stow away and walk the wings of a Battle had been disdain-
fully turned down.

3

" Good news : am posted to a new squadron of four-engined planes they are forming in these parts, but don't talk about it. Am going there round about the New Year, and will spend the next five months or so learning all about the aircraft." The aircraft referred to in Cheshire's letter was the new Halifax bomber ; and crews for 35 Squadron, the first in Bomber Command to be equipped with the Halifax, were hand-picked from 4 Group as a whole. Their station was at Linton-on-Ouse, by now a virtual home-from-home to Cheshire ; and for the rest of the winter Fred Coates of the Blacksmith's Arms and the other villagers would often stand and stare at the huge, black unfamiliar shapes skimming low in training flights over the trees and the river. There was much to learn about the complicated new machine which called for two or three extra pairs of hands in the crew ; but his early impression of power and wonderful smoothness was slowly confirmed by experience.

There were inevitable spells of enforced inactivity when he felt envious of his former colleagues who were still operating in Whitleys. At other times he was saddened by the rising numbers of casualties. Yet the prospect of flying over Germany soon in this heavier but vastly improved aircraft tempered his impatient ardour. Cheshire had already shed some of the youthful irres-ponsibility which tempted him to jump in unquestioningly where the fighting was thickest. So far the war against Germany had been a groping affair. He could see no logical pattern in the ever changing types of target chosen for attack, but put this down to the defensive needs of the moment. The formation of 35 Squadron, equipped with powerful Halifaxes, was a promise of the strategic shape of things to come.

Christopher, his brother, had meanwhile joined 78 Squadron at Dishforth and they met once or twice at mess parties or dances. His arrival at a time when Cheshire himself had just completed his first operational tour revived the strong protective interest which he had taken in him years before at Stowe, and the letters home indicate his quiet pride in Christopher's efficiency as a co-pilot already well on the way to getting a crew and Whitley of his own.

It happened that the C.O. of 78 Squadron was Charles

Whitworth, a Wing Commander now but as sociable and amiable as ever. They spent an hour together one evening discussing the war and the premature fate of many men they both knew, then Cheshire said with a touch of anxiety :

" Look after Christopher, won't you. There's no other squadron in Bomber Command I'd prefer him to be with."

Whitworth nodded, moved by what he unmistakably regarded as an " immense compliment ". He thought it a little unusual to find Cheshire even indirectly concerned about the element of personal risk in bombing operations. The truth was that though he believed too much in his own skill and luck to fear for his own skin, Christopher's skin was a different matter. Nor could he bear the thought of his mother's anguish if a raid should go wrong and his younger brother failed to return. Desmond Coutts had died a week or two earlier after colliding with a German bomber over the North Sea ; and while marvelling at the " astounding bravery " of Desmond's mother, whom he had met and tried to console soon afterwards, Cheshire somehow wanted to spare his own mother the burden of such hopeless suffering.

His parents were with him when he went to Buckingham Palace on March 11th to receive his D.S.O. from the hands of the King. They discreetly left him alone to celebrate in his own elaborate style with dinner and dancing at the Mayfair " where Jack and Eddie Eden, the cabaret artists, dedicated a song to me, much to my confusion." Quite a number of people in 4 Group would have mocked at that word " confusion ". Cheshire's quaint attempts to make the most of his decoration in public were widely discussed in the squadron messes. Many had shuddered with embarrassment and distaste on hearing how all the lights in a well-known Harrogate restaurant were switched off one evening and a blue arc lamp had singled out the calmly bowing figure of Cheshire whom the band-leader had introduced in well-rehearsed tones : " Ladies and Gentlemen, we are proud to have with us to-night that distinguished and gallant flier Pilot-Officer Cheshire, D.S.O."

Whitworth and " Dinghy " Young, who understood him better, tried to explain that this was a legacy from the Oxford period of exhibitionism and should be taken no more seriously than his habit of leaving his log-book lying about the lounge carefully opened at the page marked : " Assessment as Pilot : Exceptional." It was his peculiar way of " pulling everyone's leg, including his own ". The majority who knew Cheshire only by name or reputation, rejected such subtle excuses and tended to misjudge him a charming but intolerable egotist.

" Taffy " Roberts, who kept his ears open, was only too well aware of the strong undertow of feeling against his captain, and admired him all the more for remaining so smilingly indifferent to it. Cheshire, who commanded the loyalty and respect of every man in his crew, seemed amused rather than perturbed at the jealousy and nervous hostility he involuntarily touched off at times in the few who listened to second-hand tales about him. His weirdly theatrical sense of the ridiculous, combined with the old Oxford temptation of appearing incorrigibly defiant, made such gestures as that in the Harrogate hotel almost inevitable. The wonder is that there were not many more of them.

" My most lasting impression of Cheshire after all these years is the absolute faith he inspired in us," Roberts told me recently. " Other crews regarded him as the Elizabethans might have regarded Drake : ' You're cutting it a bit fine, old boy,' is a rather polite way of putting it. Yet we would have followed him anywhere.

" His tactical ideas in those early freelance days of bombing were unorthodox, but to us they seemed most natural if illogical. On the other hand, nothing was left to chance. He knew the technical problems each man was faced with ; and *knowing* that he knew made them less difficult. Speaking for myself, I never recaptured with any other captain the queer confidence he gave me. It was such a temptation to drop the bombs as quickly as possible and get to hell out of the target area ! Apart from wishing to avoid anything that might arouse his rare anger and the knitting of his eyebrows together in a dark frown, we felt we owed it to him to do our best. The question ' Will we get back ? ' never seemed to arise, as it did soon afterwards when I flew with another crew. And it took a prison camp for me to realise that it was an extraordinary faith in himself and us which got us back. If ever an aircraft flew on faith and little else, it was our aircraft that night over Cologne."

With the coming of spring, Cheshire could no longer resist the urge to acquire a car of his own, and drove proudly back to

the mess for lunch one day in a noisy and extremely dilapidated
old Bentley. He was greeted with loud derision.

" What's the matter with you all ? " he said. " You don't
know a good thing when you see one."

The Bentley's engine was in good condition, and he hired
two of his unexpected friends on the camp, a rigger, and a fitter
who had been a motor mechanic, to renovate his " charabanc ".
The former patched up the half-perished collapsible hood,
adjusted the collapsible doors, and gave the bodywork a bright
new coat of grey ; the latter, at Cheshire's request, " pepped up "
the engine. He took the crew into York when the car was ready
for the road on the first of many convivial evenings. There was a
special celebration at the Half Moon on March 7th, when Group
notified the award of the D.F.C. for " exceptional keenness,
initiative and devotion to duty," and for his " important role in
building up crews." The citation added with more discernment
than is usual in these stiff, cliché-ridden eulogies :

" His success has been largely due to his high personal
standards which have set an example well worth aiming at."

" Shan't be operating for at least three weeks," he wrote
home gloomily at the beginning of April. " Have to teach the
pilots here Lorenz blind landings. Bloody awful." Life on
35 Squadron had become much slower than he liked with far
too much time for reverie and reflection. Not until the middle
of the month was he able to put into practice with a new crew
over Kiel some of the tactical ideas that he had been formulating
since Christmas, when Bomber Command was issued with a
fresh directive to make " concentrated attacks . . . on objectives
in large towns and centres of industry with the primary aim of
causing very heavy material destruction to demonstrate to the
enemy the power and severity of air bombardment."

This ambitious prelude to the policy of area bombing was
scrapped a month later in favour of the strategic bombing of
synthetic oil plants ; and then Germany's massive U-boat
threat to British shipping diverted Bomber Command's energies
almost exclusively to laying mines in enemy waters and hitting
at the French Atlantic ports. The Battle of the Atlantic had
begun in earnest and was going badly ; shipping losses were
leaping upwards and concern grew apace when it was learnt
that the R.A.F. could score only four direct hits, which even so

made little impression on the battle-cruisers, in more than eleven hundred sorties against the *Gneisenau* and *Scharnhorst* at Brest.

After six weeks of this fruitless, costly raiding, the groups were ordered to concentrate on the North German ports of Hamburg, Bremen and Kiel, whose U-boat yards, docks, and aircraft factories were far more vulnerable to relatively light bombs than battleships. So Cheshire took off for Kiel on April 15th feeling that he was at last justifying his existence in 35 Squadron. The Halifax, its nose adorned with Rivaz's grotesque effigy of a Cheshire cat grinning over the head of Hitler, had a far greater ceiling and longer range than the Whitley. But the long, deep banks of 10/10 strato-cumulus cloud blotting out Northern Germany that night persuaded Cheshire to ignore what had been said at briefing and use his own discretion.

The clouds were less dense at 6000 feet, and it was from this height he attacked. Both Cheshire and " Taffy " Roberts saw the flash of their bombs in the dock area but could not tell exactly where they landed. Still, it was preferable to witness even that much of their effort. To fly across the North Sea simply to hurl one's bombs from above the cloud at a hidden target was to him a wasted journey, orders or no orders. Even in that early period, when the detailed plans for raids still left room for individual interpretation, Cheshire was beginning to feel that the minds of the planners were not always flexible enough. The individualist and the opportunist in him disliked staid, cut-and-dried tactics which left little scope for manœuvre. His business was putting bombs down, not near, but on the target, and sometimes he doubted whether the men behind the desks were in as good position to understand all the tactical factors as the men in the bombers. Wisely and typically, he kept his own counsel and went his own way.

4

That solitary raid on Kiel in mid-April was Cheshire's last operation for three months. At first he was cast down by the order from Group grounding all Halifaxes for technical alterations and virtually disbanding the squadron. Then his spirits soared on the wings of an incredible rumour, later confirmed, that two volunteers were wanted at once to ferry aircraft from

North America. Because every available pilot in 35 Squadron
volunteered, the station adjutant reluctantly decided to put all
their names into a hat ; and one morning in the middle of April
they gathered in his office for the draw. The hush of hopeful
expectancy was rent by loud groans when the adjutant unscrewed
the first ball of paper and called out Cheshire's name. His luck
was as devilishly firm as ever.

Ten days later he was clambering up the gangplank of a
Norwegian cargo ship with the other successful volunteer from
35 Squadron, a mild pleasant New Zealander named Jerry
Williams. They had been able to piece together sufficient scraps
of official information to assure themselves that the trip would
be an enjoyable if poorly earned break from routine. Although
the United States was still neutral, it appeared that the British,
Canadian and American authorities were moving more or less
in step at last to improve the trans-Atlantic organisation for
delivering to Britain new and vitally needed Hudson and
Liberator bombers. The recent passing of the Lend-Lease Act
by Congress had freed the hands of the U.S. Army Air Force,
and General Arnold's pilots had begun to fly machines straight
to Montreal from American factories. But a legal stipulation
that the aircraft should be handed over direct to a service instead
of a civilian body had created an immediate difficulty.

Hitherto the Air Ferries Department of the Canadian Pacific
Railways, directed by such experienced civilian pilots as the
future " Pathfinder King ", Air Vice-Marshal D. C. T. Bennett,
had respected the letter of American neutrality by taking over the
aircraft on the frontier itself and had gone on to make aeronautical history by flying the machines across the Atlantic in
the dead of winter. Now that the C.P.R. had neither men,
resources, nor legal right to maintain deliveries, lucky volunteers
like Cheshire were called in to keep up the trans-Atlantic flow
until the establishment of R.A.F. Ferry Command.

The tub of a ship in which they sailed to Canada flew the
flag of Norway and was no floating palace, but the slow, rough
voyage in the centre of a huge convoy of merchantmen passed
without incident. There were six other volunteers on board, all
from Coastal Command, and Cheshire more than held his own
with them at cards when the heaving seas permitted.

On disembarking at Montreal over a fortnight later they

hung about the offices of C.P.R. for a day and a half, and were slightly deflated by the critical, unimpressed manner in which a man behind a desk scanned their flying qualifications. They were asked to leave forwarding addresses, and were told they would be sent for by and by to start training. Obviously, before Williams and himself were entrusted with a new bomber to ferry back to England, they would have to submit to the indignity of learning the business all over again as co-pilots. It was an infuriating introduction to the war as seen from North America. That night they shook the dust of Montreal off their feet and took the first convenient express to New York.

For the next four weeks Cheshire trod air in an unreal world which seemed to offer the instant fulfilment of all those dreams and ambitions which had been banished to the back of his mind since the outbreak of war. An adaptable creature of circumstance, with the willing opportunist's gift of moulding events boldly and quickly to fit his own ends, he was at once enthralled by the glitter and human friendliness of the city.

As an R.A.F. pilot, he was assured of a hero's welcome wherever he went, and the uninhibited generosity and hospitality of the Americans he met were overwhelming. It was impossible not to think of them as Allies. They were not yet at war, but they made it embarrassingly plain where their sympathies lay. There had been an occasion in 1940, when Cheshire's instinctive prejudice against the mercenary self-interest implicit in American isolationism had gone to his head: he had sat down and written a stinging political reply to a kindly letter of inquiry from an American who had been an undergraduate with him at Merton. In this intoxicating atmosphere of hazy sentimentality and goodwill, however, even reasoned criticism of American neutrality would have been uncalled for and worse than boorish.

Cheshire simply " let himself go " and was led off by a company of hosts and hostesses on a sleepless round of gaiety. At one of the many parties he attended, he met a small plump woman whose vivacious personality, devastating wit and abounding energy made it almost hard to believe that she was some twenty years older than himself. Her name was Constance Binney; she had been a minor actress in the twenties but was better known as a socialite. Her sophistication and charm fascinated him.

Constance gave Cheshire and Jerry Williams the freedom of her New York flat, entertained and introduced them to her friends, drove them to her comfortable country home at Old Lyme, Connecticut, and gradually came under the quiet spell of the young English visitor. She was extraordinarily frank about herself and her outlook on life : she had been married twice before, the first venture into matrimony having ended in annulment, the second in divorce. Neither attachment had brought her lasting happiness, but then in her view marriages were certainly not made in heaven or necessarily meant to last. Her blunt proposal that Cheshire and she were well enough suited to succeed, for a time at least, in extracting unbridled enjoyment out of life together staggered him at first.

In other surroundings his better judgment would probably have asserted itself, but in the permanently effervescent company of Constance he found it increasingly difficult to look at the practical flaws in the proposal. Despite the disparity in age between them the idea of marriage attracted him more than it repelled. She was offering him wealth and comfort on a generous scale he had always coveted, in return for his mere affection. If his affection cooled and the experiment fell flat, if either tired of the other as might easily happen, there was always the divorce court to legalise their prearranged agreement to separate. Without seeking any advice, relying, as he had always done, on his own self-sufficiency, he decided to wed.

The arrangement was a bargain very heavily weighted in his favour, and Constance's understanding of the fickleness of human affection both touched him and roused a stubborn determination to prove his loyalty. If she had proposed marriage as an irrevocable step, it is extremely doubtful if he would ever have taken it.

In the social world of New York news of their whirlwind romance quickly spread. Cheshire's Aunt Edith, who had escaped from France as a refugee months before and was now living in the United States, vainly tried to dissuade him from going through with his decision. It was too late. His mind was made up. His parents were told but communications were agonisingly slow and the abrupt cable from Grey Walls imploring him to wait was delayed in transit. It also arrived too late.

When the authorities recalled Cheshire to Canada early in July for the long deferred training course in handling Hudsons, Constance followed him as planned. They were married in a little Montreal church by special licence, in the presence of two strangers who obligingly agreed to stand in as witnesses. Jerry Williams, the New Zealander who had spent so much time with them in the early stages of their rapid courtship, had already left for England. The former B.O.A.C. pilot, Captain Donald Bennett, who was still attached to the Air Ferry Service, read or heard about the sudden marriage of the American actress to one of the R.A.F. volunteer pilots from England, raised his eyebrows and casually noted Cheshire's name. Three years later, as an Air Vice-Marshal, Bennett would have quite another reason for remembering it.

5

On July 21st, 1941, Cheshire landed at Prestwick with his crew of two Canadian-trained sergeants. The flight across the Atlantic from Gander had taken just over ten hours, against the thirteen weeks needed in 1939-40 to tranship a crated Hudson from the Lockheed plants in California to the shores of England. Luck and the changing methods of supply had played superbly into his hands : for Cheshire had been gladly given leave of absence for fully thirteen weeks to ferry back a single bomber in less than a day. Most of the time had been his to kill as he pleased, and he was returning to 35 Squadron well satisfied that by marrying someone who ranked as a celebrity he had killed it profitably.

Rivaz was the only person left at Linton of the crews he had once led ; and the shock of realising that all his old colleagues, even " Taffy " Roberts, were missing, brought Cheshire back to earth with a bump. It was a salutary awakening. At all costs he must keep his mind cool, clear and untroubled until he had felt out the German defences again and recovered his old ease in the air. For that reason alone, he found immediate solace in the competent, uninquisitive co-operation of his new crew.

He liked Peter Stead, his co-pilot, on sight. Fair haired and extremely young looking, sparing of words and gestures, Stead was as phlegmatic in his way as " Jock " Hill, the wireless operator, a seasoned veteran of thirty-four trips with the biting,

native humour of a hard-headed Lowland Scot and the burring
assurance of a man twice his twenty-one years.

On Hill's recommendation, Cheshire agreed to take on
provisionally as flight engineer an Irishman called Paddy O'Kane,
who had served his apprenticeship as an air force mechanic
before graduating to aircrew. Cheshire found the smiling, cool,
O'Kane something of an enigma partly because the young Irishman had a quick tongue and was as unmoved by reputations
and decorations as he was by obvious attempts to patronise
him.

" Well, O'Kane, and how do you like flying with ME ? "
Cheshire asked him after their first practice flight as a crew.

" Oh, not too bad, sir," replied O'Kane. " So long as I'm
flying at all I suppose you'll do as well as any other pilot."

It was hardly the type of ecstatic answer Cheshire expected
and normally received from newcomers.

" Is O'Kane normally as free with his backchat ? " he asked
Hill in some perplexity as they walked across to the flight office
together, and " Jock " tried to explain that the Irishman's
penetrating wit sometimes got the better of his judgment.

Gerry Henery, the navigator, Crocker and Martin, the front-
and rear-gunners, were English, more conventional and perhaps
more deferential. All six men in the crew were sergeants, but
Cheshire made light of the customary barriers that segregated
officers from N.C.O.s. As a result, he quickly became familiar
with their instinctive likes and dislikes, their problems and their
characters. Nor is it a matter for surprise that the mutual sympathy between himself and " Jock " Hill, the strongest personality in the crew, ripened into a friendship which endures to
this day.

Only three days after his return, on July 25th, the squadron
was briefed to attack Berlin, and Cheshire's inner excitement
was intense. Once again the German capital, so distant, so large,
yet still in that high summer of 1941 so difficult and unprofitable
to strike with the force at Peirse's disposal, had become a priority
political target—this time to reassure the hard-pressed Russians.
The night was fairly clear, and they reached their objective
without trouble. On the way out Cheshire kept a close watch
on each member of the crew in turn, noting how Peter Stead
handled the Halifax, and pleased with the confident navigational

ability of Gerry Henery. They watched him with equal close-
ness, and Hill remembers how their spirits seemed gradually to
soar with his as they approached the target.

" He was an extraordinary captain. The nearer we came to
Berlin, the more gay he became. He thought of everything and
missed nothing. You'd think he'd been drinking champagne."

Over the searchlights and flak batteries, his defiant good
humour remained ; but what they noticed now was the calmness
and speed of everything he said and did. Cheshire saw immediately that the heavy guns were more numerous, the barrage more
concentrated, and the searchlights stronger and more densely
distributed than on his one and only previous visit to Berlin.
The war in the air was becoming fiercer. It was the first time
he had ever carried a 4000 lb. bomb, and prudence dictated that
on this occasion at least he should run in to drop it from the safe
ceiling of 10,000 feet.

" There's a night fighter closing in to starboard," Crocker
called out from the front turret while the others strained to see
the flash of the bursting bomb and the flames that licked greedily
upwards where it had fallen.

" Right, Crock. Keep an eye on him while I get weaving,"
Cheshire called back.

The German fighter was lured on by other prey. They
were not molested and returned as quietly as they had come.

Although he put a brave face on his nagging private worries,
Cheshire was far more deeply upset than was apparent by the
attitude of his parents towards his marriage. Their letters
reflected a degree of disapproval and distress he could not understand. Worse still, they imputed to him motives which were
anything but idealistic.

" I had either to marry on the spot or renounce her for ever,"
he wrote in reply. " It was a decision I had to make on my own,
and God knows I didn't want to have it this way : it hurts me
equally to know the way you feel . . . I have only made my
own choice of whom to marry, and if my choice is bad I am to
be pitied, not disliked.

" You probably don't know that under Constance's influence
I have ceased to waste my life as I have done for the last twenty-
three years, and that I now have an almost fantastic urge to seek
out what talents I have and develop them until I can achieve a

career that is worthwhile. I am not marrying for money. I could have had Constance's money without marrying."

Taking advantage of a cross-country flight to Abingdon, Cheshire saw his parents before the week was out and felt much happier. It was a "great relief" to be able to assure them of his utter sincerity, even though they might still harbour misgivings about the rashness of his action and the immaturity of his judgment.

"Wish I could get Constance over here," he wrote buoyantly after the meeting. "The Foreign Office won't answer me. Do you know anyone who could fix it?"

Indulgent as ever, Dr. Cheshire sent a note to an influential friend in London. He had no great desire to see Constance or to speed her arrival, but his son's happiness meant more to him than his own doubts about its duration.

On the last morning of July, after an unsuccessful raid on Cologne in very thick weather, Cheshire was warned by control at Linton not to attempt a landing. The airfield was blanketed in a swirling ground mist. He was diverted to Middleton St. George, near Darlington, where his brother was now flying a Halifax with 76 Squadron. As Christopher had been groping over the same target the night before, and it was nearly four months since they had last met, they found much to discuss at breakfast. Christopher was naturally curious about the sudden American romance which had caused such a crisis at home. He also felt slightly cheated and annoyed, remembering how on the last occasion they had a long heart-to-heart talk together on a similar subject Leonard had argued plausibly and persuasively against the folly of even getting engaged in wartime. As at Oxford and all through boyhood, it still seemed as if Leonard's bland self-confidence gave him the prescriptive right to be "different".

The friendly but idle curiosity of his fellow officers at Linton and elsewhere in 4 Group did not affect Cheshire in the least. He brushed aside questions about his wife with a smiling offhandedness which encouraged flippant whispers.

"He's married her for money," said some.

"More likely he's married her for a joke," said others.

"Surely he knows his own mind best," said the trusting few.

One morning after the briefing for an attack that night on Essen, Cheshire walked away with " Jock " Hill and led him almost furtively into his room.

" I've something to show you," he said. Unbuttoning his shirt, he undid a smart belt wound right round his waist next to the skin. It was bulging with paper money. Grinning broadly, he laid the notes in handfuls on the table.

" A present from Constance," he explained, to the puzzled Hill. " We'll celebrate with the crew in due course."

By now, Hill was beginning to appreciate his captain's bizarre sense of humour and his fondness for creating mysteries about himself. But this unexpected schoolboy charade left him wondering vaguely whether the rumours were true and Cheshire had in fact gone through the marriage ceremony purely in a spirit of levity. Whatever the truth might be, Hill felt, he had never encountered so complex a personality whose motives lay well hidden beneath an almost hypnotic charm.

His charm captivated the ground crews. For Cheshire shunned that correct attitude of chilly superiority which often marked relations between officers and other ranks. Just as he had once mixed with college servants and race-track punters on a basis of warm equality, so now he made mess waiters and mechanics feel perfectly at ease with him. Aircraftman Laurence Scott, one of his aircraft fitters, was always taken up on air-test flights before raids. The first time it happened he was speechless. He had never received such an invitation before and nervously wondered what lay behind it. Gradually he grew used to it.

" Well, Scottie, what's your verdict on the old bus this morning ? " Cheshire would say as they took off, and he would listen intently to Scott's listing of technical points good and bad.

" He gave us all the feeling that we were important and could be trusted, and I'll never forget what that trust meant," said Scott. " Regardless of what early hour he got back from the Ruhr or anywhere else, he would invariably let the crew truck go when he'd climbed out. Then he'd sit down beside the aircraft, thank us, hand round his cigarettes and start describing what had happened. We felt part of the outfit. Often he'd pass round what was left of the flying rations, talking all the while like an excited youngster back from his first film instead of a bone-weary skipper who'd probably gone through hell for seven hours or so in a cramped cockpit."

Scott and the others had been slightly sceptical to begin with, especially on the morning after Cheshire's very first raid when he said to one of the riggers :

" I want you to do something for me."

The rigger had looked a little startled, and warily waited for the catch.

" I want you to paint a good big bomb on the nose of the aircraft, and in case I forget remind me when the tenth goes on. If we come through safely after ten ops, we'll have a special celebration together in York. On me, of course."

It was a strange offer, but so obviously genuine that the ground crew accepted it as a matter of course. No air crew captain in their experience had ever gone so far out of his way to rub in gently the value of their humdrum, unspectacular work. With each successive raid, they grew more elated in spite of themselves ; Berlin (twice), Karlsruhe, Essen, Cologne. Scott admitted that they came to treat the offer as a subtle challenge to their efficiency. Every man was determined not to let Cheshire down.

Six gaudy bombs were already daubed on the nose of the Halifax when he took off to attack Berlin on August 12th for the third time in three weeks. The half-dozen small holes in the fuselage, where shrapnel came pattering through on their previous visit, had been securely patched up, but for some indefinable reason he felt a premonition of disaster at the outset. The clouds rose in sheer white precipices three miles high, and from the moment they crossed the Dutch coast at fifteen thousand feet the ground defences were ominously active. Shells kept bursting in the haze away to their left as they ploughed steadily on, and searchlights suffused the snowy murk about them with an intense blue radiance that dazzled them.

Cheshire was cold in his roll-top pullover and wished he had been sensible enough to wear a flying suit ; above the spitting gun batteries of outer Berlin the temperature gauge wavered between 20 and 19 degrees centigrade. All the way in to the centre, for a full half-hour, Cheshire pulled the Halifax this way and that, half blinded by the gigantic blue shafts of light. The crump of exploding shells was incessant ; it seemed ridiculous to linger hopefully for the sudden break in the clouds which would give them a fleeting sight of a possible aiming point below. In the end they released their bombs at random among the litter of descending flares.

" Jock " Hill remembers well the haunted look on Cheshire's face as they moved away and a bomber was suddenly held in a cone of searchlights level with them and about half a mile away.

" I hope to God that isn't Christopher," he said.

" Why should it be Christopher ? " asked Hill. " We can't even tell what sort of aircraft it is. From here it looks to me more like a Wellington than a Halifax."

Nobody could be sure what it was in that eerie light, even when the silhouetted wings glowed red and the machine fell out of the sky, but Hill's quick sympathy won him a swift glance of gratitude. Cheshire's feet were numb with the cold. He was chilled to the marrow and unaccountably depressed. He could remember no raid so overcast by this heavy feeling of foreboding. The knowledge that they had hoodwinked the enemy on their way in by ignoring the murderous short-cut laid down officially at briefing—an outdated short-cut across the greatly strengthened defences of Western Germany—no longer had power to rouse elation or anger in him. The journey home the same way seemed interminable.

They had little to say for themselves at debriefing. Hill thought Cheshire looked very pale and drawn, and watched him move off jerkily to the telephone. Above the trailing babble of voices in the room he could hear his laconic questions to someone in the operations room at Middleton St. George. After breakfast he rang through twice more. It was just as he had expected : Christopher's aircraft was missing. He told Rivaz and Hill, but his face and voice gave no hint of his inner turmoil. He rang up Grey Walls to break the news to his parents and marvelled at their stoical calm.

Cheshire felt more deeply for them than for himself. Their store of trouble had suddenly overflowed. Yet there was nothing he could do to comfort them. Fate had certainly struck back at him with a vengeance in the meanest way of all— through the anguish of his mother and father who were already badly upset by his impetuous decision to marry someone they judged unsuitable.

E

There was nothing for it but to carry on in the hope that time and routine would help him to forget. Self-reproach was not in his nature, and his nerves were strong. In the mess that evening, he put in one of his rare appearances at the bar. Talk turned to the inevitable question of duping the German defences, and Charles Whitworth, who had called to condole with Cheshire, remembers how his face lit up when someone said :

" Of course the best trick, if you can get away with it, is to feather your airscrews and glide in to attack. That's the surest way of throwing Jerry off the scent."

" Feathering " the engines by switching off the motor was a popular tactical topic at the time, though it seems that very few pilots had ever done more than discuss it. It was a daring ruse which might have been justifiable in an extreme emergency, when an aircraft was caught by searchlights and pinned down helpless in a box barrage. But Cheshire saw it in quite another light.

" What a wonderful idea," he said. " I must try it out."

The idea had the merit of steering his mind away from personal problems, and Whitworth was glad of that at least. Neither he nor anyone else could tell whether Cheshire was deeply affected by the loss of his brother. Outwardly he seemed calm and self-possessed, as though the tragedy had scarcely touched him.

Two days later, on the usual morning air test with his crew and mechanics, he tried out the " feathering " experiment. Nobody passed any comment, though Hill caught himself wondering whether this unnecessary courting of danger was his captain's perverse way of blotting out his private worries and uncertainty. In the sunlit air above the Vale of York they swung down noiselessly from nine to five thousand feet. It worked like a charm. Each engine picked up effortlessly and without protest at the end of the glide. Cheshire was boisterously happy. All his cares were momentarily forgotten in the thrill of a successful risk. " We'll test it out properly sometime," he said, and winked.

The target that night was Magdeburg, in the Ruhr, and the guns woke up as they nosed down through the lower fringes of the clouds, quickly finding their range. It was now a question of taking evasive action in the approved manner by dodging between the shell bursts and hoping for the best or diving towards the general target area in a soundless, undetected approach. Cheshire did not have to choose. His mind was already made up about "feathering". As the four powerful motors spluttered and died in turn at his touch, the Halifax spun round and lost height. Nobody spoke.

The shells were now falling above and behind them, aimed at the patch of sky they had just left. The ruse seemed to be working well. When they had glided down a couple of thousand feet, Cheshire reluctantly pressed the starter of one engine. It was simply a precaution to ensure that all was well. He frowned when the starter coughed and received no answering roar from the motor.

"Tell Paddy to come forward," he shouted to Hill.

For the next two minutes O'Kane and Cheshire pressed and pulled every button and knob on the panel. The bomber was drifting earthwards out of control. Only once did the four engines let out a simultaneous abortive roar ; then, at five thousand feet, the two starboard motors picked up together, unbalancing them still further.

"Get rid of the bombs," yelled Cheshire. There was a note of anxiety in his voice.

Even when the bombs were released, the Halifax could not keep an even keel. It rolled and yawed drunkenly on its two overworked motors before slipping several hundred feet more towards the ground, where the German gunners had spotted them again. The air around them was alive with shell fragments, and still the port engine refused to respond. O'Kane knew what had gone wrong, but to explain that the oil had probably turned stone cold would not have improved matters. This was hardly the moment for regretful technical explanations.

When a shell exploded a few feet below the sagging port wing, they were all pitched violently forward. The rear- and front-gunners, cut off in their exposed little cupolas, added to the confusion by asking on the intercom for news of what was happening. The aircraft had begun to spin dizzily and the needles on all the instrument gauges except the altimeter no longer registered. For the first and last time in his operational career Cheshire gave way to a bout of panic.

Half rising from his seat at the controls, he turned and said, "Bail out, everybody. There's nothing more we can do."

Nobody moved. They were stunned by such an order, from Cheshire of all people. "Jock" Hill, who made a point of never carrying his escape kit, gave way to a sudden surge of anger against his captain for attempting this foolhardy "feathering" experiment:

"For God's sake, Chesh, pull yourself together," he said. "You can do much better than that if you try."

Hill's fierce outspoken scorn brought Cheshire to his senses like a brutal slap on the face. Tugging hard at the jammed control column, he managed somehow to free it and right the aircraft. At two thousand feet, not far above the flashing muzzles of the guns, the capricious port engines came to life again. Slowly and unbelieving, they edged their way out of Magdeburg.

The two crises, the common physical crisis and the emotional one, were over. Cheshire shamefully admitted to himself that he did not deserve to be alive. He admitted to me more recently that he owed his survival that night entirely to "Jock" Hill's splenetic outburst. The other members of the crew were tactful enough not to refer to the incident then or afterwards. They realised that something had gone wrong with Cheshire. For the space of two minutes his self-confidence had deserted him and with it his luck; yet he had recovered both in time to save himself and them. Nobody could ask and expect more of any man, least of all one who had just lost a brother in these same skies. The incident sealed his friendship with the pugnacious Hill. It also taught him never again to take an irresponsible risk for its own sake; and Cheshire was a pilot who seldom forgot a lesson learnt the hard way.

In view of everything, he was not surprised when the C.O., Wing Commander R. W. P. Collings, normally the mildest of men, sent for him next day and stormed at him for his lapse into stupidity. As both of them knew, the borderline between stupidity and unorthodoxy in bombing operations was still of hairsbreadth fineness; but Collings was also aware that Cheshire had not been himself since returning from North America. It is probable that the C.O. would have been much sterner had the silent Flight-Lieutenant on the mat in front of him given even a vague hint that he went out looking for trouble as a remedy for his own deep depression.

CHAPTER SIX

THE LEGEND

THE tenth bomb was duly painted on the nose of the aircraft the morning after Cheshire celebrated the night of his 24th birthday in the draughty cockpit of a Halifax over Berlin. Since the incident above the Magdeburg defences, he had been cautious ; and his caution had paid off well. The synchronised photographs taken of successive targets, Colonel Ivor Jones assured him dryly, were perfect proof that excellent results could be obtained without courting unnecessary risks. Cheshire shrugged his shoulders but did not comment.

These photographs were far more important than he realised. The first airborne cameras were being distributed in Bomber Command about the time Germany invaded Russia, in June, 1941. Only the best crews were given them because cameras were still in very short supply ; Cheshire's Halifax was equipped with one on his return from Canada. Yet a preliminary analysis of the bombing photographs confirmed the suspicions of Lord Cherwell, roused serious misgivings in the War Cabinet, and sent a shudder of incredulous dismay down the spines of Air Council members and right down the chain of Command as far as Groups.

The photographic evidence was certainly disquieting. It showed that Bomber Command had been deceiving itself and the public for close on eighteen months, ever since the lethal costliness of unescorted daylight attacks had forced it to operate under cover of darkness. The British public would have been disturbed beyond reason by the unpalatable truth that, on average, only one crew in every three succeeded in releasing its bomb load within five miles of any target. The propaganda services glossed over the subject and emphasised only the new plans for bringing home the air war to the German people.

With the Luftwaffe now fully engaged on the Russian front, and the threat of any sea-borne assault on Britain indefinitely postponed, the time was certainly ripe for a drastic change in the entire character of R.A.F. bombing policy. Hitherto the pre-war supporters of precision attacks on individual targets had more or less dominated strategic thinking. They were now silenced by the incontrovertible testimony of the cameras.

The way was open in that summer of 1941 for a cruder, less ambitious policy ; and with a boldness which it did not altogether feel, the Air Council directed Peirse to aim at disrupting the vast transportation system of the enemy. In the same breath, the bombers were officially ordered for the first time to strike terror into the hearts of civilians. The euphemistic phrase used was " destroying the morale of the civil population as a whole, and the industrial workers in particular."

As a consequence of this essential trimming of strategy, the value of individual bomber captains like Cheshire, whose unfaltering verbal evidence at debriefing usually tallied with his own photographic evidence, was increasingly recognised at Group Headquarters. Thus, at a time when he was recovering from one of the most humbling experiences of his flying life, Cheshire had already been earmarked as an exceptionally skilful leader in one of the best bomber squadrons between Tees and Humber.

Although, as he said in a somewhat glum birthday letter home shortly before taking off for Berlin, " there isn't much to celebrate," Cheshire remembered his promise to the ground crew as soon as he landed. A birthday and ten raids safely accomplished seemed a reasonable excuse in the more cheerful light of a new dawn. That night he drove Hill, Henery, O'Kane and the rest of his crew into York, and picked up Scott and the mechanics by arrangement outside Betty's Bar, a popular rendezvous for the thirsty.

" This bar was out of bounds to other ranks," Scott recalls. " When we pointed that out to Cheshire, he only laughed and said, ' Up guards and at 'em. We'll sort out any who protest.' When we got into the dive, which was full of braid and red tabs, the air seemed electrified. A high-ranking army officer approached Cheshire and started protesting about our presence there. Cheshire listened to him without interrupting. Then he said very firmly but quietly :

' These men with me have as much right in this place as any of you so-called gentlemen. We work together. We depend on them. Our lives lie in their hands every other night. This is one occasion when I intend to pay back a little of what I owe them, whether you like it or not. I would strongly advise you to go away.'

"The high-ranking officer turned and walked away with no more to say. Cheshire made himself responsible for the party, and none of us stepped out of line. We had a wonderful evening at his expense. The little disturbance at the beginning apparently didn't worry him or anyone else. We were there till closing time."

Later that week Cheshire suggested that his air crew might like to go to London with him on short leave to spend some of the notes in the belt round his waist. They gleefully agreed. Hill had forewarned them that an invitation was probable.

He took them for drinks to the Mayfair, his favourite hotel, introduced them to Alf, his favourite barman, and brought Hill with him to a dog shop near Berkeley Square where he bought himself an alert, rather sad-looking poodle which was promptly given the name of Simon. Then he visited a big car dealer near the hotel and after some bargaining paid cash for a second-hand Bentley in really good condition. It was dearer but far more respectable than the old ramshackle model at Linton, for which he already had a prospective purchaser. None of the crew found these errands awkward or embarrassing. Cheshire was enjoying himself in the West End of London as naturally and unaffectedly as a child playing on the seashore. He had the money and was spending it freely on them and on goods that seemed exactly right for him.

They threw away the return halves of their railway tickets and rode back to Yorkshire as his passengers. They drove at excruciating speed along darkened roads without signposts, and somewhere on the fringes of outer London Cheshire must have taken a wrong turning. At one o'clock in the morning they pulled up in the middle of Tamworth and got out to stretch their stiff legs. The street was deserted, a few searchlights were sweeping the starlit sky; and presently a white-helmeted air-raid warden came round the corner, and hurried up to them.

"Put those cigarettes out," he shouted. "There's an alert on, and German aircraft are in the area. You ought to have more sense."

Without a word of protest, Cheshire stubbed out his cigarette and the others did the same. Hill and Henery were livid at his passive acceptance of this peremptory order from a " doddering old idiot."

" Why don t you tell him where to put his tin helmet ?" asked Hill, in a heated aside. " If you don't, I damn well will."

" No, don't, Jock. Let him have his little bit of power. It takes all sorts to make a world and it's no good arguing with some people." This unexpected meekness was a new trait in Cheshire they had never noticed before.

They were depressed to find themselves in Tamworth, with or without an air raid, for they had completely lost their way. After several false starts, Cheshire suggested with straight-faced solemnity that there was nothing for it but to steer a general course towards Yorkshire by the stars. There were smirks and some laughter as they agreed to try, and gradually, by a mixture of lucky guesswork and crude astro-navigation, they glided at half-speed through a maze of second-class cross-country lanes to join the Great North Road. Dawn was breaking, and only Hill and Cheshire were awake, when they pulled up outside the guardroom at Linton.

" There isn't much to tell you," he wrote home. " I work hard now : get up at five in the morning and fly right through the day almost without a stop. Have had my acting squadron leader upgraded to substantive rank. . . . Have you heard any more from Christopher ? "

Now that his brother was a prisoner, there was little Cheshire could do in the service to justify himself to his parents. The letters written about this time have a faint undertone of uneasiness, suggesting not only his frustration at being unable to ease their sorrow but a consciousness that he had somehow been at fault. He longed for Constance to come from New York. Her vivacious presence would restore his self-esteem and blunt the barbed hints that he was irresponsible, thoughtless, and emotionally immature.

Meanwhile, there were many compensations in his work on the squadron, to which he gave all his mind ; and the impression left on everyone at Linton was that Cheshire had not a care on earth. He had long ago mastered the art of disguising his thoughts and confiding in nobody. There were also a few compensatory interludes only remotely connected with the squadron's work. On September 11th he took off with his crew for Skebrae, in the Orkneys, flattered that Collings should have chosen him to act as personal pilot to the C.-in-C. for a few days. Peirse was on a tour of inspection of outlying stations, and had sent a signal saying that he wanted to be flown back in a Halifax.

Next morning, as Cheshire was leaving the mess after breakfast, the Skebrae catering officer approached him :

" We have some eggs for the C.-in-C." he said.

" Fine," said Cheshire. " Just shove them in the back of the car. I'm going out to the airfield now."

The officer shook his head. " No, the back of the car's not big enough," he said. " We'll be putting them in a special truck. I thought I'd let you know in advance. By the way, would *you* like some eggs ? '

" Wouldn't mind at all."

" How many would you like ? "

" Let's see," said Cheshire, thinking of dried eggs and the prevailing scarcity of fresh, " would a dozen be asking too much ? "

" A dozen," exlaimed the officer ironically. " Don't be so bashful. I'll put an extra crate in the truck."

At the airfield a small gang of airmen lifted two heavy loads into the Halifax.

While Cheshire and his crew strolled about, smoking and talking, another group of airmen walked up. A corporal detached himself from the party and asked Cheshire if he would mind giving them a flight to the mainland. They were on leave, he said, and the ordinary journey by boat and rail took two whole days which would be deducted from their leave. After a reflective pause, Cheshire said to the corporal :

" You know that this is a V.I.P. trip ? "

" Yes, sir," said the corporal, untroubled by the thought.

" Well, let's look at it this way," said Cheshire. " As pilot, I get in first and am not to know who gets in after me. If I turn a blind eye would you care to take a chance ? "

" Like a shot, sir," said the corporal promptly.

The subject of passengers was not raised until they landed for lunch at a station in North-East Scotland :

"You seem to carry an enormous crew, don't you, Cheshire?" said Peirse.

"Not normally, sir," came the ambiguous reply.

The sixteen stowaways in blue sidled off as inconspicuously as possible, while the Commander-in-Chief's eyes were on the ceremonial parade drawn up in his honour. Cheshire winked at Henery, Hill and O'Kane.

"I don't suppose he'd have minded much if we'd told him to start with," he said.

Another gift of food, this time a large case of lobsters, was loaded into the Halifax before they took off again. Then Peirse joined Cheshire in the cockpit, asked him several searching questions about the bomber and its performance, and told Henery to hand over the maps and instruments.

"I'll navigate for a bit," said Peirse. At the next port of call the crew were curious to know whether the Air Marshal had any idea what he was doing. They were inclined to think lightly and unkindly of Air Marshals masquerading as honest-to-goodness air crew.

"I'm sorry to have to say this," said Cheshire. "But Peirse knows his stuff. He surprised me, I tell you. Had it all sewn up. At times he knew where we were a darn sight better than I did."

Peirse seemed to be enjoying himself. The Air Marshal's face twisted in a grimace of mock horror each time they descended steeply towards the uneven grassy runways.

"I warn you, Cheshire," he kept repeating, to the suppressed mirth of the crew, "you'll be for the high jump if you smash a single egg."

As the wheels touched down, Peirse would scowl and turn half anxiously towards the heavy crates in the back of the Halifax, and would make a great show of examining the cargo for breakages. They landed finally on the smooth, hard tarmac at Benson in Oxfordshire without even a dent in one egg; and Peirse sent Cheshire a formal congratulatory message, with a lobster as a friendly memento.

In October the squadron was re-equipped with the latest Halifaxes and, as Flight-Commander, Cheshire was in the air as often as possible testing the new machines. Some were unsatisfactory, others appeared to have a hoodoo on them, and there were one or two serious accidents.

" Had the job of trying to fly a Halifax out of a ploughed field where it had force-landed, out of gas," he stated briefly in one of his letters. " Just managed. Cleared the trees on the edge of the field by three or four feet, much to the excitement of five hundred or so of the local inhabitants. Came back before they'd scattered and caused some panic by shooting them up."

Several times in the course of the next few weeks he pleaded and argued with the C.O. to defer the extended rest from operations he had been ordered to take after the birthday visit to Berlin. Office work and the testing of Halifaxes were a poor substitute for the exhilaration of night bombing. But Collings was adamant.

" You've done too much as it is," he told him. " You've got to give yourself and other people a chance."

The one bright speck on the horizon was Constance, with whom he had been exchanging frequent cables since July. One day there was a night letter awaiting him in his pigeon hole at the mess. It confirmed that she had managed at last to secure a passage on a Canadian troopship, and on October 20th he motored across country in torrential rain to Liverpool and was at the quayside to meet her.

She looked " a little older and fatter but nonetheless flourishing and in high spirits." The day was grey, sodden and cheerless, and it was back-breaking work struggling along with thirty-six assorted pieces of luggage from the ship to the waiting car " especially with thousands of tough Canadian troops swarming around." To add to the difficulties, the press besieged them, too. For this dockside reunion of a young bomber captain, twice decorated for gallantry, with a vivacious wife reputed to be not only an established actress, but also the first American war-time bride to cross the Atlantic in a troopship, had all the makings of a romantic " human interest " story.

Cheshire had become a marked man. Press publicity for its own sake or as a short-cut to fame no longer attracted him as it had once done. The Oxford obsession to see his name in print had lost its force, but the attentions of journalists were naturally flattering. His charm, accessibility and colourful record made him an admirable subject for ready copy ; but his enigmatic, fickle sense of humour as well as his reserve, sometimes contrived to make the copy unreliable, and he lacked sufficient interest in what they wrote either to correct errors and exaggerations or even to read it all. One can justly date from this period the growth of many half-fictitious stories about Cheshire, some complimentary, others less so, which are explained by his unfailing readiness to answer journalists' questions and his invincible indifference to the printed result.

His parents reproved him at the time for the doubtful taste of some of the material which appeared in some of the popular papers. He wrote defensively in reply :

" I don't know what makes you think I'm responsible for it. I'd rather they'd print my story than their own if they're determined to print something."

He complained acidly that journalists seemed " to follow us wherever we go, and you know it's impossible to shake them off." The complaint was short-lived. They were disturbed less and less by the press after the first hullabaloo had died away, and for nearly a year were left in comparative peace.

2

Cheshire found as time went by that his instinctive dislike of paper-work did not diminish ; and the paper-work snowed him under for two dreary months, as the only non-operational squadron-leader at Linton. The enforced inactivity was a far heavier strain for him than flying because casualties rose in November, 1941, and he suffered repeated pangs of enervating suspense while others went out on hazardous missions from which he was debarred. Writing to the next-of-kin of men who failed to return was the hardest part of it all.

Yet, badly as he wanted to return to flying duties, he acknowledged to himself that the respite was useful and necessary for domestic reasons. Constance was living in furnished rooms not far from the airfield, bravely acclimatising herself to a restricted social life and much lower material standards than she was accustomed to. The least he could do was to be near until she felt more at home. With the encouragement of Geoffrey Harmsworth, proprietor of *The Field*, who was then stationed at Linton as an intelligence officer, Cheshire settled down seriously to write a book about his early bombing experiences. It was an enjoyable pastime which took up most of his free evenings and provided a useful outlet for his unspent energy.

"Saw Hutchinsons Friday lunch to settle final details," he announced briskly in a letter home early in December. " Journey up was awful. The car broke down, but I managed to trace it to a loose connection in the petrol pump which I patched up as best I could in the dark. Later we got a puncture, and the jack folded up before the wheel was high enough to get it off."

Before Christmas the weather closed in over Yorkshire and the rest of England and days went by without a raid. The only regular target was the dockyard at Brest where the elusive *Gneisenau* and *Scharnhorst* were still immobilised. Cheshire tried desperately hard to " talk his way " into two daylight attacks on the battleships. He was repeatedly refused permission for the same old unsatisfactory reason : " I was the only non-flying squadron-leader, and so had to do all the work. . . . It was a sad blow. The last four weeks have been hell."

Like Buridan's ass transfixed between the two bales of hay he was still drawn towards flying as much as towards the quiet pleasures of home-life with Constance. The inner tug-of-war between these two opposite and conflicting loyalties swayed him first one way and then the other according to circumstances ; but typically, he told Constance nothing about his unofficial and unsuccessful efforts to have his name listed for operations. His R.A.F. career was a private preserve ; he would permit nobody, not even his wife, to intrude on it.

When he was posted on January 22nd, 1942, to the squadron's Halifax Conversion Unit at Marston Moor, about four miles from Wetherby, he resigned himself glumly to the inevitable. At any rate he would be able to escape more often from files and office routine to the cockpit of a Halifax. He was appalled by the barrenness of his log-book ; between October and late February there were only two meagre entries for short local training flights.

It was now that the war struck a second savage blow at his parents when the calamitous news came that the Japanese had overrun Malaya, engulfed its defenders, and forced the capitulation of the " impregnable " fortress of Singapore. Major-General Arthur Barstow, Cheshire's uncle, was killed in action before the white flags fluttered in surrender ; but his fate remained uncertain for months.

"What can I say?" Cheshire wrote to his mother. "I can't say, 'Don't worry! I'm sure everything is all right.' You know as well as I do that that wouldn't be truthful. . . . I can only say keep a brave heart . . . because you know that whatever happened Arthur kept smiling and fought harder than anyone else could have done.

"I don't believe that a long life counts for a thing, if only we understand the broad picture. I believe that the only thing that really counts is being able to conquer your worst fears, and, no matter how hard you are hit, being able to come up smiling for more. For nothing that is easy is worth having. . . . So, Tops, smile and take the weight off your heart. . . . The day may come when you find that Arthur has achieved for himself something which no earthly happiness or success could ever achieve."

His own determined brand of fatalism is clearly expressed in those lines. The bludgeonings of chance left him unafraid and largely untouched, but his agile mind groped at moments like these for a possible clue to explain the broader pattern. He and Constance had moved to The Granary, a furnished house in the village of Linton-on-Wharfe which was closer to the air-field; and his thoughts pivoted on the same basic mystery of existence as he struggled to finish the manuscript of his book *Bomber Pilot*.

The publishers were satisfied with most of it. The atmosphere was good. The jerky, slangy style lent itself surprisingly well to the subject, though sections of the dialogue were too slick to be convincing, and some of the survivors have rather different memories of several incidents. But here and there he allowed himself to go deeper than the surface of events to write as un-selfconsciously about the horrible muddle of human life as he had talked about it to Mavis Randle at Oxford.

"A struggle for existence in which the strongest survives is something I can well understand; in fact it is what I have always believed to be the essence of life. What I cannot understand is a struggle for existence in which survival hinges wholly on luck. Yet there must be an explanation, and so it is that I say our values must be all upside-down and that a long life does not really count for much in the long run."

Cheshire drove Constance home to Grey Walls in March to meet his parents. The visit passed without a hitch, but his father and mother were left unshaken in their private conviction that the marriage had been a sorry mistake. Constance was the product of another world with which they were in scant sympathy: however hard they tried, they could not recognise her as anything but a daughter-in-law who had virtually usurped the title. Cheshire took her to Oxford, introduced her to Innes and Bert Gardiner at Merton, and met a number of old family friends.

Back at Marston Moor Cheshire settled down to earn a reputation as the instructor who "never stayed on the ground a moment more than he could help." At this period, just after Air Marshal Arthur Harris took over Bomber Command in February, 1942, the Conversion Units were rapidly turning out trained men for squadrons of four-engined heavy bombers that existed only on paper. Many men were being sent to the Middle East as soon as they were ready, to the understandable fury of Harris, whose single-minded aim was to get on with the only offensive he believed in. The pressure of work on an efficient instructor was therefore all the greater; and as the evenings lengthened Cheshire sometimes put in a twenty-hour day.

"Likely to be at Marston for a long while," he wrote home in May. "Turning out Halifax captains by the dozen, and at it as hard as ever."

Before the full moon period he was called into his station commander's office with the other instructors and ordered to prepare for a very special operation. Harris, with that grim, irascible thoroughness which was soon to make him an object of awe and apologetic dislike in Whitehall and elsewhere, had laid his ambitious plans and obtained approval for a 1000-bomber attack on either Hamburg or Cologne. The training units and Conversion flights between them were to provide more than half the force:

"It was by no means the greatest risk that a commander in the field has had to take in war," Harris has said retrospectively, "but it was a considerable risk."

Of the 1046 bombers which converged on Cologne on the night of May 30th, thirty-nine were lost. Nearly 900 aircraft went in to stoke the monstrous fires that were already an angry beacon on the moonlit horizon, beckoning Cheshire and his crew of trainee-sergeants soon after they had crossed the Dutch coast. He had heard the casual talk round the station that Harris was a forthright man of frightening energy who scorned half-measures. Looking down on the burning city, he knew it was so. Six hundred acres of homes, factories, churches and public buildings were being destroyed. The sheer weight and concentration of the assault had saturated the ground defences. Even the packs of greedy night fighters had to content themselves with picking off stragglers. The raid was a showcase demonstration, not of Bomber Command's strength, but of Harris's scientifically backed belief that the air war could be won only by such crushing methods.

Before the huge force assembled by Harris was dispersed, a second mass blow was aimed at Essen. Cheshire flew with the same crew and with Group Captain Bradbury, the station commander; but low cloud and industrial haze baffled the raiders. Most of the bombs fell fifteen miles away from Krupps. The third final attack on this grandiose scale was no more accurate than the second.

Cheshire did not have to be told that bombing strategy and tactics were being overhauled by Peirse's successor. These three raids alone proved it. The new portable radar aid known as " Gee " was coming into its own: he remembered the extravagant hopes held for the device when Charles Whitworth led 35 Squadron in the first " Gee " attack on Essen during March. Cheshire had since lost touch with developments, but could not help wondering whether in the end the blind weight of the bludgeon Harris was shaping would be more devastating than the deadly and precise thrust of the rapier. There was no question which bombing method he preferred. The new type of mass attack, with its carefully-planned route and split-second time-table, was leaving less and less scope for individual initiative.

Such academic doubts, however, troubled him little at this time. Cheshire was enjoying a taste of home life at The Granary. His book was in the hands of the printers, and his evenings were spent scribbling short stories and even dabbling with a film script. Two or three of the stories were eventually published in Britain and the United States, but by far the most intriguing was one which never found its way into print. It described the feelings of a young airman whose brother had been shot down on a bombing raid. Determined to avenge him by his own bravery, the young airman went on flying until he was awarded the Victoria Cross. One of the men who was shown the manuscript in 1942 felt sure that Cheshire had written from the heart ; and when the story came true with the award of Cheshire's V.C. in 1944 this witness was no more surprised than Christopher in his German prison camp.

The villagers of Linton-on-Wharfe took a friendly interest in their neighbours, the Cheshires, though the owner of The Granary developed a steady dislike for Simon the poodle which chased the hens and ran riot over the flower beds. Cheshire usually greeted his wife each day by flying low over the village, and nobody seemed to mind.

He was by now quite reconciled to this unreal but attractive existence, and there were fleeting moments when he found himself idly wishing that the war would end. This curiously untypical mood is echoed in the following letter :

" I hope to goodness the war will be over this year. I've given up wanting to go on indefinitely. I'm also scared of a plague of some sort breaking out on the Continent, and the thought of Christopher locked up there gets on my nerves. Thank God, at least they don't commit atrocities on British prisoners. Reading between the lines, I feel the air war will flare up very shortly, but I don't know whether it will lead to greater things.

" You would laugh if you could see me. We practically never go out, except occasionally to a film. Hardly even have a drink. I have lost all desire to spend my time round the night-clubs and bars, and I see why it is you could never understand my reasons for perpetually wanting to go into Oxford. It's a great thing being happily married with a home of your own, even though it's only rented."

Half-way through July the Conversion Unit was suddenly switched to Dalton, a station with fewer amenities so close at hand, and Cheshire's sudden enthusiasm for gardening, writing and domestic chores evaporated like dew in the summer sun. He realised, with a start, that his six-months' rest was almost at an end, and rushed in an application for a posting to daylight bombers. He was, if anything, a little ashamed of his recent apathy.

When Dr. Cheshire tided him over a period of money

shortage with a financial guarantee, he replied, "I am very grateful. . . . I have just given one of my junior officers £30. The bank will be furious probably, but he needs it very badly and he's not much use to me as an instructor if he spends his time worrying himself sick."

A redirected letter reached him one day from the father of his former navigator, Gerry Henery. Gerry was missing, presumed dead. Rivaz, who had written a book which complemented *Bomber Pilot* and reflected a deep personal regard for Cheshire as a friend, was training to be a pilot. Out in Egypt the Western Desert squadrons of his former group commander, Air Vice-Marshal Coningham, were pounding away at the German supply lines behind El Alamein where Auchinleck, with his depleted forces, stood stubbornly but precariously between Rommel and the mastery of the entire Middle East. The blackest six months of the war had been Cheshire's idlest ; the futility of selfishly longing for peace as though he could live in a cosy vacuum struck him with sudden force. The time for such delusions was over. He made up his mind that he would wangle his return to operations even if it meant reverting to pilot-officer.

3

On August 3rd, after presenting a distressed Constance with the *fait accompli*, Cheshire admitted to his parents that he was flying again :

" I wanted daylight bombers but couldn't get them. I'm not satisfied with sitting back watching others do the work. I know it makes it harder for you as it does for Constance, but I ask you to put up with it. Unofficially I was given the chance of shortly being promoted to Wing Commander and taking over the training unit. I refused it. I will refuse again if necessary. The past means nothing to me : the fact that I have done a certain number of operations does not count. I have always lived in the present, and it's the same now.

" I went to Düsseldorf last Friday with a badly sprained foot. Unfortunately I was unable to reach the target, but we succeeded in shooting a fighter down into the sea, so the trip was not completely wasted.

" My squadron is 76."

It could hardly have been arranged better if the Air Council practised nepotism and " Bomber " Harris had been his favourite uncle. No. 76 Squadron was the small, select unit in which Christopher, his brother, had served. After that final flight most of the way to Düsseldorf, which thrilled him as much as his crew of Conversion Unit trainees, Cheshire left Dalton at the week-end for Middleton St. George.

With the posting had come through an unsought upgrading to Wing Commander. The rank meant as little to him as the past, and he made up his mind at once to ignore protocol and follow his own casual routine of " getting the feel " of men and machines by moving about alone, unheralded and often without a hat. On his very first morning he took up a fitter for a twenty minutes' air test to chat about the Halifax the astonished man had been tinkering with. The word went quickly round the station that the new O.C. was a " friendly, soothing sort of bloke who knows his onions and doesn't stand on ceremony."

" There is a lot of work but not much flying," he wrote at the end of the first month. " I haven't operated since Mainz. The weather has been positively foul. . . I've seen Constance once or twice, but not often. I don't really get much chance to leave camp. Being back on a squadron has put me right. I've gained a stone : eat a fantastic amount and feel very fit."

The raid on Mainz early in August introduced him unceremoniously to the growing hazards of the area-bombing campaign on which Harris had embarked with bleak determination. Having established in the early summer that a whole city could be set on fire from end to end by concentrating the biggest force available over the target in the shortest possible time, the Chief of Bomber Command brusquely refused to sit pretty until the British aircraft industry overtook his many needs. The results of his gigantic gamble had silenced the sceptics in high places as effectively as the unwelcome evidence of night photography had silenced the optimists in 1941.

Despite the iron resolve of Harris to press home his advantage, it was the Germans—not the Air Ministry—who virtually dictated his targets for the rest of the year. The battle had certainly been carried with a vengeance to the enemy's vital airspace, but the initiative did not lie wholly with the bombers. The German night fighters had become far more numerous and accurate, the guns and searchlights had multiplied, and Harris had no option but to attack minor industrial targets within easy striking distance of the relatively weak front-line forces at his disposal. To add to his peppery impatience, the navigational device known as " Gee " had fallen disappointingly short of expectations. Indeed the Germans managed to jam it and so cut down its operational range by nearly half in the very week Cheshire joined 76 Squadron.

As in the case of the airborne cameras, " Gee " equipment had been given only to the best crews at first, for it was in very short supply. Gradually, almost through a process of natural selection, the bombers were led to Germany by the most highly-skilled navigators in each squadron. Harris dug his heels in when Air Ministry ordered him to form a new unit with the sole function of guiding the main force to the target. It was no novel suggestion : the Luftwaffe had its own specialised path-finders in 1940, and had used them with crippling effect against Coventry. But Harris objected to " creaming off " experts into a central group. He wanted each Group to provide its own path-finders. On his own blunt admission, Harris was finally over-ruled.

The Pathfinder Force was formed on August 15th, 1942, under the command of Air Commodore D. C. T. Bennett. We shall see in a later chapter how Harris's persistent doubts about the value of this separate target-finding organisation and his understandable resentment at having it forced upon him, were instrumental in giving Cheshire the greatest opportunity for tactical initiative that came the way of any young squadron commander during the entire war.

Between August 1942, and March 1943, however, there were only rare and limited occasions for Cheshire to show as a squadron commander that brand of cold courage and that taste for the calculated risk which had distinguished him as an individual pilot. His main achievement lay in setting and maintaining extremely high standards of technical competence for air crews and ground crews alike.

" To avoid being shot down is not enough," he would tell his crews. " You must avoid being shot down in such a way as not to prejudice your chances of finding the target.

" If there are many guns and the bursts are forming a box

round you, get out of the box as quickly as you know how. If
the shells form a general, loose barrage not predicted against you
as an individual, take no evasive action at all. You may just as
easily fly into a shell as away from it."

The squadron moved to Linton in mid-September, and
Constance took a furnished flat not far away. Cheshire arrived
to find another unit sharing the airfield and buildings, and its
O.C. proved to be a man after Cheshire's own heart. Wing
Commander J. B. Tait of 78 Squadron lacked the easy social
grace and the quick wit of Cheshire, but he had a similar streak
of unorthodox daring and a similar flair for tactical improvisation. " Willie " Tait was (and still is) an airman of few words ;
but his very silences are eloquent. He accepted Cheshire as a
friend as well as a partner, and the pair of them would often
be seen together, deep in discussion.

They were doubly fortunate in the station commander,
Group Captain (now Air Vice-Marshal) John Whitley. Resourceful, but discerning, Whitley was a useful brake on them
both. For he was also bold and far-sighted enough to lend his
full backing to novel ideas which would have frightened off a
lesser man. Being well brought up in the traditions of the
service, Whitley was sometimes put out by Cheshire's rather cool
attitude to formal parades and his genial disregard for the strict
letter of King's Regulations. The station commander, however,
was no pompous martinet, and could turn a blind eye with the
best for the sake of harmony. He appreciated that Cheshire in
his highly individualistic fashion had won the unqualified confidence of every officer, man and woman on the station within
ten days of his arrival.

" He was not cast in the mould of any squadron commander
I'd ever encountered," Whitley told me. " He was a singular,
attractive personality with a mature mind that belied his years.
He could usually produce the best possible reasons for wanting
to do a thing HIS way, and could be very determined in the nicest
possible manner. I must say the results he got justified his
occasional stubbornness.

" Rations and leave passes were as important to him as bombs
and tactics. Often when going my official round of the station,
I'd come upon Cheshire drinking a cup of tea at dispersal or
handing round cigarettes in the kitchens. With it all he never

lost a shred of his authority. How he managed to do it on top
of his main preoccupation, which was bombing, I just don't
know. But he did build up one of the finest, happiest and best-
knit teams in the whole Command."

Cheshire's briefings before raids were seldom dull. He was
(and still is) a very clear and concise speaker, with a plausible
touch of the barrister in his effortless ability to marshal facts and
draw conclusions. Whitley, who is far from impressionable,
used to enjoy listening to his arresting but invariably factual pre-
views of what lay ahead in night raids over Duisberg or Karlsruhe or Berlin. For, as Whitley knew, he kept himself up to date
with the latest German defence methods by piecing together
the nightly experiences of his own crews and every morsel of
authentic information that could be squeezed from Intelligence
sources.

Air Chief Marshal Sir Roderick Carr (as he now is) ran No. 4
Group on as loose a rein as he could, and encouraged his squadron
commanders to speak out freely at the daily tactical discussions
on the scrambled telephone :

" Cheshire needed little encouragement," he recalls. " At
first some of his ideas sounded odd and risky. Soon I learnt to
treat them with respect. I came to know him as a man with a
very sharp analytical brain which worked endlessly on a problem
until he found the best answer to it. Only then, as I discovered,
would he put it forward in that slightly diffident way of his."

By far the most illuminating example of Cheshire's practical
flair for improvisation was provided during the closing weeks of
1942, when squadron losses rose in a distressingly steep curve.
After discussing the evidence with " Willie " Tait, and allowing
for the improvements in German anti-aircraft methods, he was
driven to two conclusions. Neither was original or novel, but
the two remedies he proposed to Carr unquestionably were.

Cheshire's first conclusion was that the Halifax carried too
much surplus " fat ". Her ungainliness played into the lethal
hands of night-fighter pilots. The bomber's speed and manœuvrability had been sacrificed to a dubious safety. The extra
armoured plating, the cowlings to hide the tell-tale glow of
exhaust and the heavy mid-upper turret were false advantages.

" Let me strip them off," he told Carr. " Then watch the
losses drop."

" Certainly not," said Carr.   " I want proofs, not assertions."

The A.O.C. was even more hesitant at first about the merits of Cheshire's second startling remedy, which dovetailed conveniently with the first.   German night-fighter attacks " on the blind side " had been taking a severe toll of bombers for months. As early as March, 1942, Mr. Churchill had expressed his personal concern to Air Ministry ; but no solution had been found. Cheshire now suggested as an experiment that an emergency " blister " should be fitted to the floor of the Halifax to protect the vulnerable " belly ".   He had already taken two of his non-commissioned technicians into his confidence to ensure that the modifications would do no structural damage.

Sergeant George Coates and L.A.C. Frank Layton worked " all the hours God gave us " shaping a perspex " blister " of the correct size, and Carr, yielding to Cheshire's persistent pleas, finally visited the station and inspected the experimental " lower turret."   After much close questioning, he captured some of his unconventional squadron commander's enthusiasm.

" It's worth a trial," he said.   " But we must have exhaustive local tests first."

The tests were successful, and early in the New Year the A.O.C. accompanied Cheshire to the R.A.F. research establishment at Boscombe Down where scientists went meticulously into the proposal.   Eventually, as Sir Frederick Handley Page confirmed to me, the Halifax bomber was slightly modified : excessive armour was removed, and an air-gunner's turret covering the " blind side " incorporated.   On 76 Squadron, however, Cheshire boldly anticipated the slower alterations of the designers and makers by many weeks.

" We left the steel coverings of the oxygen equipment," admitted Layton " but practically everything else was stripped off at once, including the solid engineer's door."

Most of the routine paper-work had been taken out of Cheshire's hands by Squadron-Leader " Pop " Bligh, the adjutant, for whose forbearance and understanding he was eternally grateful. Bligh, a short, cheerful, elderly man, felt he knew two distinct versions of Cheshire : the gay, dryly humorous individualist who would protect his men against all-comers from petty service restrictions and injustices, and the rigidly uncompromising leader who could be merciless to any man who failed him.

On at least three occasions, Cheshire was faced with the difficult problem of what to do with air-crew members who refused to continue flying. Bligh remembers how strained he looked as he " retired into his shell " to reach a different decision in each case. One man, an air-gunner, he " sent to Coventry " at once, coldly ordering him to remain locked in his room until arrangements had been made to remove him under escort from the station.

" It was almost as if he feared, like a doctor, that others might be infected by someone whose nerve had gone," said Bligh.

Cheshire himself can look back to-day on these harsh decisions without undue qualms :

" I was, I admit, pretty ruthless with what were technically called ' moral fibre cases '. Sometimes I tried to deal with them myself, without taking official action, but that was rarely possible. I remember once in 76 Squadron how a young chap who'd been recently decorated made a scene and declared that he couldn't go on. I put him down as a member of my own crew to show him I still trusted him. It was a risk, but it worked. He finally made the grade—though only just.

" I still think sometimes of another case when I was tempted to spare a cowardly man official sanctions. My idea was that we should administer our own punishment by giving him a bit of a beating. In the end I was persuaded against it. It was always my aim to act quickly, either getting rid of the person or taking my own line with him before others got to know what was afoot. That obviously had to be done for the man's own sake and for the sake of the other fliers."

This hard, unbending side of Cheshire's nature was rarely in evidence, even to Bligh who knew him intimately. When he took some step to assert the need for discipline it was normally a very simple, unexpected but human step. One morning, for example, he inspected the air-crew billets in a big requisitioned mansion near Linton and was annoyed by the general air of untidiness.

" Right, Pop, give me a hand," he said to Bligh. " They'll think they've been bombed out by the time we finish."

He then began to turn untidiness into chaos, emptying the contents of drawers on the floor, throwing discarded equipment and odds and ends of clothing under beds, while his adjutant looked on aghast.

"Put it round that I've been here," he told Bligh as they walked away. Bligh did so, and the air crews took the hint far better than if an order had been pinned on the squadron notice board.

During November, the first six Norwegians to fly with Bomber Command were posted to Linton. Two of them, Lt.-Col. Gunnar Halle and Lt.-Col. Eirick Sandberg, followed one another to London after the war as air attachés at the Norwegian Embassy : the third, Lt. Hallvard Vikholt, is flying still as a pilot of Scandinavian Airways.

"It made a lasting impression on us, the generous way Cheshire received us," Halle recalls. "None of us can forget how hard he tried to ease things for us. I never met any English squadron commander afterwards who got people to do things his way without apparent effort. I think this was partly because everybody in the squadron knew that Cheshire took a personal interest in HIS or HER personal problems."

Constance occasionally visited the mess for parties and musical evenings. She played the piano beautifully ; and her witty, sophisticated tongue made her a firm favourite. Bligh rang her up one dank morning early in November to say that Cheshire had been hurt in a road accident the night before, but was in no danger. Driving back from York with Tait at the wheel, in the small hours of the morning, they took a tight corner on the narrow, frozen road in top gear. The car had skidded and overturned in a ditch.

"I damaged my left arm and right hand, but at least I can write," he told his parents. "They gave me eight days' sick leave and, being forbidden to travel far, we came here to Bolton Abbey, a delightful place in the heart of the moors. The weather is gorgeous again. We have no worries, nowhere to go, and nothing to do except walk, eat and sleep. . . .

"By the way, while I was in hospital I amused myself by re-reading Pickwick, and believe it or not there was a Snodgrass and a Tupman in the same ward with me !"

Shortly before his mishap, on the night of October 23rd, Cheshire led the squadron to Genoa. The whole effort of Bomber Command at this period had been peremptorily turned from Germany to the Mediterranean in preparation for the Allied landings in North Africa. Milan, Turin, and Genoa wilted under repeated blows by day as well as night, while the great Armada of " Torch " stole through the Atlantic towards its objective.

" Yes, I was at Genoa the second night," he assured his parents. " It was the most fascinating trip yet. The Alps were absolutely dead clear in the full moon . . . Opposition, of course, was negligible, but on the way back an impertinent fighter set about us. Being a biplane, he was amazingly manœuvrable and therefore somewhat difficult to deal with. Fortunately his aim was not as good as it might have been or he would have fetched us down on his first attack. As it was, he barely missed us. He was remarkably bold for an Italian : I felt sorry we had to hit him. They are such a pathetic race."

With no access to top-secret information and only his intuition to prompt him, Cheshire came back from Genoa convinced that the " showdown " was coming in North Africa. Whitley, Tait and others listened with polite scepticism to his reasoning : they were not at all convinced. Did not the Dieppe raid in August support the popular belief that if a landing in strength came anywhere it would come in France ?

One junior officer, rasher than the rest, confidently bet Cheshire £5 that there would be invasion before the end of November, and that if any took place it would not take place in Africa. Before he went into hospital, Cheshire had collected his £5.

" The news is gratifying to my vanity," he wrote in an unusually long letter written from bed. " I was right in predicting that we would land a powerful force in French North Africa and thereby wipe out Rommel. The only thing in which I was wrong was in supposing the frontal attack (at El Alamein) would come after we had started marching against his rear. I did not dream we were so strong and prepared. . . . We could never hope to get anywhere in this war without liquidating Rommel. Not only was an entire army mobilised, but a huge proportion of our shipping, naval and air resources were engaged solely in maintaining that army, in a purely defensive role. . . . In desert warfare an army that gets worsted packs up its bags and runs for all it is worth, so fast and so far that the other side outruns itself and has to fight a battle at the extreme limit of its resources. As a result, the only sane way to annihilate the enemy is to attack him in force from both sides. . . .

" I did not believe an invasion of the Continent was possible this year. . . . One day I heard people saying that Dieppe was a preparation for the real thing. According to them, everybody down south damn well knew it was. Well, I damn well knew it wasn't, because when you invade, the enemy has his forces so distributed that he can get up five divisions to the danger area within twenty-four hours. Consequently you've got to get sufficient armour on to the Continent in the same period to deal with those five divisions. The only possible way you can do that is to establish a great many bridgeheads. . . . Therefore, I reasoned, people were saying Dieppe was the second front because they were meant to say it, and the whole thing was a gigantic piece of bluff designed to make the German put his forces in the wrong place—which indeed he did."

This letter seems to me worth quoting at some length. It gives an insight into the cool, dispassionate sweep of Cheshire's mind on the larger strategic issues of the hour. To show how extraordinarily near the mark he was in fact, one need only compare his " hunch " with the essential part of Churchill's formal reply to Stalin, during the Prime Minister's first Moscow visit, scouting the dubious merits of invading France in 1942 :

" All the talk about an Anglo-American invasion of France this year has misled the enemy and has held large air forces and considerable military forces on the French Channel coast. . . . The wisest course is to use ' Sledgehammer ' as a blind for ' Torch ', and proclaim ' Torch ' when it happens as the Second Front. That is what we ourselves mean to do."

Cheshire was far from dispassionate, however, in his attitude to unsuccessful bombing raids, particularly the severely rationed raids on which he was allowed to lead the squadron. Five of his nine precious trips were partial failures, and it amused Whitley and others to see how he chafed at the weather, the poorly placed leading flares or whatever else had ruined his enjoyment of a rare night out.

After a scattered assault on Mannheim early in December, Colonel Ivor Jones listened at debriefing to his short, mournful account of what went wrong and said bluffly :

" Cheer up, nobody's going to court-martial you for someone else's mistakes."

" It's all very well for you, Colonel," came the sharp reply. " I've only got two raids left and just look at this abominable weather."

Shortly before Christmas Whitley went away for two or three weeks, and Cheshire had the station commander's work to do as well as his own. In the office where he now had to spend hours signing unintelligible orders and shuffling uninteresting files, his exasperation was kept well within bounds. Olive Ascough, the blonde W.A.A.F. who had typed for Whitley, found him " even-tempered, friendly and most considerate ". Only in his letters did his true feelings overflow :

" Not only is Christmas fast approaching, but so is the end of my tour. Not only am I virtually forbidden to operate, but the days in which I shall be even remotely connected with active flying are speedily drawing to a close. This appears to afford Constance the utmost gratification. I view it with the utmost despondency and gloom."

On Christmas Eve, Constance came to the mess where the Norwegians jovially insisted on playing host, pouring out large glasses of their own mysterious fire-water which brought tears to the eye, rasped the throat, but slowly warmed the cockles of the heart, creating its own mood of talkative elation. At mid-night, Cheshire belatedly decided to conduct a tour of the entire camp to wish everyone a Merry Christmas ; and with Bligh, the Norwegians and half a dozen more forming a noisy crocodile behind him, he moved off. By half-past two they had visited every hut and billet.

The final port of call was the guardroom, and by now only Bligh, Hill and Halle were left with him. The others had dropped off wearily, one by one. Cheshire insisted on going into the cells to greet the few air-crew prisoners and to tell them they would soon be amnestied to fly again. Then he turned to the corporal of the guard and said rather stiffly :

" I want you to demonstrate how you'd deal with a difficult customer."

The corporal jumped up with alacrity to give a vigorous impression of a man tying himself in a reef-knot, providing his own gasping commentary as he went along. He seemed bewildered when Cheshire suddenly grabbed his wrists and slipped on the handcuffs, but gradually saw the absurdity of the situation and joined in the loud laughter at his own expense.

Handcuffs and iron bars had been in Cheshire's mind for some months, ever since the chaining of war prisoners stirred up a brief outcry in parliament and the press. He had often wondered how Christopher was faring; and musing on the miserable emptiness of life in a prison camp led him to lay his own plans against the hour when a stray shell might force him to bale out. " Jock " Hill noticed that, in addition to the escape kit, Cheshire now carried a thin, silk rope wound about his waist. He made no secret of the reason. If the worst came to the worst, he would never stay a captive for long.

Whitley, who was shot down over Northern France in April, 1943, returning to England eventually after one of the coolest and most thoroughly planned escapes of the whole war, admits that " it was far more probable Cheshire influenced me in my determination to evade capture at all costs than that I ever influenced him." Coming from a man who, as a precaution, wore civilian clothes under his uniform, and carried a compass, a razor, and even a toothbrush on the night he disappeared, this is significant praise indeed.

Only once did Whitley fly on a raid with Cheshire. That was on January 16th, a special occasion when the station commander was taken on a " Cook's Tour " of the main German night-fighter " boxes " en route. Each box was controlled by a powerful ground station of the Kammhuber defence line which zig-zagged deep across Northern Europe from the Skagerrak to Marseilles. Harris's unflagging offensive would remain in jeopardy until these stations were either destroyed or jammed, for only a handful of brave and knowledgeable pilots claimed that there were any safe loopholes through this formidable radar screen. In Whitley's words, " we leapfrogged across Germany without interference. Cheshire seemed to know where the boxes were and what was to be expected next. It was almost a leisurely trip. We sighted and hit the target untroubled by opposition worth speaking of."

On the way home, Cheshire diplomatically broke with a custom he had observed on every trip he had flown with Hill : instead of handing round cigarettes he winked at " Jock " and moved down the aircraft for a quiet smoke. He did not wish to embarrass Whitley by openly flouting a regulation. Hill caught his captain's eye and winked in turn a few minutes later when Whitley suddenly rose to his feet, excused himself and retreated with equal delicacy to enjoy a forbidden cigarette of his own.

The last raid with 76 Squadron was undoubtedly the dullest. They flew above cloud to Wilhelmshaven and back half-way through February, dropping their bombs blind on the Pathfinders' skymarkers. It was not the spectacular sort of ending Cheshire would have ordered for himself, though he had to admit that " bombing accuracy all round has reached a standard nobody would have thought possible twelve months ago."

4

" Days and nights flash by like a cinema flicker. February has been a decisive turning point in the war. I think the damage we've done must almost equal all the damage put together since 1939 . . . and last night was probably the best of all. As far as I'm concerned I've played little or no part. Try as I may, I'm unable to fly and I feel somehow my stay here is nearly ended."

In January and February heavy and repeated assaults were inflicted at the Admiralty's instigation on the Atlantic U-boat bases of Lorient and St. Nazaire. (Cheshire returned gaily from a trip to Lorient with a clear photograph of the aiming point taken from 8000 feet). Now the bombers had been relieved of this thankless naval chore which, owing to the thick concrete roofs of the U-boat pens and the lack of suitable bombs to penetrate them, Harris scornfully opposed as a " hopeless misuse of air power."

The Battle of the Ruhr opened on March 5th, the night before Cheshire wrote the above letter, with a ferocious blow at Essen ; and the corresponding entry in Goebbels' Diaries records the dismay it caused in the minds and hearts of Germany's Nazi rulers. The communiqué issued after the Casablanca Conference in January had seemed rather thin propaganda to Dr. Goebbels : it contained little more than an array of militant platitudes marching ponderously across an endless horizon in search of an idea. Even the directive to the Allied Air Forces had failed to impress him. Its object was laid down to be :

" Primarily, the progressive destruction and dislocation of the German military, industrial, and economic system, and the undermining of the morale of the German people to a point when their capacity for armed resistance is fatally weakened."

Goebbels was learning that the Casablanca directive was no longer beyond the power of the R.A.F. to fulfil. It meant in hard fact that the area-bombing policy which Harris had inherited from Peirse, his predecessor, and which he was gradually transforming with warped apostolic fervour (and complete War Cabinet approval) into an overwhelming instrument of destruction, had been solemnly underwritten as a short-cut to victory in the West. In time, many men on the Allied side with motives far less mixed than they have been given credit for, were to doubt the strategic wisdom and moral rightness of the Casablanca decision ; but in early 1943 the few critics who raised their voices against it as a bad psychological and moral blunder were regarded either as dangerous cranks or as unpatriotic poltroons.

Cheshire was different from many R.A.F. bomber pilots in that he did give some thought to this bitterly controverted problem :

" In the main we supported Harris," he recalls. " I doubt if any of us ever felt squeamish. On the actual attack itself we were far too concerned with getting through the defences and dropping the bombs to think about the people on the ground. Besides, bombing is a cold, impersonal game. You are so far removed in distance and vision from the people you are attacking that you don't really think of it in terms of human beings.

" Some of us knew, of course, that Harris believed the bomber alone could win the war by a technical knock-out. No doubt we supported the Harris view at least by implication, assuming that the leaders knew what they were doing. No doubt also we had our own private views which probably swung from one extreme to another according to whatever influences we came under.

" I remember going to a dinner at No. 4 Group Headquarters at which Harris was guest of honour. I felt flattered at being present and hearing an off-the-record opinion from him on the course of the war. At the same time he was so excessively pro-Bomber Command and so violently anti- the efforts of the other services and especially the Navy, that I'm not certain to what extent I agreed with him.

I don't think I was ever actually against area-bombing as such, but I was inclined to think, at least at times, that strategic precision bombing was more valuable. Once we discovered that we really could do precision bombing I'm sure that we thought in terms of factories to be destroyed and not houses . . ."

But Cheshire's main feeling as the Battle of the Ruhr opened was one of fretful petulance : here he was, in the best of health and brimming over with energy, foredoomed by short-sighted regulations to stagnate in a quiet backwater for the next six months. For he had now completed sixty operations, and Whitley agreed with Carr that sixty was a nice round figure at which to call a halt.

One evening, when he was helping " Jock " Hill to arrange chairs in the mess ante-room for a cinema show, Cheshire said lightly that it was months since they'd had a party and about time they had another.

" I'd wait for that party, if I were you," said Hill.

" What do you mean ? "

" Just what I say. It may interest you to know that you've been recommended for a bar to your D.S.O."

Cheshire turned pale with anger and muttered :

" You'd absolutely no right to tell me that, Jock."

Then he stalked out of the room.

Such touchiness in Cheshire was rare, and sprang from his general irritability with the obtuseness of his R.A.F. superiors, rather than from any strong resentment at the impropriety of the remark. As a matter of fact, Hill had been asked by Whitley for details of Cheshire's previous tours : he did not know that he himself had been recommended for a D.F.C. to add to his D.F.M., both earned while flying in Cheshire's crew.

They had their party before the end of March, and on April 4th, his last day at Linton, Cheshire called everyone together. He thanked the ground crews for their wholehearted efforts and the air crews for spontaneously sending a deputation to Whitley in a sincere but vain attempt to defer his posting. The gesture had moved him deeply : he had been too busy to consider whether he was popular or unpopular. The deafening cheers and clapping that broke out as he finished his farewell speech to the squadron left him in no doubt : he felt bewildered and momentarily happy.

Three years in the R.A.F. had knocked some of the conceit out of him ; the old itch for notoriety and adulation had gone. He cared less now, but was human enough to relish the unlooked-for sweets of success. For that reason, the many letters of congratulations from friends, colleagues he had forgotten and total strangers during his first three weeks at Marston Moor were a pleasant distraction.

Cheshire realised that Carr had done a good deal of pushing at the highest level to secure his promotion to Group Captain. The appointment as a station commander at the ridiculous age of twenty-five was unprecedented, but that alone did not explain the fan-mail. Throughout the winter, extracts from his book had been appearing under sensational headlines in the *Sunday Graphic*. Now, as he knew, *Bomber Pilot* itself was selling hand over fist in the bookshops of York and Harrogate.

His affability and alertness, as much as his success, had made him a quick favourite with the public relations officers at Group. He could usually be counted on, at short notice, for broadcasts and comments on raids. When three Russian officers arrived on a propaganda visit, it was to Cheshire at 76 Squadron that they were sent by Group ; when a eulogy from the R.A.F. on the Soviet's struggle against the Hitlerite hordes was called for, it was the obliging Cheshire who wrote it. He was just as easily persuaded also to send a cable to Stalin after the lifting of the siege of Stalingrad.

The legendary Cheshire, a shadow of the real man, had slowly begun to take shape in the public eye as a direct result of this jig-saw pattern of publicity ; and it is only fair to add that many officers in Bomber Command who had never met him, jumped to the conclusion that the " other " Cheshire must be a " shocking line-shooter ". They did not question his record, which spoke for itself ; they did question the doubtful taste and freakish exhibitionism of a man who was willing to regale the world in very bold type, with such nauseating offerings as " HOW I CONQUERED FEAR ", at twopence a time. The R.A.F.'s sacred tradition of studied understatement was being sabotaged from within by cheap sensationalism.

Characteristically, Cheshire was as blandly indifferent to this unfavourable current of opinion as he was to the articles themselves. What he had written in the past belonged to the past.

F

The headlines were not his in any case, and he had already registered an angry protest with the editor of the paper concerned. Public relations officers, he felt, were a necessary evil in wartime, doing a job that had to be done ; but he was alternately amused and infuriated by the dogged way they haunted him.

It would have surprised some of his R.A.F. critics to know that Cheshire was guilty more than once of mischievously embellishing the popular legend by inventing facts within the hearing of journalists in order to discover how gullible they were. " Give them the straw, and they'll drop the bricks " seemed to sum up his attitude on such occasions. During his six months at Marston Moor, he was frequently in demand for the routine public engagements that are often the fate of minor celebrities in wartime : opening Wings for Victory Weeks and visiting factories to address the workers. In nearly all cases, he was extremely successful for a very simple reason, which was expressed most pithily by an organiser in the East Riding of Yorkshire :

" He was such a pleasant surprise—much more modest and accommodating than the man we had expected."

In the spring of 1943, Harris had introduced the Base system of command as the most economical method of controlling the rapidly increasing number of bomber stations. The newly appointed Base Commander at Marston Moor, responsible for three Heavy Conversion Units, including Cheshire's, was a tall quiet, rather severe-looking man called John Kirby, an Air Commodore of many years' service. Kirby was down with 'flu in his billet when Cheshire arrived on April 5th.

The weather had turned treacherously cold. While vaguely examining his room, Cheshire noticed water oozing through the frayed linoleum near the bed. Underneath, the chipped concrete floor was covered with moisture. There and then he decided to take matters into his own hands. Going straight to the station stores, he commandeered a large bell-tent and with the help of his batman pitched it ostentatiously on the patch of grass outside his room. This practical method of protesting against the damp discomfort of his billet excited the mirth of the men and the keen interest of the Base Commander, who was still nursing a high temperature.

" I understand you've moved out into a tent," said Kirby.

" Don't you find it rather cold at night ? "

Cheshire assured him that a stove and extra blankets helped to create an illusion of warmth.

" Could you organise a tent for me ? " asked Kirby with an appreciative smile.

The prompt appearance of a second tent beside the first caused more amused discussion. The general opinion was that the Base Commander must have a sense of humour as flexible as Cheshire's. They might not be so bad to work for, after all.

A few days later, when Kirby had recovered, Cheshire walked into the O.C.'s office one morning, saluted smartly, and said solemnly :

" May I have a word with you, sir, on a personal matter ? "

" Certainly," said Kirby. " Pull up a chair and sit down."

After a pause, the Base Commander looked at him quizzically across the desk :

" Well, what can I do for you ? "

Cheshire seemed to be selecting his words with care :

" I know I've been here less than no time," he said, " but I've come to ask for a posting to an operational unit. I'm out of my depth here. Can you help to arrange it ? "

Kirby had been half expecting some such request. From odd remarks dropped in casual conversations he had already gathered that Cheshire felt lost in the role of a static Group Captain. But there was no hint of sympathy in Kirby's manner as he replied testily :

" Definitely not. I never heard a more preposterous sugges-tion in all my life. I suppose you realise the trouble Air Vice-Marshal Carr went to over your appointment ? "

Cheshire nodded.

" In that case, you've got no right to let him, me, or yourself, down. Let's look at this sensibly. You promise not to raise this subject again, and I'll promise you something in return. Stick it for six months, do your job here properly and provided you still feel the same way then, I'll pull all the strings I can to get you back on operations. What about it ? "

Cheshire shifted uneasily in his chair. Kirby's offer was reasonable, but it had the unanswerable ring of an ultimatum. There was nothing for it but to agree. They shook hands on the arrangement, and neither raised the subject again. Kirby's words pulled him round as quickly as the angry words of his Scottish wireless operator had once done over the defences of Magdeburg. Before the end of April he was running the station with that personal concern for detail which had made his reputation at Linton.

" Cheshire was 100% efficient," said Kirby, " though I expected that from his record. What I never quite got used to was his innate knack of communicating his confidence and enthusiasm to others, no matter what their work happened to be."

None was more ruefully aware than Cheshire himself of the seeming pointlessness of serving on a Conversion Unit ; and in his " Personal Message from the Station Commander ", a printed leaflet distributed to all ranks early in May, he used arguments on which he had fallen back to convince himself that the work was not entirely futile.

" If you were to walk up to a soldier in the 8th Army and say to him, ' What are you trying to do ? What is the victory you are aiming to win ? ' the answer would be obvious : ' Kick Rommel into the sea.'

" If, however, someone came up to you and asked you the same question, the answer wouldn't be at all obvious ; and unless you were very careful you might get yourself tied up in knots. . . Your objective here at Marston Moor is a clear and definite one. So long as the weather lasts, to keep two aircraft from every flight in the air for ten hours a day, and to fly every available night-flying crew until they have finished. . . .

" There are many things that can hold the objective up : a crash, a spare part that someone didn't order in time, a dirty room that spreads disease, a burst tyre from a stone on the runway, or a piece of grit in the glycol. . . . Before we can go to bed with the knowledge that the day's objective has been gained, we must have had two aircraft from every flight in the air continually for ten hours. If we have done it, we've succeeded, and if we haven't we've been defeated. There are no two ways about it."

The personal challenge was understood and taken up ; and although there were days when the station was " defeated ", the general level of efficiency rose remarkably.

In June, Cheshire had a railway coach brought by road from York. It was furnished and equipped by Constance and himself, and parked in the field behind the officers' mess. They lived in it for the rest of the summer and autumn. They had a chef of their own whom Cheshire kept well supplied with fresh meat, even though meat was frequently hard to come by " over the counter." Corporal R. G. White blinked in astonishment one morning when Cheshire responded to the doleful announcement that the butcher had failed them again, by walking out jauntily with a sporting gun. Presently there was a loud report, and he returned carrying a large hare. Well pleased with his huntsman's skill, Cheshire gradually became bolder, stalking his quarry from behind the living-room curtains. Both Air Vice-Marshal Carr and Air Commodore Kirby were treated to this routine performance on a visit to the railway bungalow for lunch :

" How would you like roast pheasant ? " he asked them suddenly.

" That sounds splendid," they said, wondering why he had mentioned it.

" Well, if you'll hold your breath, I'll attend to it. There's a brace on the fence outside."

The window was slowly slid open, Cheshire took aim, and two minutes later his chef was busy in the kitchen removing the feathers.

Cheshire went to Buckingham Palace in July to receive the second bar to his D.S.O. from the King :

" I'm awfully sorry you weren't able to come up," he wrote home, " although I must say the ceremony isn't particularly exciting. King George spoke to me for quite a long time. I was with Commander Ben Bryant, almost the first after a few knights.

" As we were waiting in the entrance a fellow in morning coat came up and asked us to follow him. We walked for hours along passages, up stairs, down stairs and through lobbies, finally fetching up in a kind of pantry place. The fellow banged on a panel. It shot up, and behind it was a bar. We had the unaccustomed pleasure of drinking beer in the royal butler's pantry."

Outwardly, he seemed to be conforming to the exacting, popular but unexciting régime he had invented for Marston Moor, and the Base Commander regarded him as an effervescent, yet wise companion. When they discussed the war, they did so in general terms ; the intensified bomber offensive on the Ruhr was in both their thoughts, yet Cheshire had no trouble in dissembling his thoughts. He was well able to discuss even the raids on the Mohne and Eder Dams without betraying any sign of frustrated longing. Kirby, it appeared, had every reason to feel proud of his firmness and common sense in handling that first tiresome little interview between them.

Yet the Base Commander would possibly have been upset by the discovery of Cheshire's real reason for flying to Scampton in Lincolnshire, towards the end of July. When his Falcon reached this airfield, on which 617 Squadron, the famous "Dambusters", was based, he at once went to pay his respects to the station commander, none other than his old friend and Oxford instructor, Charles Whitworth. Cheshire finally came to the point :

"I hear 617 has been without a squadron commander since Guy Gibson was taken off," he said. "Any chance for me, Charles ? "

Whitworth was sympathetic but straight :

"Sorry, Leonard. Not this time."

He explained that the vacancy had already been filled by George Holden, who had served under Cheshire at Linton.

"Besides," he bantered, "I doubt if you would have stood much chance in any case. I don't think Cochrane and you would ever have hit it off."

Air Vice-Marshal Cochrane, the A.O.C. of 5 Group, had a reputation for punctilious strictness, and Whitworth was at least half serious in suggesting this as an almost insuperable obstacle to the brilliant but harum-scarum Cheshire he remembered from Abingdon, Driffield and Linton days.

But if the journey to Scampton had been fruitless, Cheshire was undeterred. Having once exerted himself, he must go on ; and now the Pathfinder Force seemed his last remaining hope. Here again, however, his unofficial inquiries met with a rebuff. The Pathfinders had no vacancy for him either. As their lack of interest tended to colour his attitude then and later, it is only just to quote what Air Vice-Marshal Bennett, the Pathfinder A.O.C., said of this episode : "I knew nothing about any application from Cheshire. If I had, and if he'd been free to move, we'd have snapped him up at once."

Bennett knew no more of these secret overtures than Carr or

Cochrane. Nor did Cheshire feel any sense of disloyalty to Kirby, to whom he had given his word not to seek a move for six full months. It was perfectly true that Carr had gone to immense trouble on his behalf : but Carr's jurisdiction did not extend to the Pathfinders or 5 Group. Cheshire was rarely at a loss for sound logical or legalistic excuses to justify his own unofficial bids for freedom.

Neither his wife nor any of their friends suspected that the strain of prolonged inactivity was beginning to tell on his nerves, until one day Mr. George Muff, M.P. (the late Lord Calverley), who was serving locally as an Army welfare officer at the ripe age of sixty-six, unexpectedly called his bluff. Muff subsequently told Geoffrey Gilbey, an old friend and the O.C. of the Army unit at Wetherby, who liked and admired Cheshire.

An unworldly man at heart in spite of ample private means for cultivating worldly interests, Gilbey was well known in Fleet Street and elsewhere before the war as a racing journalist and an authority on bloodstock. He was less well known, perhaps, for the unselfish use he made of his extraordinary knack of reading minds as others read teacups, and of teaching highly strung people how to relax. Gilbey invited Cheshire and his wife to dinner, and afterwards took him aside.

" You can't continue living on your nerves indefinitely," he said. " If you'll let me, I can help."

Cheshire agreed, half joking, to let Gilbey try ; and because he was co-operative, he learnt quickly how to control his thoughts by a form of auto-suggestion.

" I've been connected for many years with people suffering from overstrained nerves," Gilbey said to me. " But Cheshire was the opposite of most people I've ever dealt with. It was plain that unless he was allowed to go back to flying, the tension would probably give him a breakdown."

Cheshire quickly mastered the process of composing his mind ; it was a new attainment and a valuable one. He had not, however, quite finished his personal search for an honourable release from Marston Moor. In September, he announced that he was not feeling well ; it was nothing physical, just his nerves. Arrangements were made for him to see a specialist : no ordinary specialist, but THE leading R.A.F. expert on the complicated inner strains and stresses of airmen.

Sir Charles Symonds has an undying recollection of that interview in London, one of the strangest and most delightful of the innumerable interviews he had during the war. Symonds had been called in by the R.A.F. as a consultant, with the rank of Air Commodore, to make a thorough study of the symptoms and effects of what was miscalled " flying stress ". Long before the war he had risen to eminence as a physician at Guy's and the National Hospital for Nervous Diseases ; and his researches into the mysterious field of anxiety neurosis in combat fliers provided a basis for developing the R.A.F.'s wartime treatment of " moral fibre " cases.

Symonds was always hard pressed for time, and his first impression of Cheshire was that this youthful, slim but extremely fit-looking Group Captain had come to squander a precious quarter of an hour on a doleful hypochondriac's tale. He soon revised his opinion : from the beginning, the interview took a startling turn which made other urgent appointments wait.

After the preliminary formalities it became quite clear that Cheshire was not going to be rushed, and Symonds humoured him by trying to answer a number of seemingly irrelevant questions :

" Am I right in thinking that it's quite common for flying people to develop an anxiety neurosis through doing too much flying ? " asked Cheshire.

Symonds assured him he was right. " I'm dealing with cases constantly," he said.

" Then it is possible, even as a hypothesis, that a man could develop an anxiety neurosis through doing too *little* flying ? "

Symonds, still unable to see where this quiet cross-examination was leading, said patiently :

" Well, that's a very interesting hypothesis. I can't say I've ever come across such a case. But why do you ask ? "

" Because I'm your first case. That what's wrong with me," said Cheshire earnestly. " I'm sure of it, and before I leave, I'd like a certificate from you confirming it."

Symonds was both intrigued and perplexed. He pointed out that he would certainly try to help, but that to sign such a certificate at the present stage of medical knowledge would be more than his reputation was worth. For the rest of the interview, he asked the questions and was completely satisfied that this extraordinary young man would go on eating his heart out like a caged swallow until he was released to fly again.

As Cheshire left, Symonds said :

" *Au revoir*. I'm sure we'll meet again. Meanwhile, don't worry about that certificate. I agree that you'd be better off flying, and you may count on me to do what I can for you."

On October 5th, exactly six months after taking over at Marston Moor, Cheshire walked into Kirby's office, saluted with an apologetic smile on his face, and was motioned to a chair :

" I was wondering whether you'd come," said Kirby. " I've been watching the calendar, too. You still want to go back ? "

" Yes, I do, I'm afraid."

Kirby was as good as his word, and braced himself to tell Carr at the first opportunity. The Air Vice-Marshal, anxious not to lose one of his most competent young leaders, made a final counter-proposal which Cheshire referred to fully in a letter to his father :

" The news I have to give you will, I'm afraid, cause you some surprise, though whether for better or worse I'm not quite sure. It's to do with my future in the Air Force, and as I haven't ever said much on that score I'll start more or less from the beginning. As you well know, the job of station commander is at times a somewhat responsible, although in the usual course of events not a very arduous one. It is essentially a job that requires a settled and patient character, and promoting anyone of my experience and years to the post was an entire innovation for the Air Force and only done after a great many exertions on the part of the A.O.C. (Carr) and a good deal of arguing into the bargain.

" The job was strange and a little difficult, if only for the reason that everyone under me was considerably older and more experienced. Nonetheless I was able to succeed and appear to have justified my promotion. As a result I was put down for a Staff College course, which would fit me for bigger jobs and in the course of time, I suppose, further promotion, provided of course that everything went well.

" However, I have never felt that my duty lies in office work and I refused to accept the staff course. It would have ensured a comfortable and well-paid life for both Constance and me and, pleasant though it would have been, I was not prepared to accept it. At the same time I volunteered to forfeit my rank in order to return to operations. I have just heard that this has been granted, and I am fortunate enough to be going to a job that can only be done by a volunteer. . . ."

The command of 617 Squadron had gone begging again, and the compliant Carr had suggested Cheshire's name to Cochrane, just as he had once suggested the name of Bennett, his finest squadron commander, when the disgruntled Harris was casting about for the best man to lead the new Pathfinder Force. Whether Sir Charles Symonds's subtle influence had speeded the happy outcome, Cheshire did not pause to inquire. He had begun to breathe freely again.

CHAPTER SEVEN

THE PERFECTIONIST

BEFORE October ended, Cheshire drove south to Moreton Hall, near Swinderby, for his first meeting with Cochrane. As he approached the headquarters of 5 Group, his feeling of excited pleasure grew. He knew enough of 617 Squadron's brief history to be thrilled by the honour of being asked to lead it. Charles Whitworth's jibe still stuck in his memory like a burr. Yet Cochrane had been sufficiently impressed by the recommendation from Carr, and by Cheshire's willingness to drop a rung in rank, to give him a trial.

Air Chief Marshal the Hon. Sir Ralph Cochrane, as he now is, had gained the respect rather than the affection of his men since taking over 5 Group from Coryton eight months earlier. An acutely intelligent and sensitive man, quick and precise in speech and manner, Cochrane's feelings were always well masked. His apparent lack of warmth was due partly to natural reserve, partly to the strain of overwork. He drove himself and others with the solemn pride and unbending conscientiousness of the Scot. An excellent judge of character, he was intolerant of slackness but scrupulously fair.

Cheshire's past record stood out at once in his favour, but Cochrane's interest was focused on the contrast between the frightening " record of bravery " and the ordinary appearance of its owner : here was someone of a surprisingly different stamp from Guy Gibson. In looks, temperament, physique and personality, Gibson had been perfectly cast for the role of training and leading the original " Dambusters ". Cheshire lacked his robust vigour and natural air of flamboyance ; yet he was unmistakably a deeper person of " exceptional mental alertness ".

Cochrane explained, while sizing him up, the crippling casualties 617 Squadron had sustained in the summer and early autumn. On September 15th, fifteen aircraft out of twenty-two had failed to return from a calamitous low-level attack on the Dortmund-Ems canal. Since that time the losses had been made good. Now the squadron must make ready for a series of high-level precision blows at targets of immense strategic importance. The enemy was preparing to hurl new secret weapons against Britain in retaliation for Bomber Command's repeated mass raids on industrial areas. When these " vengeance weapons " would be used, what they were and how much they might alter the course of the war were immaterial questions : a worried War Cabinet would have given much to know the exact answers. The weapon sites were multiplying across the Channel in the Pas de Calais region : that much was certain. They must be destroyed at all costs.

"You'll have to work hard," said Cochrane. "There isn't much time, and there are a lot of problems still to be solved."

The meeting might have profitably closed on this lofty note, leaving the A.O.C. and his new squadron commander with the usual guarded first impressions of each other, if Cochrane had not been stricken by a disconcerting afterthought :

"By the way, Cheshire, I see you've been flying Halifaxes until now," he said. "I think the first thing you must learn to do is to fly a Lancaster."

If Cochrane had been gifted with the knack of reading men's thoughts, he could hardly have hit upon a more deftly baited subject for making the newcomer bite.

"Surely, sir, I can pick that up as I go along," said Cheshire, taken aback by the humiliating bathos of the suggestion.

"Certainly not," said Cochrane bluntly. "There's a perfectly good Conversion Unit at Balderton, which isn't so very far away. I want you to go there on a short course before you do anything else."

Cheshire's composure deserted him. He seemed shocked by such strictness on a point of detail, and repeated that he would prefer to learn all there was to learn about the Lancaster in his own time. Something of the fastidious disdain of the man for time-wasting side issues flashed fitfully through his words. He had been caught off-guard, and in a sense Cochrane was not displeased at glimpsing the real mettle of this seemingly imperturbable young man. Nevertheless, he was not prepared to waive the invariable rule of the Group, that all new arrivals, whether squadron commanders or pilot-officers, should undergo a thorough check before being allowed to fly on operations. And he let this be clearly understood.

The unexpected tussle gave Cheshire a useful hint of the kind of man he was working for. Cochrane was clearly an A.O.C. less tractable than Carr, with a will of his own and a strong mind to match.

Every man in 617 Squadron was meanwhile curious to meet the new Wing Commander whom higher authority had wished upon them. Veteran flyers like the Australians Micky Martin and David Shannon, the New Zealander, Munro, and the American, McCarthy, who had flown to triumph with Gibson and survived the subsequent disasters, doubted whether there was anyone in Bomber Command who could adequately replace their former leader. They had heard of Cheshire. Who had not heard of the budding writer whose heart seemed to be pinned prominently to his braided sleeve every other week in the Sunday press? The author of *Bomber Pilot* might dupe or edify the public, but not the members of 617 Squadron, who were proud of their claim to be the most cosmopolitan, close, hard-bitten, and superbly efficient team of bombing specialists in the Allied Air Forces. Cheshire would have to be very gifted indeed to win the unswerving loyalty which Gibson had exacted as a matter of right.

On his first day at Coningsby he sensed the mood of curiosity and polite scepticism. Several copies of *Bomber Pilot* hastily bought or borrowed, had been left lying conspicuously on the table of the mess ante-room ; and there were a few covert winks and expectant nudges as Cheshire paused to examine them :

" Good gracious, this ghastly thing here ! " he said in some embarrassment. " You can't have very good taste. It's not a book I'm exactly fond of."

He had spoken quite spontaneously, and his words took them by surprise. This newcomer would never be a Gibson, perhaps, but he was not the same death-or-glory boy or the self-important collector of decorations whose photograph they had so often seen in the newspapers. He seemed at first sight simpler and more likeable than the legend, but he would have time enough to prove it.

For the rest of the day they saw little of him. Cheshire was

busy moving in, shuttling to and from his quarters and the
various offices on the station. That evening, however, he joined
them in the mess for a party ; and their suspicions melted away
with the hours. In spite of anything they had read or imagined,
there was no " side " or pretentious vanity about him. Meeting
them on their own ground, he impressed them by his friendliness,
his freakish sense of humour and his restrained irreverence for
the very things most Wing Commanders worshipped.

The egotist they had looked for was nowhere in evidence. It
was as if Cheshire, knowing how much the departed Gibson
still filled their horizons, had concluded that his past reputation counted little in this select band of highly decorated
airmen.

At midnight the bar was still open and Cheshire was standing
on it. The squadron hemmed him in, brandishing their tankards
and laughing wildly. Beer was poured ritually over him. Strong
hands grabbed him, and he was lifted bodily on to the floor
again. His initiation was complete. 617 had accepted him.

The ground crews' opportunity to sum up their squadron
commander was not long delayed. Much as he disliked formal
parades, Cheshire could not very well " cut " the little ceremony
which had been arranged to mark his arrival. In a way he was
rather glad. The parade would give him the chance to explain
his own pride at being with them.

The inspection was a half-hearted affair. He was impatient
to start his speech, a sincere and interesting exhortation which
ended with the words : " Thank you very much. That's all,
you may go now." As nobody appeared ready or willing to
take him at his word, Cheshire stood hesitantly for a moment,
then turned on his heel and strode off the parade ground. Flight-
Sergeant Powell, the senior N.C.O., found it difficult to control
the shuffling, sniggering lines of delighted airmen.

" It was a revelation," recalls Clifford Wills, one of the
squadron armourers. " What a shock for the Flight-Sergeant,
but how the squadron loved it ! The Wing Commander had
started off on the right foot. He got full marks for not knowing
enough about drill book technique to be able to dismiss a parade."

At last, on November 6th, Cheshire set off reluctantly for
Balderton and his compulsory course on the Lancaster bomber.
The instructor chosen for the task, Squadron-Leader Lewis

Gunter, was not looking forward to it in the least. For Gunter, a modest but unimpressionable man, had not taken too kindly to Cheshire's bombastic recipes for glory that had been appearing regularly in print. Nor was the prospect of trying to interest in the Lancaster a pompous ass who had flown only Whitleys and Halifaxes very appealing.

They met after breakfast on Monday morning outside the flight office, and Gunter managed with an effort to conceal his surprise. He had expected someone more formidable than this inconspicuous, unaffected young man who seemed pleased to see him. A junior officer and two flight-sergeants had been detailed to go up with them, and little enough was said until they were in the cockpit together. Gunter explained the layout and the drill with deliberation ; he was still half expecting a few haughty or impatient interruptions, but none came. The engines were started up, and they moved off down the runway.

Cheshire was watching every movement closely. Only when they were orbiting the airfield, gaining height, did he volunteer his first remark about the Lancaster :

" What a beautiful machine she is ! She handles more smoothly than anything I've ever flown."

Gunter spent the next few minutes silently digesting the compliment. Unless Cheshire was acting a part or humouring him, he bore little relation to the bumptious exhibitionist he had steeled himself against. By the time they were ready to land after an hour of dual control, the instructor's attitude of veiled defensiveness had evaporated.

They took off again after lunch at Cheshire's request. He seemed anxious to become fully proficient as rapidly as possible, and in the murk of the late afternoon Gunter, curious about his pupil's unseemly haste to return to his own unit, watched him hurtle down the runway on his first solo.

By now Cheshire was thankful that Cochrane had insisted on sending him to Balderton. The Lancaster, as he had freely admitted, was a marvellous machine ; but one needed time and leisure to master its mechanical peculiarities. To have presumed on the good nature of volunteer instructors at Coningsby during odd intervals snatched from normal training would have been unfair to them and himself : either he would have begun work under a heavy technical handicap, or the work itself would have been held up unnecessarily while he suffered the indignity of being fitted for it by one of his own men.

Two more short periods of local flying gave him the complete familiarity he wanted; and on the Wednesday evening, well muffled against the raw, damp chill, Cheshire hauled himself into the aircraft with Gunter and a scratch crew for a spell of night flying.

At the end of half an hour, the instructor brought the Lancaster gliding down, convinced that it would be churlish not to offer the controls to Cheshire. A few mature pilots took to new machines like ducks to water. He was obviously one of them.

"I'll climb out now," said Gunter. "Take her over the same course yourself, sir. You'll find no difficulty, and thirty minutes should be ample."

Cheshire thanked him. He gave the engines full boost and presently the solid, black shape of the bomber swung past and was swallowed in the gloom, the snarl of the engines growing fainter as it climbed and circled in the distance. Gunter walked back to the mess, musing. He could not recall any pupil who had worked him so hard as to cram successfully into three days a course officially intended to last much longer.

Yet it had been done painlessly, without friction, and without a hint of that unctuous, empty-headed vanity which, he had been led to believe, was synonymous with the name of Cheshire. The man was clearly a far more complex and attractive personality than the popular caricature implied. . . .

Constance, meanwhile, had been grieved and angered by the abrupt orders which had whisked her husband away from her almost without notice. Adaptable, good natured, and undemanding on other counts, she was possessive enough to draw the line at spending another six months as a grass widow. The railway coach at Marston Moor had become a quaintly pleasant haven; if its comforts were limited she had not expected to remain in it for ever. Had he not said more than once that there would be no more flying for him? It was true that he had spoken with a suspicion of regret. It was also true that in the last-minute rush of his departure, he had seemed much less dejected than was proper, as though he did not in the least object to being pitchforked back into action. The Air Force authorities had no right to take such callous advantage of the generous, short-sighted ardour of youth.

While Cheshire was finding his feet at Coningsby, his wife was moodily packing up their belongings, preparing to follow him south. As a final gesture before moving off, Constance called on Air Commodore Kirby at his house in Wetherby, and poured out a litany of reproaches against the Royal Air Force and its crude, inconsiderate, press-gang methods.

Kirby listened in some perplexity. Constance was plainly beside herself with annoyance ; but just as plainly she had seized the wrong end of the stick. He wondered how much Cheshire could have confided in her about his restless longing to return to an operational squadron : very little, it seemed. Still, it was not Kirby's place to be drawn into long, detailed explanations. In any case, he slightly resented this indignant outburst against the R.A.F. and its authority. He reminded Constance sharply that as Cheshire's former commanding officer he was answerable for service decisions to no civilian, not even to her. War was hardly the time for outraged sentimentality, and he was certainly not going to stand for it, least of all in his own home.

Cheshire had felt no regret at having had to use bold and somewhat underhand methods to regain his freedom. The end, in this case, fully justified the means. Equally he felt no sting of compunction at his treatment of Constance in the act of regaining it. To take her into his confidence would have been out of character and would have merely added to his difficulties. There was always the consolation of knowing that nobody but himself could measure the compelling urge, stronger than reason, compassion or the claims of blood, which forced him to go on flying. It had begun as an ambition, a short-cut to fame ; it had been tempered and refined by war, a muted patriotism and the give-and-take of daily comradeship into something less grasping, but its elemental driving force remained. The instinct to follow his own lonely bent had not been blunted by marriage. Indeed the ties which held him to Constance, loose and easy as they were, had frayed a little under the cutting edge of it, especially during the final weeks at Marston Moor.

Circumstances had gone against Constance, the circumstances of war and the ungovernable stresses of his own nature. For all her vivacity, courage and freshness of mind, she was far older

and more settled in her ways than he had bargained for. He was
unwilling fully to admit disillusionment, even to himself. There
had been disappointment, even dissatisfaction; but one could
always blame Hitler and hope for happiness after his defeat.
Meanwhile, he must temporise, put aside the basic problem until
better days, and lose his mind and whole being once more in
the thrill of operational flying. To thrust Constance finally out
of his life would have been a premature confession of failure;
and there were still too many people whose respect he valued
who would have wagged their heads and said, " I told you so."

2

By the time Cheshire was ready to join 617 Squadron in the
air, this remarkable team of volunteer, tour-expired fliers had
virtually mastered the technique of high-level precision bombing.
During the two months before his arrival the daily flights of
Lancasters, sweeping low in perfect formation, had become a
common sight to people in Lincolnshire. Cochrane, fearful of
any further disasters through the tree-top form of attack which
had already decimated the squadron, had provided them with a
new bomb-sight. It was an instrument of extraordinary precision, incorporating a gyroscope and a calculating " brain ",
which, in theory at any rate, greatly simplified the work of pilot,
navigator and bomb-aimer.

On Cochrane's orders, the squadron practised by day and
night over the sands at Wainfleet. The Air Vice-Marshal kept
a critical eye on progress, and on one occasion astonished everyone by flying as bomb-aimer and putting his eight practice bombs
nearer the target than the best of them. " If I can do it, you can,"
was all he said.

Gradually, by trial and error and perseverance, they were all
able to drop their practice bombs within ninety yards of the
tiny, white aiming points on the ranges 20,000 feet below. The
results were outstandingly good by ordinary Bomber Command
standards, but they were not yet good enough for Cochrane.
Nor was the fear of any repetition of the Dortmund-Ems canal
disaster the only motive which made him drive 617 Squadron
at least two miles higher than they liked to deliver their mock
attacks with splendid accuracy: there was nothing so negative

or rigid about the mind of this uncommonly gifted, far-sighted and meticulous tactician.

Cochrane already knew in general terms that before the Allies could hope to force their way on to French soil for the liberation of Europe the Allied air forces would be called on to pave the way for them, and he believed that 5 Group and 617 Squadron in particular were better equipped for the task than any other formation. There were not enough heavy bombers to knock out the enemy in advance by area-bombing, a technique he loyally supported although its untidiness did not particularly appeal to him. But there were enough heavy bombers to take decisive advantage of Allied air supremacy, provided the attacks were made skilfully and selectively.

In the June of 1943, Bomber Command had been given a new directive to this end. It had been worded broadly and tactfully, no doubt out of deference to Air Marshal Harris who clung tenaciously to his vision of a Germany scourged into abject surrender by the flattening of her industries, the razing of her cities, and the incidental killing of her citizens. Harris had been told that " as far as practicable " he should try to complement the American daylight assaults on the German aircraft industry and fighter strength. These and subsidiary industries like ball bearings, oil, rubber and motor plants were booming again. Albert Speer, the inspired German production planner, was at last taking in the slack and mobilising every available man, woman and slave labourer to forge weapons for the defence of the European fortress and the ultimate thwarting of the bomber offensive.

Harris had decided in the autumn of 1943 to keep 617 Squadron for " special duties ". Cochrane with an alert eye to the future had suggested that this precision bombing team could be trained to deal economically with small targets of exceptional importance. He understood Harris sufficiently well to realise that the Commander-in-Chief would welcome any cheap, success-ful forays which, without diverting him from his simple aim of toppling Hitler by area-bombing, would placate the Combined Chiefs of Staff who had sent him that impracticable directive.

Cochrane had already proved his genius for planning and carrying out special raids that called for daring flexibility in tactics. One of those raids was so successful that, in Churchill's words, it "had a far-reaching influence on events . . . and played an important and definite part in the general progress of the war." It took place on August 17th, 1943, when Cheshire was eating his heart out at Marston Moor ; and the target was Hitler's rocket-research station at Peenemünde on the Baltic coast. By a happy chance, the finished blueprints of the V.2's were lost or burnt, several scientists were killed, and London's ordeal of bombardment from space was postponed by at least six months.

Harris had had no hesitation in letting Cochrane take an independent role, even though Bennett's Pathfinders led the 600-bomber attack as usual. The reason was brutally simple : at all costs Peenemünde had to be wiped off the map. Harris had been warned that if the operation failed on the first night it would have to be repeated, regardless of losses, until the rocket-research station was destroyed. The Commander-in-Chief could not afford to fail. He was therefore only too pleased to find that Cochrane, the resourceful commander of his old Group, had a cut-and-dried tactical plan of his own to make doubly sure of success. It was in essence a precision bombing plan which had been tried successfully before by Cochrane at Friedrichshafen. At the special conference held at Bomber Command headquarters early in July to discuss the Peenemünde target, Harris gave Cochrane authority to dovetail the plan with the ordinary target-marking procedure of the Pathfinders.

Bennett, as leader of the Pathfinder Force (which was in effect the " eyes " of Bomber Command), resented this decision as a blow to his own authority. After all, the marking of targets at night was his sole responsibility. Air Ministry had called the Pathfinders into being for that very purpose, overruling Harris in the process. And here was Cochrane, interfering with the hallowed order of things and more or less implying that the " eyes " of Bomber Command were bad.

Technical squabbles are rarely edifying or interesting, and the public should be spared whenever possible the unutterable boredom of their petty and parochial details. On the other hand, some understanding of the differences between Bennett and Cochrane is essential for any real insight into the happenings which were to give Cheshire, as commander of 617 Squadron, the most glittering chance of his R.A.F. career, and a chance which he promptly seized with both hands. It was more than a conflict of personalities : it was a clash of ideas at a period when Allied strategy was beginning to impose big and unfamiliar burdens on the bomber forces of Harris and Spaatz. The Peenemünde raid, which at the strategic level proved a major R.A.F. victory and a possible turning-point in the war, seemed at this lower personal level to have kindled the rivalry between the Pathfinders and 5 Group.

The position of Harris was that of a distinterested judge. He was interested in facts, not feelings, results, not complexes. He had never cared for the idea of a separate Pathfinder Force, and had opposed it as long as possible. He had been forced in the end to accept it and had manfully complied with an order he disliked. His personal choice of Bennett as Pathfinder chief had been the one pleasant factor in a thoroughly unsatisfactory business. For, as he implies in *Bomber Offensive*, Harris held Bennett in wholesome respect both as a person and as a navigational expert of extraordinary competence. There might have been better candidates for the post, but there was none so acceptable to him in August, 1942.

Not even his closest friend would have called Bennett a tactful man, and his rapid promotion over the heads of other R.A.F. senior officers had not increased his popularity. Obstinate when crossed, he was no respecter of persons and tended both to ruffle the tempers of his equals and to inspire the fear of God in his subordinates. As Harris put it :

" His consciousness of his own intellectual powers sometimes made him impatient with slower or differently constituted minds, so that some people found him difficult to work with. He could not suffer fools gladly, and by his own high standards there were many fools." But Bennett's courage was as admirable as his encyclopædic knowledge of aerial navigation. And his scientific curiosity was matched by a practical experience which Harris quickly turned to good account.

Cochrane's mind was of a different calibre. His remarkable strategic sense enabled him to see beyond technical problems. It was this talent which distinguished him from most of his contemporaries, for in other ways he seemed to be a paragon of service correctness. Austere, restrained and reticent, he looked the martinet he was not and stood temperamentally at the

opposite pole from Bennett. If most of his men regarded him
as a cold, insensitive commander, who always shrank from any
display of personal feeling, none was more conscious of this
failing than Cochrane himself. For he was a cultured man who
could only conceal his sensitivity by iron self-control. He did
not lack the diplomatic touch, except when confronted with
ideas which were obviously wrong. And by late 1943 he was
convinced that the stereotyped tactical ideas of the Pathfinders
were totally inadequate for the destruction of a whole range of
new small targets which Bomber Command was being ordered
to find and hit.

Bennett had worked hard and well to justify the Commander-
in-Chief's early faith in him. First with " Gee ", already on the
way out as a radar position finder, then in early 1943 with
" Oboe " and " H2S ", the two latest scientific aids to navigation
at night, the Pathfinder chief and his staff evolved new and
ingenious methods of leading the bombers to the cities of
Germany. Until Harris put his foot down, Bennett often flew
himself.

In the pioneering days, when individual crews had to identify
and bomb the aiming point unaided by radar or Pathfinders,
attacks were usually weak and widely scattered. Bennett certainly improved matters by lighting up and marking the general
target area so that most of the bombs fell in heavy concentration
on or near the markers. But everything depended on the
accurate placing of these markers. If these fell short, most of
the bombs would be dropped in the wrong place. For the crews
of the main attacking force could no longer trust their eyesight :
they had strict orders to aim only at the red or green spots wink-
ing on the ground or at the sky markers cascading like fireworks
among the clouds when the weather was thick. As Harris put
it : " Any error in placing the marker bombs led the whole
attack astray."

The trouble was that almost invariably in the later stages of
the raids both markers and bombs tended to drift farther and
farther away from the true centre of the target. That trouble
persisted in area-bombing attacks until the end of the war. The
undershooting was often caused by bad visibility, by smoke
which blotted out the original markers and made accurate
" backing up " very difficult, and by the natural inclination of

crews to aim at the first lights they could identify and then get out of harm's way. As new devices came into service, the Pathfinder technique was modified and Bennett had his victories as well as his failures.

For example, eight Mosquito bombers carrying " Oboe " equipment were guided by pulses from ground stations in England to Essen, on March 5th, 1943. They dropped their target indicators on the centre of this heavily defended steel city, the home of Krupps and the heart of the industrial Ruhr, and so lit the way for the first successful attack on Essen since the beginning of the war. But there were physical as well as technical limits to the use of " Oboe " ; it was not always so infallible. A different marking technique had to be found for the second device known as " H2S ", whose operational range was not restricted by the strength of radio pulses from England. It was an airborne instrument which threw up the features of the target area on a kind of television screen inside the aircraft. Hamburg and Berlin were among the first cities attacked in this way, though with far less accuracy than on " Oboe ".

During all this period of experiment in early 1943, 5 Group flew as part of the main force, blindly following the lead of the hand-picked and highly-trained crews of the Pathfinder Force. But as the year wore on Cochrane, who had taken command of the Group in February, was able to show more and more convincingly his own prowess as an original tactician. The planning of the raid on the Ruhr dams was the classic example ; but the alternative tactics Cochrane employed for a long-range attack in mid-June on the former Zeppelin factory at Friedrichshafen were even more significant. In Cochrane's own words : " It was the beginning of our attempt to think for ourselves."

The Combined Chiefs of Staff had issued their latest directive a few days before, that soft-pedalling directive which suggested deferentially that Bomber Command should turn its attention now and then to the booming German aircraft industry. The Zeppelin site on the shores of Lake Constance was selected to prove that " Harris was willing ", within reason. It was known to be turning out mechanical parts for mass-produced radar sets which would be used in due course to harass the Pathfinders and the main force in what Churchill has aptly described as " the wizards' war " above the clouds. Nothing but a swift, perfectly

executed blow would do to blot out the factory ; Harris ordered
5 Group to deliver the blow. But Cochrane in his coldly
calculating way was certain that the Pathfinders alone could not
guarantee the pin-point marking that was necessary for success.

He had little difficulty in persuading Harris that he was talking
sense. Harris, while admiring and respecting Bennett, held no
brief for the infallibility of his methods. The results of the past
eighteen months had certainly not helped him to swallow the
Air Ministry's view that a separate Pathfinder force was the ideal
arrangement. Quite apart from his wrath at having been
dictated to by " young Jacks-in-office ", he genuinely believed
individual Groups were still quite capable of formulating and
carrying out their own methods of marking of targets. He had
also a high regard for Cochrane's shrewdness and independence
as a tactician. This was a clear-cut case where two brains would
be better than one, especially since the target demanded a plan
of attack quite different from the mechanical hit-or-miss which
was good enough for German built-up areas.

The plan drawn up for the Friedrichshafen raid was a
masterpiece of its kind. It also set a precedent which angered
Bennett. To make good the possible shortcomings of the Pathfinders, Cochrane was authorised to choose an experienced Wing
Commander of his own to direct and control the fifty-six Lancasters of 5 Group. The introduction of a " master bomber "
proved to be more than a simple precaution to prevent the attack
from going astray ; it was quickly seen to be a bold new adapta-
tion of the age-old principle that a decisive battle cannot be
fought unless the men fighting it are adequately led by a commander in the front line. The credit for the idea is Cochrane's,
who had grasped its wider possibilities after trying it out on a
small scale in the spectacular breaching of the Mohne, Eder and
Sörpe dams almost exactly a month previously. Gibson and
617 Squadron had rightly won glory for that historic attack ; but
the detailed tactical preparations had been Cochrane's.

Any last-minute change of plan at Friedrichshafen would
rest with the master-bomber, but Cochrane was still not satisfied.
He took a further step to ensure that any mistakes by the Pathfinders should not reap inevitable failure, and ordered his
bombers to attack in two waves. The first wave should aim as
in any area-bombing raid at the markers dropped by Bennett's

leading aircraft, but the second should ignore the markers and
locate the exact position of the target for themselves by making
a timed run from a prominent landmark over a mile away. In
the event, this indirect method of bombing sealed the success of
the operation. Cochrane's tactical precautions were more than
justified by results. For reconnaissance photographs taken after
the attack suggested that the Pathfinder markers had gone adrift
in the high wind and that most of the bombs dropped by the
first wave of attacking Lancasters followed them. It was the
bombs of the second wave, dropped at the end of the timed run,
which blew up half the factory.

It is hardly surprising, therefore, that Harris authorised
Cochrane to use the same independent tactics for the all-important
raid on Peenemünde in August. The Commander-in-Chief was
well aware that 5 Group had hit upon a method more flexible
and accurate than anything Bennett had yet devised. But this
time the Pathfinder chief, after some argument, was allowed to
appoint one of his best men, Group Captain J. H. Searby, as
master-bomber.

During the raid many of the Pathfinder markers fell wide of
the three aiming points. Flying in on their timed run, the crews
of 5 Group were ordered by the controller to bomb these markers
in spite of the fact that most of them seemed to have fallen wide.
These were technical details, however. The experimental rocket
station had been heavily damaged in a single attack.

As far as Harris and the War Cabinet were concerned, the
Peenemünde raid was a resounding triumph, well worth the loss
of the forty bombers shot down in bright moonlight by German
night fighters. Bennett, however, could not escape the bitter
conclusion that as far as he was concerned the second front had
already opened behind him. He refused to take the challenge
lying down, and belittled Cochrane's attempts to establish his
" private air force ". From August, 1943, onwards the Pathfinders' jealousy was common knowledge in the messes of
Bomber Command.

It was a case of Greek meeting Greek. Cochrane regretted
that his efforts to raise the standards of bombing accuracy should
be suspected as an affront to the prestige of the Pathfinder chief,
but was quite determined not to let misunderstandings of the
kind block his way. As long as Harris upheld his efforts,

Cochrane would not be sidetracked by irrelevant criticism of his motives. Bennett could console himself that precision attacks on the Friedrichshafen and Peenemünde models were few and far between ; and during the summer and autumn of 1943, the Pathfinders led the main force as usual in a series of crushing onslaughts on Hamburg, Hanover, Mannheim and Kassel, using H2S and yet another device called " Window " which had long been held in reserve for fear the enemy might copy it. As it happened, the Germans had already invented it themselves but were wary of bringing it into play for exactly the same reason !

" Window " consisted of long strips of metallised paper. When dropped in bundles over a target, it was indistinguishable on the ground radar screens from the " blips " made by aircraft. For the first time since the 1000-bomber raids in 1942, the German defences were taken by surprise, saturated and snuffed out. Between July 24th and August 2nd, Hamburg endured four catastrophic attacks. Two-thirds of the city was laid waste and 60,000 men, women and children died in the ruins or were burnt to cinders in the huge fire tornado which swept through the streets on the first night.

Harris was satisfied that the industrial damage to docks and U-boat yards justified the disproportionate price in innocent human lives. Rightly or wrongly, he considered that here was the fiery short-cut to victory in a total war ; his duty as he conceived it was to do to the rest of Germany what he had been able to do to Hamburg. Those who cried out that he was a modern ogre as heartless and immoral as Tamberlaine or Ghenghis Khan forgot that Harris bore no responsibility for bombing policy. The fact that he was the tenacious champion of area-bombing would have carried no weight if Churchill and his advisers had been opposed to it.

In a struggle for survival fought with weapons of mass destruction, there could be no turning back after four terrible years to reshape a strategy born of adversity and German example at a time when the bomber was Britain's one weapon of retaliation. The moralists might condemn the evil of terror bombing ; the naval and military strategists might abuse Harris for waging a " private war " with resources that could have been put to wiser use ; but at this stage in the war it would have proved difficult if not disastrous to set in reverse the gigantic war machine which had been built up slowly since Dunkirk to crush the life out of Hitler and his countrymen.

Neither Churchill nor Harris had any moral scruples or strategic doubts about wreaking indiscriminate vengeance on Nazi Germany from the air. The main difference in outlook between them was one of degree. For the Prime Minister at no time subscribed to the extremist view that a modern war could be won by the wholesale use of air power alone. As he has made perfectly clear, Churchill was not deeply affected by the efforts of Trenchard and Harris to convert him. Such special pleading reminded him of the earnest cobbler who not only stuck stubbornly to his last but insisted on preaching from the roof-tops that there was nothing on earth quite like leather.

During the second half of 1943 Cochrane's Lancasters flew as part of the main force, guided to the targets by Bennett's Pathfinders. In mid-November, Harris took advantage of the longer nights and his greater striking power to launch the heaviest and most protracted campaign of the war against Berlin. The "Battle of Berlin" went on unabated until March, 1944, in spite of the appalling weather conditions and the fierce enemy defences. Bomber Command had to rely on German propaganda for second-hand accounts of the damage inflicted in sixteen major attacks, since the night bombing photographs showed nothing but layers of cloud. Even the daylight reconnaissance aircraft could not pierce the unbroken barrier to get worthwhile pictures. The uncertainty about the results of this costly campaign seemed to weigh heavily on Harris and his headquarters staff, but nobody was more anxious or more frustrated than the methodical Bennett, who felt that the lack of evidence to vindicate his target-marking efforts was playing into the hands of his critics.

3

During the first phase of the "Battle of Berlin" Cheshire spent many hours over Wainfleet practising with the precision bomb-sight. His log-book shows how hard he worked. Squadron-Leader Richardson, the expert who had been sent to teach 617 Squadron all he knew about the delicate, complicated mechanism, flew with him every day for a week to demonstrate its accuracy. The bomb-sight's " brain " had to be " spoon-fed " with facts, especially in the crucial half-minute before the target was reached. Every member of the crew had to be on his toes, measuring the exact speed and height of the aircraft. The " brain " would take a faulty reading without questioning, translating it faithfully into an error of many yards. But the error became evident only when the bomb hit the sands thousands of feet below.

This was perfectionism of a kind Cheshire distrusted. What would happen, he wondered, when 617 Squadron were ordered to use the bomb-sight on a dark night against a defended target in the light of wrongly placed markers ? Cochrane had mentioned the secret weapon sites but had said nothing about marking the target. Would they have to limit their attacks to moon periods ? He was not immediately impressed by the persistent small talk in the mess about badly strained relations between Cochrane and Bennett. It was fairly obvious that the Pathfinders would have to mark for the squadron as long as Cochrane insisted on the high-level form of attack.

Cheshire leaned heavily at first on the experience of Micky Martin and the solid advice of Sam Patch. Martin, an Australian, was a first-class pilot and a confirmed enthusiast for the low-level form of bombing attack. He had been acting squadron commander for several weeks before Cheshire appeared. Group Captain H. L. Patch, the station commander at Coningsby, a strong capable personality whose affectionate understanding for the " toughs " of 617 Squadron was blended with a deep respect for the tactical thoroughness of Cochrane, soon realised that Cheshire had a restless tactical mind of his own. Uninfluenced by Martin or anyone else, this reserved, studious-looking young man already doubted whether the precision bomb-sight alone would yield the absurdly accurate results which Cochrane demanded. But at Patch's request he kept on trying.

" Crossbow " was the code name given to the counter-measures planned by the Allied air forces to deal with Hitler's secret weapons. Since the Peenemünde attack, an army of 40,000 conscript labourers had been building V1 launching sites along the French Channel coast. By November, 1943, sixty-four of these sites had been discovered by air reconnaissance, but there was still scepticism among the politicians, the scientists and the air commanders about the seriousness of the flying-bomb threat. The launching sites were regarded in some quarters as a huge bluff to divert the heavy bombers of the Allies from their area assaults on German industry. It was impossible to know that Hitler had already ordered Speer to produce 5000 V1's a month for " vengeance attacks " on London and the South of England.

The shape of the secret weapon sites resembled a ski, the inclined point of which seemed in most cases to be turned towards London. The structures were suspiciously similar to others that had meanwhile been photographed near Peenemünde ; and when a sharp-eyed woman intelligence officer detected a small aircraft near one of the inclined ramps, Hitler's intentions became clearer. Churchill ordered an all-out attack on the " ski-sites ", which began on December 5th.

Five further structures, bigger in size and more grotesque in shape, continued to mystify the authorities, though, as Air Marshal Bottomley, Deputy Chief of Air Staff and chairman of the special " action committee " on the secret weapons, reported to the Prime Minister less than a fortnight later :

" Evidence is accumulating that the (large) ' ski-sites ' are designed to launch pilotless aircraft."

Most of the " ski-sites " lay in woods and orchards, and more than 3000 tons of high explosive bombs were dropped by British and American bombers before the end of December. At first 617 Squadron took no part in this concerted effort : cloud lay low almost continuously over France and England, ruling out high-level precision attacks. Cheshire's patience was sapped by the strain of waiting and by Cochrane's insistence that there was no hurry. His crews were just as eager for action as he was ; they felt they had done enough formation exercises and practice bombing to last a lifetime.

At last, on December 13th, Cochrane sent for Cheshire and told him to hold the squadron in readiness for attacks on the two Pas de Calais ski-sites of Fréval and Flixecourt. Harris had agreed that these minute targets would afford a useful practice ground for 617, and one of Bennett's " Oboe " Mosquitos had been instructed to lead the way and mark for them. Cheshire was enormously relieved. He returned at once to Coningsby, chose nine of the most experienced crews, including Shannon, Martin, and McCarthy, and briefed them carefully. Provided the weather held out, they would now find out whether their high-level technique was as perfect as the A.O.C. swore it should be.

The others caught his infectious enthusiasm. The past six weeks of unremitting training had removed the last lingering doubts about Cheshire's quiet influence and subtle gift of leadership. His grip was certainly far gentler than Gibson's had ever been, but in some indefinable way his personal authority was stronger. None of them understood all the strange facets of his character, yet they were learning to trust him implicitly. He rarely gave an order or stood on ceremony, nor did he seem to mind listening to or trying out ideas at variance with his own. They liked his " dead-pan " humour and casual friendliness as much as his willingness to take every man as he found him. On one point they were unanimous : Cheshire as a pilot was more skilful and fearless than they had ever expected him to be.

For some incomprehensible reason, the operation was cancelled early in the evening. Cheshire was furious. With a touch of defiance he ordered the squadron out on a low-level cross-country flight, leading his own crew on a full-dress rehearsal of the raid, timed to the last second.

By the following morning the weather had taken a turn for the worse ; the skies were overcast with cloud and fog patches ; even local flying was out of the question. While Cheshire was moodily pacing up and down the operations room, pausing every so often to stare out at the low racing clouds, a tall, middle-aged intelligence officer entered. Arthur Pollen, a sculptor in civilian life, was new to Coningsby, but he had heard much at second hand of 617's commander. He stood a little hesitantly now, watching him. There was a drawn look on Cheshire's face. He was hatless and his tense, abstracted movements reminded the artistic Pollen of a caged panther.

Cheshire stopped in his tracks and turned as Pollen came up, saluted, and formally introduced himself. A sudden smile lit up his face removing every trace of anxiety.

" So you're on the intelligence side," he said. " You'll find very little to do. We never operate here."

The last four words were rapped out almost contemptuously, and Pollen withdrew, leaving him to resume his lonely pacing up and down.

On December 16th, after another day of unsettling idleness, the weather improved and Cheshire briefed his crews again. The ten Lancasters flew across the Channel dead on time, led by a single Pathfinder Mosquito. At this short range the " Oboe " position-finder was working at its best. The strong radar impulses from the two ground stations in England guided the aircraft straight to the ski-site. There was no reason to suppose that this blind, foolproof device would go wrong. All the conditions were favourable. Nothing stirred on the ground. The cold, clear sky was unsullied by shell-bursts or rising coloured bubbles of tracer. They were almost above the target area when the Mosquito released its markers, and in a moment two bright pinpoints of light picked out the lonely blackness of the wood where the ski-site lay.

617 carried out the now familiar orbiting drill, keeping the flickering markers in their bomb-sights and moving in from 15,000 feet for the "kill". One by one the ungainly 12,000-pounders went down, scattering the crumbs of light and starting a small forest fire. It had been almost too easy. Cheshire was as jubilant as the others when they reached Coningsby three and a half hours after take-off. Cochrane took him aside to listen to his brief account of an operation that had gone through apparently without any hitch whatever, and nodded non-committally. There were still the night photographs of the aiming point to examine ; until the A.O.C. saw these, he would reserve his judgment.

The photographs confirmed Cochrane's unspoken suspicions. It was true that the bombs had fallen less than 100 yards from the " Oboe " markers, but the markers themselves had overshot the ski-site by nearly a quarter of a mile. Even under perfect conditions, against an undefended target the Pathfinder leader had blindly led the bombing astray. It was a rude awakening for Cheshire. He realised in a flash that there were good grounds for Cochrane's reputed lack of confidence in Pathfinder marking results, at least where very small targets were concerned ; but he realised equally well that Cochrane could do little about it except vainly protest. For good or ill, Bennett had the virtual monopoly of men and equipment, if not of ideas : he probably had too many weightier problems on his hands to be concerned by irritating pinpricks of criticism from a mere squadron.

The " Oboe " Mosquito was a latterday Hobson's Choice. 617 could go on bombing till Doomsday on " Oboe " marking and still fail, yet Bennett for all his drive could not eliminate the errors. It seemed a hopeless blind alley, but its very hopelessness spurred Cheshire to an inspired pitch of private enterprise.

He must first discover what a Mosquito, untrammelled by " Oboe " equipment, could really do. For his intuition told him that if the marking difficulty could not be solved by an aircraft using the finest radar aid at high level, it might well be solved by the same aircraft daringly handled at low level. He had never lost the stubborn belief which made him sit down in 1940 and draft that precocious paper urging the advantages of attacking German targets visually from a few hundred feet. Whether or not the matter-of-fact Cochrane could be persuaded to share his faith in the vastly altered conditions of late 1943 would depend on Cheshire's own diplomacy and practical skill. For Cochrane would not dispense with the radar-guided Pathfinders until he had found some acceptable alternative, and yet a man so sternly opposed to the risks of low-level bombing would not find it easy to accept the equal risks of low-level marking.

Three days later, Cheshire paid a hasty visit to Group Captain Percy Pickard, the leader of 161 Mosquito Squadron and a famous specialist in the low-level form of attack. Pickard, whose name became known to the film-going public early in the war as the rather blasé pilot of " F " for " Freddie ", was reputed to possess a better working knowledge of exploitable gaps in the enemy ground defences along the Atlantic Wall than any other pilot. Cheshire flew to Sculthorpe with his crew and had a very useful factual talk with Pickard, who took him up in one of the latest Mark VI Mosquitos.

The demonstration flight lasted a mere twenty minutes, but before it ended Cheshire knew that this graceful plywood aircraft was the real solution to at least half of Cochrane's problem. For the Mosquito, as fast as a fighter and as sturdy as a heavier bomber, would surely take the peril out of marking from low level. The leader would have enough speed in hand to race in, pin-point the target and be up and away before the enemy guns or fighters could touch him. Pickard had assured him, however, that Mosquitos were harder to come by than diamonds.

Before Cheshire could adequately test his low-level marking

theory in a heavy Lancaster, the squadron carried out two more raids with the " Oboe " Mosquito. On December 20th, the orders were changed at the last minute and instead of attacking the ski-sites they went to Liège in Belgium. The night was frosty and cloudy. Somewhere beneath the haze lay the town and the arms factory which was their target, but they could see no glow of light on which to train their bomb-sights.

Finally, Cheshire decided to go down low enough to detect what was happening, only to discover that the Pathfinder markers were burning merrily a good quarter of a mile away from the factory. The squadron dropped no bombs that night, and the journey home was trickier than Cheshire had expected. The starboard inner engine of his aircraft spluttered and gave out as they crossed the Channel, and the bare fact was noted in his log-book. He added the sour afterthought :

" 1×12000 lb. bomb brought back because the Pathfinders failed."

Two nights later the squadron went through the same agony of frustration over one of the ski-sites, and again Cheshire recorded the reason :

" Operations : Secret Weapon : 14×1000 lb. brought back because the Pathfinders failed."

Splenetic outbursts against the Pathfinders were futile, however. Cochrane sympathised with Cheshire but would not consider letting him try low-level marking, even on the range :

" I don't mind you trying it from medium heights, say at 5000 feet or so," he said. " But you must use the bomb-sight. It will give you all the accuracy you need. That's what it's for."

Cheshire spent part of Christmas week with Constance. It was the first time he had been able to relax at Thorpe Hall, Geoffrey Harmsworth's comfortable country house at Louth, since she had moved in ; but his mind kept wandering off to Coningsby and the fascination of an unsolved technical problem. He appeared cheerful and attentive enough ; and when they visited Grey Walls to see the New Year in, he told his parents rather diffidently that he had had to abandon a secret plan for flying low over the Baltic on Christmas Day to drop gifts of food and cigarettes into Christopher's prison camp. It was not easy to tell whether he was joking, though his mother had been collecting chocolate and tinned goods at his request for some

G

time. Apparently, a meteorological officer had warned him that the German guards might mistake the bundles of gifts for bundles of arms. It was the one possibility that had not occurred to him.

4

" As you can see from the address, I've moved across the road to Woodhall Spa," he wrote home early in January. " It's a dispersed camp with long distances to travel. We live in a commandeered hotel in the village—a very pleasant one, too, but it's some three miles away from our place of work which is a considerable drawback."

Woodhall Spa had its disadvantages. But a unique factor in its favour was that it could house only a single squadron ; and Cochrane, a stickler for security, believed that 617 should train and operate in splendid isolation. They operated twice more with the Pathfinders, once while Cheshire was away on leave and again on January 4th ; but the customary lack of success affected them less. For they were training harder than ever, using the bomb-sight now to mark the dummy targets on the range from medium level. He urged them on, yet they needed little urging. The incentive of winning Cochrane's permission to carry their own flares and spot-markers was enough. One morning, as Cheshire was pulling up his undercarriage after take-off, a flock of plovers sailed headlong into the Lancaster and whirled to the ground. The crew went back later and collected " 20 bodies for consumption in the mess." It seemed a good omen.

The average error was slowly reduced to 40 yards from 5000 feet, though on one occasion (two days after the accident to the plovers) Cheshire cut the margin down to a mere 9 yards in six successive bombing runs. Such accuracy was incredible, and he was wise to dismiss it as a fluke. Between times he would go as low as possible and sight the target visually. That was the method he preferred. The more he fell back on his own eyes, nerves and judgment, the better were the results.

Carol Durrant, Cochrane's personal assistant, read the uneasiness in Cheshire's eyes as he waited outside the A.O.C.'s room one day in mid-January to report progress. She had often seen that look in the eyes of visitors, and knew at second hand of Cheshire's present dilemma. As he went in, she gave him a discreet sign of encouragement. Half an hour passed, then he came out beaming, and almost walking on air. Cochrane had relented at least to the extent of letting the squadron go alone to the ski-sites.

Two bald entries in the log-book record the only two independent attacks 617 delivered against these targets. On January 21st, after destroying the first of them, Cheshire wrote:

"Secret Weapon: Marked under flares. Successful." And on January 25th, remembering the smoking craters pitting the site at Fréval, he wrote again:

"Secret Weapon: Low level marking. Very high wind. Successful with the help of Micky (Martin)."

Cochrane had been more than satisfied with the photographs brought back from the first mission. 617 had scored a definite knock-out. He was convinced at last that Cheshire had stumbled upon a workable compromise, and was not surprised when his persistent squadron commander asked if he might mark from low level in the second attack:

"Even in a Lancaster there's no real risk, sir," he said. "And when there's haze or low cloud there's no other practical way."

If it crossed Cochrane's mind to inquire what made him so sure, the A.O.C. resisted the temptation. Very probably Cheshire was talking from illicit experience; if so, Cochrane did not want to hear of it officially. Instead, with a show of hesitancy, he gave Cheshire the formal permission he sought.

In spite of low cloud, light flak and a wind of gale force which flattened the tree-tops in the Fréval clearing, the markers were planted "almost by hand" on either side of the target. The Lancasters hovered one by one at 12,000 feet. Minutes later, the site was smothered in smoke and flame; but, far more important, a new spectacular bombing technique of great promise had been developed.

Cochrane's next move was to press Bomber Command for more targets. The Germans, having discovered too late that the original ski-sites were naked and wide-open to the constant attentions of British and American bombers, had begun to abandon them one by one. Harris was fully engrossed again with the one campaign that mattered to him, the arduous

" Battle of Berlin ", from which the temporary withdrawal .of
squadrons for the piecemeal destruction of small targets had
been a regrettable and dubious diversion.

To his credit, Harris responded swiftly to Cochrane's plea.
" I don't believe in this finicky business, but let them get on with
it " is an adequate summary of his attitude. The decisive factor
was that 617 were begging for targets—the only commodity
Harris could offer in abundance.

On February 7th, Cochrane sent for Cheshire again : " This
is your big chance to prove what can be done," he said with a
slow smile. On his desk lay a list of half a dozen towns in France,
which housed key factories turning out essential parts and spares
for the German aircraft industry. Some were undefended, and
that, in Cochrane's view, was all to the good.

" I want you to go to Limoges first," said Cochrane. " The
local aero-engine plant is on the railway two miles outside the
town. It's a distinctive target, but there are houses close by."

He emphasised the need for accuracy. There might con-
ceivably be political complications if French civilians were
slaughtered, and such complications would hold up the squadron's work. Cochrane knew Cheshire's mind well and had
judged the situation to a nicety. He had given him an excellent
non-technical reason for ensuring that the raid would succeed.
When Cheshire briefed the squadron in the early afternoon, he
dwelt at some length on the dire political consequences of failure,
as though the War Cabinet in London were watching their
every move and one bomb out of place would mean the dis-
honourable superannuation of 617. It was a pity Cochrane
could not have been there to hear him.

They took off for Limoges the following night, downcast
about the prospects. In defiance of higher politics, the weather
was behaving atrociously. The forecast gave them a fifty-fifty
chance of success. But if the whole of Northern France was
covered by stratus cloud and five of the twelve Lancasters carried
12,000-pound blast bombs, which could not be dropped below
cloud with safety, or above cloud with accuracy, Cheshire was
gloomily resolute. The weathermen could easily be wrong ;
their luck might change nearer Limoges ; at worst the squadron
could always return without bombing.

His crew, from Pat Kelly, the navigator, to Patch, the rear-

gunner, were frigidly polite to the "stowaway" whom Cheshire
had been pampering for the past week or so, but Squadron-
Leader Pat Moyna did not seem to notice their black looks and
mutterings. For longer than he chose to remember, Moyna had
been trying to interest busy squadron and Group Commanders
in the R.A.F. Film Unit. It had been unrewarding, uphill work.
Most of them refused to take it seriously, advising him to try
peddling his unwanted wares at Air Ministry. He had gone to
Woodhall Spa expecting the cold shoulder from Cheshire. To
his amazement he had been received with unaccustomed warmth.

On his arrival, a warrant officer had looked him up and down
and said : " The Wing Commander ? He's very busy, sir,
always is." At that moment there was an angry roar of aircraft
flying low overhead : " There he goes, now."

Moyna, an ex-operational pilot himself, replied with affected
jauntiness :

" Good. I'll wait."

About an hour and a half later Cheshire had come in, greeting
the warrant officer with a grin. Moyna stood up, relieved but
also a little disappointed. He had been rehearsing the usual
one-sided interview with someone older, bigger, more formidable, less frail and friendly than this neat, slim youngster who
pouted when he smiled and who appeared faintly amused at the
absurdity of life in general.

" Hallo, I'm Cheshire," he said. " Let's walk round the
station while we talk," and Moyna was led away wondering
whether the guided tour of mess, hangars and bomb-dump were
part of an elaborate joke at his expense. Presently he decided
it could hardly be that : Cheshire's searching questions and
comments suggested that he was interested in cameras for reasons
which were still obscure.

" Do you think you could film a live operation ? " he suddenly asked.

" If you give us the facilities, I'm sure we can," said Moyna
promptly. Cheshire came to a quick decision :

" We shan't be operating for some days. The ground crew
will give you all the help you need. Get your men to rig cameras
into my aircraft."

The ground crew regarded it as worse than sacrilege. Half
the door had to be cut away to make room for two 35 mm. movie

cameras, and two huge mirrors were fitted underneath to reflect
as much light as possible. Even Moyna was taken aback by the
quaint transformation of the Lancaster ; it reminded him less
of a bomber than of a film studio on wings.

As he crossed the French coast, on February 8th, a provisional
member of Cheshire's crew, he was unable to suppress the feeling
of unreality. It was like being on a joyride which had gone too
far. A searchlight began to wave in the sky near Caubourg, their
landfall, and before it went out Moyna wondered whether the
mirrors would betray their position to the German gunners.
The troubled thought passed. They flew steadily on at 4000 feet,
well below the clouds. Somewhere above them were eleven
more Lancasters. The black-out in some of the towns seemed
brazenly bad, as though the people, expecting company, were
providing a civic flarepath. The Gnome and Rhone aero-engine
factory was blazing with lights as they circled over Limoges.

" We went in very low," said Moyna. " I heard Cheshire
say that he had time in hand to warn the 500 women workers
on night shift. We could see the moon behind the Cathedral
on the banks of the river. The clouds were breaking up at the
right moment.

" Twice the Lancaster swooped in a shallow dive above the
factory, seeming almost to scrape the roof at fifty feet.

" Keep a look-out for the girls. Tell me when they clear
out," called Cheshire.

On the third low warning run, someone said :

" There they go, Skipper, hundreds of them. Streaming to
the shelters."

A thoughtful French foreman had left all the lights burning,
but a master switch suddenly plunged town and factory into
total darkness before the first markers burst in the middle of the
central bay. The reflected glare was so sudden and dazzling that
Moyna feared the aircraft had caught fire. Automatically he
fiddled with the control of his camera and took some of the most
striking low-level precision-marking pictures of the war.

One minute after midnight Cheshire called up the main force
and with a blinding flash the first of the five 12,000-pounders,
dropped by David Shannon, landed in the centre of the markers.
It was followed by Pilot-Officer Knight's stick of 1000-pound
bombs which exploded on the western edge of the factory.

Cheshire had meanwhile climbed to 5000 feet, and Moyna enjoyed an outsider's grandstand view of the cleanest, hardest, and cheapest raid yet made by the R.A.F. on a small industrial target. Only one bomb load fell wide, landing in a field 150 yards to the west. Cheshire ordered the bombers to return to base, then flew down to inspect the damage.

" Right, Moyna," he said. " It's all yours now." They cruised about at less than 100 feet for half an hour, edging close to the burning, smoking ruins.

" He was as unconcerned as an assistant arranging a group photograph in a studio," Moyna recalls. " I knew then how far-sighted he really was in his rather secretive way. His first job had been to direct the bombing ; his second was to help me to get my pictures. If he felt he was adding a footnote to the history of the war in the air, he was determined that I should record the beginning of it for him."

Some of his crew disliked loitering above the target and began to protest in a light-hearted way :

" Come on, Skipper, are you tired of life ? "

" What are we waiting for—night fighters ? " asked another.

" All right, all right. Moyna's got work to do, too," he replied.

The smoke was too dense for any but the briefest exposures, and finally they turned for home, flying west from Poitiers and hugging the Atlantic coast round the Brest peninsula. The other eleven had landed an hour ahead of them.

There were two notable sequels to the Limoges raid. One was a message from Sir Charles Portal, the Chief of Air Staff, which Harris forwarded to Cochrane without comment. It was short and to the point :

" I have just seen the photographs of the Gnome and Rhone aero-engine factory at Limoges taken after an attack on 8-9 February by 617 Squadron. The very severe damage caused by so small a number of aircraft is most remarkable and I should be grateful if you would convey my warmest congratulations to this squadron on the extreme accuracy of their bombing."

About six weeks later a pretty French girl arrived in England. She was a member of the Resistance, and her name was Jacqueline. Moyna met her at Pinewood Studios, and was intrigued to hear that she had been in Limoges on the night of the attack. The

whole town had been stirred by the chivalry of the pilot who had
given the factory workers ample warning before the bombing
began. Could she meet him? She would like to thank him
personally in the name of every " limousin." Moyna said he
would try to arrange a meeting but never succeeded. Limoges
was already part of the limbo of Cheshire's past ; his caravan had
moved on at speed to greater things.

The most solid proof of Cheshire's unbounded faith in the
merits of his own low-marking methods can be found in four
large, leather-bound cash books which give an extraordinarily
detailed and balanced account of the squadron's achievements
during the spring and summer months of 1944. He decided to
open this operational diary immediately after the Limoges raid,
and the entries were filled in regularly until the pre-eminence of
617 as exponents of precision bombing was universally recognised.

In the back of his mind, Cheshire was toying with the agree-
able idea of writing a history of the squadron himself when the
war ended. His belief in his luck and powers of survival had
been fortified by success. But his original intention was to
present photostat copies of the completed diary as victory
souvenirs to the men whose disciplined skill and raw courage are
stamped on every page of it.

Although he has neither written the history nor handed
round the photostat copies (the diary lapsed in May, 1944)
Cheshire's four cash books remain a unique quarry of information. No comparable record exists, for 5 Group Headquarters
made a fetish of security and the secret log-book kept by Carol
Durrant, Cochrane's personal assistant, has since been mislaid
or lost.

To a biographer, their interest lies less in the vivid factual
accounts of the raids themselves than in the recurring evidence
of the author's critical, watchful, shrewd, unconventional yet
infinitely painstaking mind which seemed to derive as much
inspiration from setbacks as from triumphs. For Cochrane's
reservations about the riskiness of the new system of marking
were not lightly dispelled and Cheshire had to be firm as well as
diplomatic to get his own way in the end.

On February 12th, for example, when the squadron flew
to the Mediterranean coast of France in a brave but hopeless
attempt to shatter the Antheor Viaduct, a genuine bottleneck

on the main railway line between Marseilles and Genoa, he turned the failure to good account in support of his own claims for greater freedom of initiative.

The viaduct had been attacked three times before without success, twice by 617 and once by the Americans. Nearly 100,000 tons of supplies crossed it every week, and its destruction at that moment—when Kesselring was bracing himself to push the Allies back into the sea at Anzio—would undoubtedly have eased pressure on this precarious beachhead hundreds of miles to the south. But Antheor was an exceptionally difficult target to hit, not only because the hills above it shelved down steeply almost to the Mediterranean shore but because it lay at the extreme limit of the Lancaster's range.

In his summing-up, Cheshire was less concerned with the perils which almost cost him his life than with the rigid un-imaginative attitude of those who had planned the final details of the raid :

" This attack was unsuccessful for two reasons," he stated. " In the first place the information about enemy defences was inaccurate so that the plan was inadequate to meet the opposition actually encountered. In the second place, insufficient petrol could be carried to enable the leader to change his tactics."

The squadron took off from Ford, an emergency station beneath the Sussex Downs at Arundel, in order to husband the slender stocks of petrol. At the last minute Cheshire asked for permission to fly straight on from Antheor to Sardinia. The weather had worsened, and the danger of attempting a return flight on very low tanks was obvious to everyone. He pointed out quietly that if permission was refused the chances of success would be greatly reduced, as the necessary room for tactical manœuvre would be denied him. Permission was refused. A local air-raid warning wailed dismally as he climbed into the cockpit. He set course for France not exactly in the best of tempers.

Cheshire and Martin, who were to mark the target, reached Antheor about five minutes before the others. They were met by an unexpected hail of heavy and light flak from hidden batteries of guns in the narrow valley below. The night was black as pitch ; the spurts of flame from the muzzles of the guns were the only pointers to the general target area. Cheshire was about two miles over the sea after attempting his third unsuccessful low-level run when Martin's voice broke in on the intercom :

" Hallo, leader. I'm in a good position to go in. Can you provide entertainment ? "

Martin had flown in a wide circle to approach the target from inland, throttling back hard as he slid down into the valley, then rapidly picking up speed again to flash across the top of the viaduct with a bare 50 feet to spare. Bob Hay, the bomb-aimer, was about to press the button and release his marker when a 20 mm. cannon shell hit the aircraft and blew his brains out. No marker fell, and every gun opened up on Martin as he raced on out to sea. Cheshire, who had been too far away to draw off the enemy fire, listened to Martin's breathless account of the accident and ordered him to fly on towards Sardinia. It was an unpalatable way of forcing prim planners to eat their words.

Climbing out of reach of the light cannons, he turned and made a straight marking run at 5000 feet ; but " even up there the twelve heavy guns concentrated their fire on me to the exclusion of the main force circling above." Shannon and the others watched anxiously. It seemed that nothing could live in that inferno. Then they saw a red spot marker bounce very close to the viaduct. In its glare the nine slender arches were silhouetted plainly, but the marker itself had overshot by 100 yards. It was a marvellous near-miss, but not near enough in the circumstances.

Cheshire's voice sounded calm and unhurried as he ordered them to allow for the error and bomb. They did their best but failed. Only one 12,000-pounder narrowly missed the viaduct in the few grudging minutes left by the petrol ration.

At the post-mortem, Cochrane conceded half of Cheshire's argument. The need for tactical freedom to meet unforeseen hazards was reasonable enough ; but adding needlessly to the hazards by laying markers on targets like wreaths on cenotaphs was not. In future, *he* would decide beforehand whether the marking for any raid was to be carried out from low or medium level. Dogged as ever Cheshire threw up a fresh idea :

" There'd be no question of danger if we had a couple of Mosquitos, sir."

Cochrane did not rise to it ; for the moment he was implacable. Antheor had reminded him unpleasantly of the Dortmund-

Ems disaster and he preferred living squadron commanders to
dead ones. The raid had reminded Cheshire uncomfortably of
the night he had floundered helplessly above the guns of Magdeburg ; but he felt no immediate sting of self-reproach. After
all, a Lancaster could not be expected to pick its way through
flak as nimbly as the Mosquito he had flown in with Pickard.
Gradually he must persuade Cochrane of that fact.

5

Constance had meanwhile left the loneliness of Thorpe Hall
for a modern flat in St. John's Wood, London, and midway
through February Cheshire joined her for a few days' leave. It
was the period of the German " tip-and-run " attacks, the faltering reply of the Luftwaffe to the R.A.F.'s protracted onslaught
on Berlin ; but some of the bombs fell close enough to give
him a healthy fright and one or two sleepless nights. Enjoyment and relaxation seemed his only aims—to everyone but
Charles Whitworth and one or two colleagues at Air Ministry.
Whitworth had been transferred to the Operations Directorate
some months before, and he looked up with a start when
Cheshire walked into his office one morning with a problem.

" Are Mosquitos hard to get hold of ? " he asked.

" It depends who you are and what you want them for,"
said Whitworth. " Come on, Leonard, what are you up to this
time ? "

Cheshire explained his dilemma, and Whitworth nodded
understandingly :

" Of course the first move must come from Cochrane.
Convert him, and we'll do the rest. Still, we'd better go along
the corridor and consult the man who knows all the answers."

The Group Captain in the other room listened, then bellowed
with laughter.

" Mosquitos ? " he said. " We've got lashings of them.
Seriously though, how many do you want ? "

Cheshire hedged a little :

" I'd like a couple, but I don't want to take them with me.
What I'm more interested in at the moment is how to make sure
of getting them without delay when I want them." The obliging
Group Captain gave him an infallible recipe :

" Avoid the usual channels like the plague and give me a buzz in good time."

A few days later, at Woodhall Spa, unpredictable events cut short his researches into the problem of scarce Mosquitos. Cochrane sent for him and said that a conference on the whole question of marking methods was to be held at Bomber Command Headquarters. Cheshire must accompany him : 617's experimental technique would probably be discussed, and the evidence of his squadron commander might be all-important.

The meeting in Harris's room was an oddly dramatic affair even though Cheshire was only half aware of its uneasy political undertones. At the head of the long table sat Air Marshal Sir Robert Saundby, deputy to the Commander-in-Chief, with Bennett on his left, Cochran on his right, and Cheshire next to Cochrane. No minutes of the discussion were taken, no written record exists, and even the date is disputable. But by carefully piecing together the fragmentary and sometimes contradictory evidence of all four principals, one can justifiably place the conference in late February and reconstruct in general terms what was said and decided.

The most bothered man in the room was Bennett, who fairly naturally regarded the whole affair with suspicion. For some time he had been enduring carping criticism of his standard marking technique in the " Battle of Berlin " ; and owing to the complete lack of photographic evidence he had been forced to endure it in silence. In his eyes such a conference could mean only one thing : the thick end of a wedge which had been progressively inserted under him since the summer of 1943.[1]

Saundby narrowed down the subject in his opening remarks. The purpose of the meeting, he said, was to decide on the best method of marking small targets. 617 Squadron had already embarked on a campaign against relatively undefended targets with a new technique. They had had some success. Could this technique be developed for wider use against more important targets ?

Bennett intervened bluntly. The methods used by the Path-finders had been worked out by trial and error over a long period of time. The best crews and the best equipment had been

[1] Bennett contends that the meeting was called in April, not February, to discuss the marking of lock-gates near Berlin.

employed in their development. Could anyone suppose that 5 Group or 617 Squadron, with so little experience behind them, could hope to improve on the Pathfinders? He thrust aside Cochrane's reminder that 617 had already achieved very promising results. It was one thing to knock out " agricultural targets " by low-level marking and precision bombing ; it would be quite another matter against defended targets. As far as he was concerned, they could go ahead and try. But they would be wasting their time.

Cheshire was asked for his opinion ; and he gave it with an emphatic assurance that proved almost too much for Cochrane. 617 could not complain of inexperience, he said. They had trained so hard with the hand-made precision bomb-sight that they could now guarantee to put three bombs in every ten within twenty-five yards of a target, and three in every four within eighty yards, from a height of 20,000 feet.

The squadron crews, he said, had proved the deadliness of their bomb aiming, but the " Oboe " Mosquito had let them down badly. They had since worked out an independent method by which the leader identified the target visually and released his markers point-blank in the course of a shallow dive. He was certain this method was feasible for defended as well as un-defended targets. At any rate he knew that it was far more accurate than the normal Pathfinder technique.

Bennett abruptly dismissed Cheshire's assertions as " com-pletely pointless." " It just can't be done against defended targets," he said. " In a Lancaster it would be asking for trouble. In a Mosquito, the speed of the machine and the foreshortened horizon would make it impossible to mark with real accuracy, especially at night."

He would certainly not undertake it because it was utterly impracticable, if not dangerous.

Cochrane felt bound to qualify Cheshire's enthusiastic support for low-level marking. Perhaps, he said, the best solution lay midway between the two approaches. If Bennett was unwilling to try, he would be happy to do so. In his opinion the new technique was altogether too promising to be dropped.

In his summing-up, Saundby agreed with Cochrane, and Cheshire was secretly delighted. At least the door had not been locked against him ; it was still ajar. Bennett's sturdy refusal to budge meant that there would be no competition from the Pathfinders. Provided 617 could win a few quick, bloodless victories, they might get those Mosquitos after all.

During the first three weeks of March the squadron won the bloodless victories on which Cheshire had set his heart : five in a row. Each was made possible by flexible, opportunist tactics ; for in each case the conditions were against the attackers. On March 2nd, with Munro as his deputy (Martin had meanwhile been " grounded " and sent to an unwanted safe job), Cheshire was ordered to destroy the cunningly camouflaged aero-engine factory at Albert, in Northern France. It was believed to be strongly defended, and Cochrane insisted that marking should be carried out from medium level. In the light of flares dropped by the main force, Cheshire sighted the aiming point and ran in at 5000 feet. A shout from Keith Astbury, the bomb-aimer, made him pause :

" Sorry, captain, the bomb-sight's U/S."

They circled the town twice more, hoping that the temperamental bomb-sight would respond to Astbury's frantic manipulations, but the flares were going out. Cheshire called up Munro :

" Right, Les. Mark as quickly as you can."

Munro's marker relit the target area as the last flare disappeared. Within a quarter of an hour the two factories were enveloped in flames. Every bomb but one had struck home ; and this exploded harmlessly well away from the town. Nearly a year later Allied bomb damage experts examined the broken shells of the buildings. The machine-tool section had been so badly smashed that the Germans had not even attempted to restore it, while output in the aircraft engine department was still only a tenth of what it had been before that one attack by 617. Cheshire wrote in his diary :

" This factory will produce no more engines for the Hun."

A week later, on March 10th, in the cloud-covered valley below St. Etienne, a variation of the point-blank marking system had to be improvised on the spur of the moment owing to the unbelievably bad visibility. All that morning Cheshire, Munro and Shannon had sat in the operations room, poring over maps and old photographs of the smallest target yet allotted to 617, a needle-bearings factory at La Ricamerie. It was the only factory of its kind in France, a mere 170 yards by 90 in area ; but among

the pitheads and straggling housing estates of that valley in the
Cevennes it would be no easier to find on such a night than a
wallet dropped in the black-out.

They had been promised " perfect weather conditions ", as
Cheshire recalled whimsically more than once on the way. Yet
even at 100 feet he and his crew could see little in the pale, wispy
moonlight.

It was on his seventh approach to the target that he sighted
the roof for a blurred moment and let go a stick of incendiaries;
ordinary markers would have been invisible to the squadron
wheeling round in the clouds a mile and a half overhead. He
cursed as he watched his bombs overshoot and skid away,
landing on the main road skirting the western end of the factory.
Then he called up Munro, the second marker :

" Come in, Les, and do your best to undershoot those
incendiaries."

They groaned as Munro's stick of bombs undershot—by
nearly a quarter of a mile. Without hesitation Cheshire called
up David Shannon :

" You saw what happened, David. Will you try approaching
from west to east ? That'll give you my incendiaries to aim at.
Overshoot them if you can by fifty yards." Shannon succeeded
brilliantly. His stick of bombs hit the factory roof, but bounced
back and began to burn at the eastern end. Now at least the
squadron had something bright to concentrate on. Cheshire
ordered them to direct their bombs through the clouds between
the two nearest glows.

The aiming was good, as far as he could tell ; but the sudden
change of tactics seemed to have knocked the squadron out of
its stride. On the way home Cheshire sent a despondent message
to base :

" Deeply regret attack unsuccessful. Refer to your weather
forecast."

He seemed to have the weather on the brain at debriefing
until Arthur Pollen disconcertingly changed the subject :

" Was there a chimney attached to the factory ? " he asked
rather anxiously.

" What ? "

" A chimney, sir. A factory chimney. You remember, the
matter came up at briefing yesterday."

Cheshire suddenly remembered. Pollen, in a sense, had come to his rescue at a difficult moment. It had virtually been decided that the marking should be done from medium instead of low level because of an enormous factory chimney in the target area, when Pollen brightly suggested that in all probability the chimney was no longer there. Some of the target pictures, he said, were out of date. More recent photographs indicated that the factory had been rebuilt. The raid was over; Cheshire seemed none the worse, chimney or no chimney; but Pollen was still concerned about " the only bit of original intelligence I produced in the whole war."

" Oh, yes," said Cheshire with icy deliberation. " There was a chimney all right. A whacking big one. You deserve to be court-martialled, Pollen. That confounded chimney of yours practically ruined the operation. How we missed hitting it, God only knows."

The intelligence officer's heart sank into his boots. He kept turning over the evidence in his mind and the more he thought about it, the more uncertain he grew. He slept very little that night, and as soon as he reached his office next morning the telephone rang. It was Cheshire again, with the suspicion of a laugh in his voice.

" Hallo, Arthur. About that chimney of yours. You were absolutely right. It wasn't there, and I'm grateful." Pollen hung up the receiver feeling much better. There were occasions when Cheshire's enigmatic sense of fun was too much of a luxury. This, he told himself, was one of them.

There were whistles of astonishment when the reconnaissance photographs arrived. Cheshire's regretful message about a probable failure had been premature. Over 80% of the bomb-load had smitten and burnt out the needle-bearings factory at La Ricamerie.

It seemed that nothing 617 attempted could go amiss; on March 16th, they visited the Michelin tyre plant at Clermont Ferrand, leaving untouched the single building in the confined target area which Cochrane had particularly asked them to avoid hitting. It was the workers' canteen.

" Michelin's complexion seems a trifle red," Cheshire signalled after a last low-level inspection of the blazing sheds; and a remarkable photograph of the undamaged canteen showing the selective precision of the squadron's bombing was brought to the notice of the War Cabinet.

Cochrane had been deeply impressed by the versatile switch in tactics which, in defiance of all the omens, had turned failure into victory at La Ricamerie. The squadron's manœuvrability was as great as its accuracy; nobody could have foreseen in November the astounding timeliness of the technique which Cheshire had slowly engineered and brought to perfection.

Looking back, Cochrane could not help admiring his persistence and skill in the face of endless small discouragements. Looking ahead, he could already see clearly enough the historic conjunction of events which would probably test the value of Cheshire's methods as never before. A long list of railway centres in France and Belgium which would have to be destroyed before D-Day was at this moment being stormily debated in London. There were critics who said the project was impossible. Yet what 617 could do to a series of smaller targets, the whole Group and perhaps the whole of Bomber Command would have to do shortly to a series of larger and more vital targets.

Nor had Cochrane overlooked Cheshire's broad hints about the practical difference a few Mosquitos might make to the squadron's marking. He had sounded Harris on the question, and the gruff, still slightly incredulous Commander-in-Chief had promised to let him have the loan of two before the end of March. Meanwhile 617 must complete its own campaign, and more squadrons from the Group must be schooled in the new technique.

As if to prove that his tactics at La Ricamerie were no fluke, Cheshire was forced to repeat them on March 18th when trying to mark the explosives factory at Bergerac. The factory was blown sky-high, and the powder plant at Angoulême disappeared with fewer preliminaries two nights later. Then the squadron was sent to destroy an aircraft factory at Lyons, and twice they returned to report failure: on both occasions Cheshire had accurately marked the wrong group of buildings and the perfectly aimed bombs of 617 were wasted.

The third visit to Lyons, on March 29th, was in the nature of a ceremonial farewell to the high-level method of marking on which the A.O.C. had insisted so firmly from the beginning.

For two days earlier Cochrane had broken the news about the Mosquitos to a dumbfounded but radiant Cheshire.

"There are two of them waiting for you over at Coleby Grange. They're on loan for a month only but you're not to use them on operations until I give the word," he said with one of his rare, slow smiles. That same afternoon, in exactly one hour, Cheshire learnt how to fly a Mosquito.

At Woodhall Spa the air crews re-studied the target map of Lyons as though their lives depended on it. And a white square was superimposed so that there could be no alibis for failing. They knew that even if the marking had to be carried out in thick cloud and industrial smoke from 10,000 feet, it would probably be for the last time. This was " Cochrane's benefit performance ". They must not let him down.

In the small hours of March 30th, while the Lancasters were heading back across France to Lincolnshire, Cochrane was handed a six-word message from Cheshire. It said simply :

" All bombs within the white square."

In nearly 300 sorties, the squadron had lost only one aircraft. The proportion staggered Harris as well as Cochrane, for though German cities were far more heavily defended than French, the enemy had begun switching fighters from Germany to deal with these daring raiders who never left a demolition job half finished. The low casualties, the astoundingly successful results, and the small number of bombers used were the three factors which finally swayed the planners at Bomber Command : from April onwards, Cheshire's perfectionism played its indirect part in the shaping of strategic thinking.

His constant search for new ideas and gadgets was an incalculable but real element in the squadron's success. He usually benefited from failures. After the Antheor raid, for instance, he became convinced that the squadron badly needed some form of air cover. A few days later, quite by accident, he met at a party Flight-Lieutenant Noel Holland, the senior controller of the Beachy Head radar station of Fighter Command. They fell to talking " shop ", and Holland was horrified to hear that 617 went out night after night with no protection but their guns.

" It's none of my business," he said. " But you should come down to Beachy Head and look us up. We might be able to

help." Cheshire visited the radar station at the first opportunity,
and Holland explained how the experimental American equipment served Fighter Command in its daily sweeps across the
Channel. After dark, he said significantly, most of the short-
wave channels were idle.

"That's very interesting," said Cheshire, " but how would
that help us?"

Holland replied that the unique feature about the Beachy
Head equipment was its exceptionally long range :

"It's made for you people," he said. "If you were
hooked up to us here, we could give you early warning of night
fighters in your area even if you happened to be 200 miles into
France."

Cheshire's interest quickened at once. He decided to
approach Cochrane for official permission to experiment.
Holland was invited to Woodhall Spa to " sell the idea " to the
squadron ; and as he nervously faced " the toughest-looking
bunch of fliers I ever faced in my life ", he wondered what
mystery of animal magnetism underlay Cheshire's gentle but very
sure hold on them.

With Cochrane's approval, 617's Lancasters were fitted with
crystal pick-ups and the latest Very High Frequency sets, and the
Beachy Head station gave the squadron complete radar protection
during the decisive weeks that followed. Noel Holland reached
the same conclusion as Pat Moyna, the film camera expert : any
idea or contrivance, however far-fetched, that seemed likely to
increase the efficiency of the squadron was grist to Cheshire's
insatiable mill. In his hard, calculating curiosity and practical
foresight lay half the secret of his success. The other half was a
matter of faith in himself and opportunist inspiration.

Moyna, as an observant stranger, noticed how frequently
Cheshire visited the anonymous men and women in the offices,
repair sheds and cookhouses, with Simon the poodle trotting
along at his heels. The ritual of thanking the ground crews
after every raid, often letting the crew truck go while he smoked
a cigarette, sipped a cup of tea and chatted about the night's
operation, was rarely omitted. One of the fighters, a hard-bitten,
middle-aged Cockney, expressed most forcibly a view which was
repeated in a dozen different ways by others :

"I'm too old for hero-worship," he said. "I've seen too

much of the world and the people in it. I didn't know very much about what was going on at Woodhall Spa, except that most of it was hush-hush and we had our hands full all the time. 617 did a lot of successful jobs. I don't know if they brought victory any nearer in the end, and I don't honestly care very much. I was proud to belong to the squadron not because of what Cheshire did but because of what he was. It was nice to feel all the time that we had a human being for a boss, someone who appreciated our work and wasn't too standoffish to come and tell us so. I'm not exactly a glutton for work but I don't think I've ever worked harder in my life than I worked for Cheshire. And I can't remember a happier period in the service."

6

In the week 617 took delivery of its two Mosquitos, the future of Bomber Command and of the American strategic air force based in Britain was thrashed out at the highest level. The most effective contribution which the Allied heavy bombers could make to the invasion preparations had been the subject of prolonged and acute dispute, and the controversy came to a head between March 25th and April 17th. Day after day there were meetings between political as well as military leaders in Whitehall and elsewhere, for the problems went much deeper than the nicely balanced technical viewpoints of the professional partisans.

Apart from the vexed question of targets, the operational control of the bombers was at stake ; and as Supreme Allied Commander, General Eisenhower was in no mood for pedantic, time-wasting arguments. He had only two months left to complete the aerial prelude to D-Day. He wanted the strategic bombers to paralyse all railways leading to the Normandy beaches ; only thus could he win the vital race for reinforcements and keep a firm foothold on the shores of France. Without such a campaign of interdiction, D-Day might go down in history as the bloodiest and most foolhardy gamble ever taken by a responsible commander.

In Eisenhower's view, the success or failure of the Allied landings hinged on the success or failure of what became known as the Transportation Plan, drawn up by experts on the staff of

Trafford Leigh-Mallory, his air commander, and wholeheartedly backed by Tedder, his deputy at S.H.A.E.F.

It was Tedder's resolute support for the plan, and Eisenhower's deep faith in Tedder, which gradually overcame all opposition and led to its adoption ; but the Supreme Commander and his brilliant deputy had first to meet a fierce cross-fire of criticism from Churchill, the Ministry of Economic Warfare, Spaatz and Harris. The time was certainly overripe for sending out the bombers. Yet with Allied air supremacy unchallenged from Norway to Sicily, there seemed ample room for more than one opinion about the best strategic use to which the bombers could be put.

Spaatz had cut-and-dried strategic ideas of his own. He was on the eve of an independent campaign with his Flying Fortresses and long-range fighters against Germany's synthetic oil plants. He believed that the enemy's power to resist an invasion would be fatally undermined if the life-blood of his war-machine were drained away. Harris thought otherwise ; oil plants were what he called " panacea targets ", and he would have none of them. But, like Spaatz, he was reluctant to be diverted from area attacks on industry. Both could argue with some show of realism that to sidetrack them now from campaigns which promised such rich results was wrongheaded strategy, since the enemy would be allowed a breathing space for industrial recovery and reorganisation.

But Harris, as rigid as ever in his advocacy of mass raids on cities, had a second line of argument that could not be disputed so readily. He expressed his genuine doubts whether Bomber Command was fitted to undertake such a campaign of precision bombing as Eisenhower and Tedder envisaged. His force had been employed almost exclusively with the saturation bombing of sprawling built-up areas : what likelihood was there now that it could suddenly be turned against small targets with any hope of quickly knocking them out ? As he put it in *Bomber Offensive* :

" All previous experience had gone to show that the R.A.F.'s heavy bombers, with their futile .303 defensive armament, could not operate by day in the face of serious opposition, and could not hit small targets by night except when the opposition was negligible and the weather and light exceptionally good. Any sustained campaign against a large number of small tactical targets could not be carried out in any reasonable period of time if the bombers had to wait for such unusual conditions."

The Prime Minister's objection to the Eisenhower-Tedder plan was political and therefore unanswerable. With other members of the War Cabinet, Churchill was concerned with the possible effect of the proposed bombing campaign on Anglo-French relations, especially if the attacks resulted in grievous casualties among French civilians. Finally Roosevelt was asked for his view, and the President's firm reply to Churchill on April 11th settled the question.

" However regrettable the attendant loss of civilian lives is, I am not prepared to impose from this distance any restriction on military action by the responsible commanders that, in their opinion, might militate against the success of 'Overlord' or cause additional loss of life to our Allied forces of invasion."

This, as Churchill says, was decisive.

On April 14th, the control of the strategic air forces was handed over to Tedder, who was admirably suited for the task of co-ordinating them by his diplomatic touch and great experience as an Allied air commander. He needed every ounce of tact and patience, not only to smooth over inter-service and inter-Allied jealousies but to assert his rather nominal authority without winning unnecessary enemies in the process. Lacking a staff and a headquarters of his own, Tedder was in the invidious position of a Minister without portfolio suddenly saddled with some of the responsibilities of a Premier. It is a measure of his statesmanlike stature and strategic acumen that he managed to defy the odds and make the Transportation Plan work.

Tedder had acquired a wealth of valuable experience in Sicily and Italy, where, acting on the advice of scientists like Professor Zuckerman, he had perfected a novel method of paralysing enemy rail communications. Instead of following the traditional text-book technique of blowing up bridges and cutting lines, both of which the enemy could speedily repair, he directed his aircraft against the railway workshops and repair sheds. Since most of these were situated close to big marshalling yards, he gradually deprived the Germans not only of communications but of the means of restoring them. Only when this had been done were the tactical bombers turned loose finally against locomotives and rolling stock.

The Transportation Plan before D-Day followed the same pattern, except in one vital particular : it had to be carried out so deceptively that the German High Command would be given no inkling whether the invasion was likely to be launched against the Pas de Calais, Brittany or Normandy. Fortunately for Tedder, the geography of France and the original builders of the railways in the north aided his strategy of deception : for the lines to Normandy nearly all branched off from the main network linking the Pas de Calais and Brittany to Paris. In other words, the gutting of rail junctions and maintenance centres near the Belgian frontier, in Paris or along the Seine would hamper the movement of German troops and supplies just as effectively as if Normandy itself were turned into a " railway desert ". And German intelligence would be none the wiser about Allied intentions.

The Transportation Plan was given a trial run more than a month before Eisenhower won control of the heavy bombers. On March 6th the R.A.F. attacked the marshalling yards at Trappes, a busy rail centre some miles west of Paris. Seven more of the eighty targets finally allotted to Bomber Command were attacked during March by the standard method used against cities in Germany : Bennett's Pathfinders flew in at great heights to drop markers from " Oboe " Mosquitos, then the main force followed to bomb the markers. To prevent unnecessary loss of life the crews were forbidden to bomb if they were unable to see the markers.

Even so, there were the inevitable early mistakes with the inevitable outcries from politicians here and Resistance leaders in France. The latter did not contest the necessity for destroying rail communications ; they were apparently less apprehensive about the political repercussions of severe civilian casualties than Churchill and some of his advisers. But they believed that it could be done at a far cheaper cost in human lives by sabotage than by air bombardment. When General Koenig, the Commander of the French Forces of the Interior, offered to destroy any targets the Allies cared to name, Eisenhower had to refuse. The Supreme Commander dared not court the risk of failure.

The edginess of Harris and his staff during the trial phase of the railway offensive can be well imagined. They had practically no experience of precision attacks to guide them, except the evidence of 5 Group's raids on Friedrichshafen, Peenemünde and the ski-sites, as well as the rather startling results achieved by Cheshire and 617 Squadron since the beginning of 1944. Even though the Pathfinders inflicted considerable damage and spilled comparatively little French blood during March the prickly vigilance of the politicians ruled out all complacency. Slowly the marking methods were overhauled in the interest of greater accuracy, and in the changes the influence of Cochrane's tactical ideas stood out unmistakably.

A master-bomber and a deputy were introduced to control the attacks and direct the target marking. Then, with irresistible logic, it was decided that 5 Group should be given a virtual monopoly of target marking because of its proven experience. Finally, as the supreme vindication of Cheshire's lonely persistence, his low-level technique was fully tested over France in mid-April.

It had taken him less than a fortnight to prove that the Mosquito was too fast for the defenders at low level. On April 5th, the whole of 5 Group was sent to attack an air-frame repair factory at Toulouse, and Cheshire was ordered to mark the target in his Mosquito. It was the first large-scale precision raid he had ever led, and he prepared for it with even more thoroughness than usual.

One small incident beforehand perfectly illustrates the scrupulous, almost finicky care he gave to technical minutiæ. Cheshire was not blessed with a mechanical mind, and as a rule he trusted the judgment of his own experts ; but none of the experts could answer a simple conundrum which worried him : could the Mosquito, which had been designed for high altitudes, carry him at low level to Toulouse and back without running out of petrol ?

Without more ado, Cheshire telephoned direct to John de Havilland at Hatfield who realised at once that the problem was no figment of an apprehensive imagination :

" I'll come over to-morrow, and we'll decide what's possible after a test," he said.

The informal arrival of de Havilland on the morning of an important raid created a mild stir among those who had dismissed Cheshire's doubts as fussiness carried to the nth degree. There *was* some uncertainty about the Mosquito's petrol range after all. De Havilland wasted little time, and few words.

"It can be done, but only just. My advice is—don't try without long-range tanks."

Cheshire hesitated for a second, then replied :

"Thanks, John. But I think I'll chance it."

Too much depended on the raid to "scrub" it at the last minute, and clear knowledge of the odds gave him a sense almost of relief. By spending less time identifying and marking the target, he could just scrape home. With so little margin for error, he could not afford to slip. Risks for Cheshire had little in common with the conventional phantoms of aircraft trapped by guns or night factors. The risks he really feared were the stupid, avoidable ones, the loose screw, the wrongly-fused marker, or the badly-tuned engine. That explained his endlessly roving eye and the pains he took to inspire every man with pride in his work and faith in the work of others.

Pat Kelly, the short, dark, charming Irishman who was his navigator, had some trouble keeping a straight course to Toulouse. The Mosquito's speed was deceptive, and they arrived after the main force. The bright moonlight over the target, however, guided them to the aiming point at once. Hurtling through the light flak, Cheshire put his markers on the roof of the central repair hangar on his third low-level run. The backing-up by Munro and McCarthy in Lancasters was excellent, and for a few minutes he watched the bombing with satisfaction. The needle on the petrol gauge told him when to leave.

At St. Cyr less than a week later, Cheshire was baffled by the darkness. The squadron had been ordered to "destroy at all costs" the Field Air Park and Signals equipment depot of the Luftwaffe, the most important single target of its kind in France. But the light was so faulty that he could not see even the ornate, formal gardens of the Versailles Palace, which practically adjoined his aiming point. Not to be outwitted by the weather, he did something he had longed to do for five years. Turning the Mosquito's nose straight down he dived towards the ground, identified the T-shaped central depot as it loomed up out of the gloom, pulled back the control column 700 feet above it, and released the markers. They landed on the western fringe of the target area.

When the squadron turned for home, says the diary, "all

six sheds were burning fast and were beyond any shadow of doubt destroyed."

Less than a fortnight had passed since the two borrowed Mosquitos had appeared at Woodhall Spa; in that brief span Bomber Command policy had been turned upside down as a result of the strategic arguments in London. The entire force was committed now to an indefinite campaign against the type of target in which the squadron specialised; the whole of 5 Group was keyed up for action; and Harris readily agreed to let 617 act as the spearhead in two mass attacks on marshalling yards in the Paris region.

Never a man for niggling half-measures, the Commander-in-Chief moved energetically to implement a policy in which he disbelieved; and on April 14th, he ordered the transfer to 5 Group of two Lancaster squadrons and a whole Mosquito squadron from Bennett's Pathfinder Force. Since Cochrane had made a study of precision bombing, Cochrane should be given as free a hand as possible against precision targets. It was as simple as that. But Bennett, conscious of the blow to his prestige, was sickened by what he still regards as his greatest " let-down."

617 Squadron received two more Mosquitos; Shannon, Kearns and Falke learnt to fly them; and on April 18th Cheshire led his team to the Juvisy marshalling yards, south of Paris, to mark for two hundred Lancasters of 5 Group. In the morning Shannon and Cheshire spent nearly an hour dive-bombing on the practice range at Wainfleet, calculating the exact moment for dropping markers so that they would stay put and not bounce. They found a way together, and it was one problem less for Cheshire.

Hardly any bombs shattered the homes that shut in the labyrinth of railway tracks at Juvisy. " The bombing was exceptionally concentrated and well aimed," said the diary, " especially when it is considered that this was achieved by Main Force crews practised in area and not precision onslaughts. All squadron aircraft returned safely, and so was opened a new phase in the history of Bomber Command."

That hackneyed, overworked phrase expressed the bare truth. Harris at any rate was sufficiently impressed by the results of this raid and the second against La Chapelle two nights later, to send for Cochrane and Cheshire. Low-level marking seemed an unscientific, impracticable way of clinching a bombing operation ; and false heroics had no appeal for the unsentimental Harris. Yet he had to acknowledge that this intent-looking squadron commander had reduced a crazy technique to a teachable art. Could it be used, he wondered, against targets in Germany ?

When the question was raised over dinner in the Commander-in-Chief's home, Cheshire's heart thumped madly. There could be no better test on earth for his methods than a heavily defended German target. He said so.

Harris leaned across, fixing him with his stony smile :

" There aren't many German targets that fit into the present campaign. Have you any particular preference yourself ? " The answer tripped off Cheshire's tongue :

" Yes, sir. Munich."

Munich ! 5 Group had come nearest to pounding this remote Bavarian city and rail junction where the Hitler Movement had been born; but even 5 Group had been defeated by the distance, the weather and the defences. Munich was protected by more guns and searchlight batteries than any other place except Berlin and the Ruhr. Even the stern Harris paused, consenting at last with a shrug which seemed to say :

" Right, but it's your funeral. YOU suggested it."

It was an exclusive 5 Group affair, and there was an indifferent dress rehearsal over Brunswick, where Cheshire discovered that controlling a force of nearly 300 aircraft by radio could be a confusing business. The two squadrons of Lancasters recently transferred from the Pathfinders carried flares to enable 617 to mark accurately ; but one of these Lancasters had its radio transmitter turned on, and every order Cheshire tried to give was effectively jammed.

There was no radio jamming at Munich on April 24th. The four Mosquitos set out two hours after the main force. As they weaved through the flak and searchlights on the outskirts of the city they could see the occasional outline of bombers high above, pinned like gulls against the angry sky. Cheshire put the nose of his machine down and dived steeply at nearly 400 miles an hour towards the little white house near the main railway

station that was his aiming point.   He pulled sharply out at 500
feet, and Kelly shouted excitedly :

"That's it, sir, dead on."

As far as they could see, the markers were just right, and the
white walls of the house were stained red in the glare.   The
backing-up by the other Mosquitos was perfect.   So was the
bombing, at first.   Then a clump of markers suddenly appeared
on the far side of the river, half a mile away.   As he flew over
the city at less than 1000 feet, weaving wildly through the barrage
of heavy bullets and pattering shell fragments, Cheshire tried to
warn the main force of the wrongly-placed markers.   But the
ex-Pathfinder controller, too, had seen the error and corrected it
with an accurate cascade of green spot-fires.

For days before the raid, Cheshire had badgered Cochrane's
headquarters for long-range petrol tanks.   He had not forgotten
the lesson of the Toulouse raid, but apparently everyone else
had.   His repeated demands were "not taken seriously."   Once
again, to his lasting regret, he had to leave the target area early.
Yet if he had stayed over Munich much longer it is questionable
whether he would have lived to tell the tale.   As it was, the guns
and searchlights pursued him "for fully twelve minutes before
he got clear".

Cheshire still believes that the Munich attack was his greatest
single triumph of the war, and the undeniable fact that 90% of
the bomb-load fell in the right place for once, doing more damage
in a night than the whole of Bomber Command and the American
Air Force had done in four years, supports his opinion.   Characteristically, he takes little credit for helping to revolutionise
Bomber Command tactics in the far more criticial campaign
against the French railways.   The only victories Cheshire could
recognise were the victories he contrived himself.

The Munich raid is usually accepted at his valuation, partly
because it was specifically mentioned in the citation which
accompanied the award of his Victoria Cross in the late summer
of 1944.   But Cochrane, in his detached way, does not altogether
endorse the popular sentiment :

"Munich was a triumph, but not nearly so important as is
often claimed," he said.   "Its significance as a matter of air
history is simply that, for the first time, Bomber Command
managed to hit a difficult German target by the low-level mark-

ing technique which Cheshire pioneered. Later, other squadrons, notably 627, achieved far more striking successes with the same method, and Pathfinder techniques steadily improved, too. They got no V.C.s for a good reason : Cheshire was the first man to understand the problem, to grapple with it in his own thorough fashion, and to solve it in action. The entire burden of proof was his, and his greatness as a tactical thinker was established in the process."

The most merciless critics were members of Bennett's Pathfinder Force, and some of their criticisms reflected the ill feeling that undoubtedly existed between themselves and 5 Group. The most valid objection to low-level marking, however, especially in the second quarter of 1944, was that it sometimes exposed the waiting bombers to the full fury of the enemy defences, a disadvantage which Harris was quick to recognise. I have met pilots who hold this against Cheshire almost as a personal grudge. Not long ago one of them said to me with some heat :

"We objected to Cheshire's perfectionism. He lost all sense of time in his efforts to provide the best possible point of aim, and kept heavily-loaded bombers hanging about as easy meat for German fighters. Surely no raid was so important that more than forty bombers could be sacrificed against one small target. That happened at Mailly-le-Camp on May 3rd, 1944."

The Mailly-le-Camp attack, which incidentally wiped out a whole panzer division, cost the R.A.F. 46 Lancasters ; yet the delay in attacking was no fault of Cheshire's. The aiming point was marked at zero hour, the order to bomb was given at once, but it was not passed on to the first wave of attackers by the 5 Group controller of the main force. Later, when the second wave appeared, the whole target area was already lost in a fog of dense, billowing smoke. A dim but distinctive glow showed at the far end, where the original markers were still burning. Cheshire, who could see the fierce air battle developing overhead, called up the controller, ordering him to bring in the second wave without delay. But again the order was not passed on, so that Shannon and Kearns had to plunge through the smoke, with the bombs of the first wave still whistling down about them, and re-mark a target which could no longer be seen. The facts are in the operational diary ; the personal conclusions

Cheshire drew from them are still applicable to the new age of atomic jet-bombers flying through the stratosphere at 500 miles an hour :

" Everything would have gone smoothly if the controller had reacted quickly to the sudden change of tactics. He can't be blamed. Sudden changes in tactics were part of 617's technique : but it was only through long, hard training that we became perfect. At Mailly the second wave of attackers was unprepared for new orders. They belonged to a Group untrained in the technique.

" I never could understand the normal Bomber Command method of planning an attack. Everything was wound up and pre-set like an alarm clock hundreds of miles from a target, as though all the unknown factors could be predetermined infallibly and the raid conducted by the remote control of unseen experts. No battle in history was ever fought without a local commander to adjust his tactics to the needs of the situation. The system often went wrong and I felt in my wilder moments that even if it meant building an enormous aircraft for an Air Vice-Marshal and his staff, we should have someone responsible on the spot. Flexibility of tactics is as essential in an air as in a land or sea attack. All 617's victories were due to it. Mailly-le-Camp was a small but terrible example of what can happen to an attacking force which has not been trained to fight its own battles. We wiped out a whole panzer division but at an unnecessarily high cost."

7

Late one night, towards the end of the first week in May, Danny Walker, the Canadian navigation officer at Woodhall Spa, walked into the lounge of the mess. He had been to a party in Boston with Dave Rodger, a fellow-Canadian and the rear-gunner in McCarthy's crew. The pair of them were surprised to find Cheshire sitting alone with a drink in front of him.

" You're just the man I want to see, Danny," he said. " You're going to be busy for the next six weeks."

That morning Cheshire had attended a pre-invasion planning conference, and had seemingly startled some of the more senior service delegates by sparring tentatively with Harris. The Bomber Command chief had barked back in a menacing tone

that 617 Squadron would simulate an invasion fleet crossing the
Channel on the night of June 5th-6th, learn how to do it meanwhile, and like it.

Over a bottle of whisky, Cheshire reconstructed the scene
for them, explaining why he had opposed the offer of this dull
yet brilliantly imaginative " spoof " mission.

" The Pathfinders are the navigators ; 5 Group, and particularly 617 Squadron, are the precision bombers. Surely this is
Bennett's pigeon."

Cheshire's chagrin was all the keener because he already
knew that by D-Day the squadron would be equipped with an
exciting new bomb, another product of the teeming brain of
Barnes Wallis, the chief designer of Vickers-Armstrong.

" They also serve who only sit and wait," he mumbled
cynically. " What's the use of talking? Let's get to bed."

The scientists were scrambling for the services of 617 now,
and Barnes Wallis had been momentarily nudged out of the
lead by Robert Cockburn, one of the most versatile men in
Telecommunications Research. Cockburn arrived a day or
two later, walked with Cheshire to the loneliest stretch of the airfield, and there expounded the D-Day mission of the squadron.

All aircraft would have to be flown on instruments in short,
overlapping orbits, dropping " window " as they went. This
would require phenomenal navigational skill and exact mathematical timing if the German radar stations near Le Havre,
which had been deliberately left intact, were to draw the wrong
inferences. Those metallised strips of paper called " window "
had worked wonders of confusion among the radar defenders
of Hamburg and other German cities. A flawless flight now
would give a flawlessly false impression of a vast convoy steaming
towards imaginary invasion beaches, perhaps pinning down an
army in the wrong part of France for two or three vital days.
The scheme was a keystone in Tedder's vast edifice of deception.
It must be carried out without a mistake, and absolute security
was imperative.

" I'd like you to tell the squadron what you've told me,"
said Cheshire. Then, seeing the slightly shocked look on
Cockburn's face : " Don't worry about security. Leave that to
me."

Cockburn addressed the squadron, went carefully through

his rather incredible brief, invited questions, and left. He liked
Cheshire's air of dry confidence, but wondered at his half-
apologetic attitude in introducing the subject of the D-Day
mission to his men. It seemed as though Cheshire believed it
unworthy of 617's talents, calling for blind efficiency rather
than courage or creative imagination. All the imagination had
been supplied already by Cockburn and his colleagues.

The month of May, then, tended to be one of the most
insipid in the squadron's short history. Every day the Lancasters
took off on monotonous navigational flights, rehearsing in two
formations, seven miles apart, the intricate movements on which
the possible safety of tens of thousands of Allied soldiers would
depend. For Cheshire it was a month of preparation at half his
usual pressure, consulting the " boffins " at Farnborough and
elsewhere, overseeing the training and playing tennis or squash
to relieve the idle hours between.

Constance, whose patient good humour seemed endless, came
north and settled in Skegness. They saw much more of one
another than for months past ; and her unaffected charm made
the squadron happy for Cheshire. She appeared uninterested in
his service activities and amusingly innocent about his decorations. A second star had mysteriously appeared on his D.S.O.
ribbon, awarded a few weeks previously for his " magnificent
achievements " over France. More than one man was irritated
by her naïve admiration of its " prettiness " and her lack of
curiosity as to its meaning. Cheshire was never embarrassed ;
his sense of the ridiculousness of such baubles was too real.

In any case his mind was already ranging ahead to a campaign
which promised to compensate for this interlude of dullness.
He knew from Cochrane that the secret-weapons sites beyond
the Channel were springing up again and that the Tactical Air
Forces were vainly trying to knock out these multiplying, deftly
camouflaged, targets. The flying-bomb menace could be light-
ened but not removed. That seemed clear from the rapidity of
the German preparations.

The impending rocket threat was more of a mystery, the
heart of which lay hidden under fifty or sixty feet of reinforced
concrete in the five grotesquely-shaped underground launching
structures. There was still no agreement among War Cabinet
members as to the purpose of these strange buildings. Were they

a hoax to draw off the bombers from real targets ? Or were they, as some fragmentary reports said, the invulnerable casements for multi-barrelled V3's, rocket guns that could rain four huge shells a minute on London ? Whether a hoax or a fact, no chances could be taken : 617 Squadron was earmarked to destroy them with the one bomb capable of doing so.

The " Tallboy " was the invention of Barnes Wallis, the impatient visionary who designed and built the weapon for breaching the Ruhr dams. An old friend and Great War colleague of Cochrane's, he privately deplored the wanton waste of area-bombing and the crass timidity of most wartime policy committees. Wallis's ideas were often too breathtakingly simple for small men with " committee minds ". One might call him an instinctive " strategist ", but far in advance of his time. When he told Beaverbrook in 1941 that he knew how to win the air war, the hustling Minister looked at him with benign incredulity :

" Give me facilities to build a ten-ton bomb and a modified bomber," pleaded Wallis, " and Germany will lose her oil, coal and water power. That's the short-cut to victory."

It was also something of a pipe-dream in the straitened circumstances of 1941, when the outmoded, weak bomber force could not even locate the cities of Germany by night. The man who had proved his all-round ability as a designer by constructing the Wellington on the geodetic air-frame principle ignored Beaverbrook's brusque scepticism, crossed his fingers, put a bridle on his tongue, and went on hoping.

After his original vision had been partly vindicated by the raid on the dams, Wallis was still frowned upon by lesser beings as a bumbling old eccentric with the fire of the fanatic in his belly. A notable exception was the Chief Executive of the Ministry of Aircraft Production, Sir Wilfred Freeman, who, on his own initiative, with no formal authorisation from anyone, had asked Wallis to design a ten-ton bomb when the secret weapons scare was at its height in the summer of 1943.

Later Freeman had second thoughts which remained positive : no existing aircraft could carry the ten-tonner far, and it was rather late in the day to build one. Could Wallis design a scaled-down, portable version of his big bomb ? The inventor agreed with alacrity to try. Very soon the designs were ready

H

and passed. The new bomb would be a 12,000-pounder, with the explosive power of an immense blast weapon and the penetrative force of an armour-piercing shell. "Tallboy", as it was called, was something of a contradiction in terms. If it could do all that Wallis claimed, it would certainly destroy Hitler's supposed V3 sites.

Cochrane had given a broad hint of what was in store during the spring, and it was then that Cheshire met Wallis for the first time. The inventor's office was littered with instruments and neat drawings ; on the wall was a scale replica of one of the mysterious sites, and Wallis led Cheshire to it, explaining the need for unfailing accuracy. A direct hit might not be good enough, he said. The bomb might bounce off the concrete into the air. What he wanted was a deliberately contrived near-miss, so that the earth would be convulsed by an artificial earthquake and the foundations of the structure sucked down by the tremendous subterranean shock of the explosion.

"If you can do that, the whole thing will collapse like a pack of cards," he said. "You know, Hitler's engineers should have put fifty feet of concrete under the foundations. That might have saved them."

While Wallis idly stuck pins in the drawing to show the weak points where the bombs would do their work best, Cheshire could not resist remarking facetiously :

"Of course we can't guarantee to score near-misses from 20,000 feet as accurately as you can put pins into that drawing."

The grey eyes of the inventor narrowed under his beetling brows, the rosy farmer's complexion deepened, and the cropped white hair seemed to bristle :

"If that's your attitude, I'll say no more," he snapped. "These bombs are NOT meant to be flung about the French countryside like handfuls of seed. I didn't invent them for fun."

Cheshire was shaken. Wallis evidently had a robust sense of humour—about everything except his own sacred subject.

During the squadron's spring campaign, the inventor had analysed the bomb-plot charts with growing approval. The rising curve of 617's success pleased him almost as much as the delays in the production of the bomb infuriated him. On the day the prototype was tested, Cheshire saw another facet of Wallis's character. The glistening, shark-like bomb had shivered into a thousand pieces on impact ; it seemed as though all those months of work and hope lay in fragments, too. The realisation must have been reflected in Cheshire's face, for the inventor patted him on the shoulder and said :

" Don't worry, my boy. I'm used to this sort of thing. You'll see, all will be well in the end."

After dinner one warm evening just before D-Day Munro and Cheshire stopped a truck that was moving slowly down the perimeter towards the bomb-dump. The driver leaned out of his cabin and said he was carrying " aircraft spares." Lifting the tarpaulin cover, Cheshire peeped at the cargo to make sure : one could not be too careful about security in these last days before the curtain rose. Then his heart leaped, and he had to suppress an exclamation. The first consignment of " Tallboys " had arrived. Wallis had been right. Everything had " turned out well in the end."

About dusk on June 5th sixteen Lancasters rose into the sky and headed south-west. " Operation Taxable ", the squadron's unexciting, exacting part in supporting the Allied invasion, had begun. They flew on instruments, with the windows blacked out. Beyond Dover they picked up the eighteen ships far below, with their barrage balloon attachments, and the painfully slow manœuvre began. Hour after hour the aircraft flew forward, orbited, and doubled back, dropping bundles of " window " every twelve seconds. They returned after dawn, scornful and tired. The entry in Shannon's log-book expressed the general feeling :

" June 5th : Tactical Exercise to simulate spoof landing . . . Involved hazardous task of flying straight and level at 3000 feet in bright moonlight, dropping window at the same time. Successful, but bloody browned off."

On June 8th, their morale soared again. Cochrane ordered an attack on a railway tunnel near Saumur to complete Bomber Command's part in the Transportation Plan. It was the green light at last. They were to carry their first " Tallboys " and seal off one of the main railway lines leading from south-west France to Normandy where the Allies were consolidating the beach-heads.

Cheshire's markers fell in the deep cutting approaching the tunnel, and two of the bombs dug cavernous craters more than

100 feet wide. A third " Tallboy " shattered the roof, causing
it to cave in; the rest landed equally close to the markers.
Months afterwards, the liberating armies discovered that the
main line through Saumur to Normandy had remained blocked
to German troop trains from June 8th onwards.

The sun was not yet down on the evening of June 14th when
the squadron, after days of waiting for the weather to brighten,
took off on their first daylight raid. As the Lancasters orbited
over Le Havre with the drilled perfection of a Guards' platoon,
Cheshire's Mosquito was already speeding down headlong
towards the massive E-boat pens in the harbour, flattening out
below the flailing fire of many guns. His markers settled near
enough to the thick concrete tops to give 617 the fixed aiming
point they awaited. Once more there was an answering ava-
lanche of " Tallboys " and the E-boat pens were very heavily
damaged. The next evening, at Boulogne, nearly a hundred
E-boats were engulfed in the tidal wave created by " Tallboys ".
It was in effect a major naval victory. The fabric of Cheshire's
Mosquito was pitted with countless bullet holes and rents.
According to the law of averages he ought never to have survived the deadly barrages loosed against him in those two
suicidal dives.

Finally, on June 19th, it was the turn of the V3 sites. The
new bomb's proven power of devastation was tested against the
targets for which it had been specifically designed. The structure
at Watten was first on the demolition list, and in the late afternoon
Cheshire's smoke-marker plummeted down. In the distance he
could see the oncoming Lancasters like a flight of gnats, three
and a half miles high, wheeling as if by instinct, then breaking
formation and closing in with bomb-doors open, among the
smoke-plumes of Watten's heavy defences. Then, swift and
straight as an arrow from the blue, a " Tallboy " streaked
towards the earth. Ten seconds passed before Cheshire and
Kelly heard the cataclysmic roar as it burst in the bowels of the
earth :

" God help the Germans," muttered Kelly.

Into the air there shot a tumultuous geyser of stones, soil,
steel and rubble which spread out fanwise as more bombs found
the mark. But if one visit to Watten was enough, the Wizernes
site needed three. Twice Cheshire abandoned the operation

over the target : the third time they made no mistake. He had not forgotten Wallis's horrified disapproval at the thought of squandering " Tallboys " on the fair fields of France. The Siracourt structure was wiped out shortly before the sun set on the longest day of the year.

" Do you never feel any strain living on your nerves like this without a break ? " The questioner was Arthur Pollen, whose candour seemed to attract Cheshire.

" I never think about strain or nerves, so I can't answer," he replied.

It was perfectly true. The rare occasions he betrayed signs of jumpiness were when the weather took a clumsy hand and sabotaged flying. During the leaden weeks before the invasion, the Griller Quartet had visited the mess to give a concert. The station commander, a lover of good music, was beside himself with delight. At his suggestion, all but the essential duties were suspended for the evening ; and everyone but Cheshire accepted the unexpected holiday with satisfaction or indifference. To boycott the concert would have been childish and churlish ; but his face was a study of scowling impatience as he sat in the front row tapping his foot restlessly until the magic of Mozart and Beethoven and the appreciative hush about him restored his sense of proportion.

" How did you enjoy it ? " one of the musicians asked him afterwards.

" Quite well after a while," he answered. " To be perfectly honest, though, Duke Ellington would have suited my mood much better."

The musician gave him a wan smile, then admitted furtively that he was a jazz devotee himself. Cheshire's face lit up ; the fag end of the evening had been saved. The pair were overheard speculating with some animation on the hideous hash an unrehearsed Griller might have made of Duke Ellington.

Most of the important visitors to Woodhall Spa were drawn by curiosity and interest. They included the American Air Force Generals Spaatz and Doolittle, who arrived one day to inspect the bomb charts and photographs. Cheshire explained how the 617 technique worked in practice.

" Of course there's one problem we've never really managed to solve," he said.

" Yeah, and what's that ? " asked Spaatz.

" Well, we sometimes forget to readjust the bomb-sight after use, and that can be pretty wasteful."

" You mean the bombing goes wild ? "

" Oh, no. It's just that we go on lobbing bombs into the same holes made by the first crews."

Spaatz glowered, then joined in the general laughter. He left deeply impressed, and remembered the young wing commander whom he was to meet half a world away twelve months later.

A crated Mustang fighter, a gift from the Americans, was delivered on June 25th, and Cheshire asked his ground crew if they could fit it together without delay. He wanted it that evening ; the squadron had a rendezvous before dusk above the V3 site at Siracourt, and this new American machine was the aircraft in which he intended to mark the target. The ground crew worked without a break, removing the guns, testing the engine and scooping out the thick grease which covered everything. An hour before the Lancasters took off, the Mustang was not yet ready ; an hour after they had disappeared beyond the horizon, Cheshire took a final swig of tea from his fitter's mug and taxied down to the main runway. There was a bigger crowd than usual to see him off, and nobody spoke until the wheels left the ground.

They knew that Cheshire had never handled a Mustang until that moment.

The Base Commander was on edge for the next three hours, wondering if the raid had been imperilled by the Wing Commander's stubborn whim. But Cheshire seemed to have forgotten the incident at debriefing. He was full of praise for the Mustang, admitted that he had not enjoyed navigating, but swore that he would improve with practice.

After his hundredth operation on July 6th, when the fifth and final site at Marquise was destroyed, Cheshire was led aside by Cochrane :

" I think you've done enough," he said, and quietly thanked him. The A.O.C. had noticed a tell-tale sign of the prolonged strain. Now and then Cheshire's right eye flickered as though he had a nervous tic. His protests were so much wasted breath. This time Cochrane would not change his mind.

CHAPTER EIGHT

THE CLIMAX

IT was one of those oppressively hot August afternoons when Nature had lazily put her feet up and persuaded the majority of weak-willed office workers to follow her example. As Squadron-Leader G. C. Heseltine, a short, energetic man of middle age, walked across from the operations section at Bomber Command Headquarters towards the mess, he seemed to sweat harder at every step. The beeches along the path hung limp green heads in surrender to the sun. The shimmering heat seemed to have sucked the vitality out of the atmosphere so that the act of breathing was a conscious, uncomfortable effort of will, like swallowing a glass of tepid beer.

Heseltine, a man of strict routine, remembered the day and the conditions well. It was nearly tea-time and there were few people about. The stifling weather seemed to have cast a spell of inertia on the place. An officer was standing bareheaded on the steps of the mess as listlessly statuesque as any beech. The stranger did not notice Heseltine approaching. His eyes seemed to be with his mind, thousands of miles away from the sun-drenched uplands of Buckinghamshire. Only when Heseltine greeted him did he turn with a start, like a man brusquely roused from a day-dream. It was Cheshire and he looked drawn and flustered.

" Hallo, Heseltine. I didn't expect to see you. I'm just leaving."

" If it's transport you're waiting for, you've got a hope. You'll have a long wait on a day like this unless it's already laid on," said Heseltine. " Have you had tea ? "

" No, I wasn't going to bother about tea."

" Well, why not change your mind while I take care of the transport ? "

Cheshire hesitated, then agreed, and walked on into the mess where Heseltine joined him a few minutes later. As Bomber

Command security officer, he had met Cheshire several times before ; and his respect for the late commander of 617 Squadron had grown with each encounter. To most squadron commanders, visits from Heseltine were regrettable invasions which could be quickly repelled only by a mixture of firmness and rudeness.

Skirmishes with high-handed C.O.s were not to his liking but he possessed the patience and pertinacity of the lawyer. A First War pilot and a cultured man of taste who had cracked bottles in his time with G. K. Chesterton and his associates, he rarely paused to mourn over imaginary pinpricks to his vanity. By contrast, he could scarcely forget those commanders who put themselves out to lighten his unwelcome work. Cheshire was one of the few who invariably " unrolled the red carpet" whenever he put in an appearance.

He had always impressed the security officer as an " almost secretive character ", lacking the simple exuberance of the average pilot and the haughtiness of many commanders who " did not exactly hate themselves " ; but his refreshing " difference " communicated itself practically in an intuitive grasp of the need for water-tight security regulations. Heseltine did not then know that Cheshire's devoted regard for an unpopular subject could be traced back four years, to the day when his R.A.F. career hung on the thread of Air Commodore MacNeece Foster's indulgence. Nor, for that matter, did Air Marshal Harris, from whose room Cheshire had walked into the sultry afternoon stillness less than half an hour before.

He was still too stunned by what Harris had said to encourage Heseltine's efforts to make conversation. The inert unreality of the past seven weeks, sitting out the war as a Group Captain at Group Headquarters while the Allies blasted their way out of the Normandy bridgeheads deep into France under a massive air umbrella, had suddenly ended. For that at least he could be thankful. Though there was not the foggiest hope of his returning to lead a squadron against a target in Europe, Harris had hinted broadly that an overseas posting might offer an outside chance of flying again. The Far East was the obvious choice, and Cheshire was pleased to think that Harris had recommended it personally.

" Are you here for anything special ? "

Heseltine had to repeat the question.

" No, nothing special.   The C.-in-C. sent for me, and I kept turning over the various things he might have discovered against me all the way down."

" And he discovered nothing of interest ? "

" No, thank goodness.   I shan't be drummed out—yet."

Cheshire was holding something back, and Heseltine prudently changed the subject.   The security officer reflected that there were depths to this strangely aloof young man which could not be reached in a few minutes' random fishing.   His thoughts were far away again and the slightly dazed look was returning.

" What's it like being grounded again ? "

" Pretty dreary.   I can't get used to the feeling of being left out."

As Heseltine saw him into the car and wished him the best of luck he noticed again the repressed air of confusion.   What lay behind it, he wondered.   He had not long to wait for part of the answer.   It started as a shapeless rumour that same evening, and Heseltine pricked up his ears when a friend came up to him in the mess lounge :

" I expect you've heard the latest ? "

" No, what's it this time ? "

" They say Harris has dished out another V.C.   It's supposed to be going to that chap who ran 617 Squadron.   You know, Cheshire."

" Good God," exploded Heseltine.   " So that was it." Everything fell into place : the shyness, the reticence, the overwhelming sense of bewilderment.   He might have guessed it. At the bottom of Cheshire's elaborate conceit lay an extravagant humility.   Heseltine saw the puzzled expression on his friend's face :

" Cheshire was here this afternoon.   He looked as though he'd seen a ghost and didn't have a word to say about it."

Just over a week later, the newspapers picked up the official announcement from the *London Gazette*.   The familiar boyish face beamed above the columns of printed praise which recalled the exploits of a legendary operational career.

About breakfast-time that morning, Air Vice-Marshal Bennett answered the telephone at his home.   A Pathfinder colleague was on the line :

" Have you seen the papers yet, sir ? "

" No, why ? "

" Another V.C., and it's a gong for target marking."

" You mean it's gone to a Pathfinder ? " asked Bennett incredulously.

" No, not a Pathfinder. Cheshire. I wondered if you'd recommended him for it ! "

The officer found the situation morbidly ironic, and expressed gloomy disapproval of the stress laid on the Munich raid in the citation :

" After all, the ex-Pathfinders kept that attack going long after the 617 Squadron Mosquitos had left. It's a bit gruesome."

Bennett, who related this anecdote, was not impressed by the excuse that Cheshire and his deputy leaders had to leave the target early because their Mosquitos were not equipped with long-range petrol tanks. He disliked on principle the citation's reference to a marking method whose validity he doubts to this day.

" I have the greatest respect and admiration for Cheshire's guts and courage," he said. " But I hold no brief for his low-marking technique. It was spectacular and little more."

The reservations of the Pathfinders, which turned on a fine point of professional pride, were understandable. But none disputed that the supreme award recognised the unique personal qualities of a young man who had made an art of dicing successfully with death in defiance of all odds. The Victoria Cross is usually conferred for a single act of heroism, which explains why it is so often conferred posthumously. In Cheshire's case it was awarded in effect for four years of sustained courage, as the citation clearly implies :

" He led his squadron personally on every occasion, always undertaking the most dangerous and difficult task of marking the target alone from a low level. . . . Wing Commander Cheshire's cold and calculated acceptance of risks is exemplified by his conduct in an attack on Munich in April, 1944. . . .

" In four years of fighting against the bitterest opposition he has maintained a record of outstanding personal achievement, placing himself invariably in the forefront of the battle. What he did in the Munich operation was typical of the careful planning, brilliant execution and contempt for danger which has established for Wing Commander Cheshire a reputation second to none in Bomber Command."

There can have been few men in England more intrigued by
the news that September morning than Sir Charles Symonds,
the distinguished Harley Street neurologist, whom Cheshire had
consulted a mere twelve months before. The details of that
farcical interview with the likeable and inscrutable young man,
who had come complaining of anxiety-neurosis through doing
too little flying, were sharply etched in his memory. Subsequently, in the course of his ordinary duties as a service specialist,
he had visited 5 Group, met Cheshire again, and heard officially
of his inspired individualism.

" I am not competent to speak about his tactical contribution
to the air war," said Symonds, " but his personal contribution
to the morale and fighting efficiency of Bomber Command was
remarkable. By his own example, he certainly succeeded in a
short space of time in raising the normal standards of courage
and risk-taking. That is an achievement I was able to judge for
myself."

Events had indirectly justified Cheshire's startling self-
diagnosis ; but the more Symonds pondered, the less easy he
found it to fit him into any fixed category of fighting men.
Since the war, the neurologist has come to know Cheshire better ;
yet with all his experience and specialist knowledge to draw on,
he still places him in a class apart as a " brilliant eccentric " and
an outstanding exception to normal rules. Courage is a singular
virtue harder to define than to recognise. A great deal of glib
rubbish is written about it, especially in the life-stories of men
of action. For that reason, Sir Charles Symonds's evidence is
of unusual interest, if only for its dispassionate precision :

" I would say that Cheshire was 90% fearless and only 10%
courageous," he said. " There is a real distinction between
fearlessness and positive courage. The latter is a state of mind
in which fear is endured or overcome for the sake of attaining
some object.

" Normally it's the introspective man who knows the sweat
of apprehension before an attack and has to summon all his
powers of will to carry on. Cheshire, though an acutely sensitive
and introspective man, seemed as completely immune from
apprehension as the most phlegmatic and unimaginative types,
with whom the stolid quality of fearlessness is invariably
associated. He had the heart of a lion and the incisive brain of

the practical planner, so that risks appeared to him as impersonal obstacles made to be overcome.

" He had the foresight courage gives with none of the fear-fulness beforehand. Possibly Cheshire acquired this extraordinary habit of cold detachment by experience and the stimulus of success : for fearlessness born of courage is a far greater prize than courage itself. Yet it is improbable that any person, however great his strength of will, could go on consciously ringing down a sort of steel curtain between mind and emotions before every raid. Cheshire has always seemed to me, despite his frail appearance and his reflective nature, a man rarely if ever beset by natural fear. He was born fearless—or as nearly so as makes no difference."

Symonds's opinion may be scoffed at as a pseudo-scientific shot in the dark, as a tentative piece of intelligent guesswork with little bearing on the subject of this book. Guesswork or not, it seems to me an admirable commentary on a key element in Cheshire's character. For the basis of fearlessness is confidence ; and the dominant trait that had begun to distinguish him from his contemporaries even at Stowe was an overweening self-confidence born of loneliness and self-sufficiency. Ambition nurtured it at Oxford ; an almost superstitious belief in his own luck thickened and toughened its roots during the early years of war.

If Cheshire's self-consciousness saved him from becoming an unbearable egotist, his personal charm and healthy curiosity in other people and their affairs offset the secretive side of his nature. Without being wilfully selfish or oversensitive to the rights of others, his abundant self-confidence enabled him to make a virtue of impulsiveness. He was not content to wait for things to happen if there was the slightest chance of forcing the pace to make them happen first. He never seemed to doubt his capacity for inspiring others to follow him, and in war, success is the absolute yardstick of greatness.

Yet there was a gentler element, at first sight contradictory, entwined with Cheshire's basic self-confidence. It might be described as a negative kind of humility, which expressed itself in a steady awareness of what he owed to others. A man without true friends because he had never felt the need to open his heart fully to anyone, he was nevertheless surrounded always by reliable comrades who admired him enough as a personality to reciprocate the complete trust he placed in them. If he feared anything, Cheshire feared the possible failure caused by slipshod work before or after raids. The occupational risks of flying left him unafraid. He would rationalise them as factors in the game ; it was the business of a good commander to anticipate them by leaving no item in his planning to chance. Provided his weapons were perfect, he could have no cause for alarm.

That is why, with half his complex mind, Cheshire regarded his V.C. as an undeserved decoration. The fact that he had had to bear the sweat and strain of responsibility for the outcome of repeated missions meant little to him : he knew his strength too well to falter. Yet for all his vast self-confidence, he seemed eternally surprised that his men should go on trusting him. At least in the small air force world that revolved smoothly round himself, he took nothing and nobody for granted, so that the supreme award was somehow a collective tribute to the team-work of every member of a great squadron.

With the other half of his mind, the romantic and acquisitive half which thirsted for fame and was very susceptible to flattery, he had no difficulty at all in welcoming it. The role of " the shy V.C.", who privately derived not a little perverse amusement and pleasure from seeing his name and photograph splashed across the pages of newspapers and magazines, fulfilled an ambition and satisfied an old yearning.

2

Yet decorations were about the last subject Cheshire expected Harris to discuss when he entered his office at Bomber Command Headquarters. On the journey to High Wycombe he had been anxiously wondering whether the C.-in-C. had somehow un-earthed some half-forgotten military " crime " to hold against him. Cheshire did not mind that in itself, but the gambler in him was speculating how far such a discovery would lead Harris to oppose his request for a posting abroad.

" The work here is not to my liking, but I've made the best of it," he had written in a letter to his parents from 5 Group Headquarters. It was the same chronic complaint, with the same chronic symptoms of unrest and impending flight. Cochrane, knowing that Cheshire was thoroughly allergic to the obscure safety of desk work, had supported his application for a transfer.

For the whole half-hour he spent in Harris's presence, Cheshire's brain was in a whirl. A hard and belligerently practical man, the C.-in-C. had a " soft spot " for pilots who did not realise when they had done more than their stint of operations. The gruff gentleness of his welcome was the first shock ; the second was his statement, still in those velvety tones, that he wanted to congratulate him before anyone else on winning a V.C. Cheshire was reduced to a stunned silence. The V.C. of all things ! He had never thought of Harris as a " fatherly man " with feelings and a heart. The interview was like a fantasy with wish-fulfilment, a triumph of hope over experience.

Harris did not seem to notice his bewilderment. He was used to the spectacle. (" On every occasion when I informed anyone that they had been awarded that very high honour, they have invariably been overcome with astonishment and given me the impression that it was the last thing they expected or deserved," he told me.

" I have never known any recipient of the Victoria Cross not to be astonished at the news of the award—but I have sometimes met others astonished that they have not been awarded the Victoria Cross.")

Only when Harris asked him what he wanted to do did Cheshire recover his poise. The V.C. was a kind of unearned increment from the past ; Harris might shed his fairy godfather guise if pressed for a favour affecting the future, yet only the future mattered now. He must have freedom to fly, and this was the moment to secure it. His second shock was Harris's readiness to oblige.

" I'm going to a staff job," he told his parents in a jubilant letter the following day. " A very important one, with my old rank back. It was arranged personally by Harris, and I'm really fortunate. I have suddenly got my marching orders, and have to leave next week. Constance is going to the U.S.A. and from there, all being well, to India. . . ."

The short week for winding up his affairs lengthened to three while Constance waited for an exit permit. Her disillusionment might be deep, but experience had given her a buoyant sort of patience. She made the best of Cheshire's lonely craving for adventure, which had come between them like a jealous stranger and turned their marriage into an unheard-of version of the eternal triangle, with the R.A.F. at the apex and her husband always at its beck and call. For his part, Cheshire seemed content to maintain the unnatural relationship while there was serious work to be done.

He stayed at the Ritz during his last few days in England, was toasted by his former 617 colleagues at a send-off party to celebrate his V.C., and left Bournemouth in a Sunderland flying-boat on September 10th.

Just over a week later, in the clammy heat of the monsoon period, he reported to his new commanding officer in a converted jute mill outside Calcutta. Some of the R.A.F. officers on the Anglo-American staff of Major-General George Stratemeyer looked askance at the white-kneed newcomer from England who, with an exaggerated show of coyness, omitted to wear the ribbons of his decorations. Their early critical disapproval soon gave way to respect. He was eager to learn from scratch the difficult art of planning strategic bomber attacks on a tough, mobile enemy whose domains stretched unbroken across mountains, plains and steaming jungles from the Indo-Burmese border to the East Indies.

To the ordinary soldier in the forgotten 14th Army, or to the average airman servicing or piloting bombers and fighters, the war against Japan seemed a stagnant, dreary, interminable business. To the commanders in Delhi, Ceylon and the front line, there was always the comforting hope that a fanatical foe, who lived off the land over which he fought, callously indifferent to disease and superbly trained in the art of jungle warfare, would one day overreach himself. Brigadier Orde Wingate's first attempt at long-range jungle penetration had already proved that British troops could fight and win local success far behind the Japanese lines in that unnatural green hell.

The tactical air-arm had been the key to success, at last enabling the planners to see the skies as the only sure supply route over that roadless, disease-infested wilderness. While Stilwell prepared for an independent offensive in North-East Burma, which would keep pace with his new highway and pipe-line through the jungle of Northern Assam to the age-old Burma Road to China, Mountbatten kept up his own limited campaign,

in the centre and south, deploying aircraft and troops to harass
the enemy. In February, 1944, he snatched his first major victory
out of the jaws of probable disaster by the intelligent use of air
power.

An Army Corps of three divisions, under General A. P. E.
Christison, had pushed down the Arakan coast of Burma to
clear the Maungdaw Peninsula and seize Akyab. The Japanese
waited, then suddenly counter-attacked, outflanking the British,
Indian and West African troops and threatening to cut them to
ribbons as so often in the past. A quick change of tactics saved
the day for Christison. Instead of falling back and allowing the
enemy to surround and decimate his men in batches, Christison
stood firm. A hasty system of independent " boxes " was
organised in the heart of the jungle as it had once been organised
against Rommel in Libya, and each strong-point was kept
supplied by air. Then the heavy bombers struck at enemy
communications, so that the action became not a battle but a
struggle to maintain opposing lines of supply.

This was the turning-point. The Japanese had at last been
pinned down and robbed of mobility on the ground. For three
weeks British and American air crews dropped food, ammunition,
fuel and medicine ; then the intact forces of Christison regrouped
and advanced again. They were halted only by the start of a
fiercer and more critical battle hundreds of miles away in Upper
Burma.

Powerful Japanese thrusts were directed against Imphal and
Kohima, keypoints astride the one major highway winding like
a dark blue ribbon through the scrub-covered hills of the Indo-
Burmese frontier. If the road and the two towns fell, there
would be little to prevent the enemy from sweeping down the
Manipur Road into India according to plan.

But the Japanese lunges were checked and turned by a still
bolder and more flexible use of air power.

Before the Japanese could clinch their advantage of tactical
surprise, the 5th Indian division was lifted from the Arakan over
the heads of the enemy. Further reinforcements were flown
into beleaguered Imphal from India. It was harder to build
up the sparse defences of Kohima ; the nearest airfield lay many
miles down the road and the Japanese lost no time in cutting
off the town. Yet throughout the bitter battle from April 4th

until April 20th, when British troops finally broke through to raise the siege, non-stop supply runs were made by Dakotas threading up the steep Manipur Road and releasing their canisters over the shrinking battlefield itself.

Cheshire had been revelling in the triumph of his own tactical ideas nearly 6000 miles away during that ferocious, unequal clash between an entire Japanese division and an exposed, weakened force of a battalion and a half—odds of nearly ten to one—on the hillsides at Kohima. He had a personal reason for grasping its historic importance: Jack Randle, his closest companion at Oxford, had died a hero's death when the siege was lifted and the winkling out of Japanese from bunkers dominating the road to Imphal had begun. On May 6th, Randle attacked a bunker single-handed, silenced the machine-guns with a hand-grenade, and—mortally wounded—sealed the aperture with his bullet-riddled body. His gallantry had rallied his company; his self-sacrifice had saved many lives; it made Cheshire feel small to think of Jack's posthumous V.C.

The indomitable defiance of the defenders of Kohima and Imphal halted the enemy offensive; but their will to resist was heightened by the close tactical support of the air-arm, directed by Air Chief Marshal Peirse, whom Cheshire had once flown from the Orkneys in a Halifax. Had the aircraft not been available to switch reinforcements from one Burmese front to another, drop supplies in the thick of the fray, and deny the enemy infantry the cover of their own army-air force by superior aggressive skill, the Allies would have suffered one of the most catastrophic defeats of the entire war. The conquest of India at a jog-trot would undoubtedly have followed.

During the summer of 1944, the strategic situation was transformed. The Japanese pulled back, leaving the bodies of 30,000 men behind. Slim's "Forgotten Army" pushed on and forced the Chindwin River. In the north-east Stilwell's American-Chinese columns took Myitkyina. By mid-September, when Cheshire took up his appointment on Stratemeyer's air planning staff, the tide had turned in Burma.

Although aircraft had been used repeatedly to help ground troops out of tight corners, by no means all the Army commanders yet regarded their use as essential for victory in the jungle. It was still commonly assumed that the throwing of

bombers and fighters into the battle had been imposed by the
exceptional threat of calamity. This narrow outlook sprang
naturally from the independent traditions of the two services
and it flourished during the two months Cheshire spent in the
Far East. The Supreme Commander, South-East Asia, Lord
Louis Mountbatten, fortunately possessed a mind as broad and
as lively as Eisenhower's or Tedder's; he saw the strategic
problem in a more positive light. Not until early 1945, however,
were the revolutionary possibilities of an integrated army-air
campaign fully demonstrated.

Cheshire, like many other staff officers, was baffled and
depressed at first by the discrepancy of service interests and the
endless array of tactical problems. The number of individual
irons in the fire sometimes seemed to him ominously likely to
put it out. For the South-East Asia Command had long been
the starved Cinderella of all Allied theatres of war.

There was nothing to do but gloomily accept the poor supply
position and acknowledge the daily miracles of improvisation
performed by the air maintenance units. Yet Cheshire still
nursed the belief that his own brand of low-level strategic
bombing could be carried out in the Far East with even greater
effect than in Europe :

" Conditions are favourable to its employment," he wrote in
an official paper. " It requires a very small force as opposed to
the large force required by the Pathfinders, and, given a high
enough priority in crews and equipment, could be guaranteed to
produce the same results as it did in 617. The success of very
long-range bombing will depend entirely on whether or not a
satisfactory solution can be found to the problem of providing an
adequate aiming point. Unless this solution is found, the R.A.F.
will compare unfavourably with the U.S. Army Air Force B29s
which already possess many advantages over the Lancaster."

In this paper, copies of which were circulating at Air Ministry
early in 1945, Cheshire seemed already to be anticipating the day
when the best crews in Bomber Command would join the
Americans in delivering the *coup de grâce* against Japan. 5 Group
was in fact alerted for that purpose in the spring of 1945, but the
proposed switch was partly forestalled by the tempo of events in
the Pacific.

Early in November, 1944, the single long-range precision

bombing raid which Cheshire had a large say in planning took place in dazzling moonlight. The target was Bangkok, over 1100 miles away from the bases in India. A small force of Liberators of the Strategic Air Force, then under the command of the late Air Commodore F. J. W. Mellersh, carried incendiaries and attacked from very low level. Bangkok stood at one end of the infamous " Death Railway ", built by Allied prisoners at a cost of nearly 25,000 lives. This experimental attack was only one of several heavy blows against the rail link which carried half the supplies for the Japanese facing the 14th Army. But the technique and timing were novel, the results devastating. Cheshire's secret sorrow was that he was not allowed to lead the raid himself.

In off-duty hours, he gave an impression of preferring his own company ; and the studied reserve of the " shy but collected V.C. from England " was the trait which others remembered. Everyone knew and respected the legend ; none, not even General Stratemeyer whom Cheshire genuinely liked, could penetrate the aura of mystery to the man behind it. Only once did he seem to extend himself socially in a way that attracted mild wonder. That was when an Air Vice-Marshal from England loomed up like an unfriendly ghost to spend two or three days at headquarters before completing his journey to China as the head of a military mission to the government of Chiang Kai Shek.

MacNeece Foster, his former base commander at Abingdon, was almost as embarrassed as Cheshire by the encounter. Neither had forgotten the burning humiliation of the incident more than four years before, which almost led to Cheshire's summary discharge from the R.A.F.

" Who's the A.V.M. Cheshire's making such an awkward fuss of ? " an observant Wing Commander asked his friend one evening.

" Don't know. He looks like an old family friend or something."

Cheshire's deferential show of attentiveness was puzzling. Only MacNeece Foster understood its meaning. And each was dumbly grateful, and relieved beyond measure, when the slow ordeal ended.

One stray flash of originality lit up the last days of Cheshire's short stay in India as a staff planner. There was much discussion of an air plan for the invasion of Akyab, an island off the Arakan coast which Mountbatten regarded as a first stepping-stone in his sea-borne campaign to catch the Japanese in the rear. A colossal air attack was considered necessary to silence its supposedly strong defences. The S.E.A.C. Commander insisted that nothing should be left to chance; intelligence reports indicated that saturation with the heaviest bombs available was the safest remedy for Akyab's hidden gun batteries and bunkers. Cheshire was sceptical. It seemed to him a prodigious waste of effort, as ill-conceived as a 1000-bomber attack on the Black Forest in Germany. Putting a shrewd finger on the weakest point in the plan, the flimsy and unconfirmed reports of enemy movements in the Akyab area, he was calmly prepared to back his own " hunch " against everyone. Between November 3rd and November 8th he called on several high-ranking officers, including General Christison, Commander of the 15th Corps, which was advancing down the Arakan coast. Christison pointed out the Japanese dispositions as far as they were known. When Cheshire asked whether the information about the enemy order-of-battle on Akyab was reliable, the General retorted rather acidly that fragmentary intelligence was better than no intelligence at all. Still far from satisfied, Cheshire decided to do a little reconnoitring on his own account.

On November 13th, with only a map to guide him, he walked across the airfield at Cox's Bazaar and climbed into a Hurricane. Two hours and ten minutes later, he climbed out and startled local senior officers by stating that he had been on a reconnaissance flight to Akyab, where there appeared to be no defences at all. From tree-top level, the place looked entirely deserted.

At first nobody would believe him. It sounded a typically tall story, especially from a Group Captain who had never handled a Hurricane before, or operated against the Japanese, and who was indeed forbidden by his position as a man " who knew too much " to fly over enemy-held territory. But Cheshire insisted that he was telling the sober truth; and Air Marshal Coryton, Cochrane's predecessor at 5 Group, who now commanded the Tactical Air Force, listened with perplexed interest as they flew back to Chittagong next day in a Flying Fortress.

Cheshire described how he had hurtled across the jungle

and approached Akyab respectfully at 8000 feet. No guns fired at him, so he circled lower and lower until he could examine the ground closely. He had seen no defenders or defences. In fact the abandoned huts and absence of all military movement suggested that the Japanese had already pulled out.

It incensed him when his written report was taken lightly for the irrelevant reason that his reconnaissance mission was unauthorised. Even the realistic Stratemeyer seemed to regard his solitary evidence as too slender to justify any drastic revision of the Akyab air plan.

The official incredulity flicked his vanity on the raw. Nearly two months passed before an authorised reconnaissance sortie confirmed Cheshire's evidence. By then, his premature discovery from the cockpit of a borrowed Hurricane was tactfully forgotten. Had he remained in India, he would probably have prodded his superiors into reluctant action. But within a week of his clandestine flight, Cheshire was on his way to the bedside of his sick wife in New York. He did not return to South-East Asia, so that the R.A.F. historian could afterwards write with impunity and a good conscience :

" On 2nd January, 1945, the pilots of two Hurricanes, flying low over Akyab, saw a number of inhabitants waving their arms to signify that the Japanese had left the island. A few hours later a former judge of the island, Wing Commander J. B. G. Bradley, of the Royal New Zealand Air Force, landed in a light aircraft to be greeted by the local doctor. Akyab was occupied without opposition and Christison's offensive had attained all its objects."

3

The wire from Constance's sister was laconic, but its effect on Cheshire was instantaneous. His wife was seriously ill, he had been urged to come at once, yet the message had taken nearly three weeks to arrive. For all he knew, Constance might already be dead. Without a second thought he applied at once for compassionate leave. It seemed a hopeless gesture, until General Stratemeyer intervened on his behalf.

" He cabled straight to General Arnold in Washington and got me an answer in twenty-four hours," Cheshire told his father.

" Stratemeyer also arranged an air passage to New York. I shall be going there as soon as I get R.A.F permission. They've already been three days making up their minds."

Shortly before Cheshire left Calcutta on November 20th, Stratemeyer handed him a sealed letter :

" I want you to give this to General Arnold personally," he said. " Remember, I'm counting on you to return within a month. Don't let me down."

Somewhat hesitantly, the R.A.F. had accepted Stratemeyer's strong recommendation that Cheshire could and should be released temporarily on compassionate grounds ; for his part Cheshire readily promised not to overstay his leave.

He regretted having given his word on reaching the New York nursing home and discovering how ill Constance really was. The specialists left him in no doubt where his duty as a husband lay. She was suffering from a severe nervous break-down and he must stay with her as long as the crisis lasted. They were not concerned with his undertaking to Stratemeyer ; as doctors familiar with Constance's case-history, they were at pains to point out that the responsibility for her state of health was his alone.

Cheshire, who had spent much of his twenty-seven years extricating himself smartly from quandaries contrived by himself, hardly knew where to turn. Unwilling to let Stratemeyer down, he could not bring himself to abandon Constance in her distress. The feckless past seemed to have caught up with him at a most inopportune moment. Trapped again between opposite and conflicting loyalties, but moved now by his wife's utter depen-dence on him, he explained his dilemma to Air Marshal Colyer, of the British Joint Staff Mission, when handing over Strate-meyer's sealed letter to Arnold in Washington.

With the problem out of his own hands, Cheshire ceased to be perturbed by any misunderstandings that might arise in the impersonal exchanges between Calcutta and Washington. Legally he was in the clear ; and the possibly outraged feelings of Stratemeyer, when presented with the accomplished fact of his " desertion," seemed suddenly less important. His decision to remain with Constance was as clear-cut as earlier decisions to leave her for further tours of operations. Any qualms about the inconsistency of his behaviour, any concern about the good opinion of Stratemeyer or others, were driven out by the over-riding claims of compassion, an unsuspected chink in his adventurer's armour which had never been put to such a test before.

His leave was extended ; and Cheshire spent the Christmas of 1944 with his wife in the New York nursing home. This harrowing existence continued until early in the New Year when Constance was well enough to accompany him to Washington. He had not felt equal to the unpromising task of excusing himself to Stratemeyer for a seemingly flagrant breach of trust. Meanwhile, there had been no difficulty in attaching him to the British Joint Staff Mission.

One or two letters of the period suggest that he was conscious of having landed on his feet too easily. Gradually, however, he put aside his uneasiness and began to enjoy the specialised work of keeping abreast of Allied technical and tactical developments in the air war. From March until June scarcely a week passed without an official visit to factories, service depots or training centres in various parts of North America. Cheshire's log-book shows that he piloted himself on the longest journeys, shuttling between Washington and Nassau, Toronto, Los Angeles, Pensacola and Ohio in a neat little Beechcraft, a machine which he had quickly learnt to handle in India.

The war had by-passed him again. Yet the hustling, dynamic earnestness of the American approach to it, and the massive scale of their preparations for settling the final account with Japan, tended to keep the remote Pacific battlefield in his mind's eye. Cheshire found himself reflecting fairly often on the strident patriotism of Americans, comparing its form favourably and unfavourably with the British. A gigantic slogan above the gates of the embarkation depot at San Francisco, shrieking with lusty pride : " Through these portals pass the best damn soldiers in the world," epitomised a way of living and fighting with which he was only partly in sympathy. He once tried to express the difference on paper :

" The greatness of the American forces lies not in the personal courage of the individual serviceman, but in mass organisation and mass output. These are qualities which no other military machine in the world has equalled. In Britain, mass production is limited to industry. In America it extends to the battlefield."

Cheshire was too judicious to blurt out such private thoughts, but he could point the moral without giving offence when called upon to write and speak about the point-blank bombing technique he had developed with 617 Squadron. A method which depended far more on sharp eyes and cool nerves than on mechanical infallibility had a paradoxical old-world flavour which seemed to intrigue the American officers and business executives who read or heard Cheshire's words.

The gay informality of the social round in Washington and farther afield revived wistful memories of the summer of 1941. The happiness he had counted on from marriage had dwindled into a dull dutifulness. Life with Constance in 37th Street was emptier than the hours he spent in the huge Public Health building where the Joint Staff Mission worked. None of his colleagues guessed that he was often a worried man.

What held him to Constance was a strong sense of loyalty in which pity outweighed affection. The very qualities in her which once attracted now bored him. The meaning had gone out of the match, and with it the harmony; but he could not yet bring himself to unmask his true feelings and demand his freedom. Official Washington was a small, talkative world.

There were portentous happenings, too, to distract his mind. A wave of genuine grief swept through the capital when President Roosevelt died in the middle of April. One of the two great architects of victory had disappeared. His prosaic successor was at first a subject of curious and sometimes jocular interest over cocktails. Yet within a month of his moving into the White House, Mr. Harry S. Truman, the newly constituted Commander-in-Chief, had to face the fact of a terrible weapon which science was perfecting in the utmost secrecy. His Secretary for War, Mr. Henry L. Stimson, has graphically described the occasion :

" I did not see Franklin Roosevelt again. The next time I went to the White House to discuss atomic energy was April 25th, 1945, and I went to explain the nature of the problem to a man whose only previous knowledge of our activities was that of a senator who had loyally accepted our assurance that the matter must be kept a secret from him.

" Now he was President and Commander-in-Chief, and the

final responsibility in this as in so many other matters must be his. . . ."

Major-General Leslie R. Groves, the military head of the project, was at that momentous White House meeting with Truman and the ageing Stimson. There had been inspired whisperings that the mysterious Manhattan Project was " costing the earth " and might well be " a dud " ; but the detailed memorandum Stimson now placed before Truman disposed officially of the rumours :

" Within four months," it began, " we shall in all probability have completed the most formidable weapon ever known in human history. . . ."

The wrongheaded rumours were regarded by the security services as a good form of insurance against any serious leakage of information. But if they reached the cupped ears of Congressmen, they never reached the ears of Cheshire. His thoughts were already romping ahead to the future, when the war against Japan had been won by the same conventional weapons as the war against Germany.

One of the firm business openings he seriously considered was an offer to join a large American radio concern. Building speculative castles in the air had been a hobby of his at Woodhall Spa, and the aircrews of 617 had unanimously welcomed his plan for a luxury hotel in the Bahamas. It was a pity Nassau seemed so overcrowded with luxury hotels when he cast a prospector's eye about him during a brief but pleasant stay there.

Dreams of the future were thrust aside in July when Cheshire boarded a B.O.A.C. Clipper at Baltimore. Christopher, his brother, had been repatriated after four years in a German prison compound ; and Cheshire ingeniously found a way of arranging an official visit to London at the psychological moment. Once established in the Ritz, with his brother as his guest, the intervening years receded as though they had never been. Among the soft lights and discreetly expensive surroundings of the clubs and cocktail lounges he had haunted since his undergraduate days, Cheshire quickly recovered the infectious *joie de vivre* that Christopher well remembered.

On the flight back to Washington he wrestled with the problem of his marriage. The nostalgic break from routine enabled him to view it with new impatient eyes as a pathetic farce that had been unduly prolonged. By the time the aircraft landed, he had decided to tell Constance that he was leaving her for ever.

4

The remaining days he spent with his wife were embittered and desolate. Yet it was a relief to have laid bare at last the thickets of small annoyances which had been stifling him for so long. He had announced at once his intention of going his own way, though for the present, until the R.A.F. posted him elsewhere, he would continue to stay under the same roof for the sake of convenience and appearances.

The emotional tension was miraculously eased and ended by service commitments which this time owed nothing to his own contriving.

During the third week of July he was unexpectedly sent for by Field-Marshal Wilson, the head of the British Joint Staff Mission. Wilson told him of his recent trip to Potsdam, where the Allied leaders had swiftly decided to use the atom bomb against Japan. An experimental weapon had been successfully detonated in the New Mexican Desert on July 16th, and the dramatic news had been rushed to President Truman immediately. Considerations of prestige warranted that Britain should be officially represented when the weapon was brought into action. The War Cabinet in London had insisted on this as a matter of right ; the President had agreed in principle at Potsdam ; and the American authorities, though reluctant to admit Allied " spectators ", had finally consented to let a distinguished British scientist fly in the raids, accompanied by one R.A.F. representative.

As he left the Field-Marshal's office, Cheshire's brain seethed with an excitement Wilson had expressly asked him not to show. The need for absolute secrecy had been made very plain to him ; and for two awkward days he had to keep a sharp rein on his tongue. Yes, he was going out West for a while. . . . No, nothing to write home about . . . San Francisco and the Conference, probably . . . Playing messenger boy to some pompous politician planning to rebuild a better world or something equally dreary. . . . Evasion and quick mental reservation became the conscious order of the day. He was like a secret

agent marooned and tongue-tied in his own family circle on the
eve of a perilous mission.

After further briefings from Major-General Groves, the
military director of the Manhattan Project, and Professor
Chadwick, the head of the British nuclear team of scientists,
Cheshire flew to San Francisco, spent two or three more watchful
days in the company of friends, and on July 24th started off on
his long westward journey by air, in the track of the sun, to
Guam.

The thrill of this final operation blotted out the morbid
memories of his broken marriage ; Constance was already someone he had met in a previous existence. Everything pointed
like a signpost to the mysterious adventure that lay ahead ; and
Guam itself, the administrative heart of the Marianas, 8000 miles
from San Francisco, teemed with solid symbols of the American
gift for organising battles on unanswerable terms.

The busy four-lane military roads, the broad runways of
dazzling coral for endless streams of aircraft, and the new military
town that surrounded the headquarters buildings had not existed,
even on paper, a year ago. The " Seabees ", as the Americans
nicknamed their naval construction battalions, had moved in
nonchalantly with the first waves of attacking Marines as though
the outcome of the battle were never in doubt. The simple
local people, squeezing a living out of small plots of land or
doing unskilled jobs for the new conquerors, reminded Cheshire
with a start that the physical transformation of Guam was a
tactical move in a campaign and not a measure of enlightened
colonial policy.

The metamorphosis was even more breathtaking on Tinian,
where Cheshire landed as a passenger in a C47 transport aircraft
on July 26th. The green top of the island seemed to have been
cut back to the bone. Working round the clock in shifts, pausing
only when air-raid warnings at night extinguished the naked
lights, the naval engineers had used bulldozers to flatten hills,
fill in valleys, and turn Tinian into the largest operational airfield
on earth. Empty trucks still moved in assembly line order to
the lips of the huge quarries, then surged on again with fresh
cargoes of the hard, porous coral.

The first runway, 6000 feet long, had been laid within three
months of the landings almost exactly a year before. The last

had been completed in May.   But the B29s had been pounding
the cities of Japan from neighbouring Guam and Saipan since
the closing weeks of 1944, redoubling their blows as more and
more runways in the Marianas were completed.   Fire-raising
attacks had begun in the spring, when Tokyo, Yokohama, Kobe
and Osaka were scourged as mercilessly as Hamburg had been
scourged by Harris.   The results were baldly stated by General
Arnold in his Second Report, on February 26th, 1945 :

" Over 100,000 tons of bombs were dropped in the course of
more than 15,000 sorties against sixty-six Japanese cities. . . .
Nearly one hundred and sixty-nine square miles were destroyed
or damaged in the sixty cities for which photographic reconnaissance is available, with more than one hundred square miles
burned out in the five major cities attacked."

Cheshire's respect for the prodigious American art of running
the Pacific air war on Big Business lines was unbounded during
his first few days on Tinian.   He could not get away from the
tangible proofs of its supreme reasonableness—the giant Superfortresses, alone capable of 20-hour missions to the home islands,
the airfields, the well-furnished huts, tents and warehouses, the
pipelines for water and fuel, the hospitals, swimming-pools and
cinemas, the new harbour, even the prison camp of Churo three
miles away in what remained of the bush, where Japanese
civilians were interned in material conditions far better than
they had ever known.

The British scientist whom Wilson had mentioned arrived
soon after Cheshire ; and the man was much more *sympathique*
than he expected.   Sir William Penney, as he now is, had none
of the " stuffiness " of the long-haired scientist of popular
caricature.   His straight, fair hair occasionally flopped down
over his broad forehead when he moved his head.   A captivating
grin was the badge of his unassuming simplicity.   It broke out
at the corners of his mouth, into which a pipe was perpetually
clamped, and spread across the whole face until the humorous
eyes behind the horn-rimmed spectacles disappeared in wreaths
of wrinkles.   The American nuclear experts on Tinian regarded
Penney as one of the finest mathematicians on earth.   Cheshire
took to him as " an ordinary chap " with no affectations and
unusual human understanding.

Being the only two Englishmen on the island they shared

the same tent in the atomic compound assigned to the scientists, special observers and senior officers. Penney was a good listener, and he could admire without always condoning Cheshire's unrestrained enthusiasm for the American pattern of war. He had never met a young man so steeped in the techniques of mass destruction : he seemed to the scientist an outstanding symbol of a generation which had reached manhood on the battlefield and found its only ideals there.

" He was a slight young man," Penney recalls, " with very black hair and dark brown eyes. He tanned easily and his skin was already brown when we met first in late July, 1945. One of his many remarkable qualities was his ability to wear his clothes as if they had just been pressed and put on. In that hot, steaming atmosphere khaki shirts and drill trousers rapidly lost their shape and became wet with perspiration. . . .

" His lively manner, through which showed at once the authority of his brain and his combat experiences, made a great impression on the American Air Force officers of the two special squadrons which were part of the Atomic Weapons Group. At once he became warm friends with several of the pilots, most of whom had also experienced the horrors of aerial warfare in Europe.

" Ours was one of about twenty tents assigned to scientists and service officers of the Manhattan District. In the tent nearest to ours was Captain W. S. Parsons, U.S.N. (the late Rear-Admiral Parsons), while on the other side were the two security officers !

" For about two weeks there was little work for any of us to do. The bombs were not ready, and there were few technical preparations to make. The aircraft were kept tuned up for immediate flying, and a few practice flights were made. Although there were many thousands of men on the island, and hundreds of B29 bombers, we saw little of the other groups. Rumours of what we were to do had spread, and sometimes in the swimming-pools curious glances were thrown at us but nothing was said."

Every night, without fail, there was the angry droning of mighty supercharged engines, and streams of Superfortresses would take off and head out into the starry sky towards Japan. Everyone sensed that the climax of the war was near. Wild, contradictory reports spread like luxuriant tropical creepers. Everyone assumed that the Japanese had rejected the Allied

ultimatum of July 26th, stressing the catastrophic consequences
that would follow if the final demand for immediate and unconditional surrender were ignored. But nobody knew for certain,
and speculation in the atomic compound became wearisome and
morbid. When the bombers left Tinian carrying leaflets as well
as bombs, they feared that the Allies were giving the people of
Japan too broad a hint of their impending fate. Copies of the
ultimatum and warnings that their city would be next on the
target list were being dropped on a score of places. Would
they take the hint, would their rulers let them, before the atom
bombs could be assembled and used ? That was the paralysing
obsession that gradually laid hold of Cheshire and others.

" During those final days before the atomic attacks," Cheshire
wrote to me five years ago, " a more authoritative rumour began
to circulate. It said that the Japanese were on the point of
surrender. We learnt later that it had been true. Far from
causing us to hope that the attacks would be postponed, it only
served to aggravate our obsession to see the bombs explode.
Indeed I and the majority of the others were determined that if
the surrender took place, some means should be found of keeping
the war going until the attacks had been launched."

When the two atomic cores arrived, the first by battleship
and the second by air in a portable yellow box, the obsession
became a palpable, nerve-racking duel between hope and fear.
The noisy routine activity elsewhere on the island, the harsh
reverberations of drills in the coral quarries, the constant throb
of aircraft, the ceaseless movement of trucks up and down the
chequer board of roads named and numbered after the main
avenues of Manhattan, New York—all this formed an unreal
background to the only reality that mattered. The scientists set
to work at once in the steel huts ; yet their enviable air of
detachment as they handled the cores and discussed technicalities
in the half-secret language of their rite was not wholly convincing.
Even they were reluctant victims of the dull, stabbing uncertainty
which robbed the ritual of half its meaning.

" We were expecting that some gestures would be made by
the Japanese, causing Washington to order us not to proceed,"
Penney stated dryly. " But nothing like this happened, and the
weapons team acted on the orders to which they were working."

Cheshire spent hours listening and watching in the steel

hut, following the abstruse conversation in snatches. He could always turn to Penney for brief, sensible explanations of parts he missed.

The uncertainty continued until August 4th. Then the incredible happened. That morning Cheshire discovered with a shock of horror and dismay that the " orders " excluded Penney and himself from flying on the atomic raids. He burst into the tent and told the scientist what General Farrell had just told him :

" It's fantastic, Bill," he said. " I reminded Farrell that we came here officially and that we don't intend to be pushed about to suit them."

" Did he give any reason ? " asked Penney.

" He said they'd decided it would be risky taking extra people."

" Meaning us ? "

" Meaning us. A damned likely story."

Cheshire was angry in a cold, controlled way. Penney, more accustomed to the inscrutable workings of the bureaucratic mind, agreed that they must protest but seemed unsure whether protesting would be of any avail.

" I think I'll go right over Farrell's head and tackle LeMay," said Cheshire suddenly. " At least he may know what's behind this maddening decision."

He had a reason for believing that the American Tactical Air Force Commander, General Curtis LeMay, might be more helpful. Cheshire had already met him briefly and had been flattered by his close interest in the low-level marking technique of 617 Squadron. The general had gone so far as to suggest that Cheshire would be doing himself a favour and the Allied cause a service by joining his staff to train American pilots. The friendly invitation might possibly be used now as a bargaining counter. In an emergency as uncalled for as this, half a foot in any door was better than none.

LeMay rose from his chair as Cheshire entered.

" Come on in, Group Captain. What can we do for you ? "

A sixth sense told him that LeMay already knew the real purpose of his sudden visit. The general's smile and the heartiness of his welcome seemed forced and bogus, as though he were uncomfortably conscious of playing the diplomat.

" Remember that proposal you made to me about teaching low-level marking ? " asked Cheshire. " I've been thinking a lot about it, and I'd like to take you up on it."

" Proposal ? " echoed LeMay blankly. The mask of bon-homie had disappeared. He was his wary self again.

" Now let's get this straight. I never made you a firm proposal. And right now I'm too busy to be interested. Maybe I'll think again later on, but we'll have to see."

It was the heavy stalling of a man who had no intention of being lured into a false position. Yet if Le May was unable to grant favours, he should at least explain why two Allied observers were all of a sudden being treated like potential spies :

" You know, sir, about the predicament Penney and myself are in ? "

LeMay confirmed with a nod that he knew.

" Can you use your influence to smooth it out ? We think there's some misunderstanding somewhere."

" Sorry, there's nothing I can do. And there's no mis-understanding. We have our orders, and we're carrying them out. That's all."

A happy afterthought came to the general as he showed Cheshire to the door :

" I can guarantee you this. After the raids, I'll see you both get the official reports at once. Beyond that I can't go."

The absurdity of the offer irritated Cheshire. He asked quietly whether the general imagined the British Government had sent Penney and himself all the way to Tinian to sit and wait complacently for second-hand reports. LeMay shrugged his shoulders indifferently. Even generals were inhumanly con-ditioned by the massive, mechanical rigidity of the American pattern of war.

Penney was inclined to agree with Cheshire's opinion that they were the unwitting victims of a higher policy decision. The attitude of General Carl Spaatz, who arrived unheralded the next morning, appeared to confirm it. Spaatz was genuinely delighted to see Cheshire and chatted informally about his visit to Woodhall Spa in 1944. But the Pacific Air Force Commander-in-Chief's geniality froze into embarrassment when Cheshire asked for his help.

" You may not believe it," he said at length, " but I can't

raise a finger for you. This is a Washington ruling. You'd need
the personal authorisation of President Truman himself to fly
to Japan, and I doubt now whether you could get it in time."

Spaatz at any rate had stated the exact, hopeless, damnably
frustrating position. Penney and Cheshire retired to their tent
and cast desperately about for some loophole in this front of
iron indifference. They had been idling in the sun for two whole
weeks without the faintest hint from anyone that their credentials
were valueless. It seemed as though they had been purposely
misled, yet there was nobody within eight thousand miles who
could right the injustice. Tinian was shut off from all direct
communication with the Allied world by a tight security censor-
ship. Any message they might send to Washington would
almost certainly be . . .

"Wait a minute, Bill," said Cheshire excitedly. "I think
I've got it. Let's send a really stiff signal to the Joint Staff
Mission, not mincing our words about the fix we're in. I doubt
if the American censors would dare to stop it."

Penney reflected for a moment. It was a long shot, worth
trying. The time factor was against them, of course ; any delay
at either end would probably be fatal. They settled down and
drafted the message, making it unambiguously clear that the
American refusal to let them fly was the result of a higher policy
decision and not of a local technical hitch. The message was
handed in with a top-priority grading, creating the diversionary
panic among high-ranking American officers it had been designed
to create. Spaatz and LeMay thought better than to stop it.
The formal protest of two aggrieved Englishmen was too full of
political dynamite to be conveniently mislaid by the censors.

Cheshire's ephemeral satisfaction did not survive the briefing,
next day, of crews and scientific observers for the attack on
Hiroshima. Penney and himself could not sleep for frustration
after the aircraft took off without them in the small hours of
August 6th. A week before they had all been in the hands of the
Mikado : one faltering word from him would have forestalled
the atomic fury. Now the pair of them were just as powerless
in the grip of these unimaginative Americans. Only the immediate intervention of Field-Marshal Wilson in Washington could
release them in time for the last act.

The agonising suspense lasted for another day and a half,

I

shadowing Colonel Tibbets and his crew in the lone B29 all the
way to Hiroshima, battening enviously on the incredible, halting
descriptions of atomic violence when the *Enola Gay* returned.
The reprieve came through just when Cheshire had begun to
give up hope.

"By midday on August 8th," said Penney, "weather conditions were judged suitable, and almost at that same moment
permission came from Washington for Cheshire and me to
fly. . . .

"During the evening, the air crews, scientists and observers
were briefed. We were given the standard type of briefing
together with a few extras such as not looking at the bomb
with the naked eye. The information which made the strongest
impression on me was the position of two sea-rescue ships,
should we have to come down in the sea.

"The three planes took off successfully in the early hours of
the morning on August 9th, and we got to our rendezvous
without incident. We had flown fairly high to take advantage
of the winds, and we were ready. Round and round we went,
but never saw another plane."

At this point, off Yakoshima island and within easy reach of
their alternative targets, Cheshire went through the wind-tunnel
to the forward pressurised cabin of the B29. Major Hopkins
the pilot, his navigator and his bomb-aimer seemed unaccountably worried. Sitting bolt upright in their steel-framed parachute
harnesses, they looked like men in strait-jackets :

"Everything under control ?" Cheshire asked.

"No, it's not," said Hopkins. "Something must have
happened to the two leading aircraft. They should have reached
the rendezvous minutes ago."

"They've probably gone ahead," said Cheshire. "I think
we've kept them waiting, not the other way. We're 20,000 feet
higher than we should be according to last night's briefing."

Then one of the Americans noticed that Cheshire was not
wearing his parachute harness :

"Do you want to die young ?" he asked indignantly. "You
should be wearing one of these things."

Cheshire brushed aside the interruption. He could see that
Hopkins was in two minds whether to fly on or return to base.
Hovering over the pilot, he used all his powers of persuasion

to make him continue. The thought of turning back after coming so far was unbearable. At length Hopkins agreed to proceed, but not before ordering his wireless operator to send to Tinian the disturbing message which betrayed his apprehension and plunged those left behind into an agony of sweating uncertainty :

" Has the aircraft with the bomb aborted ? "

" Finally," concludes Penney's tactful narrative, " we decided that the other planes had gone on and that we also should proceed to the primary target. When we got there, the clouds were thick and we seldom saw the ground. After spending half an hour there, we decided to go to the secondary target, Nagasaki.

" We were about forty miles away from Nagasaki when we saw a flash, followed by the billowing mushroom cloud. There was little we could do except circle in the air, well away from the cloud, and try to see what was happening on the ground. Cheshire's experience enabled *him* to see things that were not apparent to the rest of us. The whole of the city was hidden in dust and smoke, but very few fires were visible. Cheshire drew a sketch of what he thought was happening, and the description he gave later, with the aid of the sketch, was remarkably accurate.

" The smoke pall seemed to be ever-increasing, and after watching for nearly an hour we left for Tinian. However, our fuel was low, and we landed at Okinawa for further supplies. We got back to Tinian about six in the evening, to find that the other planes had been back for several hours.

" All of us were in a state of severe emotional shock. We realised that a new age had begun and that possibly we had all made some contribution to raising a monster that would consume us all. None of us could sleep. We argued well into the night, and in our talks were raised the same tremendous issues that have been debated ever since."

The scientists were more articulate and dispassionate than the service officers, whose awe and numbed bewilderment were slowly replaced by varying degrees of apathy, approval or condemnation. The common reaction of wholesale condemnation was one Cheshire could not understand. Like everyone else, he had been appalled by the unimaginable power of the plutonium bomb ; but he refused to let his trained airman's

mind be dominated by irrational details. Instead, he listened
with respect to the scientists discussing the deeper implications
for all mankind.

The late United States Secretary for War, Mr. Stimson,
publicly admitted in 1947 that the nuclear experts were consulted
and their views made known to President Truman before the
successful atomic test in the Mexican desert. At that time
scientific opinion on the question of using the bomb against
the Japanese had been divided, with a majority favouring the
course adopted at Potsdam. Opinion was far more evenly
divided on Tinian in the lurid afterglow of the two raids. A
large minority argued hotly that a " purely technical demonstration " would have sufficed to force the Mikado to yield, and
that the responsibility of opening this terrible Pandora's box
had not been properly weighed by the statesmen and their
advisers.

But Cheshire, while appreciating these intellectual and moral
doubts, swung to the small majority viewpoint which emphasised the incalculable saving in Allied lives and the securely
held prize of an unprecedented deterrent against war and its
miseries.

He went further than most of them in concluding triumphantly that atomic energy was the absolute key to peace :

" We've got to have the biggest and best bombs. That's the
first principle of survival."

The definiteness of such views had brought down on his
head the disgusted fury of men like the New England colonel,
whose remorse was as deeply felt as Cheshire's elation.

CHAPTER NINE

THE REACTION

FIELD-MARSHAL WILSON's questions were few, brisk and to the point. The early cables had given him the unadorned facts; his inside knowledge had filled in the general background. But Cheshire, in the last half-hour, had injected cold words and dead generalities with pulsating actuality. The obsession on Tinian beforehand, the fretting anxiety on the flight out, the haunting memories on the long flight back, were revived as he spoke. So was the aftermath of remorse or elation. The matter-of-fact Group Captain, for all his sensitive awareness, sounded suspiciously like one of the elated.

"So you think the bombs stopped the war?" asked Wilson curiously.

"I'm absolutely sure of it, sir," said Cheshire eagerly. "Japan could do nothing to stop the bombers, so she stopped the fighting. She had no choice. The alternative was atomic extinction."

The Field-Marshal leaned forward and said with deliberation:

"You're right, of course. It was a gamble, but it came off. And as you say, it stopped the war."

Looking back, it was hard to realise that just a week ago Nagasaki was still intact, a busy seaport on the west coast of Kyushu, vibrant with life but doomed, and invincibly ignorant of its own death warrant. That had been the day when the urgent wire of protest arrived from Penney and Cheshire:

"The question of their flying was very difficult," Field-Marshal Lord Wilson recalls. "The opposition came from the U.S. Air Force, not from those in the Atomic project. The idea of a Britisher flying over Japan in an American bomber, whatever it carried, was viewed with disfavour. One was handicapped by the supra-secrecy, and most of the individuals in the Pentagon were not 'in the know'. There was little trouble over Penney as he was wanted to help in the assembly of the bombs. For

Cheshire there was more difficulty—overcrowding was mentioned
—but I was able to overcome that objection before they left for
the Pacific.

"When their plea for help arrived, I went at once to Major-
General Leslie Groves, the 'managing director' of the project.
He approached Stimson, the Secretary for War. That was how
sanction to fly was obtained for Cheshire and Penney at the very
last minute."

Men like Groves, Wilson and Professor Chadwick were
untouched by the sensationalist rumours which formed the
staple of morbid conversation wherever one moved in the
United States. The man in the street, even the majority of
Congressmen, did not yet know the size of the gamble that had
been taken. After the Japanese spurning of the final call for
unconditional surrender, two atomic bombs had been earmarked
for two of four selected targets. In Stimson's words : " They
were the only two we had ready, and our rate of production at
the time was small."

Relief at the success of the gamble was an impregnable
defence against the shock-wave of horror which had begun to
infect the minds and hearts of civilised men with guilt. The
garbled reports spoke of total devastation, of life immediately
extinguished by the triple effect of blast, flash-burn and radioactivity. Photographs had fostered the illusion of apocalyptic
destruction. The great moral debate had started prematurely,
without the men in possession of most of the facts.

Hysteria was a poor substitute for accurate observation and
military logic. The fevered popular imagination might play
with loose fantasies of an Absolute weapon, of scientists bowing
to the decrees of irresponsible statesmen, but Cheshire had
talked to the scientists, had seen the weapon used, and knew
better. It was not as though these men had closed their minds
to the wider issues. Individually, they had been grappling with
them for months ; they had continued their discussions on
Tinian, and he had learnt the arguments—for and against the
weapons.

It was all a question of how much weight was allowed to
expediency, how much to principle. As far as Cheshire was
concerned, circumstances, the whimsical currents of chance,
created the only principles he could recognise. The Allied right

to use the atomic bombs could not be challenged. He had listened to the sincerely held views of men who disputed that right, and had admired them all the more because they did not claim special proprietary interests in the weapons they had helped to build.

The pricks of distaste he still felt were on points of detail. Cheshire's lingering grievance was against the American Air Force. The overstrung nerves of the crew in the steel-plated parachute harnesses high above the range of bullets or shrapnel ; the sneaking reconnaissance flight of a B29 before the attacks, conditioning the inhabitants to the harmless droning of an invisible enemy ; the high-handed official exclusiveness, sullenly revealing itself only when it was nearly too late to react. These were the unseemly antics of a jealous giant.

Washington had ceased to be anything but a base which he was about to quit. He had seen Constance off at the station, a subdued inwardly distraught Constance who had finally taken him at his word. He was now free to go his own way as he wanted ; his only ties were the official odds and ends which took little time to trim. There had been one early shock. An Air Ministry posting to Pensacola cut wickedly across his private plans. The prospect of wasting two years of the atomic age teaching low-level markings to Americans was unendurable. At all costs he must find a lawful excuse for returning to England. So, with fragrantly hopeful memories of Sir Charles Symonds, Cheshire went to see an official psychiatrist ; and by a mixture of bluff and special pleading he secured a sympathetic hearing— and an air passage to London.

In mid-September, Cheshire turned his back on the broad, tree-lined avenues falling away in neat, dead, mathematical patterns from the Dome on Capitol Hill, homesick for the bright uncertainties of peace. He was looking forward to his meeting with the Prime Minister : there were one or two incidental points about atomic developments which Mr. Attlee might be interested to hear. . . .

The interview at No. 10 Downing Street later that month had its lighter moments, but Cheshire stuck to the brief he had planned since leaving Tinian. The Prime Minister sat well back in an arm-chair opposite him, his eyes half closed, his hands fumbling with an unlit pipe. He gave an impression of Oriental impassiveness, as though he had all day to spare for the intent, rather tired-looking young officer so full of his tale of atomic violence.

Mr. Attlee was indeed weighed down by many problems far more pressing; in particular the strain on Anglo-American relations had become more severe in recent weeks. The abrupt foreclosing of Lend-Lease, and the heedless return to "normalcy" as though the war had been a regrettable cosmic distraction from business, was a bad start. Now, it appeared, there were unforeseen difficulties over the continued collaboration of British and American nuclear scientists. The Prime Minister found himself listening attentively to Cheshire's account of his experiences on Tinian.

He seemed to indicate approval of the steps which Penney and Cheshire had taken to outwit the U.S. Air Force leaders. (" The Americans were rather tiresome at that time about these atomic secrets, and it wasn't so much the men at the top as their subordinates. It was all very well getting the President's signature. Unless you got the counter-signature of the office-boy, you would be probably wasting your time.") But the dryly sympathetic Mr. Attlee seemed to grow restive as Cheshire plunged into his conclusions.

As a strategic weapon, said Cheshire, the uranium and plutonium bombs were unanswerable. Simple to assemble, easy to carry and drop, they had more than justified the expectation of the scientists. If he might venture to express his own opinion (the Prime Minister showed no sign of dissent), Britain should build her own atomic stockpile. He realised the immense technical and financial outlay this would involve. There were also practical dangers in an island so heavily industrialised and densely populated; but Britain, like the United States, had a lead which she would be well advised to keep.

Mr. Attlee appeared to shoot up in his chair and open his eyes a little when Cheshire suggested a scheme for storing the future stockpile of atomic bombs:

" A space platform would be the ideal place," he said. " That would eliminate most of the dangers. If all our bombs were put up there out of harm's way, just floating around above the atmosphere and controlled by radio, we'd have no worries wondering how to stock them in safety."

The Prime Minister, who had worries enough without having to consider where to put mythical hoards of atomic bombs, grunted noncommittally and let the fancy peter out like a damp squib. Apart from the far-fetched notion of space platforms ringing the earth like satellites, Cheshire had talked sense. Mr. Attlee cupped his chin in his hands and asked him kindly what he hoped to do now that the war was over.

"I'm thinking of going in for some form of scientific research," said Cheshire.

The Prime Minister grunted again, this time a little less sceptically. The rather weird suggestion of floating platforms for atomic bombs seemed more understandable.

2

For nearly eighteen months after his return to London in 1945, Cheshire's outlook on life changed only gradually; and the atomic explosion he witnessed had no direct bearing on the change.

The Cheshire who reported to Wilson in Washington and Attlee in London was a man both fascinated and highly elated by the omnipotence of the new atomic weapons. Being also a realist and a man of imaginative intelligence, he could foresee the strategic vulnerability of Britain as well as the political dangers of any misguided attempt to create a monopoly in atomic energy. In an article which appeared in the *News Chronicle* on September 18th, 1945, he expressed his ideas for the first time in this country, prefacing them with a personal description of the Nagasaki attack. One particular passage in that article has been eagerly seized on by the propagators of the post-war legend as evidence of a suddenly acquired "feeling of guilt":

"I had seen what were probably the two greatest chemical explosions of the world, the destruction of the naval ammunition dump at Wilhelmshaven and the destruction of the powder works at Bergerac. . . .

"When Wilhelmshaven blew up we felt a sense of elation; we had set out to destroy and we had destroyed. When Nagasaki blew up we felt nothing but an overwhelming sense of awe, not because an unusual number of Japanese had been killed but because something had happened which altered our fundamental concepts of life."

What Cheshire meant by that hackneyed phrase, so battered and beloved by reformers down the ages, is implicit in his next paragraph :

" About the future there has been much conjecture and speculation. From the confusion and uncertainty, however, there emerges one fact we should do well to grasp and digest. Atomic energy is a stern reality and is not in the realm of religion or magic. It is a staging post along the road to scientific knowledge and is not a secret locked in the bowels of the earth, which may either be uncovered or hidden at the will of man.

" Scientific knowledge is the property of the world and not of nations. It is not a physical possession like territory, and therefore cannot be denied or withheld except by denying the right to carry out research. Its progress cannot be halted any more than the development of industry or of medicine could be halted."

Cheshire's natural antipathy to politics was a tower of strength against comforting illusions about the future. The world of national rivalries was as outmoded as the primeval world of the flint axe. He was determined to make people sit up and take note of the awesome potentialities for good and evil in this latest scientific discovery. His mind, employing its familiar pincers movement of an intuitive leap forward and a slower, more calculating march to outflank disagreeable facts, clung to its foregoing conclusion that atomic strength was the master-key to peace. After all, the article was written within a week of his visit to No. 10 Downing Street.

War had been his only business. He was untrained for the ordinary tasks of peace. Yet atomic energy also opened an endless vista of personal opportunity which the romantic in him found irresistible, and the mature man of action mysteriously challenging. Penney had not risen to the idly cast bait of a leading appointment in the proposed Anglo-American research corporation ; it was becoming plain that no nuclear scientist would be free to offer his services to a private concern. Governments were jealously concentrating the fruits of atomic knowledge in their own hands ; and the breaking up of the Allied scientific partnership was already imminent. His private hopes and ambitions for the future were also at stake; but these were incidental to the main argument.

His scientist friends advised him to think of a career less specialised than nuclear physics. Much as they sympathised with his aspirations, they could hold out no worthwhile future for a young man whose sole qualifications were determination, boldness and a versatile brain. The Labour Government's plans for the post-war development of atomic energy were still being formulated; but these would almost certainly preclude the headlong scramble for position which he seemed to envisage.

As it happened, Cheshire already had a promising second string to his bow. Rockets might supersede aircraft, but rocket research experiments would surely make room for skilled airmen. Mr. Attlee had been given a startling glimpse of science reaching for the firmament, of atomic platforms orbiting in outer space, untrammelled by Government restrictions. Cheshire seriously intended to devote himself entirely to this or any other branch of science which offered quick returns for enterprise and enthusiasm.

His consuming interest in scientific day-dreaming was treated less seriously by members of his family. His mother, especially, was more immediately concerned about the state of his health.

Rest and quiet were what he obviously needed; rest and quiet he obstinately dispensed with, until the R.A.F. doctors examined him in October and sent him to St. Luke's Hospital, Muswell Hill, at that time a rehabilitation centre for service officers. During the weeks he spent there, secretly chafing at the " confinement " which nevertheless left him free to move in and out more or less as he pleased, none of his fellow-patients saw much of him. The only person who succeeded in drawing him out a little was an Anglican army chaplain, recuperating after months of treatment for severe head wounds received in Belgium. He found Cheshire gravely polite, but given to bouts of dark depression and inspired at such moments " by very little faith in God or man."

It was the friendly understanding of Sir Charles Symonds, whose advice Cheshire valued, which confirmed his half-formed resolve to leave the R.A.F. The fact that he had a permanent commission was a small formality. He seemed to realise as clearly as Symonds that he would probably be a misfit in the peacetime service. What he wanted now was the freedom to strike out independently as a civilian. There was no motive of " conscientious objection ", no suspicion of any lack of mental balance, in this wish to leave the R.A.F.

It would be impertinent and distasteful to raise the matter at all, were it not for the persistent reports that have circulated ever since that Cheshire's reason was at least temporarily un-hinged by the Nagasaki explosion, or that his conscience was so revolted that the R.A.F. had to drop him as gently and rapidly as possible. There is not a shred of positive evidence, medical or otherwise, to support these rumours.

On November 13th, Cheshire took a taxi to Buckingham Palace to receive his V.C. and the third bar to his D.S.O. from the hands of the King. It was his fifth visit to the Palace, and his name was first on the list. The King asked him a number of questions about the later activities of 617 Squadron. Guy Gibson had still been in charge when he had called on the " Dambusters ", and though he seemed to remember Cheshire quite well he had not connected him with the later and greater victories of the squadron. When the King asked whether he intended to remain in the R.A.F., Cheshire replied that he expected to be out before the end of the year :

" I'm interested in scientific research," he added.

" And an excellent thing too," said the King. " You'll be doing work that is very important and rewarding."

The sentiment was unoriginal, but the way it was said—with an indefinable touch of solicitude suggesting that at the moment no other person in the Kingdom mattered but himself—heartened Cheshire greatly. He went out into the gravelled forecourt to face the press photographers and the heedless din of London, easier in his mind than when he had entered.

3

Before the end of November, Cheshire viewed and took the lease of a modern town house in Kensington, paid a £500 deposit on a Bentley car, and restocked his wardrobe with expensive civilian clothes from a fashionable tailor in Mayfair. He was not evading his self-appointed responsibilities as an acolyte of science ; he was simply making adequate provision for his needs until a suitable opening came his way. If a situation commensurate with his vaulting hopes were not offered at once, he could afford to wait; meanwhile there was much to keep him busy and amused.

Cheshire's unique position as the only British eyewitness willing and free to discuss Nagasaki played into his hands. Both as a journalist and lecturer, he was in great demand; and because he felt a sense of mission about this open invitation to speak out in public, he seized it with both hands. A more avaricious man would have promptly sold his services to the highest bidder. Characteristically, he spurned at least one tempting offer before agreeing to contribute a fortnightly article to the *Sunday Graphic* at a relatively moderate fee. He could not overlook the fact that this was the newspaper which had first introduced him to the public by serialising *Bomber Pilot*.

His inability to say " no " to the organisers of lectures took a heavier toll of Cheshire's time and limited energy than he could prudently spare; but on the whole he quite enjoyed deducing the dire consequences of the strategic use of atomic weapons in any future war. The intellectual effort stimulated him, and gradually he seemed to fall under the spell of his own gloomily incisive logic.

Some critics, in the R.A.F. and elsewhere, believed that he was playing to the gallery. Others felt that he was grossly exaggerating the revolutionary importance of atomic weapons. Re-reading his lecture notes and articles to-day, however, one cannot but admire a detached, tightly-woven consistency which many a practised politician might envy. Cheshire, as has been suggested, was suffering from his excessive exertions during the war; he was physically and nervously worn out. His moods fluctuated between depression and optimism, which indirectly coloured his thoughts, yet his strategic insight was objective and steady.

The two constant factors in his arguments were the physical vulnerability of Britain to atomic attacks, and the political complacency of statesmen whose bickerings over the international control of atomic energy might well end by destroying Britain.

" In the next ten years," Cheshire told members of the Publicity Club of Manchester early in November, " the bombs produced will be very much stronger. In fact the figure of a

hundred thousand times as powerful as the present bombs may
not be very far off the mark. . . .

"If there is a possibility of war, then we must prepare to
make the best we can of the situation. We know that we cannot
rely on any form of defence to stop the atomic bombs from
reaching us. We could no doubt stop a proportion, but we
could never stop them all. We can certainly never stop an
atomic bomb exploding, any more than we could stop a high
explosive bomb exploding. . . .

"We could perhaps save some of our population by putting
them out of reach both of the explosion and the effects of radioactivity which kill human life. . . . We must either disperse
or go underground, and we haven't any room to disperse in
this country. Russia has to a certain extent and so has America ;
but we haven't unless we choose to go out to the Empire.

"The alternative is to go underground.

"We would have to abandon the surface of the earth to some
other form of life. What we'd become I don't know, but we
wouldn't be men. . . . In other words, we are faced with the
end of this country or no war.

"How we can rule out the possibility of war is a question
that doesn't fall within my sphere.

"But this I do know : for us the necessity to end war is a
biological necessity, a choice between survival and extinction.
It's no longer enough to say there are good reasons against war,
to reduce the argument to something that's moral, or social,
or political or even economic. It's biological. If we take this
as the cornerstone on which we build our efforts, we should
succeed in ruling out the possibility of war. But if we forget it,
saying to ourselves that it's so bad we'll shelve it, then the
danger is obvious. We'll fall into the same trap we fell into
before 1939."

The "principle of the Big Gun" did not, on reflection, help
Britain. The facts of geography were against her. Even if she
had bigger bombs and more space platforms for storage than
any other nation, these would not necessarily insure her against
the ultimate peril of atomic extinction.

In the company of his friends he never wore the mantle of
the prophet. The Voice crying in the wilderness of Rotarian
Clubs and British Legion halls, was stilled in his own home and

in the West End night-clubs which he patronised as freely as his leisure would permit. He seemed to some of his closer companions a split personality, untroubled by the obvious contradiction between his luxury-loving gaiety in private and his austere, Cassandra-like gloom in public. A Freudian might jump to the easy conclusion that Cheshire was merely compensating for his insecurity by indulging in the one form of escapism he habitually enjoyed; but such a conclusion omits the rather important fact that he adopted the role of a man-about-town quite deliberately. He felt without any affectation that he owed it to himself as a public figure to live and be seen to live in lordly comfort while awaiting the ideal outlet for his talents.

In 1944 he had promised David Shannon, his trusted Australian lieutenant in 617 Squadron, that he would employ him in England after the war. Shannon had since left the R.A.F. and was eager to start work without delay; he was a married man with a small family to support. The need to find an interesting occupation for Shannon and himself was strengthened by the pleas of ex-service colleagues who wrote expressing their dissatisfaction with the monotonous conditions of post-war life. In December, Cheshire sent a note to Dr. Penney, asking him to pass on to his scientific friends enclosed copies of the following letter:

" There are a number of ex-servicemen, mostly drawn from those who served in the various volunteer units, who are anxious to devote their energies to some good cause. They do not feel inclined for the time being to settle down to the normal type of business, and are keen to undertake some work which would take them into new fields as pioneers. . . .

" It has, for example, been suggested that an expedition could usefully be mounted to the Arctic to study weather conditions and perhaps to set up meteorological sounding stations. This is exactly the type of work for which these men are looking, but there would be little object in undertaking it unless some concrete gain were likely to result to the world."

It was a discouraging period for would-be pioneers. The response to Cheshire's letter could hardly be described as overwhelming. An Oxford professor eventually showed a vague interest, and Shannon called on him to discuss a possible expedition to the Tundra in search of rare shrubs. Nothing came of it, and by then Cheshire's interest had moved on with disconcerting rapidity to other outlandish projects. The invariable factor in all of them was the desire to serve the community, with little thought of profit-making ; but his mind strayed far and wide for unconventional challenges to satisfy his craving for the unusual.

" I should be glad if you would send me, in addition to my existing order, the following : news report on

" REVOLUTIONS
" CIVIL WARS
" RIOTING."

That terse little message to a press-cutting agency reflected the frustration he felt in a Britain which was sluggishly turning its back on the real perils of peace. He had no more stomach for well-meaning suggestions to stand for Parliament than for invitations to join the boards of City companies. The idea of shackling his freedom of action for a possible seat in the Commons or a few unearned directors' fees was ludicrous.

Cheshire's thoughts anchored nearer home as the trickle of letters from disgruntled ex-servicemen broadened into a torrent. The discovery that many shared his longing for the comradeship engendered by war became a turning-point in his own quest for useful adventure. He had no political axe to grind, belonged to no party, and could work up no interest in the controversies at Westminster. But his fortnightly articles furnished him with a platform from which to preach the need for preserving fading ideals which seemed incapable of flourishing except in the soil of a worthwhile cause. From January, 1946, when he was discharged from the R.A.F. with a disability pension for psycho-neurosis, Cheshire began to draw increasing attention to himself as the unsettled ex-serviceman's unofficial champion.

It was not in his nature, however, to discuss problems and leave the solutions to others. He was the born entrepreneur, as full of novel suggestions as an egg is of meat, but constitutionally incapable of distinguishing those which were practicable from those which were not. That is why the record of those early months of peace is so disconnected and untidy. There was no logical sequence in the schemes he conceived and produced with the over-anxious dexterity of a conjurer pulling rabbits out of a hat in an empty hall.

4

Apart from the schemes for bettering the lot of others there were others for increasing his own earnings, which trailed snail-like behind his personal expenditure. For though his acquaintances assumed that he must possess capital or a private income, Cheshire possessed neither. Money matters worried him less than they had ever done at Oxford, and he saw no reason for depriving himself of the luxury that befitted a person of his standing. His credit stood as high as his reputation, and he consoled himself when the bills came in that his prospects were even better.

His father had seen it all before and nervously wondered how long this unsettled spendthrift phase would last.

" Tell your son that a man can live on his reputation for a few months at most," was the advice given to Dr. Cheshire by a former Oxford colleague who had risen to eminence in public life. " And tell him I'm talking from experience."

If the advice was passed on, it fell on barren ground. The moral maxims of the established were unlikely to influence a restless young man of generous but stubborn impulses groping for a higher motive in life than doing a mundane job for its own sake. Once or twice Cheshire did bestir himself as though to prove that he could make money when necessary, even if his heart was not in the game. His first intention of turning himself into a company called " Enterprises Ltd.," to co-ordinate all his activities from lecturing to polar explorations, was dropped in favour of running each venture on a separate basis. Government restrictions thwarted his attempt to set up as a wines and spirits export agent for the American market ; and Government policy on emigration fortunately ruled out an impracticable scheme for transporting intending emigrants to Australia in renovated landing vessels. In the spring of 1946 he abruptly decided to become a shopkeeper, when a legless ex-serviceman sought his help. A high-class flower store in Kensington, providing floral decorations for exhibitions, banqueting halls and hotels seemed to him an uncomplicated way of earning a comfortable living.

With Shannon and two women partners, he gradually built up a small clientele, and was beginning to " break even " when

he sold his interest about a year later. " Flower Deliveries ",
which to-day is a flourishing little business, was never the success
he had hoped, partly because of his own inexperience, but
mainly because the shop in the Old Brompton Road was just
another side-show to which he could give only a fraction of his
scattered attention.

Of his many facets—man-about-town, half-hearted businessman, journalist, social reformer, and gay companion—it was
the last-named which seemed to his close acquaintances the most
natural and likeable. His generosity and kindliness were prodigal.
When Noel Holland, the Fighter Command radar officer who
had collaborated with him from Beachy Head in 617 days, was
laid up with mumps in his small bed-sitting-room, Cheshire
brought him to his house in a taxi and let him stay on as his
guest. Holland kept the books of " Flower Deliveries ", passed
on the mumps to Cheshire, whom he chided for his extravagant
business ideas, and was drawn into conversation on many topics,
grave and gay. Occasionally talk turned to the atom bomb, but
at no time did Cheshire betray the least qualms about its use.

There were lively discussions on religion, a subject which
had begun to stir his faint curiosity. Cheshire claims that his
interest in religion was momentarily awakened more than six
months previously, during the brief leave he spent in London
after Christopher's release from a German prison camp. One
evening he wandered into the Vanity Fair club in Mayfair for a
drink. Two or three people were propping up the bar, chatting
amiably about the aimlessness of human existence. The talk
drifted idly on to the problem of man's origin and destiny. Was
he the plaything of blind forces, as the muddle and misery of life
suggested ? Or was he a creature fashioned in the image and
likeness of a personal God, as Christians alleged ?

Cheshire, who had fairly definite ideas about the struggle for
existence, joined in the conversation. It was absurd, he said,
to imagine that God existed, except as a convenient figure of
speech. Man had invented God to explain the voice of conscience, but it was doubtful whether right or wrong existed outside the human mind. They were words affixed like labels to
customs and laws which man had also invented to keep social
order. While Cheshire sat back, pleased with his worldly wisdom, a woman friend who had been quietly listening rounded

on him and demolished his self-assurance, if not his arguments :

What did *he* know about God or conscience ? He should be ashamed of himself, talking such rot in a public place. Of course there was a God. And He was a *real* person, not a figure of speech.

This incident confronted him for the first time as an adult with the Christian attitude to life ; and his surprise was all the keener because the woman who contradicted him was one of the last persons on earth he would have credited with such rooted convictions. But the incident seems to have made no lasting impression. On the flight back to Washington he had dipped into C. S. Lewis's *Screwtape Letters*. The witty, mannered epistles from one devil to another told him something about human frailty but disappointingly little about the unknown God who somehow governed everyday existence. In the emotional upheaval of his break with Constance, in the excitement of his mission to Tinian, and in the exaltation afterwards, the episode sank into obscurity and the problems it raised ceased to matter. It was only in later years when, as a convinced Christian, he began to scour his past for dimly remembered landmarks of the search for Faith, that the incident in the Vanity Fair began to loom impressively larger than it appears to have done at the time.

Some of Cheshire's friends seriously doubt whether it could have happened in 1945. He is very positive that it did. Undeniably there were frequent arguments of a strikingly similar kind in the Vanity Fair in early 1946, when the persuasive influence of a close woman friend of strong religious views kindled or rekindled his interest. It may well be, as he suggested, that the seed sown months before now began to show belated signs of life. The fact that someone for whom he felt deep affection, someone who in other respects shared his worldly tastes and standards, paid lip service to religious values, was sufficient to fire his imagination.

People and their incongruous differences had always influenced him more directly than books and abstract ideas, and it was natural that his introduction to religion in the broadest emotional meaning of the term should come through a person who herself was influenced by it. Cheshire was too logical to accept without questioning a higher way of life inspired by little more than a

funny inside feeling, too hardened in the ways of the world
and too fond of his own pleasures to let it affect his behaviour.
He was quite prepared to discuss the notion that men were the
" children of God " and that " a spark of divinity " ennobled
everyone ; but it brought him no closer to the unknown God
who seemed to have performed His creative handiwork in a fit
of absence of mind.   During the first quarter of 1946, at least,
religion remained for Cheshire a conversational hobby, though
God had become something more than a figure of speech.

CHAPTER TEN

THE IDEALIST

THE man's voice at the far end of the wire came through faint but with a rasping edge of urgency.

" That is PARK 4038 ? "

" It is."

" May I speak to Group Captain Cheshire, please. It's urgent."

" Speaking."

" Oh, thank heavens you're in. Major Murray-Smith's agent here. I'm sorry but you can't come to-morrow. The house is still locked up, and none of the furniture's been moved."

It was the estate agent at Gumley Hall, a big, red-brick country house, near Market Harborough, which was to be the headquarters of Cheshire's first public experiment in peace-winning.

Since the announcement of his colony scheme for ex-service-men exactly nine weeks previously, there had been many setbacks and good-intentioned warnings ; but this trunk call at ten-thirty on a June Sunday night, a few hours before the departure of the advance party, was a malevolent stroke of fate. When a man is on the point of burning his bridges behind him, he does not care to have the torch dashed from his hands.

Cheshire hid his vexation and said :

" That's all very well, but we can't call it off now. It's too late to warn the others. Anyway files are already on the way to Gumley.

The estate agent hesitated now. The bridge seemed to be well alight already.

" I see," he said hopelessly. " In that case we'll try to sort out the muddle when you arrive to-morrow."

Cheshire replaced the receiver with relief. In the morning he would catch the train at Euston, place a hundred miles of countryside between himself and the time-wasting vacuum of

London, and put his convictions to the sure test of action. For the best part of a year he had been frittering away his energies in quest of a cause, an unstable combination of the hedonist and thwarted idealist, weary of living enmeshed in a web of shining trivialities.

Cheshire had at last stumbled on his cause as a moralising journalist, disturbed by the plight of thousands of men and women newly released from the services, like himself. For many of them the fine promises of the politicians rang with the mocking hollowness of echoes ; the planners had trodden on their dreams of peace with heavy ammunition boots. The victims of a generation ironically displaced and dispossessed by a war they helped to win, Cheshire sprang to their defence with an alacrity and an imaginative understanding which were almost personal.

Instinctively he identified their plight with his own, feeling not for and with but IN them. What modern psychologists call empathy is a greater gift than sympathy. This rare quality of insight, which enables great writers to identify themselves with the creatures of their invention, has also inspired social reformers down the ages, giving an enduring effect of selfless greatness to the compassion of an Elizabeth Fry among her prisoners, a Peter Claver among the slaves, or a Fr. Damien among his lepers on Molokai. Cheshire used his limited newspaper space to console those in immediate need ; but the realisation that he must offer a lead broke only gradually.

" To the impartial observer," he wrote on March 17th, 1946, " we in Great Britain must appear a collection of madmen. The half of us are crying out that we cannot find labour, and the rest that we cannot get employment. And, therefore, the rest, in order not to starve, are planning to emigrate, if only the Government will let them. If this were all, it would not perhaps be too bad because it might offer a solution to the ex-serviceman's problem. Unfortunately, it is not all. The ex-serviceman must not be sent out untrained. . . .

" The task is by no means impossible. If the Government was able to take accountants and draughtsmen and turn them into pilots and gunners, I am unable to see why they cannot reverse the process. It is failing to do so because, in its opinion, there are other problems of more immediate urgency, and it is not likely to act until enough people make enough fuss. . . ."

Cheshire's compassionate anger fed on the enthusiastic response of ex-servicemen : the letters continued to pile up ankle-deep on the hall mat each morning, a tribute to his intuitive grasp of the problem but equally a spur to personal action. If the Government or industry would not raise a finger to help, he would have to find a way.

His friends refused to take him seriously. This was just another amusing distraction which would not outlast the next brainwave. How could he expect them to believe anything else ? Had he not already sunk a lot of money in " Flower Deliveries " which would be opening for business before the end of March ? He must not let his impulsive generosity run away with him. They regarded his reformer's zeal as part of his journalistic stock-in-trade ; apparently he could not resist dramatising a minor symptom of national instability in those early, insecure days of peace.

Their devil's advocacy did not deter him in the least. During the next ten days he drafted a plan of action to test the sincerity of the hundreds who had written to him. It appeared on March 31st, under the bold headline :

" I OFFER A CHALLENGE."

Addressed to those " who are now stranded by the turning tide of peace," the plan was simply and clearly put :

" There are at the present time in this country 680 aerodromes surplus to requirements. What is going to happen to them no one knows, not even the Government, and in the meantime, through want of attention, they are becoming even more derelict. Let those of us to whom this article is addressed join together and by our common efforts let us acquire one of these forgotten sites. Let us move in as colonists with our families.

" In order to earn our living and not become a drag on society we will farm the land and carry on any productive occupation that we can. We will turn the hangars into workshops and the billets into homes. Our objective will not be to settle there for the rest of our lives but to establish a base from which we, and others like us, can go out into the world armed with enough qualifications to stand on our own feet."

The decaying aerodromes of Britain were for Cheshire a striking symbol of the nation's imperceptible decline from its wartime greatness. In late January he had travelled to Yorkshire on a sentimental visit to an airfield from which he had operated in the early days of the bomber offensive. He had sat smoking on the bench in the well-remembered crew room, fascinated by the weather-stained poster still fluttering on one damp wall. The door, which had never closed properly, now swung to and fro in the whistling wind, groaning on its single rusty hinge.

There had once been laughter as well as tragedy in these ghostly surroundings and life had been simple ; in four years the sense of purpose sustaining air crews, ground crews and a whole people behind them had withered. He saw the aerodrome as a mark of the futile emptiness of life without a common cause ; a symbol of mute reproach like the untended grave of a lover. On his return to London, Cheshire tried to express his feelings in an article. The symbol was pushed away into a cranny of his mind for reference. Momentarily he forgot it and resumed his life of desperate gaiety.

Now, like a lucky charm, the symbol had dropped effortlessly into place as part of a new pattern.

Cheshire's visit to the aerodrome followed an equally significant visit to All Souls College, Oxford, where he dined with the author of a book which had helped to gather his sporadic thoughts on questions of post-war reconstruction. Lionel Curtis's *World War—Its Cause and Cure* stated in coherent fashion some of his own intuitive fears and doubts. He agreed it would be useless offering ex-servicemen the prospect of something to live *for* until they had been guaranteed something to live *on* ; but he advised Cheshire against rushing into any ill-conceived scheme of land resettlement :

" I told him that, having served under Milner in South Africa, I knew from experience that there are few things more difficult than settling men on the land. The past is strewn with the wreckage of such schemes, and it seemed to me of vital importance that he should not court a fiasco which would do positive harm to the cause of establishing a real peace."

There was a delightful interlude of mistaken identity when Cheshire approached Peter Scott, the artist and ornithologist, under the misapprehension that the son of the explorer shared his anxieties and uncertainties. He had been told that Scott was an authority on rural development, not realising that there might possibly be two men of the same name and of more or less equal stature in two quite separate fields.

Cheshire promptly wrote suggesting an early meeting, and was slightly puzzled by the rather guarded reply. When he rang up Scott to confirm an appointment for lunch, the puzzlement deepened. They seemed in their telephone conversation to be talking charmingly at cross purposes, yet the invitation to come and discuss matters was firm and courteous enough. Whether Cheshire misunderstood the arrangement, or Scott forgot about it, remains a matter of conjecture. At any rate the son of the explorer was not at home, and many months passed before Cheshire learnt that the Peter Scott he really wanted to meet lived all the time in Monmouthshire.

When his brother came to stay for a few days, Cheshire was disappointed to find Christopher more sceptical of his plans than anyone. As a former prisoner of war, Christopher warned against relying too much on the virtuousness of human nature, above all in the claustrophobic atmosphere of a closed community.

" It just won't work in practice," he said. " It's an unnatural mode of living with or without the barbed wire."

Cheshire believed that his brother exaggerated the difficulties, and that the analogy of a prison compound did not apply. There might well be personal animosities at first, but the knowledge that they were freely shaping their own common destiny would outweigh these petty human foibles. He was equally confident that the very act of building up from scratch a self-governing community would engender social virtues which seemed to be perishing from neglect.

His friends shook dubious heads, wondering how long the philanthropic craze would last :

" If you can convince yourself of that," they seemed to say, " you can convince yourself of anything."

His self-assurance gave an infinite impression of candour and a total effect of obstinate naïveté. Addicted as he was to luxury, he had found a stronger counter-attraction. Nothing they could say now would prevent him exploding into premature action.

On April 14th, ninety-three ex-servicemen and women arrived in London to discuss the proposed colony scheme.

Before leaving the West End hall where they met, they unanimously agreed to launch the project at once. When the second public meeting was held on May 19th, a number of would-be pioneers had quietly dropped out ; but others had taken their places and there was an encouragingly long queue of applicants.

Reluctantly, Cheshire had to abandon his earlier inspiration to hire a disused aerodrome. The de-requisitioning process would take time, and the Government experts had tactlessly advised him to " spend nine months planning before thinking of starting." It seemed to him " a perfect example of one of the evils we are up against ". Then, in May, Major Murray-Smith offered them rent-free, for twelve months, the use of his forty-five-bedroomed house and grounds. It seemed a happy omen, the appearance of a well-disposed benefactor at a critical moment.

Half yielding to those who insisted that any enterprise not based on Christian principles would surely fail, half echoing the sentiments of the woman who remained closest in his affections, Cheshire publicly announced a new long-term objective : " belief in God and complete selflessness." It was as much a conciliatory gesture as an expression of sincere personal conviction. The colony had inevitably attracted its quota of religious-minded men and women. What could be more respectable than to proclaim the ideal of the Second Commandment as the touchstone of their efforts ?

The practical problem of raising money was eventually solved. Every member should have a minimum stake of fifty £1 shares in the project, paying an extra sixpence per share into a central welfare fund.

By the end of May, with about £400 in the bank and a further £800 outstanding, Cheshire and the Committee were ready. The name of the colony, chosen after some mild disagreement, explained itself :

" As all members know," said Cheshire, " the letters V.I.P. stand for ' Very Important Persons,' a priority prefix allowing them to travel without hindrance and with all speed. We can think of no more suitable title. We propose to jettison everything in favour of speed, and, so far as moving in goes, are working to a deadline of June 7th."

The estate agent of Gumley Hall was still mystified by the extraordinary emphasis on speed when he disconsolately replaced the telephone receiver late on June 6th. For good or ill, the advance party of V.I.P. would be descending on him in the morning.

2

The twelve members of the advance party, eleven men and one woman, sat on packing-cases in the kitchen and reviewed their unpromising dilemma. The agent was walking down the drive towards Gumley village in the slanting rain. He had just shown Cheshire over the rambling, echoing house. Its rooms contained enough dust-sheeted furniture to fill thirty average homes, but no inventory had yet been taken. With the best will in the world, V.I.P. would have to wait for the removal men.

Almost apologetically, as though half conscious of Cheshire's disapproval, the agent had put forward an alternative proposal of his own.

" If you want to stay," he said, " there's always the stables. It'll be rough—and a bit of a squeeze, but it'll be a roof over your heads at any rate."

This was an unnecessary early setback. The four rooms in the stables had no water and no heat, except for a broken kitchen range. The roof let in the weather, and there were tell-tale signs that rats had enjoyed the freedom of the place for months.

" Well, what's it to be ? " Cheshire asked hesitantly.

" We'll stay," they said unanimously. " We've slept rougher than this before now. Besides, if we stick around, it may encourage the owner to shift his furniture."

It was the decision Cheshire had hoped they would reach.

" I'm glad you feel that way," he said with relief. " It's going to mean a great deal to the others. Some of them can't afford to wait."

Within a week they had renovated the stables and were starting to move the furniture into one wing of Gumley Hall. Their energy and determination impressed the owner. Once his possessions had been safely stored, he told them they could occupy the rest of the house. Cheshire was jubilant. The first hurdle had been cleared.

About the middle of June, the main party of colonists arrived. The extra hands were welcome ; for Gumley Hall, like the stables, had stood empty since the Army left in 1945. They redecorated offices, repainted bathrooms, fitted a new Aga cooker in the kitchen, converted a derelict laundry into a workshop, and rewired part of the electrical system. They swept chimneys, cleared roof gutters, and replaced broken tiles and window panes. It was satisfying but wholly unproductive work, which ate steadily into their small reserve of capital.

The weekly wages and domestic bills for twenty-two adults and four children amounted to a round £75 ; but the financial outlook worried Cheshire less at this stage than the unpromising opportunities for expansion. There was no room for any more members, and some of those waiting to enter were, he felt, in desperate straits.

The V.I.P. Finance Director, budgeting on shrinking re-sources, had to choose between many unlikely plans for taming the wilderness and creating plenty. The land, equipment and goodwill of a two and a half acre market garden were secured for £500 ; a mechanical all-purpose saw-table was ordered for the woodwork section ; essential stock was bought for the livestock experts.

There was an air of disembodied enchantment about the early production plans which betrayed their inner unsoundness. They were based on the topsy-turvy economics of Wonderland. Cheshire, as hopelessly out of his depth as Alice, was quite content to be guided by the committee, whose members had been appointed for their specialist knowledge as craftsmen or smallholders. His faith in their abilities was matched by their respect for his good-natured tolerance. The minutes of the first meeting indicate that the colony was already thriving on its unearned expectations :

" The market garden has been taken over and five members are fully employed in its cultivation. It is expected to yield a weekly return of £35. . . .

" Livestock : Rabbits and Mice. Nine hutches have been completed for the rabbits, twenty-four cages have been com-pleted for mice. The mice are to be sold as pets and also for laboratory and research work. The eight rabbits (of which six are chinchillas) are for breeding, exhibition, etc. More rabbits are being bought.

" The rabbits will have paid their way by the end of the year, at which time we shall have some £300 of capital stock. The mice will yield an initial profit of £3 per week, which will gradually increase.

"Livestock : dogs. Two pedigree Labrador puppies have been bought for breeding and gun training, also three guard dogs for the poultry. The director intends to train guard dogs for use in factories and on business premises and for police work, if possible. The trained guard dogs alone will bring in a weekly profit of £10.

"Woodwork, Arts and Crafts. Plans have been drawn up for the production of toys and household woodware. The sales department have been provided with samples and are negotiating with various London stores. They expect to be able to place £75 worth of orders."

If there was more than a trace of elfin fantasy in these estimates of future income, the colonists had no means of telling at that time. Many of them were would-be " back-to-the-landers ", people who pined for the simple, unvarnished values of a lost age. Farming to them was not an industry but a romantic way of life that could be taken up without tears, if not without sweat. A few resented having to go out and find temporary work until the " minor industries " could absorb them, realising only slowly that V.I.P. was in no position to buy a single acre.

Clashes of temperament are probably less avoidable in the unsettled atmosphere of a new community than anywhere else, and Christopher Cheshire's warning was vindicated quickly. The tendency to splinter into cliques gave rise to friction, which soon threatened to wreck the experiment. Cheshire had to be harsh and suavely diplomatic by turns. A teacup storm becomes as perilous as a violent hurricane when one's horizon stretches no farther than the rim of the cup at the end of one's nose.

"We have had a great many difficulties, particularly in the matter of personalities," Cheshire wrote to Lionel Curtis at the end of July. "It is now obvious that a high percentage of members came up here after their own ends. These, however, are no longer with us. . . ."

Cheshire gave up his London house. V.I.P. was a material gamble for idealistic stakes which he was determined to win. He had deliberately cut himself off from many of his old friends, some of whom began to reflect uneasily that perhaps they had underestimated his knack of overcoming mundane obstacles by simply ignoring their existence. For Cheshire's press articles on developments at Gumley, and the statements attributed to him in the general press, were tinged by the same studied disregard for the facts of business life which had characterised their discussions before the scheme was launched.

" Now at last that there is no further doubt about our success, we can begin to expand up to our commitments," he wrote on August 18th. " To-day, we have the house and the land, but the waiting-list has grown out of all proportion to the numbers we can handle and is increasing every week. It has come not only from this country but from America, Australia, Canada, Holland and the Far East.

" Like every other organisation we can expand. But we can never keep pace with the present flow of applications, and our expansion, therefore, now needs to include associate membership. Mankind is entitled to food, to a home and to a secure environment in return for work. Now that we are beginning to provide these within the colony itself, we need to do something for those who will never be able to join us.

" To accomplish this we need work or service, either full time or part time, to increase our local income. With the money that it yields we are setting out to build a holiday and rest camp, a training centre and a welfare organisation open to all members. We are planning an Air Charter service, initially to increase our income and ultimately to provide free, or at least cheap, travel facilities. The world needs to create a fellowship and understanding between nations, and these are unlikely to come about until ordinary men and women of all countries come together and learn to know each other."

It was hard for the average reader to separate the wheat from the chaff in glowing prospectuses of the kind. But Cheshire was able to convince himself that they were objectives within easy striking distance. If only ten thousand members of the public became associate members, there would be endless possibilities of development.

In early September he paid a brief visit to *emigratio-vereeniging*, a Dutch community scheme similar to V.I.P. which still existed only on paper. The business efficiency of its leaders, in the face of restrictions far more severe than any in Britain, filled him with admiration. Their belief that overseas settlement was a sound prescription for peace echoed his own views. Herr Brinkker, the director, had been in touch with him since the late spring of 1946, when news of Cheshire's " challenge to ex-servicemen " was flashed round the Western world by the press agencies. They now agreed to help each other as freely as conditions would permit ; and Cheshire drafted into his first quarterly report a number of thoughts provoked by his visit to Utrecht :

" Although V.I.P. has made no attempt to obtain publicity other than through the medium of articles in the *Sunday Graphic* a considerable response has been received. Applications for membership amount to nearly 1000. . . . The numbers of men and women passively interested are probably well in excess of 20,000. If a deliberate programme of publicity were inaugurated, there is little doubt that the reaction would be very great.

" Within its limited sphere V.I.P. has provided a healthy basis for living which clearly appeals to the more serious thinking type of family. . . . If, however, it is to succeed in establishing contacts and colonies overseas, it needs to be governed by a Board of Directors whose experience, wisdom and public standing are sufficient both to guide it towards its objective and to earn the confidence and loyalty of its members. In reaching this conclusion I am not in any way relinquishing my interest in, or devotion to, V.I.P. I am merely acknowledging that the issues are beyond the scope of any one individual or any ordinary committee."

If Cheshire was learning by experience that idealism would not make two blades of grass grow where one had grown before, he could not forgo the temptation of letting his imagination run riot in public. When he bought two Mosquito aircraft, for example, his oracular explanation bore little relation to anything but his bounding hopes for the future.

" Eventually we hope to have colonies all over the world so that peoples of all countries can learn to know each other and sink their differences. In order to make this possible, we are building up our own communications flight and our own radio network : the former to circulate members and goods, the latter to enable us to hold daily conferences with all the colonies, wherever they may be."

This extract from a talk on the B.B.C.'s General Overseas

Service in late November, typifies the incurably sanguine outlook Cheshire adopted in public. In spite of gloomy evidence to the contrary, he believed that in the end his cause would secure the public backing it deserved.

When an Australian woman offered to sell him 60,000 acres of freehold land near Perth, in Western Australia, he eagerly examined the proposition. The price asked was £2 per acre, on easy payment terms; and Cheshire's imagination, leap-frogging gaily ahead, could already visualise this vast estate, peopled with settlers from the mother house at Gumley, as the first link in a chain of colonies which one day would girdle the globe.

" Our idea," he wrote to an Australian official in London, " is to form teams in Europe, train them in local knowledge of the place to which they are going, finance them, and send them out with a ready-made plan. We hope, by tying them closely together through a Central Headquarters, to promote a spirit of international co-operation and friendship."

The purchase price of £120,000 was far beyond the resources of V.I.P., but Cheshire was unwilling to let the offer go a-begging. The woman was anxious to sell; he was just as keen to buy. The possession of land overseas would be the making and saving of V.I.P.; so a scheme to raise the necessary funds was drafted.

On the friendly advice of a Finance Company Director, trial letters were sent to a selected list of people inviting them to subscribe to V.I.P. 3% interest bearing loan stock. At the same time, hundreds of circulars went to R.A.F. stations, book-makers and firms, emphasising the advantages of V.I.P. associate membership.

The campaign evoked little response, and economies were introduced at Gumley Hall. Instead of the original arrangement of pooling earnings and dividing profits according to needs, every member was expected to contribute to the community's running costs and allowed to keep the surplus. Meanwhile, however, the continued overcrowding, and the competition for limited local jobs, forced the executive committee to fling caution to the winds. A second site, preferably with land attached, must be found quickly, regardless of the lack of money.

By a stroke of good fortune, one of the few replies to Cheshire's loan stock letters came from Mrs. Nancy Barstow, an aunt by marriage. She was anxious to sell her home, a large Victorian mansion perched on a spur of the gently undulating hill-country of Hampshire and surrounded by 280 acres of sprawling farmland. Le Court, as it was called, seemed the ideal site, and Cheshire was given first refusal.

Being a family transaction, the terms were generously scaled down. Dr. Cheshire, who had little faith in V.I.P., came forward nevertheless with the 10% deposit. A mortgage was arranged to cover the balance. Then, as if to seal the altruism of the deal, the obliging aunt-in-law promptly handed back to her nephew several thousand pounds of the purchase money. The loan came as a godsend.

During October, the majority of the colonists left Gumley Hall to start afresh at Le Court. There was still a nucleus of loyal, trusting men and women whose idealism seemed proof against the shocks of mismanagement and the frequent evidence of amateur muddling ; yet even they were sometimes bewildered and angered by Cheshire's sudden changes of tack.

He went to endless trouble easing the way back for many who left convinced that their small savings had been uselessly squandered. The numerous letters of reference he wrote, and the money he gave from his own pocket to hard-pressed ex-colonists, were a token of his willingness to let others have the benefit of the doubt.

A note from Air Chief Marshal Sir Ralph Cochrane in mid-November put a shrewdly critical finger on the fundamental flaw in V.I.P. :

" I am interested to hear that you have not succeeded in finding a means of training a man as well as making him productive. . . . The two things are, of course, incompatible. There is no alternative but to shoulder the cost of a proper system of training which will ultimately produce some return to the individual and the nation, if not to the organisation which trained him ! "

Cochrane's comment arrived at a useful moment, when Cheshire was ill in bed with ample time to take stock of the situation. When he was on his feet again, he approached the voluntary financial expert who had been insisting that any serious colony project must attract capital and must base itself on agriculture ; and the response to the new development plan they

K

evolved together was gratifying. In mid-December, a syndicate
of city businessmen agreed, on certain conditions, to sink £33,000
into Le Court. Its potential promise as a soft fruit farm, under
contract to sell the bulk of its products to a leading fruit juice
firm, appeared to interest them.

Cheshire flew to Western Germany in his Mosquito early the
following week, happier than he had felt for six months.

3

The purchase of the two Mosquitos for the knitting together
of overseas colonies still unfounded, had one concrete and useful
result. Early in October, the editor of the *Sunday Graphic*, with
a realistic eye to the present, proposed that one of the machines
should be pressed into service at once. It was a timely flash of
inspiration. Cheshire welcomed it as such.

With a range of 3000 miles and a cruising speed of 300 miles
an hour at 27,000 feet, the Mosquito would annihilate the
distances between peoples, bring nations into closer focus, and
so promote the dual causes of world peace and the sales of the
Sunday Graphic.

" By spring," he told readers, " we shall have opened up at
least one overseas branch."

Cheshire's log-book, which he seldom filled in immediately
after a flight, does not contain the entry of his first brief trip to
Western Germany as a " flying reporter " at the beginning of
November. His impressions were published on November 10th ;
and they reflected his uneasiness at the " complete mental and
moral collapse " of the German people in the British Zone, his
contempt for the feeble cavortings of the Control Commission,
and his sympathy for the occupying forces :

" You might well suppose that the Germans, seeing their
predicament, would throw everything they have into their
common cause and pull together ; but they do not. Their creed
has become a question of each man for himself. . . . They no
longer believe in National Socialism, but equally they no longer
believe in anything else. The older people, knowing that they
will never find material security or happiness on this earth, are
turning to Christianity, but they have no organised lead. . . .
And so it is in every other department, politically, socially and

economically, they are leaderless. It seems to me that we have one alternative only. Either we claim that the Germans are unfit for civilisation—in which case we ought to destroy them—or we allow them to survive; in which case we should give them orders and force them to play their part in the cause of world peace. I think they would do it. I think, also, that if we do not, and if we try to compromise between the two, a national leader will ultimately arise. And if ever he does, we will have a third war on our hands."

It was the same kind of drastic logic, the *reductio ad absurdum* of hard and fast alternatives, which had characterised his public statements on the atom bomb twelve months previously. He gave the facts without revealing his innermost feelings. And the paradoxical point is that Cheshire was more deeply moved by the ugly bomb damage in Cologne than he had ever been by the perfect symmetry of the surging pillar of fire and smoke above Nagasaki.

This was his first glimpse from ground zero of a great modern city half reduced to ruins by conventional bombs; and the first nightmare shadow of what atomic warfare meant in terms of human suffering flitted fitfully across his mind like a cloud across the sun. The thought did not register for long; his German visit was too brief. He flew home, spent three weeks ill in bed, rose to open the delicate financial negotiations which promised V.I.P. a healthier future, and settled the final details of a long-standing R.A.F. lecture tour of Western Germany.

When Cheshire returned in mid-December, it was in the twin roles of " flying reporter " and official lecturer. He stayed for the best part of six weeks but half the visit was wasted musing and reading in a West Berlin hospital bed.

Air Marshal Sir Philip Wigglesworth, A.O.C. of the British Air Forces of Occupation, had arranged his itinerary; and on every station he visited his talks were well received by large gatherings of officers and men. It was two years since he had tasted the easy, companionable atmosphere of mess life, and undoubtedly this short, busy interlude revived in him a nostalgia for the ready-made values of the R.A.F. What he missed most as a civilian was the moral backing of an established organisation which had unobtrusively done much of his wartime planning for him. For in V.I.P. he had partly overestimated his own

abilities. Doubt is a canker which eats slowly into the brain :
during that lecture tour Cheshire began to wonder whether he
had been wise to leave the service so precipitately.

The R.A.F. stations were like little oases in a man-made
desert. Only by moving into the desert itself and inspecting the
destruction caused by Allied bombing could he link his thoughts
together and see himself detachedly as someone who had had a
hand in it. Even so, he felt no remorse, no personal sense of
responsibility at first.

As he drove or walked through streets where the faint
stench of death still seemed to linger above the mountains of
rubble, the disproportionate misery caused by modern war was
finally brought home to him. He could put himself at last into
the place of the victims. He could see with his own eyes that
the fruits of victory were Dead Sea fruits for victors and vanquished alike :

" I think Cologne depressed me even more than Berlin,"
Cheshire recalled in a letter. " The devastation, the cold and the
despair on people's faces helped me to grasp for the first time
what saturation bombing meant to the victims. Piloting a
bomber was a cold, impersonal game. We were too far removed
in distance and vision from the people we were attacking. We
were concerned with switches and markers and flak, not with
life and death. Now I understood the other side of the problem."

Yet, he could still hide behind the argument that the Germans
had brought it on themselves, and that the grisly lesson had
been necessary.

His unannounced arrival in Berlin was as hazardous as any
wartime exploit with 617 Squadron. On the way, the Mosquito
ran into fog, and neither Harry Parker, his flight engineer, nor
himself could see ahead. Cheshire suddenly recognised the
control tower of Gatow below ; but on turning for a groping
touchdown the ground was lost again in the yellow murk.
Overhead there was a muffled snarl ; they both glimpsed the
outline of a Dakota losing height and preparing to land.

" We'll tag on and hope for the best," said Cheshire.

The Mosquito rapidly overhauled the heavier aircraft ; and
as he flashed underneath its wings, a runway suddenly loomed
up below at a crazy angle of forty-five degrees. Cheshire twisted
in a steep turn, watched the startled flare party scatter like nine-

pins, landed safely, and walked back to apologise for his abrupt arrival.

Early in January he fell ill again and remained in a Berlin hospital bed for nearly a month. There was nothing organically wrong. He had merely overtaxed his strength. He finally decided that on his return to London he would apply to re-enter the R.A.F. The overwhelming need to sit back and let others do the arranging for him seemed momentarily to outweigh every other consideration.

On February 3rd, Cheshire landed at Abingdon, and a few days later put his request personally to Marshal of the Royal Air Force, Sir John Slessor. It threw the Chief of Air Staff into a mild quandary :

" Much as I liked and admired him, and would normally have welcomed him back, I felt sure he was not up to it. I remember my impression that he felt a bit adrift and did not really know what he wanted to do."

Slessor diplomatically referred the question to Sir Charles Symonds, who had been on the medical board which discharged Cheshire. But the specialist was as emphatically against it as ever.

After confessing to Slessor that he was " somewhat put out " by Symonds's decision, Cheshire returned to Le Court. In his absence the affairs of V.I.P. had gone from bad to worse. Most of the wage-earners had had to seek outside work ; only the men with trades—the carpenters, metal workers and kennel keepers—succeeded in supporting themselves on the premises. Those who doubted, as well as those who trusted him, wondered uneasily what had become of the fine plans laid before Christmas.

In March, after representatives of the City syndicate had visited Le Court, the dispiriting rumour spread that the bottom had fallen out of the £33,000 deal which was to have brought V.I.P. commercial prosperity.

Determined to keep a tight hold on affairs until the colony was on its feet, Cheshire twice put off another R.A.F. lecture tour through the Middle and Far East, from Tripolitania to Japan. Experience had taught him that extensive outside en-gagements were an excessive drain on time that he could no longer afford. Given two months of uninterrupted effort, he should succeed in consolidating Le Court. With the support of

Turner, the new farm manager, and a qualified works manager who would be arriving in April to direct the " minor industries ", there was no reason why they should not pay their own way at last.

" Apart from V.I.P., I am not quite certain what to do," Cheshire wrote to a senior R.A.F. officer in late March. " It doesn't of course leave me much time over, but what there is, I would like to use constructively. I have been invited to join Churchill's United Europe Committee but don't yet know whether to do so. I am not quite certain whether they are likely to achieve anything or whether they merely confine themselves to talk."

The invitation to join the Churchill Committee followed a widely acclaimed Home Service broadcast he gave at the beginning of the month. It was one of a series of talks on atomic energy in which a panel of noted scientists and writers, including Dr. Bronowski and Sir George Thomson, took part ; and Cheshire's address was the profoundest he ever made on the issue :

" Of all worldly attractions," he said in one of the key passages, " the most vicious is that of power, and atomic energy spelt power. It spelt power of destruction, power of delving into the realms of the unknown, power of being able to achieve our objective. . . . As we lay on the beach sunbathing or sat at table eating, or even as we flew across the Japanese coast under a faultless, sunlit sky, we gave, I am afraid, little thought to the human life that we were to cut short so abruptly. The end was too overpowering for us to pause to consider the means."

There were two simple and connected reasons for his sharper insight into the moral as opposed to the military implications of Nagasaki. In the first place he had seen with his own eyes the wanton misery and havoc caused by the area-bombing of Germany, which had paved the way for the subsequent atomic attacks on Japan. In the second place, Cheshire was beginning to grasp the link between man's inhumanity to man and the loss of religious belief in the Western World.

At Gumley Hall he had become an occasional churchgoer. He felt that Christianity, which taught men to love their enemies, might be a surer means than science of removing the causes of war, though it was sometimes hard to reconcile the secular values of nominal Christians with the infinite personal love of an Almighty Being who really cared. His prayers seem to have been tinctured with the anguish of the man in one of Cardinal Newman's books, who cried out : " Oh, God—if there is a God—save my soul—if I have a soul." When in the spring of 1947 an itinerant Anglican Franciscan visited Le Court, Cheshire fell quickly under his influence, and Brother Hugh was asked to stay as long as he wished.

As soon as finances permitted, Cheshire planned to set apart a dormitory for six disabled ex-servicemen. A small contingent of Dutchmen arrived to work in the greenhouses. The words behind the initials of V.I.P. were changed to suit his hardening Christian sentiments ; and the " Very Important People " became rather puzzled members of the " Vade in Pacem " Association. The promise of stability appeared to be within reach at last, despite the continuing ebb and flow of enthusiastic newcomers and disenchanted pioneers. Then Cheshire mysteriously ran out of strength again and was ordered to take at least six months' complete rest, preferably out of the country.

To Dr. Cheshire and his wife the colony was a mare's nest, and had been so from the beginning. Their son's health was more important to them than the misguided communal experiment which, they felt, had systematically undermined it. They made their own arrangements ; and Cheshire compliantly fell in with them. On May 21st a delegation of colonists saw him off at the airport. He was touched by the surprise parting gift of a poodle in a portable kennel, which the uniformed officials eyed with cold disapproval and the other passengers petted and spoilt on the long flight to Gander.

CHAPTER ELEVEN

THE CHRISTIAN

THE two heavy red locomotives panted to a standstill in the small, sun-dappled station, throwing off their last hissing plumes of steam, and Cheshire climbed stiffly down to the platform with his poodle beside him. Through the brightly-clad press of passengers streaming towards the barrier, beyond which lay the streets of Nelson and the towering cloud-capped peaks of the Rocky Mountains, a handsome middle-aged man came forward with a conspiratorial smile of half-recognition. " This," thought Cheshire, " must be the Bishop in person, though he does not dress like one." " This," thought the Right Rev. Hugh Embling, " must be Leonard Cheshire, though nobody mentioned a dog."

It was ten years at least since the Bishop had met him at Grey Walls, as a young undergraduate, but there could be no mistaking the striking family resemblance. In the pout of the lips, the appraising stare of the serious brown eyes, the firm cast of the long jaw and the slight stooping of the shoulders above the supple frame, he could see the living image of Dr. Cheshire. Embling confidently introduced himself, and they shook hands. He had hardly expected to identify his guest so easily.

A widely travelled man with a critically observant eye and a witty tongue, he had been pleased and flattered when Mrs. Cheshire wrote asking whether he would take care of her son for a while : his friendship with the family dated from the year of the boy's birth. As he led him out of the station, he said briskly :

" The first thing you need is a wash and a meal. You look all in. I'm afraid it's been a long journey, and we've still quite a drive ahead."

" If you don't mind," said Cheshire, " I'd rather not eat. I'm not particularly hungry."

" Nonsense," replied the Bishop firmly. He recalled well

enough his own sensation of torpor on clambering out of the
same train not many months before. The smooth rail journey
across the plains from Calgary on the Lower Main line degener-
ated into an anti-climax of monotony once the long haul up to
the Crow's Nest Pass began. There was a limit to anyone's
enjoyment of the panoramic grandeur of the Rockies viewed
from the windows of a stuffy train pulled by over-heated,
asthmatic engines which had to halt for breath and water nearly
every twenty minutes. Cheshire seemed to him more bored
than physically jaded, and he fully sympathised.

Embling had left England after the war to enjoy an early
retirement in the far west of British Columbia. A long career
in various parts of the world, notably in Korea where he had
served as Assistant Bishop, had taught him to look on human
nature with kindly tolerance. His experience in Western Canada
had already proved to him that travellers could be divided into
four categories : " Those sick in trains, those sick in buses,
those sick in cars and those who don't get sick at all." He was
unimpressed by Cheshire's loss of appetite. He assumed that,
for the moment, his guest had joined the ranks of the train-sick.

" Come and watch me eat at any rate," he suggested.

He had risen early that morning for the drive from New
Denver, a small village of three hundred inhabitants, where he
had made his home. The fresh mountain air had given a sharp
edge to his own appetite ; and, as he had expected, the sight of
food automatically seemed to restore Cheshire's. Embling
admitted over the meal that he was not really surprised to see
Vicky, the poodle pup. His earliest and most vivid memory of
Cheshire was of a small visitor to his home who had suddenly
been galvanized into a ball of fiery energy by the discovery that
he kept chickens in the garden. That had been almost a quarter
of a century before. When finally he had cornered the cockerel
of his choice, Cheshire had pleaded successfully to be allowed to
keep it as a pet. Afterwards, Embling was told that his indulgent
generosity had not increased his popularity. The bird was
coldly tolerated by Cheshire's parents and detested by the next-
door neighbours ; for it ran wild and would permit none but
its owner to touch it.

The lengths to which Cheshire had been prepared to go on
behalf of Vicky, his latest pet, amused the independent-minded

Embling. He was glad that the childhood passion for animals had not been stunted by the hard, eventful life his young friend had led since; and as he listened to the story, he was sure Cheshire would enjoy his stay among people who, in a different sense, were equally kind-hearted and individualistic.

It seemed that the captain of the American airliner, who had connived at Vicky's presence on the flight across the Atlantic, turned the other way at Gander where Cheshire changed planes. But the airport officials had been more obdurate than their counterparts at Heathrow:

"Sorry, you can't take that dog to the mainland," they said. "It's against the law."

"Oh," said Cheshire, taken aback. "In that case, I'd better cancel my booking on the next plane out."

He needed time to think. Whatever happened, he had no intention of leaving Vicky behind, having come so far with him. Renting a rest-room for the day, he eyed his suitcases thoughtfully but decided against stowing the poodle away among his clothes; even a pup must breathe, and air vents cut in the fabric might be a little too obvious to deceive wary officials. A large cardboard box, disguised as a parcel, would probably be the best conveyance, but where could he find one without arousing premature suspicions? Cheshire went round to the airport canteen to reconnoitre.

An obliging girl in the kitchen provided him with the box, and he returned to his room to cut it down to the right size. Then he went back cautiously to the swill-bins behind the canteen, came upon a pile of discarded straw, hid a handful under his coat, and returned five times more to remove the rest. Vicky joined in the game with destructive zest, tearing each fresh handful of straw to shreds, and scattering it over the floor.

"Inevitably," said Cheshire, "he got the idea that I was providing a makeshift lawn for him to do his business on. That didn't help much. In the end he went into the box. I tied it up, made sure he was breathing, and walked across to the office to pay for the room and fly out on the next westbound aircraft."

The man behind the *guichet* scrutinised Cheshire's ticket and looked at him cautiously:

"Ha," he said triumphantly. "Aren't you Group Captain Cheshire?"

Cheshire admitted it with a sinking feeling.

" And you've got a dog you want to take with you ? "

" I beg your pardon ? "

" A dog. The one you want to take across to Canada ? "
The official's smile was amiably omniscient, as though seeing
through clumsily tied cardboard boxes were all in the day's
work. To bluff one's way past a man like that would be impossible, and Cheshire owned up despondently :

" Yes, I have a dog. A poodle puppy."

" I was sure you had," said the official. " If you'd care to
step over to the other office, you can buy him a special ticket.
I've been making inquiries. It'll be quite in order to take him."

So Vicky travelled openly to Calgary after all, dividing his
time between the laps of various passengers and the kennel with
its V.I.P. markings. Embling chuckled at the story : Cheshire's
stock stood high in his estimation.

On the car drive from Nelson through the hills, he began
to appreciate the wild magnificence of the countryside. The
Bishop was busy at the wheel, concentrating on hugging the
craggy elbows of rock that rose sheer above them. The road
was strewn with small boulders and scarred with potholes, but
the constant jolting was not unpleasant. As they twisted upwards in a haze of powdery dust, Embling remarked laconically
that the other side of the track was unfenced and one could not
always trust the edges. They had been known to crumble
under the weight of tyres, and it was rather a long drop into the
valley.

As far as the eye could see stretched the serrated peaks of
the Selkirk mountains, bare, grey and majestic under the bright
blue sky. Every now and then there was a flash of quicksilver
as the sun's rays glanced off the surface of the river tumbling
like a tiny stream through the gorges of dark green pine below.
They bumped past abandoned workings in the outcropping
rocks where prospectors, lured by the hope of striking silver,
had dug and blasted in vain. The market town of Nelson had
absorbed most of them, leaving isolated places like New Denver
to shrink with the years into " ghost towns ".

When they reached its single street of rough timber houses
standing along the western shore of the Kootenay Lake, the
Bishop pointed out his home. " Wild, woolly and a bit hilly-

billy " was Embling's description, but the crude wooden arm-
chairs and the iron cots in the bedrooms seemed to Cheshire
quite adequate comforts. That night he slept more soundly
than he had slept for months.

Time assumed a new meaning for him during the golden
summer months that followed. Often he would accompany the
Bishop on his journeys to villages across the lake or beyond the
valley. The people he met, young and old, accepted him as one
of themselves. Farmers, miners, lumberjacks and storemen,
carpenters, mechanics and local officials, all of them had long ago
come to terms with their surroundings ; and the neurotic tempo
of life as he had lived it for nearly ten years suddenly appeared
empty and artificial. Cheshire made many friends in the valleys
of the Selkirk Hills.

One of them, George Pumphrey, a storekeeper in the village
of North Bend, met him first when he entered his shop one day
with the Bishop to buy provisions. Pumphrey still has Vicky,
now a full-grown poodle, and the field-glasses through which
Cheshire looked down on the radio-active ruins of Nagasaki ;
but he cherishes far more the memories of numerous visits, of
" yarning " round the stove at night, of an argument with the
Bishop when the poker-faced young Englishman suggested a
radical tightening-up of the lax Canadian gaming laws and was
told for his pains " not to be a B.F." Cheshire intrigued many
with his accounts of the struggle to found self-supporting
colonies in England ; and they hoped Le Court's predicament
would never drive him to crashing his Mosquito and charging
sightseers to inspect the wreck, as he humorously asserted it
might.

" Money meant nothing to him," said Pumphrey. " He
loved good food, especially big salmon steaks, and had an
enormous appetite. He was popular with everyone."

Though he enjoyed the company of men like Pumphrey in
North Bend, and Harris, the farmer, in New Denver, Cheshire
learnt to value even more the opportunities for solitude. As the
bushes and trees flamed into autumn browns and reds, he often
wandered off alone into the pine forests, pondering problems
which had been shelved in the past for lack of time. The con-
templative side of his nature, no longer drugged by the craving
for distracting excitement, was allowed to develop free and

unfettered. The conflicting thirsts for action and contemplation were partly reconciled at last; and with the new sense of proportion came a serene acceptance of his surroundings and an awareness, surer and subtler than ever before, not merely of God's existence but of His living presence at the root of all this panoramic glory. Religion, like time, had taken on a new dimension for Cheshire. It had become more than a mumbling of the fixed formulas, a Sunday routine which left the rest of the week unaffected, or a frantic search for solutions to complex social problems. From a disturbing, irresolute instinct it grew into a powerful conviction that enabled him to raise his heart and mind in prayer whenever he was alone. God, the Creator of all this magnificence, was always within earshot.

"During this period," said Cheshire, "I also became attracted to the Virgin Mary. For some reason or other, I wanted to find out what the Hail Mary was. I went to great trouble to find out, and then I used to say the Hail Mary frequently, especially when I was out in the woods felling timber. I was astonished at the sense of peace it gave me; it was a source of great comfort and help."

The Bishop, a rich mine of information on other matters, discouraged pointed inquiries about the differences between the Christian churches. He disliked theological hair-splitting.

"I am not," he said on one occasion, "a potted meat merchant."

His principal concern was with the health of his young guest; and he left him to puzzle out the divisions of Christendom for himself.

Looking back over the years, from the dreams of easy wealth at Oxford to the threadbare ideal of a closed community founded on selflessness, Cheshire saw that his gravest error had been to trust too much in himself. All through the war, before it, and since, he had been impelled largely by an intuitive faith in his own predestined luck; now that he could discern the hand of a personal God in the works of nature and the world of men, he realised that a better and more accurate name for that uncanny "luck" would be Providence. In spite of his vaulting over-confidence, he had been protected, guided and spared through countless hazards for a reason. One day, perhaps, he would understand it and begin to repay the staggering debt of gratitude

he owed.   Unemotional and logical as ever, Cheshire started by
searching his own conscience.

" I'm afraid I have always had a tendency to make people's
minds up for them," he wrote to a V.I.P. member in England,
who criticised the tottering organisation of the colony.   " It's
taken me a long time to realise that it's a very selfish thing to
do and only leads to unhappiness."

To another member of V.I.P. who held no official position,
he wrote in a similar vein :

" I am beginning to see a few of my many shortcomings.
Thank God, though, it looks as if what I wasn't able to do is
now being done by the few who remained, and when I come back
I may well find something that I could never have built. . . .
I absolutely agree with you that the thing which counts most is
the spirit in which it's done : but it's awful how easily one can
imagine one's self to be doing something perfectly altruistically
when in point of fact it is purely for one's own ends.   However,
I am sure it doesn't help to dwell on the past.   The main thing
is that we should all be a little better for our mistakes."

At times these far-off echoes of V.I.P. seemed remote and
unreal ; then he would be filled with enthusiasm at the idyllic
thought of an overseas colony in British Columbia.   During the
summer, he trekked alone across country to the Arrow Lake
valley.   A friendly Canadian ex-serviceman he had met at
Okanagan told him the land was cheap, unspoilt and very suitable for emigrants who were really keen on pioneering.   Embling
was scathingly critical :

" Whoever said that can't know much about pioneering,"
he said.

Cheshire returned from the trek, sunburned and dispirited ;
the Bishop knew without asking that his young friend had learnt
the unsatisfactory truth for himself.   The inhospitable Rockies of
British Columbia were hardly a good training ground for a
group of raw pioneers from England.

It surprised Cheshire to hear that New Denver itself had had
its lean years, and that until 1939 it had been in danger of
becoming a deserted village.   By an ironic accident, its inaccess-
ibility had proved its greatest asset after the Canadian declaration
of war on Japan.   A large internment camp for Japanese civilians
brought renewed prosperity to the almost bankrupt local shop-

keepers ; indeed many of the internees took a perverse liking to the place and decided to stay on indefinitely, as Cheshire sometimes felt tempted to do himself.

One of his friends in the village was the elder son of a remarkable English settler, J. C. Harris, who had given the valley hydro-electric power and its own piped water supply years before. Old man Harris was still a local legend ; he had brought from his native Dorset the Fabian ideas of his youth and a little money, and had developed a dairy farm on the rocky soil to provide the people with fresh milk. Then, with the aid of volunteers, he had extended the road to the next village, built a dam and installed his own generating plant.

It was lack of pocket-money rather than any strong desire to emulate the philanthropic enterprise of Harris which persuaded Cheshire to seek work in September and October. Embling admired without approving his diffidence about accepting help :

" The amount of money he had been allowed to bring out with him was too meagre for anything. He was much too independent to allow even a friend to finance him : he wanted to feel free and I suppose that in its way was very natural."

But the Bishop discreetly passed the word round that Cheshire wanted to earn his keep, and presently his hands were full. The school trustee needed trees cleared away for a new classroom annexe ; tactfully he offered the lumberjack's job to Cheshire :

" You can have the trees or fifty dollars," he said. " Whichever you prefer."

Very soon, with the active advice of two ex-marines, the clump of pines behind the low schoolhouse was felled.

Jim Draper, the village carter, then took him on as an assistant roundsman. Draper's heavy truck delivered groceries, coal and logs, carried the sick to and from hospital in an emergency, and acted as hearse for the dead on their last journey to the cemetery. It was as a grocery boy and driver rather than as an apprentice undertaker that Cheshire proved his worth and willingness. Draper recalls no funeral at which his handy assistant stood in for him. The regular work, in Embling's words, " provided him with enough odd cash for his needs and an occupation for his idle hours, though he had few of those."

In the first cold snap of winter, Cheshire's health suddenly broke. The Bishop made arrangements for him to be taken to the Veterans' Hospital at Shaughnessy, a town several miles to the West, for a thorough " overhaul ". Embling blamed himself for not being more observant : in spite of the good-humoured, uncomplaining attitude of Cheshire to his spare-time work, he had obviously overestimated his physical strength. A few days previously, he had written happily to another friend in V.I.P. at Le Court :

" I have been more fortunate than I can say in coming here. I lead a pretty simple life, earn my own bread and butter by working as delivery boy for the grocer, carrier for the coal and wood merchant, and in various other ways. It's the greatest possible fun, and I'm getting quite strong. By next summer, when my time is up, I should be very fit."

But Cheshire's days in Canada were already running out. Soon after returning to New Denver at the end of November, an urgent cable arrived from Le Court. It swept aside the vain hope to which he had clung for nearly seven months that those who remained behind would succeed where he had failed :

" Please return as soon as possible," said the cable. " V.I.P. in serious trouble."

2

Cutting short his convalescence, Cheshire made hurried preparations to return at once, and recrossed the Atlantic by air in mid-December. In thirty years of personal upheavals, he had shown a consistent disregard for his physical surroundings. The ups and downs of war had strengthened his cool indifference to places, especially when crisis or opportunity loomed on the horizon. A man without roots, he had trailed over the globe collecting no trophies but the incidental memories. A place had usually meant a target, a departure point, or a means to some end. He would change his surroundings and go on a journey as gladly as he would change his mind and go off at a tangent. Now suddenly it was different. He could not have believed that leaving British Columbia would be so severe a wrench. Maudlin sentimentality did not enter into it. Attachment to any particular person or place had nothing to do with it. His whole outlook had undergone a subtle change in the sublime solitude of the Rockies, and there was a sense of dread in breaking the spell.

Less than twenty colonists were left at Le Court after he had summarily dismissed the ringleaders of a " rebel " faction during the week before Christmas. The exchanges were curt, one-sided and unpleasant. The breakaway group had planned to move V.I.P. lock, stock, and barrel, to another site, under new management, using Cheshire's name to ease the transfer. It was a sickening but not altogether unexpected blow, and he was glad at least that the plot had been forestalled in time. Everything had gone downhill at a disastrous rate. Several of those he had trusted to pull the colony through had apparently decided this could best be done by pulling it down and rebuilding it. Most of the survivors were single with no close family ties. They were free to go if they pleased, but none did. Cheshire was touched by their personal loyalty and secretly surprised that anyone should deliberately choose to see the experiment through to its inglorious end.

The first two months of the New Year were an interlude of sporadic activity in an atmosphere of unnatural calm. It was, as they all guessed, the lull before the final storm. For all practical purposes, V.I.P. had already foundered and could be written off. While the accountants frowned over the books, assessing the full liabilities, the twenty survivors, led by Brother Hugh, spent their days trying to help Cheshire salvage a little from the wreck.

They formed an ill-assorted but untroubled family. The evenings were the most memorable part of the day. Sitting before a blazing log fire in the downstairs recreation room, they discussed many things with unusual openness and friendliness. It saddened Cheshire to think that only on the eve of its downfall could V.I.P. capture the spirit of give-and-take which should have been its permanent mainspring. Those talks by firelight meanwhile showed the others that in some indefinable fashion Canada had softened his exuberant air of optimism. He was more considerate, even of opinions he disliked, and far more diffident about proposing minor communal ventures. Yet there were one or two he insisted on trying.

Harry Sawyer, the carpenter, spent two or three days in the damp cellars under the house, fixing corrugated iron frames to

the walls for the cultivation of mushrooms, and wondering
where they would all be when the crop was ready. It was rather
a come-down after the brewer's contract for half a dozen inn
signs which had once kept the workshops busy for three months.
Sawyer's fiancée, Kitty McQuillan, who had served at Woodhall
Spa when Cheshire led 617 Squadron, realised later that the
scheme was a desperate version of the wartime dream of growing
mushrooms in disused tunnels. Then, before the end of February, half-hearted attempts were made to plant watercress in a
stream which ran through the grounds.

A pinching self-sufficiency had gradually been forced on
them owing to the antagonism of people in neighbouring villages,
where V.I.P. had acquired a bad name. He heard that several
former colonists had been involved in humiliating scenes with
impatient shopkeepers, best typified by an incident in the late
autumn of 1947. An irate little laundryman had turned scornfully on one of the married women when she called to collect the
weekly basket of clean linen for the colony :

" V.I.P.", he had stormed, " Very Important People, to be
sure. Too damned important to pay your laundry bills. This is
the last time I want to see any of you." And he had slammed
the door behind her. Other shopkeepers had followed suit.
Now Le Court was partly blacklisted in the vicinity, and Cheshire
knew that until the local creditors were placated they would
either have to pay cash or go short of goods.

The accountants finally sorted out the books early in March,
and Cheshire was momentarily staggered by the debts that had
piled up in less than eighteen months. He had to find nearly
£20,000 within seven weeks. His father, hardheaded and realistic,
advised him to cut his losses and sell up the entire estate if
necessary, and went down to help with the legal arrangements.
By the middle of April new fences marked the truncated bound-
aries. Only the house and grounds, two fields, and the kitchen
garden were Cheshire's ; but the biggest debts had been wiped
out by the sale.

Since returning from Canada, he had kept well out of the
public eye. But if the newspapers overlooked or ignored his
activities, there was still the unfailing trickle of visitors who had
heard of V.I.P. and were vaguely curious to meet its founder.
One of the few who accepted Cheshire's characteristically warm

invitation to " stay for a while and decide if you like it " was an ex-public schoolboy called John Turner. Turner came up the steep uneven drive one bright spring Sunday afternoon and was met outside the main door by a short, grey-haired man in faded brown corduroy trousers and a grey roll-top pullover, whose hands were buried in the side-pockets of a shabby tweed jacket.

" Do you want the Group Captain ? " he asked.

" Yes," said Turner, " but I've no appointment."

" He's resting, but I'm sure he'll see you. I'll show you up."

The man's face was lined and had the unhealthy tinge of faded parchment. In the pale sunlight his rather taut smile had made Turner think inconsequentially of a tired orange. He introduced himself on the way upstairs.

" My name's Arthur Dykes. I should have told you in the first place. I've been here quite some time." His voice trailed off, and he added as a kind of apologetic afterthought, " You'll like the skipper."

Dykes left Turner at the bedroom door, and shuffled self-effacingly down the corridor. They saw each other daily for the next few weeks ; but neither Cheshire nor anyone else seemed to pay particular attention to the kindly but forlorn little man with the ugly sallow mask of a victim of chronic jaundice. It was a mystery to them how anyone as ill and as old-looking had managed to join the R.A.F. during the war ; how he had been released with a clean bill of health was a bigger mystery still. Dykes had entered V.I.P. in 1947, and until the kennels changed hands had put in a hard twelve hours a day which would have taxed the strength of anyone half his age. Dogs were his life, and he hated leaving them.

As a younger man he had trained to be a " vet ", but times had been bad. Ill fortune seemed to have hounded him for years. Now his back ached unbearably at times, so that a routine task like weeding a path or a flower-bed proved too much for him. He would pause, half-bending but without a murmur, until the spasm of pain had gone. Then he would straighten up with a hangdog grin and watering eyes to face the good-natured taunts of his companions that old Dykes was " slacking again ". Nobody, not even Cheshire, for whom he had a deep but distant respect, could then have foreseen the part this timid, ailing, prematurely aged man of fifty was destined to play in the resurrection of Le Court, though Dykes himself seemed to have a faint glimmering of what the future might hold in store.

" Arthur used to talk as we weeded the path of ' something good ' that was sure to happen," said Mrs. Marjorie Cowey, an ex-V.I.P. member living at Empshott Green, a mile and a half away, who still came to help in her spare time. " He used to say : ' I don't think Cheshire can fail. He's too big. Some good will come out of all this.' It was something he felt most strongly. Arthur Dykes was perhaps the only one of the two hundred people involved in V.I.P. from the start who believed Cheshire was not finished."

The mushrooms and the watercress were swept away with the debris of older ideas while the estate was being sold. To guard against further financial loss, Cheshire decided to convert part of the house into a number of self-contained flats. He told the colonists that after the formal winding up of V.I.P. he would have to charge them a fixed rent. Meanwhile they should look for independent jobs. It was a bitter decision, forced upon him by circumstances. He had flown once too often in the face of Providence, only to fetch up against the walls of a hopeless blind alley. In the process he had become a Christian ; but understanding the reasons for failure did not make the humiliation any the less oppressive. More despondent and weary than he appeared, Cheshire turned his back on Le Court for a spell.

For months he had rarely glanced at a newspaper. But he knew with a certainty born of faith that the mass of mankind was as sick at heart as himself. The lessons of the last war had been learnt no better than the lessons of any other war in history. The western democracies had forgotten the aim of true civilisation as surely as the avowedly godless states which had sprung up in the wake of the liberating Soviet armies.

He had no taste for mastering the idealistic subtleties of the Marshall Plan : as far as he could see, no nation or group of nations would find lasting strength in life-giving transfusions of dollars alone. The economic recovery of Europe, of Britain, of the world, could not guarantee peace until the statesmen and citizens of every land were at peace with God and themselves. These glum reflections of his own contrite mood became semi-public property in May when Cheshire went to the Congress of

Europe at The Hague as a delegate of the United Europe Movement.

He accepted the invitation after much thought, and astonished the vicar of the Anglican church nearest his parents' home by insisting on going to confession beforehand. Cheshire regards his brief visit to The Hague as a landmark in his life. For it was the first time he ever stood up on a political platform as an impromptu champion of Christian values and principles. With eight hundred M.P.s, authors, churchmen, and other distinguished delegates from nearly a dozen European countries, he attended the formal opening of the Congress on May 7th, in the 13th-century Knights' Hall of the Netherlands Parliament, and heard Churchill's rhetorical call for a Europe united to save its unique inheritance of freedom which "we have almost cast away." That evening at his hotel he met the Rev. L. J. Collins, then the Dean of Oriel College, now a Canon of St. Paul's Cathedral, and Mr. Douglas Woodruff, the editor of the *Tablet*, a weekly Catholic review. Both of them seemed indignant at the secularist tone of the Cultural Committee's resolution. They felt that a stand should be made against the agnostics and humanists who headed it ; some kind of protest was called for. Cheshire listened, saying little. He was not used to lobbying tactics. Besides, he had already decided to act independently.

His intervention in the Committee's debate next day was starkly simple and sincere. After the late Anglican Bishop of Truro had criticised the resolution for failing to recognise the need for " Christian Humanism," Cheshire caught the Chairman's eye and obliquely criticised the Anglican Bishop for flirting with humanism in any shape or form.

" The primary tasks of man on earth," he said, " are to love and serve God. These admit of no compromise with humanists or politicians or anyone else. Humanism isn't Christianity, whatever else it may be. The whole movement towards European unity as defined in the resolution of this committee is to my mind anti-Christian."

According to Collins and others, " Cheshire's forthright, uncompromising stand had an electrifying effect on the meeting and encouraged other delegates to speak their minds." It certainly put the chairman, Señor de Madariaga, and his committee colleagues on the defensive ; and in the end the wording of

the offensive resolution was amended. It was a hollow victory.
The Congress as a whole appeared to Cheshire a dismal waste
of time. Whatever else he did with his life, he would certainly
avoid trying to influence delegates to political congresses.

Canon Collins was impressed by the marked change in his
outlook. He had last met him about eighteen months before,
when V.I.P. had begun to be a burden. Cheshire at that
time seemed to have " wispy and very vague ideas about
religion." The full-blooded Christianity of his new views was
startling :

" I wouldn't be at all surprised if he ended up a Roman
Catholic," Collins said to his wife during that May week-
end at The Hague. " Something tells me he's heading in that
direction."

No thought could have been further from Cheshire's mind
at that time. Catholicism, in his eyes, was a vaguely outlandish
creed, obviously unworthy of grown Englishmen with the
intelligence to think for themselves ; and he was hardly flattered
when two Dutch Franciscan friars, congratulating him on his
uncompromising little speech before the Cultural Committee,
mistook him for a Catholic. The Hague Congress had disappointed him. The affably spineless discussions had merely
accentuated the divisions among Christians on what seemed
unassailable questions of principle, defying him to find the
elusive key which would exactly fit the eternally reliable lock of
divine revelation. Nothing had happened to alter his view that
the key and the lock lay rusty and disused in one or other of the
Protestant churches.

His consciousness of past failure and of uncertainty for the
future could not brook delay. Like an injured but undaunted
man pinned beneath the ruins of old ambitions, his instinct was
to stretch out for strong hands to release him and guide his own,
so that life could begin afresh. In that mood of half-hoping
expectancy, he met two men who partly restored his sense of
proportion before he left The Hague. The first, a German
Evangelical Bishop, quietly described the unequal struggle to
keep despair at bay in the festering cities and the vast slums of
the D.P. Camps ; the second, a learned, congenial Anglican
cleric from Lambeth Palace, yielded to Cheshire's request for
spiritual direction. If one had thrown down a practical challenge

to his compassion, the other would perhaps help him to take it up worthily.

The resolve to settle in Germany as a relief worker was still strong in him when he returned to Le Court on May 12th. Little had changed in his absence. There had been a further thinning out of tenants, and Brother Hugh had departed. Cheshire had at last discarded the religious ideas of the unattached Franciscan, who firmly believed in the transmigration of souls and could usually detect plausible " signs " in prosaic situations as happy manifestations of God's will for himself and others. This short-circuiting of the humdrum ways of Providence had greatly attracted Cheshire, until a visiting Anglo-Catholic curtly noted that one drawback in Brother Hugh's system was its possible tendency to short-circuit the rights of others.

The big house had grown quieter. Colonel Weddell and his wife still occupied their self-contained flat upstairs ; the Scotts and their child had not moved from the converted billiard room, nor the Macraes from their apartment on the ground floor. George Swinton, who cooked and tilled the garden, had made himself comfortable in a bed-sitting-room close by. But the former estate office was empty ; the bed and its occupant had gone. Cheshire was momentarily stunned to hear what had happened to the tired, little man with the ugly, sallow complexion. Arthur Dykes, they told him, was lying in Petersfield Hospital with incurable cancer of the liver, and the shock drove from his mind the challenge of the German D.P. camps. Here was a displaced person on his own back doorstep, a victim of circumstance for whom he felt a surge of compassion and belated responsibility.

He bristled with indignation on learning that Dykes was dying in apparent ignorance of his true condition. The hospital authorities, for reasons of their own, were unwilling to let him know the worst, and none of his ex-V.I.P. visitors had the heart or the " nerve " to pronounce sentence of death on him. It seemed incredible that anyone should be allowed to perish slowly in the dark, suspended between the devil of lonely helplessness and the deep, cold sea of public care. Cheshire decided to demand an explanation.

The doctors and matron emphasised that the diagnosis of Dykes's fatal illness had placed them in an extremely awkward position. Here was a patient beyond medical aid. They were powerless to save his life. Yet, with the best will in the world, they could not keep him until he died. Rules were rules, and there was already a queue of curable patients for the hospital's few beds. Their hands and tongues were tied ; they could not bring themselves to darken the last agony of a dying man with the useless knowledge of this fate. For Dykes had no known friends or relatives to turn to and nowhere else to go.

It was a dilemma more cruelly involved than Cheshire had imagined :

" If you could find a place for him," they said " it would ease things a lot."

" I'll do what I can," said Cheshire. ' But I still think he should be told the truth. He has a right to know."

For nearly a week Cheshire vainly pestered nursing homes, benevolent associations and influential friends, frantically trying to rouse their practical sympathy. None seemed to appreciate the urgency of the case or the plight of the victim. When the Health Authorities proposed with chilly formality that he would do well to reapply in six months, the blow to his sense of justice proved too much. With a bare three twilight months to live, Dykes had become almost a symbolic figure, whose cold rejection cried out for instant redress like the despairing *De Profundis* of a whole agonised humanity. Cheshire decided to act alone. And on his next visit to Petersfield, he gently told Dykes what the authorities had been so anxious to keep from him.

His relief was great when he saw the rueful grin wrinkling the discoloured, sad face above the straggling beard the patient had grown during his seven weeks in hospital. In a life dogged by misfortune, the last unkindly stroke was not unexpected. Instinctively Dykes had reconciled himself to the grim probability of death. But his spirits sank during the day. The knowledge that he had become a burden to the doctors and nurses seemed to deepen his unspoken self-pity. He had no wish to be kept on secret sufferance to die unwanted, yet where else could he turn ? His doubts were answered when Cheshire reappeared the following morning :

" How would you like to come back to Le Court, Arthur ? "

A beam of astounded pleasure flickered over the lined, yellow face on the pillow. Then the happiness faded, and Dykes shook a mournful head :

"I couldn't," he said. "It wouldn't work. I'd only be in the way, and I don't want that."

"Don't talk nonsense, Arthur. I've spoken to the others. They want you back. If you don't mind risking it, you can come straight away."

He left him to "think it over", promising to return as soon as possible. There were still a few preparations to be made. From Nurse Roberts, who was on the hospital staff, he took a quick course in bed-making and treating an advanced cancer case. From Mrs. Weddell, who was having second thoughts about nursing Dykes herself, he borrowed a bed, sheets and blankets. She was eager to help in other ways, and together they cleaned and distempered the large, bright room on the first floor which had been set aside in readiness. A cheerful fire was burning in the grate when they tucked Dykes carefully between the sheets on May 22nd. He grinned at them in dumb gratitude, sniffing at the lingering smell of fresh paint. The hospital had given him his final discharge with solemn alacrity. He had come home gladly, and Cheshire had taken the leafy, winding road from Petersfield in his small Standard saloon at half the usual speed.

Some of the patient's regular visitors began to stay away after his return to Le Court. The fact puzzled him until he discovered that they despised Cheshire the Nurse as an unfeeling charlatan. They deplored his vain self-conscious posing in a white coat, using a dying man for what they regarded as the latest ill-chosen venture in dramatic make-believe. Their misjudgment of the man and the situation prompted Dykes to write what was probably the last letter he ever wrote. The scrawled, pencilled note, dated May 29th, was a brave attempt to demolish their bitter distrust :

"I do assure you that you are entirely mistaken if you think he just came and snatched me away from the hospital. The matron had told me the position. . . . There seemed to be no object in going to another hospital when the doctors could not do anything for me. It would have meant planting me down among strangers, very likely a long way from my friends.

"You can imagine the terrible quandary I was in and how

anxiously I was wondering what on earth was going to happen to me. Neither my one or two friends nor any of my relatives could possibly manage to take me. Then along came Cheshire. When he heard the position, he absolutely assured me that the good people here were really keen to have me back and more than willing to look after me. . . . They have done that and more. You cannot imagine what a relief it was to me to know that the Good God had sent some kind friends to my rescue, for that is just what He did."

3

On the last Saturday of June, Cheshire walked out into the hot sunshine after lunch, shouldering a scythe. The lawn in front of the house, sloping down towards the stagnant lily-pond, was growing rank and coarse for want of attention. He had formed the new habit of mowing a patch each day to maintain a semblance of order and to placate the nagging of his essentially tidy mind. The daily exercise was not unpleasant, nor did it impede the free-wheeling of his thoughts.

Arthur Dykes was far less of a physical burden than he had supposed he would be. The dejected air of the man whose last rags of self-respect are in pawn had soon vanished. There was no improvement in his health, but the improvement in his moral and spiritual stature had already been startling. Dykes had recovered some of his long-lost dignity and independence ; and Cheshire, who had suffered beforehand all the fastidious man's horror of unpleasantly close contact with disease, could afford now to mock at his own squeamishness. The patient, by insisting on doing nearly everything for himself, had initiated him painlessly to the more squalid chores of the daily round.

It had become clear that Dykes feared death far less than waiting for it in helpless loneliness. A lapsed Catholic who had abandoned the practice of his religion years before, he had raised no objection when Cheshire suggested sending for the priest at Petersfield. And Father Henry Clarke, a tall, solid, dark and unobtrusive personage, had called nearly every week since to administer the sacraments. The priest remained a shadowy figure in the background with a kind of decorative walking-on part, though he had known Le Court since first visiting its handful of Catholic colonists in the days of V.I.P. His comings and goings did not touch Cheshire's interest or curiosity. He treated him as a stranger, with courteous reserve ; yet grudgingly he had to recognise that Dykes invariably seemed happier for his regular half-hours with this uncommunicative man in black. The patient had found solace at last in the neglected faith of his childhood.

There were moments when Cheshire almost envied him. For if the unsought role of Good Samaritan had given him a new, fixed purpose, it had also aggravated the old crisis of spiritual indecision. The isolation of Le Court was forcing him more and more in on himself. Though he had long broken with the worldly ties and habits that once shackled him, there was nothing sure yet to put in their place. He was full of self-questionings about the Christian's right to turn a convenient back on the wreckage of the past in a pious flurry of determination not to compromise the future. It seemed too easy a solution to be anything but suspect. As an earnest Anglican, convinced that his religion had the answer to such recriminating doubts, Cheshire had begun to put his problems fairly and squarely to the half-dozen clergymen he knew and respected most.

From the beginning, living people had always had a more enduring influence on him than dead books or theories. His clergy friends represented a variety of viewpoints, from High to Low Church, and he was satisfied that between them they would eventually show him what he must do to wipe the slate clean. Ten years as an exuberant pagan, two as half a Christian with a foot in both worlds, had proved that existence without God was endurable but unintelligible. If one accepted the Christian revelation, one had to accept the Church as the official guardian of that revelation. For Cheshire that still meant the Established Church. Nor was his confidence weakened at first by the conflicting advice of his friends. Anglicanism seemed to be an inalienable part of his birthright, like the British Constitution. He would no more have considered changing his religion than changing his citizenship ; and to have considered either would have struck him then as treasonable folly.

As the weeks went by, however, his dissatisfaction with the vacillating and often contradictory answers of his friends steadily mounted. There must be, he felt, a clear-cut Christian solution to the problem of his broken marriage. Yet he was told by

one that he should seek a divorce and marry again, by another
that he should return to Constance, and by others that he should
let well alone but on no account remarry. Their verdicts were
similarly confusing when Cheshire asked what his obligations
were to the men and women whose lives had been entwined
with his own since late 1945. Had he a strict duty to go back
and redeem the havoc ? Or ought he to stay put rather than risk
being caught up again in the garish whirl from which he had
escaped ? The local High Anglican vicar suggested the confes-
sional as the simplest means of atoning for past sins. Cheshire
loyally tried it, but his instinctive lack of assurance in this spiritual
remedy was confirmed after the vicar's replacement by a church-
man with different views, who spurned confession as a meaningless, unauthorised rite which undid nothing.

    From each discouraging visit he would return home with a
borrowed religious book or two ; and during the summer
evenings he read widely and avidly. His general knowledge
and grasp of history were flimsy, but his common sense could
hardly recognise the " Church " described by the erudite authors.
It seemed an impossibly ideal society far removed in spirit from
the ministers who were, for him, its lawful but earthbound
representatives. Only the High Anglicans of his acquaintance
had ever asserted the need for rigid religious discipline in everyday life ; but he sometimes wondered whether their assertions
were more soundly based than the highly personal creed of
Brother Hugh. As Cheshire's doubts spread from his own
unsettled private problems to the credentials of his clergy friends,
another uncertainty overclouded his mind. Had he the right,
as a Christian, to go on looking after the Arthur Dykes of this
world, without qualifications, money, helpers or prospects ?
For once the clergymen were emphatic and unanimous in saying
" No."

    As he scythed the unkempt lawn that June afternoon,
Cheshire's self-searchings were interrupted by the crunch of
quick, unfamiliar footsteps on the gravel walk behind him. He
turned and saw an attractive, smartly-dressed girl approaching.
She stopped at the edge of the turf some yards away, and called
out :
    " Excuse me, who owns Le Court these days ? "
    " I do," said Cheshire curiously. " Why do you ask ? "

"Oh, I just wondered. I was passing and thought I'd look in. I've a kind of soft spot for the place. You see, I worked here as a Wren during the war. It was a hospital then."

"Really?" said Cheshire. "That's very interesting. It's a sort of hospital now. Not much of one, I'm afraid."

"Is it always as quiet as this?" she asked hesitantly. "Or do the staff go out on Saturdays?"

"Not exactly," he said carefully. "I'm the entire staff. I've only one patient, a cancer, and I can just about cope."

The stranger's friendly composure vanished. She stared down with withering politeness, as if he had said something in doubtful taste. Then she moved away, remarking half contemptuously:

"The thing's impossible, and I can't say I envy you. I hope you realise what you've taken on. As a one-man hospital Le Court's as good as finished now."

Cheshire watched her disappear round the side of the house. Then he picked up the scythe again, musing on her parting shot. The girl was not alone in her frank scepticism. Most of the local people, his own bank manager, and more recently his clergy friends, believed that he had rushed headlong into another quixotic undertaking without a pause for breath. From any business standpoint, he had to admit they were probably right. Apart from Dykes's weekly twenty-five shillings and the irregular sums raised from garden produce, Le Court had no income. The house was heavily mortgaged; and the small balance left from the April sale had dwindled away. Happily, their daily needs were few. A vegetarian diet could be had for the picking in the overgrown kitchen garden. Occasionally he would shoot an unwary rabbit when there was no ready cash for meat. There were little windfalls of delicacies from ex-colonists living permanently in the district, some of whom were saddened, depressed or angered by the sordid appearance of the sick-room. Its underlying spiritual drama, developing with the slow passage of the weeks, was beyond the grasp of most of them.

Even the Le Court tenants barely suspected Cheshire's inner turmoil or the unwitting power of Dykes to relieve it. For the suffering, emaciated man was the only person in whom he could fully confide. He had come to know him as well as himself: to anticipate his thoughts, to put up with his simple vanities and to admire his considerable virtues. He liked him for his independence, his contagious cheerfulness in the teeth of habitual pain, and an unsophisticated gratitude for small attentions which made pity unspeakably cheap. Cheshire had stopped worrying about the tubes of toothpaste Dykes kept handy to swallow when his heartburn caused acute discomfort; he no longer opposed his stubborn whim of staggering alone to the commode. He was far more impressed by the patient's deepening serenity and detachment from his ills. It was a spiritual transformation in which sheer physical " guts " or innate stoicism had little place.

Cheshire's respect for the uneducated cancer victim grew. Sometimes they discussed religion, sometimes the uncertain future of Le Court, and Dykes would speak with passionate but inarticulate conviction about both. He did not mind dying now that he was prepared for it, and he longed to dispel the mysterious religious doubts of the benefactor who had become his friend. He fumbled for words to convey something else he believed, something which fired Cheshire's imagination far more than the clumsy, repeated pleas to "become a Catholic". Dykes's certainty that Le Court's recovery had started on the day he returned to die came from the heart. Perhaps only a dying man could believe in a dying cause, for Dykes had no supporters.

Of all the Anglican clergymen Cheshire consulted, the Lambeth Palace adviser had tried hardest to dissuade him from founding a nursing home. Spiritual immaturity was a poor basis for practical mercy work of the kind, he said; and Cheshire reluctantly agreed to let the future take care of itself. For the moment he would confine himself to Arthur Dykes and cease crossing bridges until he reached them. No doubt God would show His hand in good time, provided he did not rush Him. It was in that slightly uneasy spirit of resignation that Cheshire invited to Le Court for August Bank Holiday a man called Harry Rae.

Rae had never heard of Le Court or Cheshire until his chance encounter in London with a former member of V.I.P. a week or two before. Bill Williams, a Welshman and ex-paratrooper, shared a canteen table one lunchtime with the short, middle-aged man who had lost a leg during the war and who seemed intrigued by his account of the defunct colony scheme. When Rae said calmly that he was about to launch a similar project for Welsh quarry workers disabled by silicosis, Williams at once suggested that he ought to meet Cheshire. As a result, Rae travelled down to Hampshire on August 3rd.

"I was greeted," he recalled, "by a quiet, slim young man in khaki shirt and grey flannels. He was carrying a cup of tea up a staircase which must have once been used by the domestic staff when the house was a private mansion. . . . We sat down to lunch in the big kitchen, five people in all, including Bill Williams. When the others left us, Cheshire told me why he started V.I.P.

"'The scheme was a flop,' he said. 'The only thing it taught me was that man's happiness isn't determined by his surroundings but by something deep in himself.'

"'In that case,' I said, 'it wasn't a complete flop. Some people go through life without learning that lesson.'"

Cheshire was more interested in Rae's spirited plan to open a small carpet factory in a Merionethshire village. His discovery that the stranger was a Catholic did not surprise or upset him. Rae, at any rate, seemed ready to give Providence a chance; and he sympathised with Cheshire in his awkward spiritual quandary. Later he visited Dykes and marvelled at the patient's mental alertness. Disease had stained his thin face and arms a splotchy brown. They looked as brittle as withered autumn leaves, and as likely to shrivel at the touch.

Before Rae left for London, Cheshire admitted that he still hoped to turn Le Court into a Home for the Sick. He could not yet decide alone whether the idea was "just another spectacular whim" or a true vocation, and was content to let the problem solve itself.

"I knew then," said Rae, "that I must try to help him, whether he wanted me to or not."

When the postman delivered a small book-parcel later that week, Cheshire read the enclosed letter but had neither time nor inclination to do more than acknowledge Rae's thoughtfulness. Events had forced the pace again; the immediate future was suddenly less obscure.

Like a whispering conspirator, the psalmist had pointed the way ahead. Cheshire had opened the Bible blindly one evening, looking for some relevant consoling word, and his finger had fallen on the boldly defiant verse :

" It is better to trust in the Lord than to put confidence in man." The simple faith of the child, putting its tiny hand in God's, would cut through paralysing scruples about the right course of action. The telephone call soon afterwards removed the last whiff of doubt. It was the hall porter at the flats off Knightsbridge, where his Aunt Edith lived, begging him to take an aged invalid relative. Cheshire had agreed at once and an L.C.C. ambulance brought his second patient to Le Court next day.

Mrs. Haynes was ninety-three and apparently stone-deaf, and as the uniformed attendants bore her upstairs on a stretcher, dressed to the nines and with a colourful feather stuck rakishly in her battered straw hat, she glared at them in toothless enmity. They set her on the bed, and left the house looking furtively relieved. Cheshire's early efforts to win " Grannie's " confidence were useless. Her deafness seemed a diplomatic affliction only slightly less exasperating than her loud and repeated demands to be taken home. He was on the point of admitting defeat after more than a week at loggerheads when " Grannie " suddenly " thawed out ", asked gently whether he loved her, assured him that she loved him and threw her arms about him in a remarkably strong embrace.

The little religious book sent by Rae was put aside. Beyond noting its title, he did not look at it. For the moment, his work was cut out, and when Bill Williams came for a night and agreed to stay longer, Cheshire was grateful for the extra pair of hands. With Dykes and " Grannie " to feed and keep clean, his search for religious truth was temporarily sidetracked.

" Since you left, I have decided to pursue my original line and not pay attention to direction, other than is necessary and appropriate for confession," he wrote briefly to Rae. " I feel the issue has resolved itself. . . ."

About midday on August 19th, Dykes struggled out of bed and tottered across the room as he had been doing for three months. He was as gamely independent as ever, a living skeleton who hardly knew his own excessive weakness. Cheshire's arm, guiding him back, was suddenly bent and almost jerked from its socket. The old man's limbs had involuntarily stiffened in

one fierce reflex action of anguish. By main force, Cheshire
half dragged and half lifted him on to the bed. An anxious
glance at the sweating, contorted face told him that Arthur
would be lucky to outlast the day. He lay there, now limp, now
doubled up and quivering, as each searing shaft of pain dragged
from him a sharp groan and the hoarse, incongruous ejaculation
of " Lumme ". There was little Cheshire could do but arrange
the sheets and hurriedly telephone the hospital. Nurse Roberts
listened to his bald description of the symptoms. She was
glumly sure that an internal hæmorrhage had begun which nothing
could stop. She explained carefully what he must do before
and after Dykes died, and rang off. Then Cheshire called Father
Clarke and asked him to come round as soon as possible.

The long summer's day was nearly over when the priest
finally arrived. All afternoon Cheshire had sat by the bed
watching Dykes struggle closer to the borderland of oblivion.
The ominous rattle in his breathing had gradually lessened.
He was unconscious when Father Clarke entered the
bedroom.

" Do you mind very much if I stay ? "

The priest glanced at Cheshire in faint astonishment.

" Of course not. Stay if you like. There's no need to ask."

The light from the single oil lamp looked pale in the lingering
afterglow of sunset. Cheshire dropped to his knees at the foot
of the bed, straining to catch dimly remembered words in the
low, liquid murmur of Latin prayers. The quick, formal movements of the priest's anointing hands, mysterious yet meaningful,
distracted him. The last rites over, Father Clarke knelt for a
few moments in silence, then scrambled to his feet. On the
way downstairs, Cheshire tried desperately hard to hold him
in conversation. Emotionally, he was drained dry. He was
conscious only of an overpowering sense of his comparative
uselessness, and of a deep desire to put off the long night vigil.
But the priest could not wait. He was already late for another
sick call.

The tail light of the car winked red and disappeared between
the trees. Cheshire closed the front door with a shudder and
returned to the bedside, realising how much he already missed
the plaintive voice of the cancer victim who had become a
secret source of strength to him. About eleven o'clock the

L

arrival of Mrs. Weddell enabled him to visit " Grannie " Haynes, who abused him mildly for his slipshod casualness then, honour satisfied, settled down for the night. Mrs. Weddell was still watching at twenty past twelve, when he felt for Dykes's pulse. The faint beat had stopped ; and the wrist he held was stiff and growing cold. Death had come unobserved, and for the first time Cheshire felt a mild onrush of repugnance.

Walking swiftly from the room, he closed the door, crossed the corridor, and sat down in the small closet he had been using as a pantry. Three hours must pass before he could fulfil the nurse's instructions and lay out the corpse. He dared not sleep. Searching vainly through his pockets for a cigarette, he suddenly remembered the half-empty packet on the bedside table by the corpse. Minutes went leadenly by, until his longing overcame his reluctance to move. Tiptoeing into the darkened death-room, he seized the packet, and returned quickly to his cubby-hole. As he lit up and inhaled deeply, the house grew uncannily quiet again. Every creak from the staircase, every slight stir in the eaves or in distant rooms, seemed to jar in his ears and jangle his overstrung nerves. The preternatural stillness crowded in on him with the stealth of an unseen enemy, as though waiting for him to make one false move into the gloom beyond the narrow circle of lamplight. His senses were playing tricks on his reason, he told himself ; with a sharp effort of will Cheshire pulled himself together.

He forced his mind back to his meetings with the clergy, reconstructing the intellectual doubts which had led him round and round the same unanswered questions like a blinkered, tethered animal treading the same worn patch of ground. If God could neither deceive nor be deceived, every seeker should be able to find the truth. He had picked up enough scriptural knowledge to accept the Church as the sole teacher of truth, in the light of which man must strive to live. But did the Church always uphold divine truth ? If she hesitated about her own God-given authority as a teacher and guide, how could any man know what to believe or how to behave ? The clerics had spoken with several voices, leaving him more confused and bewildered than ever.

Cheshire was weary with too much thinking when he went back to lay out the corpse at half-past three on the Friday

morning. Dykes lay as he had left him, rigid and composed ;
but while he was stripping off the first of the dead man's four
vests, a loud, life-like noise midway between a gurgle and a
rattle escaped from the throat. He drew back quaking, letting
the body slump back on the mattress. His first fearful thought
was that Dykes might still be alive, but then he saw the absurdity
of it. More gingerly, he removed the rest of the clothing and
set about his unpleasant task, holding his breath as he carried
each pail of slops to the bathroom. It was nearly dawn when
he stole out of the room for the last time.

Time seemed to hang heavily after Cheshire completed the
funeral arrangements the following afternoon. One of the pivots
of his life had been kicked away, and nothing he did could ease
his restlessness. Wandering aimlessly from the sunlit garden
back into his own room, he sat down and idly picked up the little
book Harry Rae had sent him nearly a fortnight before. Rae
wanted it back ; he himself had nothing better to do than read.
It was a slim book, barely two hundred pages long, and its subject
quickly explained itself. *One Lord, One Faith* was the apologia
of a High Anglican clergyman who, against every cherished
instinct and prejudice, had been attracted to the Church of Rome.
After a painful internal conflict, he had finally submitted to the
unmistakable tyranny of that monolithic, un-English institution.

The early chapters tended to bore Cheshire. They were
cluttered up with strange personal sentiments. Like the contents
of someone else's overnight bag, the details seemed banal and
trivial. The town of Lisieux was familiar only as a place-name
behind the Normandy beaches ; its pious associations with a
tuberculous girl called Thérèse Martin, who became a Carmelite
nun, lived obscurely, and died a saint, were far-fetched and
unreal.

" The saint of Lisieux pointed me to the Catholic Church,"
stressed Monsignor Vernon Johnson, the author. " The
Catholic Church sent me back to Holy Scripture, and Holy
Scripture sent me back to the Catholic Church." To that
extent, perhaps, the rather glutinous opening was justifiable.
Cheshire read on. He grew slowly absorbed in the sober reasoning of a man who had gone through some of the same theological
hoops as himself, but who scarcely raised his voice above a
mild whisper in describing the unsettling ordeal. Every stage

was understandable. The total effect, including the surrender to Rome, was one of disturbing consistency.

The late Duff Cooper once noted in a crisp half-truth that " for the majority of Englishmen there are only two religions, the Roman Catholic which is wrong, and the rest which don't matter." As Cheshire finished the last page of the book that same evening, his matter-of-fact faith in the Anglican position remained unaffected. He had no ready answer for Monsignor Vernon Johnson's pro-Catholic arguments; but he had every confidence that his Anglican friends would easily make hay of both.

The basic Catholic claim to absolute authority in all questions of faith and morals both attracted and repelled him. Its cut-and-dried simplicity was almost too good to be true. The vision of a unique authority teaching one unalterable doctrine exactly fitted his own intuitive notion of a God who would hardly have bothered to speak to mankind without making sound arrangements to ensure that what He said was handed down intact. The untidiness of the Protestant assumption that the Church had many branches argued a deficiency in the Almighty's wisdom. Yet, by contrast, the Catholic assertion was altogether too arrogant. It stuck in the gullet. Rome was not just another half-way house to heaven. According to its own fantastic pretensions, the Popes from Peter onwards held the Keys of the Kingdom in divine trust for Christ Himself. The monstrous impertinence of the claim revolted his English sense of moderation and decency.

" If this is false," he told himself, " it's nothing less than vicious. And it'll be a pleasure to expose it as never before." Yet, what if the claims of Rome were true ? It was a laughably remote possibility, yet oddly disquieting. Who was he to pit his untrained mind against the persuasive cunning of experts ? Cheshire made immediate arrangements to approach his clergy friends again. He went straight to the point with them ; and their thin-skinned intolerance shocked him as deeply as the breath-taking presumptions of Rome. The ten empty days before and after Dykes's burial at Petersfield were tense with a succession of heated little interviews which left him more gloomily perplexed than before. He had fully expected to hear at least one commonly held reason which would dispose convincingly of the Catholic case ; instead, each clergyman seemed hurt and somehow betrayed by his anxiety to consider with an open mind a question which was closed for ever to any self-respecting man of intelligence and good taste. His lack of restraint was offensive. It was as though they had caught him red-handed in the act of pilfering their offertory boxes. Yet the more they cautioned him against " playing with fire," the keener grew his perverse anxiety to unbare the hidden roots of their prejudice. Surely there must be a more reasonable defence against Rome's monopoly than scornful anger ?

When one of them warned that he would imperil his immortal soul by becoming a Catholic, Cheshire was stung into replying :

" Who said I intended to become a Catholic ? Anyway, you're going the wrong way about trying to stop me. The last time we met you said that all sincere Christians, no matter what they believed, belonged to the true Church. Do Catholics all go to hell ? You must make up your mind."

If most of the arguments whizzed harmlessly over his head, two penetrated his defences. One cleric, for instance, stressed that the choice before any intending convert to Rome was between religious freedom with some doctrinal uncertainty and complete intellectual serfdom. A religion which deprived man of the right to think for himself could hardly be true. That was obvious. Then when his Anglo-Catholic friend, taking it for granted that he was about to break with the Church of England, said sadly that he was " selling the pass " and " taking the easy way out ", the appeal to his sense of loyalty held him fast. Many weeks passed before Cheshire decided that the High Anglican had made a successful appeal to his sense of vanity.

He could not sleep at nights for worrying. His brain seethed with endless variations of the central riddle, and he often yearned for the unquestioning trust that had buoyed him up before Dykes died. He had already returned to its owner the little book which had provoked this sickening crisis of confidence. With characteristic honesty Cheshire told Harry Rae in the covering letter :

" I have read it with the greatest interest and find it hard to deny the claims of Rome."

The intransigence of the Anglican clergy had made those still-repellent claims all the harder to deny :

" Had their reactions been milder," said Cheshire, looking

back, "had they listened calmly to my misgivings, they might well have convinced me that I was attaching undue importance to it all. Their stalling as much as anything else convinced me that by a fluke I had hit the nail on the head."

The next step was the hardest of all. The Anglicans had had their say; now it was the turn of the Catholics. But he shrank from making the first move. It seemed like a direct answer to prayer when Father Clarke rang up unexpectedly on August 31st and innocently suggested a drive to the sea. The priest had noticed Cheshire's pale and haggard appearance on the day of Dykes's funeral. Knowing nothing of his inner tumult, he had put down the strain to the admirable but somehow exaggerated work that was reshaping Le Court into a home for the dying.

"Leave the arrangements to me," said the priest. "The sea air will do you good, and we'll be at West Wittering within an hour."

But Father Clarke was a taciturn man, and Cheshire's opportunity did not come easily. The beach was fairly crowded, the weather hot and enervating. They swam and relaxed on the sands, yet Cheshire felt ill at ease. Only towards the end of the afternoon did he draw the priest into a halting discussion of Catholic beliefs. He mentioned "the little book" he had read, and the powerful impression it had made on his mind. He was anxious, he said, to test the truth of Catholicism. The priest did little talking, but his few questions were phlegmatic and searching:

"As an Anglican," he said finally, "you should be quite sure before doing anything else that arguments in *One Lord, One Faith* can't be pulled to pieces. You ought to read the Anglican answer to the book. The title's from the same scriptural text—' One God and Father of All.' I don't have a copy myself, but you could easily borrow one."

Cheshire was nonplussed. He had expected more interest, more desire to help. The priest seemed unsure whether he was entirely curious, and half sensed Cheshire's disappointment:

"You know, I've no right to recommend heresy to anyone," he said with a slow smile. "But you read that book, then we'll see."

At Le Court Cheshire managed to borrow a copy from

Mrs. Weddell, and read it with the neutral detachment of a man whose loyalties were already disengaged. The arguments against Rome were too high-flown to sway his reason. In his own words, they were " right above my head—like a boxer hitting the air and never once landing a blow."

Early in September, he visited Father Clarke to tell him that the Anglican reply had only increased his doubts about Anglicanism. But he was crestfallen by the priest's refusal to accept him for formal instruction at once :

" I suggest you wait another two months," he said. " There's no need to rush it and it would do no harm to talk further with your Anglican friends."

Father Clarke admired Cheshire's free and almost ruthless approach to momentous questions from which less nimble minds would have shied, but disliked his breathless sense of urgency. He wondered, too, whether the ultimate cost of breaking with the Church of England had yet been counted. He still had no inkling of that rocklike self-sufficiency which would make the break for Cheshire comparatively easy to bear. He finally compromised and agreed to let him call twice a week for " a fuller explanation of Catholic teaching, without any obligation on either side."

During the second week of October, when they were half-way through the explanatory course, Cheshire suddenly announced that his remaining doubts about Catholicism had vanished. This time the priest yielded at once to his request for formal instruction :

" I was now entirely convinced that the Catholic Church was the true Church," wrote Cheshire, " not because of this, that or the other arguments, but because all arguments pointed in one direction. I was faced with unity of doctrine, unity of organisation, unity of worship. If God exists and has spoken to us, then the facts He has revealed are no more capable of private interpretations than the facts, say, of aerodynamics. When I became a pilot, I had to learn the laws of aerodynamics and went to a training school with the authority to teach me. There I expected and found teachers to give me the facts—not their own personal ideas. To gain the freedom of the skies I had to learn the laws of flight and submit to them."

Personal submission to an absolute spiritual authority no

longer seemed to involve the slow stifling of reason he had once
feared. In every other department of knowledge men submitted
to the discipline of infallible truth. They showed no inclination
to jump off high buildings merely to disprove the law of gravity,
to ignore the principles of Euclid in a vain endeavour to square
the circle, or to deny the existence of America because they had
not been there. If the human mind accepted these lesser dogmas,
what was so odious and degrading in accepting religious truths
revealed by God to an infallible Church?

Cheshire's fearless reasoning was profound enough, but the
priest knew by experience the wisdom of Pascal's saying that
" the heart has its reasons which reason knows not of ".
Through some mysterious channel of grace Cheshire's heart had
undoubtedly been touched by the influence of the dying man he
had adopted and befriended.

More patients had meanwhile arrived to take Dykes's place
and keep " Grannie " Haynes company. Alf Wilmot, the first
of several T.B. cases, was sent by a London chest clinic on the
very day of the funeral. The decision whether or not to establish
a Home for the chronic sick seemed to have settled itself as well.

4

Squadron-Leader Jock Hill held open the door of the car
while his wife and four-year-old son climbed out. It was about
five o'clock on a chilly November afternoon. Dusk was falling,
and the big grey house had an eerie, oddly deserted look. They
had noticed on the way up the drive that the windows were
uncurtained. Not a welcoming light shone anywhere.

" You're sure this is the right place? " Freda Hill asked
dubiously.

" The village people should know," he answered. " Anyway, we'll find out soon enough," and Hill knocked at the front
door.

It seemed ages since he had last seen Cheshire and he was
looking forward to meeting him again. By all accounts, his
old skipper had changed a good deal since their palmy days
together at Linton and Marston Moor: quite the reformed
character, they said, with eccentric ideas about helping the homeless. It would have been discourteous not to call, especially as

they were more or less passing the door. Besides, they both felt
that Cheshire would probably be quite pleased to meet Murdoch,
his young godson.

Minutes passed and still no one stirred within. Perhaps
Freda was right and they had come to the wrong address after all.

Hill hammered at the door again, long and hard enough to
startle a colony of rooks sheltering in a clump of tall trees not
far away. From inside there came the soft slow shuffle of slippered
feet and then the loosening of a stubborn catch. As the heavy
door opened slightly, a gaunt, weirdly flickering face peered out
suspiciously. Hill stepped back involuntarily as the full figure
of the stranger loomed above him holding a guttering candlestick
in his left hand. In the uncertain light the threatening angle of
the man's upraised right arm had for one moment alarmed him.
Then he saw the white plaster encasing it from palm to half-
bent elbow, forcing it up to the level of his staring eyes in a
kind of petrified salute.

" What do you want ? " demanded the apparition gruffly.

" Sorry," said Hill. " I think we've come to the wrong
address. I was looking for a Group Captain Cheshire. He lives
somewhere in the neighbourhood, but I must have mistaken the
directions."

" Come in," said the apparition, and pulled the door wide
open.

They followed him into a large hall, watching their grotesque
shadows dancing on the walls and stairs. Freda Hill gave her
husband a nervous little smile of reproach. Round a corner
another door opened and Cheshire, wearing flannels and an old
blue battledress top, sidled towards them out of the gloom :

" Hallo, Jock. This *is* a nice surprise. I'm afraid the
electricity's gone again, but you'll stay for a cup of tea."

His face was thinner and more drawn than Hill remembered,
but the disarming charm was as compelling as ever. He shook
their little boy by the hand and showed them into a barely
furnished room where five or six people were sitting in the
wan glow of hurricane lamps. Cheshire introduced them one
by one, from Ted French, the laconic individual who had led
them in, to Alf Wilmot, a morose but irrepressible Cockney.
Two of the patients, on Cheshire's cheerful admission, were
suffering from tuberculosis, and the standards of hygiene seemed

to be of the rough-and-ready variety. Freda shuddered inwardly at the delicate problem that would inevitably arise when the tea was brought in. Murdoch, at any rate, would have to go without.

Hill concealed the strange sensation of total unreality as best he could. Only " Chesh " could have dreamed all this up ; only " Chesh " could have given the dream this unearthly substance. He listened to the familiar voice describing in that bland, matter-of-fact way he knew so well the ups and downs of life since the war. V.I.P. had been a wash-out, of course. He had never expected to become the founder of a nursing home, but the choice had been partly thrust upon him. His first patient had died in August ; since then others had come, some sent by hospital almoners, some simply because they had nowhere else to go. He had resolved never to close the door to anyone in genuine need, and so far he had not had to break this resolution.

" What do you use for money ? " asked Hill.

" We just don't worry about it," said Cheshire. " That works up to a point. The patients pay what they can. Sometimes we get a contribution from the hospitals which send them, sometimes we don't. But nobody's had to starve yet."

Everyone pulled his weight. Ted French, handicapped by osteomyelitis in that semaphore-like right arm, stoked the fires and looked after the boiler every day. He had once been a cable-layer and was still as strong as an ox. Anne Fisher, another tuberculosis victim, had been a nurse. She was invaluable. Those who were not very handy at specific tasks made themselves useful by attending to the lesser wants of the bedridden. And even the invalids, the aged or the wholly disabled, were encouraged to add their little quota by doing needlework and mending.

Hill was taken aback when Cheshire told him casually he was going to become a Catholic. Was it a joke, he wondered. His mind flashed back to their flying days with 76 and 35 Squadrons. Incongruously he thought of O'Kane, the quick-witted Irish flight engineer whom Cheshire had seemed to treat more coolly than the other members of the crew. Luck, calculated daring, and an unquestioning belief in himself had been the only laws he had recognised then. God had been a back number.

" Do you ever visit London now ? "

" Very seldom," said Cheshire. " I'm pretty busy here."

" You wouldn't think of coming over to the mess at Bushey Park to meet some of the old crowd ? It'd do you good—and would make a change. We've a dance the week after next."

" It might be difficult to arrange," he replied. " Still, I'll think about it. You never know."

He saw them off in the darkness, and as they drove towards the Portsmouth Road, Hill and his wife found it hard to believe that they had not been imagining it all. The primitive nursing home on the hill was somehow " out of this world ". The fact that its existence revolved round Cheshire was natural ; but its effect of unreality was a measure of the distance they had moved apart in recent years. Their surprise was therefore all the keener when Cheshire decided at the last minute to attend the dance.

It turned out a most successful evening. Cheshire, though quieter and less effusive than of old, seemed to enter fully into the spirit of it. Hill, who had a shrewder working knowledge of his character than most of the others present, was gratified to discover within five minutes that in one way at least his friend had not changed :

" Cheshire hadn't been told or had forgotten it was to be a dress affair. He was furious with me in an icily controlled way for not warning him, and kept digging me gently all evening about my carelessness. For once his annoyance made me feel relieved."

Such breaks were extremely rare. The Home and its many problems, financial and human, tied Cheshire down. He would not have had it otherwise, for he knew now that nursing was his true metier.

Outside help had not been lacking. Lord Selborne, who owned the neighbouring estate and had actually bought land and cottages from Cheshire when V.I.P. failed, came to lunch shortly after Dykes's death. He suggested the Church Army as a likely source of assistance, and his indirect influence produced £200 worth of Church Army beds and equipment in September. Then new patients had filtered in : an ex-sergeant-major with galloping consumption, who had died almost at once, Anne Fisher and Ted Willis. As more hospitals heard of the Home, more patients arrived. The partly empty house slowly shrugged off its old memories and became a Home.

A widow from Liss village came to cook and clean ; Toc H

in Portsmouth and a few Quakers discovered and adopted them ; curious nurses paid visits on their days off ; old neighbours like Cyril and Marjorie Cowey still walked in to lend a hand :

" At that stage it was a real Fred Karno affair," said Cowey. " The spirit of the place was remarkable in spite of the difficulties. Cheshire learnt as he went along."

The token segregation of T.B. patients sprang partly from inexperience, partly from inadequate facilities. But it was prompted, too, by a justifiable instinct of compassion. He believed that the natural atmosphere of a home meant far more to his new friends than the chill comfort and bleak efficiency of a modern hospital ward. Up to a point he was absolutely right. In 1948-49 the chronic sick with no relatives of their own to relieve what was soullessly described as " pressure on hospital bed space " far outnumbered the places earmarked for them. A thousand Le Courts might have absorbed them : but for all the political cut-and-thrust of the Health Service controversy, their needs seemed to have been largely forgotten. Cheshire's concern was to provide for some of the unwanted and to restore their integrity and self-respect as human beings in a home that was theirs as much as his.

The re-emergence as " characters " and distinct personalities in their own right of neglected, lonely men and women who had been starved of affection and care for too long amazed the visitors and part-time helpers.

Cheshire's patience and encouragement, impelled by a trust in Divine Providence which seemed at times almost to verge on presumption, had created the new " family atmosphere " of Le Court.

At night, in his study-bedroom on the first floor, he read a good deal, and the books were mostly on religion. Step by step he examined the doctrine and moral teaching of the Catholic Church with a keenly critical eye as the priest from Petersfield continued with the twice-weekly instructions.

" By this time," said Cheshire, " everything had fallen into place. None of the basic arguments put up against the Catholic Church by the Anglican clergy turned out to be true. If I had discovered only one that was true I'm sure I would never have become a Catholic."

Oddly enough the only objection on which his Anglican

friends had been unanimously agreed, the corrupt lives of individual Catholics through the centuries, from Popes to peasants, seemed to him the weakest and least relevant. Objections rooted in ignorance or prejudice, like the taunt that confession was a licence to sin or that the worship of idols and the adoration of the Virgin Mary were standard practices, he could more easily understand. Cheshire's reaction to the charge that Catholicism was a whitened sepulchre resembled Boccaccio's five hundred years earlier, who dryly remarked to a friend unable to reconcile the divine character of the Church with the diabolical churchmen who ruled it :

" Only the true Church *could* survive such evil." The historical paradox of Rome's undiminished vigour in spite of the conduct of its adherents was for Cheshire an indirect proof of the indwelling of God's Spirit.

On December 23rd, he was formally received into the Catholic Church at Petersfield by Father Clarke ; and after Midnight Mass on Christmas Eve he returned to his little world of Le Court at peace with himself at last. . . .

" Don't worry, God will provide."

During the early months of 1949 Cheshire's soothing motto became a jocular catch-phrase ; but it summed up an imperturbable outlook which local tradesmen sometimes misunderstood. Nevertheless, the Home was growing without the clamorous " build-up " of publicity. He had made known his decision to shun the press. Le Court, he said, would manage well enough on their own combined efforts and the providential goodness of others.

" Patients seem to be pouring in," he wrote to a friend in April, 1949. " I shall have to buy another house ! "

It was no idle threat. Regardless of the difficulties, Cheshire was determined to expand. Few of his skeleton panel of nurses and part-time helpers took him seriously. They did not know him well enough. Though Le Court's happy spirit induced visitors, as one put it, " to remove your coat and join in," the shortages of staff, money and equipment made it impracticable to think of founding another Le Court before the first was established.

Towards the end of May, Cheshire inserted a small advertisement in the personal columns of *The Times*. He needed £8000, on which he was willing to pay 4% interest, to " equip a second non-profit-making home for homeless and helpless invalids." The property he had in mind was Lord Tennyson's beautiful house at Haslemere which was up for sale.

" I now have seven helpers and thirty-one patients," he told Dr. John Keevil, the librarian of the Royal College of Physicians, and one of the two people who answered the advertisement. " Fifteen are T.B.s, two cancers, two disseminated sclerosis, two paraplegias, one asthma and one diabetic and eight aged and infirm. They pay what they can afford—from nothing to £3 a week. Some who came have died, others have left fit for part-time work.

" I am completely full here, and have fourteen on the waiting-list with more arriving each week. In order to help them I want to open another place for which I have a skeleton staff."

Tennyson's house was to be for T.B.s only, and Cheshire's mind was so set on it that without more ado he engaged a married couple from the East End of London as resident caretakers. Sam Jenkins, a T.B. victim himself, gave up his job and went to live at Le Court with his wife. They did not stay long. When negotiations fell through for lack of funds, Jenkins left feeling he had been " led up the garden " and bitterly thankful that he had not given up his home as well as his job.

It is only right to note this " blind spot " in Cheshire's make-up, so much at variance with his more outstanding trait of sincere selflessness, which explains other instances of callousness, if not of actual injustice, to individuals. They were the victims of his headlong impetuosity. Deeply compassionate by nature, he could still be ruthless with anyone—especially a member of his staff—who came between himself and the smooth attainment of an objective. It was a fault he could recognise with painful clarity, but usually when the damage had been done.

" My nature and the training of the war have conspired to make me live very much from day to day," he wrote some months later, acknowledging the resignation of a member of the nursing staff. " I realise that I have been irresponsible in the past when it came to ' influencing ' other people."

Against this, one must set the occasionally mixed motives of his full-time helpers, some of them incurably ill and not always emotionally stable, others irresistibly misled by his habitual graciousness into thinking themselves indispensable to the Home or to him personally. Like a giant who does not know his own strength, he commanded an almost unhealthy degree of trust from individuals ; and when, for motives which were not always fully understood, he suddenly withdrew his own support, the personal grief and sense of cruel loss were just as unhealthy.

Having shelved the idea of founding a second Home immediately, Cheshire had his hands full. Frances Jeram, the almoner of the Portsmouth Chest Clinic, joined the small permanent staff in June and will never forget the extraordinary air of almost unbroken tranquillity which compensated for the overcrowding and the grossly inadequate nursing facilities :

" We had a small invasion of convalescent T.B.s from London, and the very day I arrived Cheshire had gone all the way to Switzerland to escort a seriously sick woman who wasn't allowed to travel without a nurse. She died peacefully at Le Court soon afterwards.

" His greatest gift was undoubtedly the consolation he brought to the dying. He would never leave them, night or day, until they had stopped breathing ; he hardly bothered to eat or sleep, and every one of the seven or eight men and women who died that summer seemed to die happily and without fear.

" There was nothing unnatural or morbid in his devotion. Once, after a bedside vigil that went on for days, he stole out of the room, heaved a sigh of relief as though some sort of physical burden had been removed from his shoulders and said : ' Thank God that's over.' He lost the look of strain at once, lit a cigarette, and was himself again. It was at times like those that we saw him at his best."

5

Dr. Cheshire resigned his Oxford chair at the end of the 1949 summer term, sold Grey Walls and retired with his wife to the newly reconverted cottages he had bought at the time of the V.I.P. sale. Le Court was only three minutes' walk away. The mysterious chain of circumstances which had transformed the house into a struggling Home for the sick had been less of a shock to them than Cheshire's decision to become a Catholic.

His mind was irrevocably made up before they knew; they simply reconciled themselves to the accomplished fact, wondering how long the phase of religious fervour would last.

Hitherto, Cheshire had never had any reason to question whether nursing the unwanted sick might not be his true calling. He had been so immersed in the work itself that speculative doubts about it seemed a ludicrous luxury. The inner logic of events suggested from the start that in doing this work he was doing God's will. Conscience and intuition confirmed that his vocation lay at Le Court. Then, out of the blue, there had come a contradictory sign which slowly unsettled him. It was the first of several; and it darkened the latter part of the brief holiday he spent on the island of Skye with a priest friend in July.

The weather was glorious, and the first ten days went by uneventfully. Cheshire discussed Le Court quite openly with the priest, an unimpressionable, plain-spoken Englishman he trusted and respected. The priest, in stressing the Christian's plain duty of obedience to the Church, was distressingly critical of the practice of leaving God to do the providing as though trust could lawfully be expected to replace ordinary prudence. He also disliked what Koestler has aptly called the " language of destiny " almost as much as Cheshire liked it. He was allergic to reading hidden signs into ordinary circumstances, and had no hesitation in hinting that when other people's lives were affected, as at Le Court, then there were extra reasons for caution. To treat intuitive deductions in the light of private revelations, at the expense of ordinary considerations of common sense, could sometimes be a subtle form of selfishness.

The suggestion that nobody had the indisputable right to undermine his own health or to throw away his natural talents in pursuit of personal intimations of perfection forced Cheshire back on himself. He needed time and peace to think alone. One morning, a few days before they were due to return to the mainland, he announced that he would stay on and retire for some weeks to a rocky, uninhabited island about a quarter of a mile offshore. There he would live as a recluse until he had reached a firm decision about the future. He would bring food with him. If he got into any difficulties, he could always light a distress beacon.

The priest promptly exploded : " That's one of the maddest and most unnecessary ideas I've heard for a long time," is a kind of summary of his indignant reaction.

After Cheshire had recovered his own temper, he discarded the plan. It was a hard decision, and outwardly trivial as it may appear, he still regards it as a definite turning-point in his spiritual development. In his own words, " it was my first practical lesson in obedience." He submitted to the rather heated advice of a friend more qualified to pronounce on the workings of Providence than himself ; and he resolved to be guided in future less by the highly personal language of signs and symbols than by the impersonal and objective counsel of others.

During the next three months certain changes at Le Court took some of the staff and patients by surprise. Cheshire's wild but inspiring interpretation of the motto " God will provide " no longer appeared to apply. Formerly he had spent long spells praying in the chapel, sometimes at rather inconvenient hours : he modified the habit. What was more, his aversion to publicity softened, and in September a reporter from the *News Chronicle* came down, interviewed him and was shown over the Home. Cheshire seemed also to be conserving his strength more wisely than in the past. He called a halt to the ascetical rule he had imposed on himself of making do with a minimum of food and five hours' sleep a night. Did all this mean that his interest in Le Court was dwindling ? The doubt flickered through the minds of more than one of his permanent helpers.

There was a note of elation in the letter he wrote to Dr. Keevil on September 23rd : " The *News Chronicle* published an article about us on September 10th. I tried to avoid publicity, but wasn't successful. It was a good write-up and has brought in a tremendous response, so much so, that we have not only been completely taken aback but also completely up to our eyes, trying to keep pace with over 5000 letters of various sorts. We have been sent a mass of donations, still coming in, totalling £720 — also furniture, clothes, books, etc. In fact, we can hardly believe our eyes and our morale has gone right up."

Cyril Cowey, who threw up his outside job when offered a lower-paid post as book-keeper at the Home, had never been so busy. Night after night he sat up with Cheshire, answering

letters and ruefully recalling odd little incidents which had shaken
his good-natured agnosticism in the recent past.

One morning he said gloomily to Cheshire, after counting
the money in the cash-box :

" There'll be no wages for anyone this week."

" What do you mean ? "

" We're ten pounds short, and it's Wednesday."

" That's all right. You see me again on Friday. We've two
days left for things to happen."

By the first post on Friday a registered letter had arrived from
the almoner of the clinic where Alf Wilmot had once been a
patient. Coincidence ? The just reward of sheer trust ? Cowey
was not sure. Nor was anyone else. They feared, however, that
with Le Court basking in the limelight again, such breathtaking
little happenings would no longer yield the same thrill of
infectious pleasure ; the £1200 given by sympathetic readers
of a newspaper tended to put them in the shade. Instead of
wondering where to-morrow's food was coming from, they were
almost in the opulent position of capitalists. Builders were
called in to resurface the drive so that the wheel-chairs of patients
would no longer be bogged down ; the kitchens were being
renovated ; and Dr. Keevil, in an access of generosity, had made
a loan of £100 towards a new Aga cooker. While these startling
proofs of changing fortune were going on, Cheshire fell ill.

He regarded the illness as a further sign that his priest friend
on Skye had been right. And as he sat up in bed in the room
his mother always reserved for him, he was more disposed than
ever to listen to advice. Since July he had hardly put a foot
wrong, and with far less effort than ever before. But while he
strove to be more prudent, he clung to his own private " language
of destiny ". So long as his intuitive processes kept in step with
common sense there would be no cause for concern. In a letter
to a friendly benefactor half-way through November, Cheshire
described the mechanics of one such flash of intuition :

" We have had in a minor way a miracle. Being anxious to
start an indoor home industry, partly to help finances, partly to
occupy the patients, and being unable to think of the right
industry, I asked the house to hold a meeting and talk it over
last Monday evening. I myself was here in bed, and I prayed to
St. Teresa of Lisieux to help us.

"I woke up the next morning with a start, and thought : ' Ornamental Fish ! ' In the post was a notice from the Goldfish Club (never heard of it before). I felt so certain that this was the right thing that I telephoned Olive Selkirk, the matron, and told her so. She then said that that was precisely what the meeting had decided. So I am now setting about collecting information in order to make a start."

The fact that the Goldfish Club was not for ornamental fish breeders but for airmen forced down over the sea hardly mattered. Minor discrepancies of the kind paled before the dazzling point of intuitive coincidence, which was confirmed by a second letter in the same post from a girl in Singapore. Ivy Angelo had read all about Le Court in the press and was on her way to help in any way she could. When she eventually arrived, Ivy was put in charge of the ornamental fish ; but the enthusiasm for this indoor industry did not long outlast her arrival.

Bigger events intervened to harden Cheshire's underlying doubts about his true vocation. Before the end of November, bowing to the combined advice of his parents, the local doctor, and Father Henry Clarke, he left for an extended holiday in Paris, staying, as he had often done in boyhood, with his Aunt Edith, who had reopened her home and business interests there after the war. Cheshire set off with an uncanny feeling that this interlude would almost certainly involve him in a crisis of decision ; for while still in bed he had had a strong presentiment that soon, but in a way he could not fathom, a girl would enter his life. For himself, there was nothing he desired more than to continue his work at Le Court. His whole heart and mind were steeped in it. Yet, as he said to me later in a moment of regret, " from the day I became a Catholic practically everyone did his utmost to dissuade me from carrying on with my work for the sick, saying it was quite out of keeping, that I would inevitably end up a crank, that what I ought to do was settle down to a normal routine life."

In his scrupulous desire to seek God's will in a spirit of humble obedience, Cheshire deliberately shut out his " selfish interests " and tried to reconcile himself to the uninviting idea of marriage and a career. He knew that in the eyes of the Church, Constance, as a divorced woman, had never been his wife. The marriage had been invalid from the start. He had been urged repeatedly to use his freedom wisely, legalise his separation from Constance by asking her to divorce him, and wed again. And when, through his Uncle Gabriel, he met Hélène, a dark, quiet, sensitive and highly-intelligent girl, soon after reaching Paris, he put himself out to be attentive. His mind was still dominated by the unexpected sign that had stared him in the face on the boat train journey from England. It had been a sullen day, with heavy rain. He had sat musing in his corner seat, watching the raindrops streaming down the carriage window. Then he noticed a quite ordinary phenomenon which suddenly took on a quite extraordinary personal significance. Two silvery drops of rain met and merged, then streaked down the long pane of glass far more quickly than any single drop. It happened again and again, and he saw in it an instantaneous answer to his dilemma, so that the meeting with Hélène a few days later seemed somehow providential and not very surprising. She responded to his thoughtful attentions by falling in love with him, and when he returned to Le Court six weeks later, his mind was clearer about the future. Hélène and he were tacitly engaged.

Early in 1950, failing health forced him to retire to bed for a second long period of complete rest. Hélène came over to live at his parents' cottage and nurse him ; and he finally agreed to the suggestion of Frances Jeram, the almoner, that Sir Charles Symonds should be sent for to give him a thorough medical check. Frances, like Cheshire, knew Symonds well. She had worked as his secretary during the war ; and her respect for the specialist's judgment was great. His advice was firm and to the point. He urged Cheshire to take an outside job and lead a more normal life. That would be the surest way to recover his health. He could still maintain a close interest in Le Court, while leaving the work and management to others. The staff and patients accepted the decision with glum gallantry. A Le Court robbed of its founder's drive and daily inspiration, except at week-ends, would become a shadow of its true self.

" Now that the pioneering stage is over," he wrote to a friend, " and in view of my habit of wanting to force the pace, I have decided that it is in everyone's interest that I should leave Mary MacDonagh (the new matron) and Mrs. Jeram to work out the best way of carrying on the work at Le Court. . . . It's been a bit of a wrench, but having taken the plunge I feel happier and more confident. . . . The trouble is that it's such fun going full out at something which, on the odds, looks a fair impossibility. And I find it difficult to resist when the opportunity comes along, as it seems to do so often at Le Court."

Some wondered how Hélène would fit into the changing pattern of his life. When he was well enough to get up, he had introduced her to all of them. A charming, reserved and attractive brunette in her early thirties, Hélène smilingly scorned make-up and most certainly did not need it. As a Catholic, she understood well enough what Le Court meant to Cheshire. He had grown up with it, found his Faith there, deepened his love for God there. To give it up would, she knew, be a costly sacrifice. Yet, as a woman, as his fiancée, she knew that the sacrifice would have to be made and that in time he would probably be glad of it. Hélène's gentle, logical reasoning was added now to Sir Charles Symonds's. It carried decisive weight, and Cheshire agreed to find work as soon as he felt strong enough.

By a strange irony, it was also Hélène who, realising his taste for solitude and his need for a complete change of atmosphere, suggested that he should visit Solesmes. He had vaguely heard of this great 11th-century Benedictine Abbey in the Department of Sarthe, one of the most illustrious religious houses of France, and a leading centre of the Catholic liturgical revival; but its fame meant less to him than the attractive idea of spending Lent in the unfamiliar peace of a monastery. At the end of the first week in February he set off, having arranged to stay at a little *pension* within easy walking distance of the Abbey church.

To say that Cheshire enjoyed his visit to Solesmes would be a gross understatement. Its impact on him was overpowering. The letters he sent to friends dimly reflected his enthusiastic discovery of an ordered harmonious mode of communal living which seemed to span the depressingly wide modern gulf yawning between earth and heaven, the natural and the supernatural. The rhythmic balance of prayer and study or manual labour had been tested by centuries of experience and hallowed by the example of a whole calendar of saints. The monks had their signs and symbols, but there could be no mistaking the language or where it led. It was defined for them by rule. Whether eating, or sleeping or working or praying, all their actions were directed to the praise and glory of God. They were grave, silent but happy men, untroubled by the present or the future ; and the carefully divided hours of each day were like the spokes of a wheel whose hub was the austere yet splendid pageantry of the liturgy.

Cheshire had already formed the habit of privately reciting the daily office whenever he could. His ear for music was poor ; but the solemn singing of the daily " hours " by the monks in choir gave a new breadth and meaning to prayers that were familiar. The heavy bell pealing across the little town under the Abbey gates and the open countryside beyond, the swelling chant of the Psalms, rolling round the tall, bare spaces of the church's nave in the darkness before dawn, the long rows of still figures in black, and the sense of privilege he felt at merging his own tuneless voice with theirs, taught him more about the spiritual richness of monastic existence in a few days than he could have learnt in half a lifetime of reading.

" Solesmes is a real tonic to me," he wrote to Frances Jeram at Le Court. " I have always liked and wanted solitude, but solitude pure and simple brings many dangers in itself. Here, fortunately, there are the offices to keep one steady and set the whole day in its right proportion. Other than the little maid at the *pension* and the Father doorkeeper at the Abbey, I don't speak to a soul, yet the day seems to fly. . . .

" It was the Benedictines here who, over the course of twenty years, succeeded in retracing the old Gregorian Chant which dates back before the 5th century and gradually faded out after the 10th. Their rendering of it is beautiful beyond words, and holds me completely enthralled. I am quite sure it is true that there is no work on earth comparable to the Divine Office, that's to say the praise of God in the name of all creation, either for its dignity, its importance or the results it achieves."

Returning even to Le Court was like coming down from the rarefied air of a mountain peak, for he knew he would not be returning to nurse the sick. An outside job far from his patients, with all the artificial worry that would entail, awaited him. He formed a small management committee to run the Home in his absence, and tried not to notice the edginess of the staff and patients. Some imagined that he was secretly bored with it all now that the rough pioneering days had ended.

6

Barnes Wallis of Vickers Armstrong was not as co-operative as Air Chief Marshal Sir Ralph Cochrane had hoped.

"You know my view of wartime pilots," he said testily. "The best of them don't necessarily fit in, and the rest expect too much money for work they're not qualified to do."

"That's a matter of opinion," said Cochrane. "Anyway, Cheshire's different."

Cheshire? Wallis had to rack his memory before he could even begin to place him, and Cochrane seemed to sense his hesitancy. Hundreds of pilots had visited the inventor during the war, all of them on reasonably urgent business. Some, like Guy Gibson, he had seen too often to forget.

"I can't put a face on him yet," he said, "but the name's familiar. Didn't he follow Gibson at 617 Squadron? The Tallboy period?"

"Quite right," said Cochrane. "He's a first-rate man, as you know."

Wallis reflected for a second:

"I still don't want him," he said with an air of gruff finality.

"Please, as a personal favour to me, just *see* him before deciding," urged Cochrane. And "just as a favour" Wallis yielded reluctantly.

Cheshire went to Weybridge for his interview early in May, passing the outer door of the office where a full-scale model of the Tallboy stood sentinel. The inventor scowled over the top of his spectacles and opened the conversation with blunt lack of ceremony:

"I've only one vacancy. The money's poor by the standards you ex-R.A.F. people expect. And my guess is that you'll be no good at the job itself."

Cheshire grinned, and the scowl faded from Wallis's face:

"I'm not interested in the salary," he replied. "All I want is something worthwhile to do—preferably with you. You're dead right about the third point, though. I've no qualifications whatever for research work."

Disarmed by his candour, Wallis relaxed, gave him the job and seemed to lose all sense of time as he fell to discussing his latest and most exciting experiment. Before the week was out,

Cheshire reported to the National Aeronautical Estabishment at Thurleigh, in Bedfordshire, and spent several days getting the feel of the place and the job.

The exact nature and purpose of the experiments with which Cheshire was linked for the next twenty-two months cannot be disclosed. They are still on the secret list. Wallis, with his genius for turning conventional ideas on their head, wanted to produce his own original type of guided missile well up to the demands of the age of supersonic flight. Because of his past reputation for being right after Ministries and even colleagues had closed their ranks and sworn he was wrong, he had been given facilities to develop the project, though these were still too niggardly for his liking. Development was in its early stages when Cheshire arrived. The experimental prototypes were far from satisfactory ; and the technicians were concentrating on improving them.

" Naturally, Cheshire was a bit out of his depth on that side of things," said Wallis. " He wasn't efficient as I understand the word because he lacked the necessary training and knowledge. That didn't stop him pouring out intuitive suggestions of his own, one or two of which weren't bad at all. His colleagues could make scientific rings round him, and I remember one who proved something of a thorn in his flesh. He seemed to enjoy trussing Cheshire up in his more impossible theories."

Not all the work was at the drawing-board or desk. To assist the experts in their trial-and-error elimination of faults, flying of the most exacting kind was called for in response to signals from the ground. Here, according to Wallis, Cheshire was invaluable. The air tests started in late July and continued at intervals until the end of September. First in a slow, old Moth, next in a familiar Mosquito, then best of all in a two-seater Mark 8 Spitfire, stripped of its armaments, he set out to give the lie to Wallis's rueful axiom that " the average pilot's best accelerometer is his own backside." In other words, he had to forget all he had ever learnt by instinct and wartime experience, schooling himself to act and react like a robot.

" The work is quite fascinating and suits me very well," he wrote to Dr. Keevil. " It's far from being exclusively devoted to war, which is all the better."

The Korean War, however, had broken out in June. The

possibility of a wider conflict was in his mind when he answered the wounding charge of a member of the staff at Le Court that he had simply grown tired and deserted them.

" I once told you all at a meeting that I would never leave except for war. When I was suddenly asked to take this job, it was clear that the authorities considered war as a not entirely remote possibility. . . . I felt a sense of urgency to get Le Court ready for any such eventuality. Should the worst happen, it would be better to have it staffed by people who were not going to be needed elsewhere."

He still visited the Home regularly at week-ends, as Hélène and Sir Charles Symonds had suggested, and his short stays were eagerly awaited. It is doubtful whether he yet realised how much Le Court had depended on his continuous presence ; and the belief that he had lost interest and " passed on " grew in September when Cheshire was sent by Vickers Armstrong to select a new testing ground for Wallis's experiment. The choice of Predannack airfield, on the windswept Lizard peninsula, an abandoned wartime landing ground two miles from the old-world Cornish fishing village of Mullion, was determined by its remoteness and isolation. Cheshire surveyed the site during the summer ; by the end of October the research team and staff had moved in. His log-book began to fill up with entries again.

Flight-Lieutenant Bob Dickinson, a fellow test-pilot who had served with Fighter Command during the war, admitted that there was no holding Cheshire once he had left the ground. Low flying and aerobatics were officially sanctioned, partly to keep their hand in, partly for checking radio ranges. They were in constant touch with flying control at Culdrose, the huge naval air station across the moor outside Helston ; but sometimes the Culdrose controllers were glad to turn a blind eye to Cheshire's practice " stunting ".

His official role now, apart from the periodic experimental trials, was that of an administrator. His popularity was universal. Wallis, on his visits from Weybridge, slowly began to appreciate the worth of the man he had been so reluctant to employ. The new station on the edge of a marshy wilderness, where labour was hard to come by and harder to keep, had grown into a model of happy efficiency without overstrain on anyone's part. Cheshire, it seemed, simply had to ask, and the job was done. He never had to snoop or check or reprimand. Wallis himself fell under the insidious spell of his personality. A practising Christian himself with a flair for apt biblical quotations, the inventor readily understood why Cheshire rented a damp, four-roomed white cottage on the Mullion-Helston road rather than occupy his ample and more comfortable official billet on the airfield. It was not standoffishness. He would probably have made the same move ; for he, too, relished peace and recognised the need to be left alone to thoughts and prayers.

"For someone so young, Cheshire had an uncanny insight into human nature," said Wallis, " and an even uncannier sympathy. He invited confidences. Sometimes we went walking in the evening, discussing without a trace of self-consciousness things which I, at any rate, could never have discussed with any other person."

My own clearest recollection of the period was Cheshire's diffidence in airing his opinions on the moral legitimacy of indiscriminate bombing. We sat up late one night in the cottage, and he seemed to be far more curious about the precise drill for picking his way blindfolded through the Roman breviary. I was of very little help. He impressed me as someone who distrusted himself almost violently on matters of opinion which did not immediately concern him ; mental gymnastics for their own sake he seemed to abhor. He preferred discussing the liturgy to practising mental prayer. Like many men who live alone, he tended to forget meals and ordinary creature comforts.

Something enigmatic he said about Le Court stuck fast in mind :

" To sell what you have and give to the poor looks all very nice on paper, but it counts for little. It's giving up yourself that counts, and I never did that. I shouldn't like to give the impression that I did."

The Home in Hampshire was often in his thoughts, and at week-ends he frequently used the Spitfire with its distinctive red markings to sweep across country and save himself the long rail journey to Hampshire. The usual landing ground was near Weybridge but he would occasionally make a detour to signal his impending arrival to the patients. The " beating up " of Le Court was a rare Saturday ritual. The distant drone of the aircraft alerted everyone, and then he would come with a glittering waggle of wings between the trees, flashing at 200 miles an hour over the lawn he had once scythed, and lifting the nose of the machine at the last minute so that it seemed almost to scrape the sloping roofs. These week-end flights were cut short early in 1951. Dickinson vainly tried to dissuade Cheshire from taking up the Spitfire one Friday because of the hopeless weather conditions. A dense sea mist was swirling across Predannack airfield, wrapping the hangars and Nissen huts in its clammy, impenetrable folds. Visibility was down to zero, but Cheshire had an appointment at Odiham and was clearly determined not to miss it.

Flying control at Culdrose proved to be unhelpful. The mist was of the worst persistent type, and would probably thicken during the day.

" No aircraft will be leaving the ground down here," said the control officer complacently.

Dickinson was about to commiserate with Cheshire, but a glance at the set expression on his face warned him not to be too " previous " with condolences. There was a stertorous pause at the other end when Cheshire casually asked for a clearance to take off in ten minutes. The control officer seemed to be having difficulty with his breathing.

" You must be mad," he said at length.

" Not mad," said Cheshire. " Just anxious to go."

" Very well," came the reply. " But don't say I didn't try to stop you. It's your funeral."

Dickinson shrugged helplessly, walked across the hardstands with him and watched the mechanics point the nose of the machine into the mist straight down the hidden runway. Cheshire climbed in, smiled at them, " opened up ", and vanished with a half-muffled roar into the white wall ahead of him. They waited tensely for the inevitable crash and explosion. None came. Five minutes later, back in the control room, Dickinson sighed with relief when the nonchalant voice came crackling over the speaker :

" Can't think what Culdrose was fussing about. It's a heavenly day up here. Thanks, everyone, and sorry for worrying you. I can see it's not good for you."

Cheshire had some explaining to do at Odiham where there

was thick fog. From Odiham he had flown over to Binbrook, his official destination, to spend a couple of nights with John Kirby, the former Base Commander at Marston Moor, who had not seen him for seven years.

"He was as lively as ever but more settled and happier than any sandboy," said Kirby. "I'd often wondered what went wrong with his colony scheme, and he told me frankly. He also spoke of the Home that had taken its place—and about Hélène. We were a little puzzled as to how he would fit it all in : his normal work with Vickers, the Home for the sick, and the domestic life of a married man. But he talked with the assurance of someone quite contented with things as they were. His religion, he said, had given him a broader perspective, and he certainly sparkled with gaiety all that week-end."

By now Cheshire was formally engaged. The divorce proceedings had taken several months to wind up, but he was legally free to marry at last. Le Court had become a Registered Charity, admitting only the chronic sick. The T.B. patients had been removed elsewhere. The King Edward's Fund had made a grant for repairs. The management committee was shouldering the main weight of responsibility, and the arrangement seemed to suit him admirably :

"I am learning that this job is exactly what I needed. . . . The more I settle down the more I am able to be sensible over Le Court. . . . For the first time in my life I am enjoying a good deal of peace and quiet. I wonder how long it will last ? "

The answer came with unpremeditated suddenness in February, and Bob Dickinson was the first person to be told. He had noticed as others, including myself had done, that Cheshire could scarcely pass a ruined building without a half-indignant comment. The sight of a disused barn or an empty hovel seemed to distress him, as though he felt the dead stones were a desecration in a world where homeless and afflicted people abounded. When Cheshire walked Dickinson along the airfield boundary one afternoon in late January, 1951, led him mysteriously into a derelict Nissen hut, and asked him what he thought of it, the puzzled test-pilot wondered what was in the wind :

"It depends what you want it for," he said cautiously.

"My idea is to spruce it up, and open it as another Home."

" Come off it," said the disbelieving Dickinson. " Try pulling the other leg."

" I'm perfectly serious," said Cheshire. " The place has great possibilities."

Looking round the dim interior of the hut, Dickinson could not see beyond the filth and the broken pieces of concrete strewn everywhere. Cattle had slept here ; the walls were splashed with animal dirt and hairy with cobwebs ; marshy grass poked through the cracked floor. They were probably the first people to cross that uninviting threshold since the last airman had packed up and gone. Trust Cheshire, thought Dickinson, to pick the unlikeliest site in England :

" What about the airfield—and Vickers ? "

To bring patients into the wilderness was one thing ; to " park " them a few hundred yards from the testing-ground for Wallis's rather dangerous " toys " was another.

" We'll worry about that when we come to it," said Cheshire. " Will you help me meanwhile, Bob ? "

Dickinson promised, and they started the rough work of clearing away the debris and dirt almost at once. They were joined by Douglas King, the station storeman, a Cornishman who had been in and out of R.A.F. hospitals with T.B. for six years and had obtained his first steady job when Cheshire opened Predannack airfield. King, like Dickinson, was sceptical at first ; but Cheshire's persuasiveness was too much for him.

" If he had asked me to pull out my back teeth and lend them to him," said King, " I'd have thought twice before refusing. He somehow gave you a feeling that you were really doing yourself a favour in helping him."

Within a week more volunteers were coming across to the Nissen hut after working hours : Maxwell and Trussler (" Big Bill " and " Little Bill "), the airfield firemen ; Matthews, the electrician and general jack-of-all-trades ; and Michael Gibson, an ex-naval frogman from the Midlands, subject to violent epileptic fits, whom Cheshire had invited to stay as his permanent guest because he had no relatives or friends of his own to look after him. I felt a little guilty about Gibson's descent on Predannack ; apparently it was after reading something I had written about Le Court that Gibson approached Cheshire. Without a moment's hesitation, he was asked to come down to the White Cottage as his guest until "other arrangements" could be made.

"Michael Gibson has arrived and is hard at work on the building," Cheshire wrote to me on February 2nd. "He hasn't had a fit yet—the change has done him good. He's only twenty-five and very impressive. The local officials are doing their utmost to find a way in which I can take over the building legally. There's no water or sanitation for miles and the place is in a terrible state, but it's really terrifically suitable. It's also great fun. Do you know of any other strong men who don't know what to do with themselves?"

Douglas King's wife, who used to call regularly at the White Cottage to do the cleaning, heard the crash of splintering glass as she let herself in one morning. The small kitchen seemed to have been in the path of a whirlwind : smashed cups and crockery lay on the floor, the table leaned at a tipsy angle, and the walls, ceiling and floor seemed to be stippled with hot tea-leaves. She pushed open the living-room door to see Gibson clawing the air, wild-eyed and frothing at the mouth, with Cheshire stealing purposefully round him picking up stray ash-trays and vases that had escaped the whirlwind of arms and legs.

"Stay where you are. He'll be all right in a moment," he told her in an aside. "It came on suddenly, and won't last long."

A furnished cottage which was only rented had many disadvantages, and Gibson's fit forced Cheshire to quicken the pace of his reconversion work. The original pace-maker, however, was not the ex-frogman. It was a small, grey-haired, rather dowdy middle-aged woman called Hilda who had unwittingly shaped the decision to start a second Home. She worked in the airfield canteen ; and when she failed to appear one bitterly cold day in January nobody took much notice. A shrinking, timid person who looked rather anxiously on life through red-rimmed eyes behind large spectacles and limped to the airfield in all weathers on her own rickety legs, Hilda (like Arthur Dykes before her) was not the sort of person whose presence or absence would excite comment. In any case it was the open season for influenza, an ailment to which Cheshire was becoming increasingly prone himself.

There was a buzz of surprise, therefore, at his swift reaction on learning that the canteen hand was missing.

" Where does she live ? " he asked insistently. " I must go to her at once."

Intuitively he seemed to know that she was in trouble. Driving fast down the narrow, rutted road across the moor to Ruan Minor, Cheshire eventually found the dark, cramped hut, knocked on the door and entered. The atmosphere in the airless room was nauseating. Hilda, pale and confused, looked up feebly from the untidy pillow. She lay on a straw mattress covered with sacking, a quilt and a coat. He took her temperature. She was suffering from violent dysentery ; and her pulse was ragged. On a trestle bed in another corner of the small room her small son tossed and cried : he, too, was ill with a raging fever. Wrapping them both up, Cheshire bundled the mother and son into the car and drove back at top speed to Predannack.

Sands, the catering manager, saw him arrive and went out to help him :

" I'll put them in my quarters," said Cheshire. " So don't worry about them. Leave them to me while they're here. They're my guests or patients, whichever you like."

Hilda and her son remained in the comfortable billet its owner never used for the next ten days, but the normal working routine of the airfield continued as placidly as before. That was the remarkable fact which silenced the few who might otherwise have reasonably criticised Cheshire's quixotic act of charity.

" It simply knocked us sideways," one airfield worker said, " because he took the whole thing in his stride and didn't let it interfere with business."

Cheshire had succeeded in making Hilda a freely devoted slave who works for him still and would follow him to the ends of the earth ; he had equally succeeded in conditioning the others for his next precipitate move, which he took as " a matter of desperate urgency."

His concern was evident by the questions he asked not only at Predannack but in the villages. How many down-and-out chronic sick must there be in Cornwall alone, if in this sparsely peopled corner of it working women like Hilda could suffer so needlessly when taken ill casually ? Nobody seemed to know. Some, he suggested, did not seem to care. The complacency was a challenge in itself. He would find out part of the answer, solve part of the problem, as he had done at Le Court. And so he chose a Nissen hut that was structurally sound and enlisted the help of Dickinson, King and others with time on their hands.

By the end of March, the inside of the hut had been renovated.

" I'm getting a lot of assistance," he wrote to me jubilantly. " In fact it's bewildering."

An odd-job man came along one evening and Cheshire, inexpertly laying bricks, grinned when he caught the frown of professional disapproval on the man's face :

" Here, let me show you," said Barney impatiently. After that, this trusty handyman from Ruan Minor turned up as faith-fully as the volunteers from the airfield or the naval ratings from Culdrose. The careful people of the district soon came to hear of the " strange goings-on " near Predannack. Passing farmers and tradesmen, interested or merely inquisitive villagers, inspected the transformed hut and spoke to the confident, rather tired young Group Captain whom they had known before as a distant and rather important official at Predannack. Their distrust and caution gradually melted. Cheshire and Gibson borrowed picks and shovels and a wheelbarrow from the station stores to dig a six-feet hole for a septic tank personally provided by the area Clerk of Works. His hands were bruised and blistered tearing up the rocks and the work went for nothing ; for it was pointed out to him that the Urban District Council's one sewage cart would have to be attached permanently to the Home if he made do with a medium-sized tank.

The daily communications by wireless with the naval air establishment were a constant source of help. The Commanding Officer, who admired Cheshire as a person, admired still more his selfless initiative. This naval captain's discreet habit of turning a blind eye to the unofficial activities of working parties brought valuable mechanical aid at vital moments. A bulldozer scooped out earth and boulders for stowing a bigger forty-feet sewage tank, and a mobile crane laid it in position.

" Things are going well," Cheshire wrote in mid-April. " The first patients will be in on May 11th, when we open. I've a good local committee, and we've almost finished the chapel. I've brought my altar and fittings from Le Court."

An anonymous benefactor sent an ancient Aga cooker that

needed a complete overhaul, but the man from Camborne who came to estimate the cost of repairing it shook a pessimistic head :

" It's useless. There's only one place for it, the scrap heap."

Cheshire did not argue. He showed him over the freshly painted rooms off the narrow central corridor, explaining who had donated this bed and where those curtains and that arm-chair or tallboy had come from. The man said little until he was about to start up his van outside. Then he said confidentially :

" On second thoughts we'll have a shot at that cooker. Before we finish it'll be the most up-to-date in Cornwall."

7

A few days before the Home was opened, Cheshire had lunch with me in London. He had managed to steal away to Solesmes for the Holy Week ceremonies ; and he had gone on to spend Easter week at Hélène's home :

" We've had to put off the wedding from June till August," he said. " It'll probably be on the 4th, a Thursday. Hélène's been having a lot of trouble with a knee injury, and it's slow in mending."

Then he changed the subject with disconcerting cheerfulness.

He seemed far more preoccupied with the problems of the Home than with the postponement of his marriage. The unforeseen delay was indeed partly welcomed. He needed extra time to give St. Teresa's a fair start. For a man on the point of marriage he gave the distinct impression of being remarkably disengaged and detached, but I thought I knew his secretive ways well enough not to be misled by such off-handedness. Cheshire's adroit knack of gently stage-managing conversations is an art in itself, as his closest friends will agree.

The name of the Home had automatically suggested itself. Since becoming a Catholic, Cheshire had revised his first, unfavourable opinion of St. Teresa. He had come upon her in the opening chapters of Monsignor Vernon Johnson's conversion story, but had not dallied. Nevertheless, the obscure girl who took the veil in the Carmel of Lisieux, then led a life of such outward ordinariness, even for a cloistered nun, that her superiors hardly knew what to say by way of formal tribute when she died

M

of T.B. still in her twenties, was no longer an unintelligible bore. He knew now that by a divine paradox, this saintly girl had transformed the humdrum particles of her hidden daily life into a radiant " little way " of spiritual perfection. Her entire self-surrender had made her a practical mystic, a great saint, and a tantalisingly difficult spiritual model to imitate.

He was deeply grateful to Monsignor Valentine Elwes, the brother of Simon, the portrait painter, for lending him the saint's autobiography. Monsignor Elwes had met Cheshire about the time of his engagement to Hélène ; he saw little of him after the transfer to Predannack, but understood his inner restlessness well enough to recommend the example of St. Teresa, whose heroism lay in concentrating on little things and keeping her sights well lowered. What better patron could he choose for the Home ?

The staff at Le Court were furious for being kept in the dark until the Nissen hut Home was ready to be opened. To one or two it confirmed the long-held suspicion that Cheshire had outgrown his interest in them and had moved nonchalantly on. This was not entirely true. He saw the two Homes as complementary to each other.

" I intend taking the more serious patients from Le Court," he told me. " We'll manage those they can't cope with."

One of his first patients was Bill Conway, a wiry, quarrelsome Welshman in his late forties with intestinal tuberculosis. He had been the most unpopular patient at Le Court by a long chalk, but Cheshire had always liked and defended him. He believed that a lifetime of friendlessness had stuck the permanent chip on Conway's defiant shoulders ; and he refused to " fire " him even when the truculent Welshman crept back cold, worn and dishevelled one frosty morning after a disturbing disappearance of three days :

" Hallo, Bill," said Cheshire stiffly. " What've you been up to ? "

" I had to go to Cardiff."

" Why Cardiff ? You don't have any friends there, do you ? "

" No, of course not. I wanted to watch Wales in the rugby international, that's all."

Cheshire gave up playing the heavy uncle, and grinned with pleasure :

" Who won ? "

" I don't know. I got there all right, and slept the night in the open. Then I had a few drinks and was too late to get into the ground."

Nearly everyone but Cheshire was happy to see the back of Conway when the last T.B.s were transferred from Le Court. He kept in touch with him, visited him in hospital as he passed through Winchester, and finally secured his release when St. Teresa's opened. The Winchester authorities were unwilling to move him, for they doubted whether Conway would survive the long journey to Cornwall.

" We'll have to chance that," said Cheshire. " He may be dying, but he wants to die in my Home."

They let Conway travel in the end, and his excitement grew all the way to Predannack. It abated when he arrived and saw the bare, bleak prospect. Very soon he was his old, growling, cantankerous self again—and Cheshire felt relieved at the unending cataract of complaints :

" I don't think much of the bloody view. . . . It's easy to see why nobody lives here. . . . Aren't there any buses to brighten up this godforsaken hole ? . . . What about heating ? This dump will be the death of me. . . . Who's your perishing cook, I'd like to scalp her."

But Cheshire recognised the grey look on Conway's face one night towards the end of June. As he leaned over the bed, the Welshman glared at him. He had just made his will, leaving £40 in post-war credits and three pile suppositories to Cheshire, and a further £30 in notes to Mrs. Cheshire, of whom he was extremely fond. His breath smelled strongly of whisky, which he had been drinking copiously to lighten the monotony :

" What's the matter, want me to hurry up and die or something ? "

" Don't be stupid, Bill. Is there anything you want ? "

" I know," he said wearily. " You mean a clergyman, prayers, candles and all that junk. No thanks. I don't hold with that sort of lark."

" Well, I do," said Cheshire. " And it makes a lot of difference."

" Difference ? What sort of difference could it possibly make ? "

"One hell of a difference. Just that. The difference between hell and heaven."

"Oh, for God's sake go away and leave me in peace."

But Cheshire stayed, and changed the subject. Eventually, to humour him, Conway agreed to let himself be baptised, grunting at the chill of the water. Later, he quietened down, and muttered the Lord's prayer after him.

Before Cheshire stole out of the room, the dying man said:

"Now, do me a *real* favour."

"Of course, Bill. Anything."

"Don't rush it. I'm not dead yet. But when I am, I don't want to be put in the ground. I never liked the idea of earth-worms. Can you have me cremated or buried at sea?" Conway had been a sailor once. That was a good enough reason. Any hint that there might be some obscure religious objection to cremation and Conway would almost certainly insist on it.

"Right, Bill. It'll be a sea burial," he said.

Conway died the next night, while Cheshire slept. He was momentarily annoyed with the duty nurse for forgetting to wake him in time. . . .

A few holidaymakers watched the cortège creep down the steep cliff gradient from Ruan Minor to Cadgwith Cove on June 29th. The car rounded the last right-angled bend and backed slowly down the shingle among the lobster pots and nets and ropes. Two bareheaded fishermen in long sea-boots and blue jerseys came forward and helped Jerry Rule and his son, the local undertakers, to shoulder the shining elm coffin plugged with holes and weighted with cement. Six other fishermen stood by while it was lowered into the *Winifred*, where "Lamby" Stevens, the owner, crouched over the engine. Then they climbed aboard and the fishermen shoved her off into the shallows. Stevens started up his motor, and they headed out into the open sea.

Cheshire was the only mourner. And as the floppy waves lapped sluggishly against the sides of the boat, he could still scarcely credit the puzzled benevolence of the local authorities. Nobody had seemed to be very sure whether a sea burial was within the law: the Customs at Falmouth could not give a straight answer, the Coroner at Penzance thought it unusual, but would not commit himself, and the police could quote no precedent for or against. He was told he could grant Bill Conway's last wish provided he went outside territorial waters. Hubert Luke, the Methodist minister at Mullion, had suggested that a new field of thought had been opened for writers of crime fiction. A post-mortem on a corpse lying under fathoms of water would not be so easily arranged. Luke had readily agreed to sail with him and read the burial service when Cheshire explained :

" If Conway had been anything, he'd have been a Methodist."

It was a pearly grey day, with a strong sun above the overcast of haze and the dull glitter of a calm sea. Stevens stopped the engine and broke in on their thoughts when they were beyond the three-mile limit :

" This is about it," he said.

They stood silently during the prayers, then Rule and his son raised the coffin together and slid it slowly overboard. The boat rocked lazily for a few seconds and the two wreaths of flowers were carried slowly away in opposite directions as the coffin listed and sank with a quiet gurgle and a faint gleam of brass handles. As they watched, with not even a gull to shatter the warm stillness, the parted wreaths drifted idly back to form a last splash of colour on the unbroken surface of the sea where Conway's bones had been sucked down. They chugged back towards the shore for twenty minutes and no one spoke. It was as though they could not trust themselves to put their thoughts into poor words. Their reverie ended unwillingly when Cheshire handed round his cigarette case.

Every man who took part in that simple ceremony, from Rule, the grizzled undertaker, to Tonkins, the young hearse driver, looks back on it still with a reverence devoid of all romantic or superstitious awe. None but Luke and Cheshire could be called religious men. Stevens the fisherman put it most feelingly when he said with a touch of envy :

" I'd like to go that way when my time comes."

Cheshire's raging energies were not wholly spent in St. Teresa's. He wrote to say that he had his eye on a ruined church at Ruan Major, a pre-Reformation husk of a building which he planned to buy and restore. It stood in the only knot of trees

for miles around and there was an adjoining plot of ground
on which he could already visualise the perfect shape
of a REAL Home for the dying. It seemed a hazardous venture
for a man with two precariously established Homes already,
a full-time job and a fiancée whom he was due to wed very
shortly.

Hélène, I was sure, did not yet understand what this voluntary
work for the sick meant to Cheshire, how it absorbed his whole
being and relegated all else to the background. It was not
improbable that she would be presented in due course with the
accomplished fact of his dual allegiance ; and unless she was
gifted with the grace of an almost unwomanly detachment or
could emulate his single-minded passion for helping the afflicted,
Hélène was going to be badly hurt.

Cheshire and I saw little of one another that summer, though
we corresponded frequently. Some of my misgivings undoubtedly crept into the letters. I did not know the extent of his own
anxious self-searching until months afterwards, for in all his
replies there was only a single reference to his fiancée. It came
in a note written towards the end of August, describing in outline " a large programme I have for building or rather restoring
chapels down here." There was a harsh note of abruptness in
the eight words added almost as a footnote :

" For your information only, the marriage is off."

The decision was dictated by the inescapable force of common
sense and was clinched by his faculty for reappraising stubborn
problems with startling swiftness. In this case, Hélène's leg
injury was responding to treatment very slowly ; he had learnt
that there might be a further delay while the Church authorities
formally satisfied themselves about the nullity of his original
marriage to Constance ; but above all, the overwhelming local
interest in St. Teresa's and the speed of its growth had gradually
changed his outlook. He now saw with agonising clearness that
his true vocation all along had been not in marriage but in sheltering the suffering. Hélène belonged to a pattern of life which he
had instinctively disliked from the start. He had sincerely tried
to adjust himself to it, on the unanimous advice of others, ever
since that unfortunate holiday on the island of Skye ; for two
years he had been deceiving himself—and Hélène. Whatever
others might think, he felt that the eleventh-hour decision to

break off the marriage was for her ultimate good as well as his own. Hélène, brokenhearted and desolate, valiantly tried to understand, but it was almost impossible for her not to feel that she had become the victim of a fickle whim.

Cheshire had few regrets. Nor, looking back, does he attempt to pin the decision in any way on the grave infection which was already eating into his system :

" My illness had nothing to do with the matter whatsoever. It was purely that my heart was with the work and not in marriage. I had listened too readily to others since 1949 ; I had convinced myself, after reading the life of St. Teresa, that sanctity for me lay in renouncing my work for the sick and leading a normal life in the world. The pendulum had swung too far in the wrong direction."

The pendulum was his again to control or swing as he pleased. And for the next twelve months until he was struck down by tuberculosis, it swung him more and more towards a new extreme. Not more than a dozen close friends knew the seriousness of his intention to " try his vocation " as a monk or a priest. It seemed that nothing short of renunciation of the world would satisfy his soaring aspirations now that he was free again. Just as he had become engaged more from a conviction that it was " the right thing to do " than from any romantic feeling of attachment to Hélène, so the pull of the cloister and the monk's habit drew his head rather than his heart. For years he had been caught between the conflicting tensions of the rest-less will to action and the longing for solitude and contempla-tion. Half-measures appealed to him even less now than in the past. What more natural than that he should seek peace in the austerity of a monastic cell ?

By taking vows as an obscure member of a strict religious order, he would no longer be a prey to doubt, impulsiveness and uncertainty. He had seen the monks at prayer, working in the fields, busy about the many tasks of a great Abbey. They were men conscious of doing the divine will, which was enshrined for them in the rule and the authority of their Abbot. He might find rest at last as one of them. For the heart of their life of worship was that close harmony between work and prayer, between action and contemplation, which he recognised as his deepest need.

The main obstacle, of course, was the work to which he was already committed. Le Court and St. Teresa's were heavy responsibilities. Until some means could be found of entrusting the Homes to good caretakers, he would have to shelve his hope of becoming a religious. Cheshire consulted several priests and one or two friends during those months. When Hubert Luke, the Methodist minister, was told of his new ambition, he tried gently to dissuade him. His admiration for Cheshire's zeal was unbounded. With an invalid wife of his own to nurse, he believed that his friend possessed exceptional gifts which it was his duty to use in the world. If he forsook his work for the sick before it was soundly established, it would probably fail.

Cheshire was preoccupied with the material and financial difficulties, as I discovered one foggy December evening in London when we met. He was on his way back to Cornwall. A few weeks before he had written :

" There are signs of Le Court's foundations cracking due to the subsidence caused by an underground stream. Unfortunately, it knocks my idea out of building a chapel in the crypt."

It was unusual to hear him discussing money matters, but the surveyor's report was admittedly disturbing. The provisional estimate suggested that something like £35,000 would have to be found to save Le Court from falling down. Then, changing the subject with habitual swiftness, he said :

" Keep this under your hat for the time being. I want to become a priest. If all goes well, I should start my studies in Rome next September. What do you think of the idea ? "

" I don't think much of it at all. What about the Homes ? What about that £35,000 ? "

He was not really concerned about it, he said. The money would turn up from somewhere. He did not mention that Sir George Dyson, vice-chairman of the United Kingdom Carnegie Trust, had already inspected Le Court and that his fellow-trustees were sympathetically considering the question of a substantial grant for rebuilding the Home. Cheshire had been taking discreet steps to put his affairs in order. His father had joined the recently formed Cheshire Foundation Trust, which was to be further strengthened by Lord Justice Denning and Lady St. Levan. He could console himself that if circumstances warranted his leaving, the Homes would be in good hands. Would the

Homes be forgotten as quickly as Hélène, if the way to the priesthood were cleared for him ? It was a rhetorical question, for within a month Cheshire had decided, on the advice of clerical friends, not to become a diocesan priest.

St. Teresa's had meanwhile been adopted by the people of the Lizard. The Home, because of its isolated position, had graver problems than Le Court in its infancy ; but the warm generosity of farmers, fishermen, tradesmen and professional men throughout the district made up for much. Cheshire had not yet left Vickers, but his job had become an empty distraction. His interest in the airfield had waned since Hélène was thrust out of his life. He felt a misfit, though the occasional test flights were a boon. In addition, he suffered increasingly severe attacks of a mysterious influenza which laid him up in the cottage four or five times that winter. Nevertheless, he held on at Predannack, deferring to those who advised him not to abandon a well-paid post, which gave him independence and leisure enough to continue his loftier work for the sick.

The readiness of the Cornish to assist him in that work was breaking down the traditional barriers of religious bigotry. Life-long inhabitants of Mullion and Helston, used to the hard and fast divisions between neighbours in tiny communities, were learning tolerance. Within a few months there had been a startling change of atmosphere, so that a Methodist minister could now open a Catholic garden fête without being denigrated for flirting with the Scarlet Woman, and men and women of diverse creeds could sit on the management committee of St. Teresa's.

The Harvest Festival in 1951 had brought food and fruit to last a month. On Christmas Eve fishermen joined the crowd of villagers and the choir in a derelict building near the Home where the patients and volunteers had spent days building a crib. A baby calf nuzzled the straw at the feet of the life-size figure of the infant in the lantern-lit manger, while the Mother and Foster Father in their garish rags glared straight ahead out of papier mâché eyes at the nuns, schoolchildren, Methodist choristers and patients in wheel-chairs. Later, during a lean period, the last spare bed-pan broke on the very day an A.A. patrolman drove up from Falmouth with a small library of books and a parcel of

household articles. A benefactor had died and left them all to
St. Teresa's in his will, explained the patrolman. When the
yellow motor-cycle combination had disappeared in a cloud of
blue exhaust, they found among the utensils a brassbound bed-
pan large and solid enough to be mistaken for an answer to
prayer. They were amused, but as impressed as Cyril Cowey
had been during the " Fred Karno " period at Le Court.

The break with Vickers came in March, 1952. Cheshire
actually wrote accepting the firm's offer to renew his contract,
but in his letter he was rash or subtle enough to mention officially
the Home he had founded. He must have discretion, he said,
to give time to it. Vickers promptly replied that either he
worked for them on their conditions or not at all. His choice
was clear. He sent in his resignation at once, satisfied that even
those whose advice he had tried to follow could hardly complain
of impulsiveness this time. Barnes Wallis was annoyed, and also
sorry. The old unofficial arrangement had worked well enough ;
everyone had gained, Vickers, the patients, and presumably
Cheshire. Why did he have to end it on an impossible point of
principle ?

On March 19th Cheshire took up the Spitfire for his last
nostalgic joyride. He might hear the distant whine or hum of
aircraft in the solitude of the fields around Melleray, the Cistercian
Monastery in Brittany which he intended to enter as soon as
his affairs were in order ; but he would probably never handle
the controls of a machine again. Howard Dawson, who was to
succeed him at Predannack, sat in the rear cockpit, holding his
breath as the Spitfire skimmed low over the fields and the narrow
twisting lanes, then zoomed up for a final bird's-eye view of
Mount's Bay. Through rents in the fleecy clouds, they could see
the castle and the causeway and Penzance lying like toys at the
bottom of a blue well of light. It was plain to Dawson that
Cheshire would miss the flying.

That evening Cheshire sent a forlorn little note to the O.C.
Flying of H.M.S. *Seahawk*, at Culdrose :

" Now that I am leaving Vickers Armstrong to settle down
in this part of the world, I shall have no further opportunity of
flying. Since, as a member of the Reserve of Officers, it would
be helpful if I could keep my hand in, I wonder if arrangements
could be made for me to do some occasional flying at Culdrose.

Although I realise that this request may well be impracticable, I should be very grateful if you could give it your consideration."

He would have been too busy in the spring and early summer of 1952 even if his request had been practicable. Since the arrival at Christmas of Frank, the ex-bomber pilot, Cheshire had been at slight loggerheads with the committee. Frank was a schizophrenic, with no interest in life or work. Like Michael Gibson, he was out of place in St. Teresa's among the chronic sick. So Cheshire set to work with a will to restore and make habitable yet another empty hut a few hundred yards away. He wrote to me triumphantly early in April :

" The third Home for people who have problems other than physical ones has started. I am living there temporarily. All goes well."

He had given up his cottage at the same time as the job. Before the end of Lent he had built " a realistic and truly God-forsaken looking Calvary " with a sepulchre beneath, outside Holy Cross, his new-born third Home. Apart from one of his regular visits to the French monastery in Easter Week, he divided his time between St. Teresa's and Holy Cross until priests of the Catholic Missionary Society visited Cornwall in June to preach to the people in a dozen towns and fishing villages from Bodmin to St. Ives. Eager to assist them in any way they wished, Cheshire gladly seized the invitation to speak himself about his own conversion to Catholicism. Thousands of Cornishmen and summer visitors heard his open-air talks ; but after the last in Helston towards the end of August he retired to bed sick and exhausted.

Father Francis Ripley, one of the visiting priests, suspected the worst and took him by car the following morning to St. Michael's Sanatorium, Hayle. The Polish staff doctor was horrified at the result of the X-ray : the left lung clearly showed an ominous cavity. His voice faltered as he told Cheshire, who was sitting up in bed talking to three priests. One of them, Father Austin Delaney, O.S.B., of St. Ives, was thunderstruck by his cool reaction :

" It must have been the worst news he'd ever had, a kind of atom bomb on all his hopes and schemes, whatever they were. Yet he didn't wince or complain or signify by folded hands and bowed head his acceptance of what the old Irishwoman called the ' unscrupulous providence of God.' He just gave a typical broad grin and almost laughed out loud."

I saw him a few days later at Hayle and asked how long he had suspected that he was gravely ill. His reply seemed rather guarded. He had known for some months that something was radically wrong, but had never dissembled to doctors. Once he had even suggested an X-ray himself but did not demur when the specialist replied that an X-ray would not be necessary. There seemed little to say that August day. Surrounded by books, his pen and paper close at hand in the sunlit, snow-white bedroom, he was already resigned to the unknown future. It was the end of a chapter, perhaps the end of a career, and I could not rid my mind of the persistent impression that it had ended with a dramatic abruptness which even Cheshire found slightly ironic.

EPILOGUE

CHESHIRE first mentioned the idea of a full biography in the last quarter of 1953. By then, he had been over a year in the King Edward VII Sanatorium, near Midhurst, in Sussex, and was recovering slowly from the first major operation (in two parts) on his diseased left lung. The inroads of infection had not run their course, nor yet completely revealed themselves : neither of us knew that he would have to undergo a second operation in the high summer of 1954 and that another twelve months of enforced inactivity lay ahead. I remember my feeling of flattered pleasure when, almost immediately after the subject was raised, Cheshire decided that a full biography should be written and that I should be the author. Only gradually, as I came to grips with the task, did I realise what I had taken on.

This has not been an easy book to write. Any biography about a famous man who is still young, alive and in mid-career, is bound to be difficult, if not actually invidious, for a close friend to write. One's knowledge of the subject is an embarrassing encumbrance, like the weight of the dead albatross round the neck of the Ancient Mariner. There is an element almost of treachery in striving both to be truthful and clinically objective and to strike a fair balance at the end. The task in the case of Leonard Cheshire is all the harder, for, as anyone who has read what goes before will have gathered, he is an extraordinarily complex mixture of introspective and man of action. On the other hand, the real Cheshire seems to me a far more fascinating character, warts and all, than the simple, synthetic, glossy and slightly "phoney" legend with which his name has been increasingly and mistakenly identified in recent years.

To my mind, it is part of his complexity that Cheshire, who once derived a little fun and a little vain enjoyment from the popular cult of his mythical other-self, has indirectly encouraged its spread of late by a monumental personal indifference to public opinion. His memory for detail is poor and does not go back very far, which is fairly understandable in a man who has done so much in half a lifetime. He tends to be off-hand about factual accuracy. To him the dramatic or edifying effect of an incident is infinitely more important than the incident itself.

Cheshire's highly developed flair for the limelight is a " hangover " from his Oxford and wartime days. Since his conversion to Catholicism he has been at times chary of seeking publicity, and he accepts it to-day not for its own sake but for the sake of the wholly admirable work to which he is devoting his life and for which he made the perilous sacrifice of his health. Underlying all his activities is a simple principle : " No genuine offer of help will be refused. No genuine call for help will be ignored." That broad principle of action mirrors the height and depth of his love for all who are afflicted and, in particular, for the " unwanted " chronic sick. It also mirrors a paradoxical flaw in his character : an impulsiveness which tends to jump the bounds of normal prudence when the occasion arises. It is rare for him to be guided by the advice of others. Cheshire prefers, as he has always done, to be the final judge of what is possible and practicable, and what is not. Some would say it is a sublime failing, and in a theoretical sense they are right. But in practice it often throws unexpected and heavy burdens on his voluntary helpers, not all of whom share either his formal religious faith or are endowed with his gloriously wild trust in Providence.

Cheshire's ends are unquestionably lofty and selfless. The means he adopts to reach them are sometimes less so. With the highest possible motives, he gives the impression of being a dedicated man in too much of a hurry. As always, he is the pace-maker; and those who cannot keep up must drop out in his headlong chase to succour the needy. Nor have the lessons he learnt during the twenty-eight months of discomfort and intermittent pain he spent as a T.B. patient in Hayle and Midhurst changed him appreciably in this respect.

No man could pass through such an ordeal unscathed ; no man of Cheshire's courageous faith could pass through it untouched by grace. I was not surprised when, on November 22nd, 1952, he took a major decision which brought him peace at last. It involved giving up all idea of becoming a monk and becoming instead a man pledged to the relief of suffering. It was as if he saw in his own protracted illness the clearest and least controvertible sign of all. Apart from enriching him spiritually, it settled his mind finally about his vocation.

His twofold mission, partly modelled on the work of priests with whom he had collaborated in Cornwall, began over a year before he left the Sanatorium, still under doctor's orders, in December, 1954. Its purpose is best defined in his own words :

" Between my work for the sick and my missionary venture there is a close connection. They are both concerned with suffering—the one to relieve it, the other to make its significance understood. In order to understand suffering, we have to understand Christ, for it is Christ alone who explains it. Without Christ, suffering remains a horrible and meaningless misfortune."

There have been several landmarks since. His two missionary buses, complete with tape-recorded talks on simple religious themes, have been seen by many people in London, Leeds, Hampshire, Cornwall and elsewhere. He has founded new Homes at Bromley, in Kent, at Ampthill, in Bedfordshire, at Angmering, in Sussex, at Staunton Harold Hall, in Leicestershire, and has others in view. Apart from foundations in Britain, he intends to carry his work to the Far East ; and in autumn, 1955, he will start work on his first site in South India. He has also discovered the Holy Shroud, which has become the chosen symbol and central motif of his mission. He is convinced that this piece of linen, rather narrower than a single bed sheet, is the winding sheet of Christ, and that marks imprinted on it are the marks of the Sacred Wounds. He has written a small booklet and two widely-read articles outlining the history of the Holy Shroud and accepting without reservation the scientific hypothesis that it shows in reverse, like the negative of an inexplicable natural photograph, the image of Christ's Face.

It was the " spontaneous and bewildering " response of the ordinary passer-by to a pictorial tableau of the Holy Shroud, laid out in the tomb-like interior of one of his two buses during Holy Week, 1954, which largely persuaded Cheshire to concentrate on propagating it. The fact is important ; for his small religious mission is not aimed particularly at Christians but at pagans, in other words at people who no longer believe in God. He considers that " by and large the Englishman doesn't respond well to an argument from reason alone. He responds much better to something that moves his will, and that is precisely what the Holy Shroud does. It excites the intellect by providing direct evidence of the Death and Passion of our Lord and circumstantial evidence of his Resurrection."

If its history is true, then unquestionably that faded strip of linen, which is kept, venerated and occasionally exhibited at Turin, in Italy, must be regarded as one of the most arresting relics in the world. But its authenticity remains a matter of opinion. Formidable historical and even scriptural objections were raised half a century ago when the Shroud was the subject of intense and not very dignified controversy. It was then that the theory of a sort of photographic negative was first mooted. There are pious and learned men who accept it for what it purports to be. There are others, equally pious and learned, who do not. It is, essentially, an open question.

The official attitude of the Catholic Church to the Shroud is in keeping with its traditionally cautious attitude to all matters which cannot become dogmas. It is well known, for example, that the Church cannot require the faithful to accept as part of Christian doctrine the apparitions or miracles of Lourdes or Fatima. The Church does not make infallible pronouncements on what are called private revelations. In the words of an eminent theologian whom I consulted : " The Church allows the honouring of the Shroud as a reminder of the Passion of Christ, but she has never declared that it is the actual grave-cloth from the tomb of Christ. She cannot be expected to pronounce ' photographs ' to be good or bad, true or false."

Cheshire's zeal springs from an eagerness to share with others his living faith, just as the Homes have sprung one by one from spontaneous impulses of charity. I do not think it is going too far to describe him as a monk in all but name, following a general rule of his own which has already been defined as harking to all genuine calls for help and accepting all genuine offers of assistance. So far the rule has worked quite well. Money, goods, and services have not been wanting for any of his new Homes, and on practical matters he tends to listen more readily to the advice of experts. He himself lives entirely on his small R.A.F. pension and occasional earnings, paying his secretarial and other expenses as he goes. He has never had capital of his own, whatever impression he may sometimes have given to the contrary.

It is natural that his life should be based on the monastic ideal since, but for his illness, he might well have joined a religious order. But one vital factor is missing. A monk takes a vow of obedience, and his rule maps out every moment of the day for him so that the will of God is clear for him at all times. Cheshire has chosen a typically steep way of perfection, full of possible pitfalls for a man of his lonely, impulsive nature. No doubt some will say that the results so far fully justify his partial reliance on intuition. To my mind, it is the kink in the logic of his religious enthusiasm. The inspired " hunches " of the airman are to-day the " signs " of the self-appointed missionary who is putting charity into tight-fitting seven-league boots.

A man does not change his nature with his religion ; he changes his values, his ends, his direction and his habits if he is sincere, but only gradually. That is the short answer to those who idly wonder whether Cheshire is merely " stunting ", to those who are busily trying to canonise him as a saint before his death, to those who question his sanity, and to those who speculate whether he is likely to " move on " from the Catholic Church. Nothing can be said with certainty of any man until he is under six feet of earth, and even then the last word and the last laugh are not ours. For the moment it is enough to salute the strange genius of this sensitive, good, ruthlessly impetuous, elaborately humble and intensely religious man, whose subtle knack of " making things happen ", with or without signs, has started a minor landslide of charity.

Talleyrand's remark that the love of glory can create only a great hero, while the contempt of it creates a great man, might have been tailored for Cheshire as he is to-day. His reckless, selfless zeal suggests that he understands the truth of that profounder saying of Thomas à Kempis : " How quickly passeth the glory of this world." Though, like the rest of us, he has his own precarious spiritual tight-rope to walk, he sees beyond the dazzle of the tinsel suns. He seeks, and one day may find, no passing glory.

LIST OF BOOKS CONSULTED

ANDERSON, W., *Pathfinders*. Jarrold, London.

BALDWIN, H. W., *Great Mistakes of the War*. Redman, London.

BRODIE, B., *The Absolute Weapon : Atomic Power and World Order*. Harcourt, Brace, New York.

CHESHIRE, G. L., *Bomber Pilot*. Hutchinson, London.

CHURCHILL, W. S., *The Second World War* (5 vols.). Cassell, London.

DOUHET, G., *The Command of the Air*. Faber, London.

FALLS, C., *The Second World War*. Methuen, London.

FULLER, J. F. C., *The Second World War*. Eyre & Spottiswoode, London.

GOEBBELS, J., *The Goebbels Diaries*. Hamish Hamilton, London.

HARRIS, A., *Bomber Offensive*. Collins, London.

HILLARY, R., *The Last Enemy*. Macmillan, London.

HUSKINSON, P., *Vision Ahead*. Werner Laurie, London.

LAURENCE, W. L., *Dawn Over Zero*. Museum Press, London.

LAWRENCE, W. J., *No. 5 Bomber Group, R.A.F.* Faber, London.

LIDDELL HART, B. H., *The Revolution in Warfare*. Cassell, London.

MACMILLAN, N., *The R.A.F. in the World War*. Harrap, London.

MARSHALL, G. C., *The Winning of the War in Europe and the Pacific* (Biennial Reports). Simon & Schuster, New York.

OWEN, R., *Tedder*. Collins, London.

RIVAZ, R. C., *Tail Gunner*. Jarrold, London.

Royal Air Force (1939-1945 : 3 *volumes*). H.M.S.O., London.

SAUNDBY, R., *Air Power—Air Mastery*. Article in *Air Power*, Vol. 1, No. 2. Winter, 1953.

SEVERSKY, A. P. de, *Air Power : Key to Survival*. Jenkins, London.

SPAIGHT, J. M., *Air Power and the Cities*. Longmans, London.

SPAIGHT, J. M., *Bombing Vindicated*. Bles, London.

STIMSON, H. L., *The Decision to Use the Atomic Bomb*. Harper's Magazine, Feb. 1947, New York.

TEDDER, A., *Lees Knowles Lectures on Air Power*. Cambridge University.

U.S. Strategic Bombing Survey (*Europe & Pacific*). U.S. Government Printing Office, Washington, D.C.

WILMOT, C., *The Struggle for Europe*. Collins, London.

WOODWARD, E. L., *Some Political Consequences of the Atomic Bomb*. Oxford University Press, London.

INDEX